Valencia
& the Costa Blanca

Miles Roddis

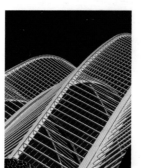

LONELY PLANET PUBLICATIONS
Melbourne • Oakland • London • Paris

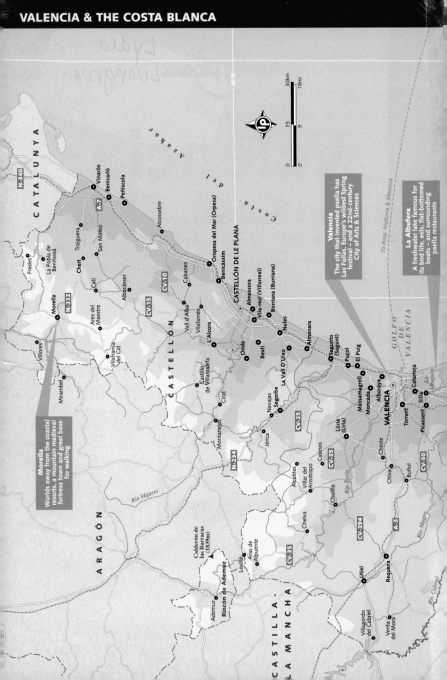

Morella
Worlds away from the coastal resorts, a mountain medieval fortress town and great base for walking

Valencia
The city that invented paella has Las Fallas, Europe's wildest Spring festival – and a 22nd-century City of Arts & Sciences

La Albufera
A freshwater lake famous for its bird life, eels, flat-bottomed boats – and surrounding paella restaurants

ELEVATION

2000m
1000m
500m
250m
0

MEDITERRANEAN SEA

39°N

To Ibiza & Mallorca

38°N

To Oran (Algeria)

Guadalest
Most picturesque of Valencia's inland villages

Altea
The prettiest *pueblo* on the Valencian coastline

Benidorm
With two superb beaches, Benidorm can belie its tacky image

Alicante
A bright, bustling port and holiday city with nightlife second only to that of Valencia

Alcoy
The region's most spectacular Moros y Cristianos (Moors & Christians) parades take place here

Elche
Venue for a magnificent medieval mystery play, and home of Europe's largest date grove

Denia
Pedreguer
Xàbia (Jávea)
Moraira
Gata de Gorgos
Benissa
Calpe
Callosa de Ensarrià
Altea
Isla de Benidorm
Benidorm
Puig Campana (1406m)
La Vila Joiosa (Villajoyosa)

Playa de El Grau de Gandía
Oliva
Pego
Guadalest
Tàvernes de la Valldigna
Gandía
Simat de Valldigna
Muro de Alcoy
Benigànim
Cocentaina
Alcoi
Albaida
Jijona (Xixona)

Sueca
Benifaió
Algemesí
Alzira
Carcaixent
Canals
Xàtiva (Játiva)
L'Olleria
Ontinyent
Bocairent
Banyeres de Mariola
Biar
Villena
Ibi
Elda
Monòvar
Novelda
Aspe
Pinoso

N-332
N-330
N-340
N-430
N-332
A-7

B l a n c a
C o s t a

SANT VICENT DEL RASPEIG
ALICANTE (ALACANT)
El Altet
Santa Pola
Isla de Tabarca
Elche (Elx)
Crevillente
Guardamar del Segura
Almoradí
Orihuela
Callosa del Segura
Torrevieja
Pilar de la Horadada
San Miguel de Salinas

Río Vinalopó
Río Segura

Alginet
Carlet
L'Alcúdia
Alberic
Villanueva de Castellón
Enguera
Aiora
Almansa
Jalance
Jarafuel

Río Cantabán
Río Júcar

V A L E N C I A
A L I C A N T E
M U R C I A
MURCIA

Cullera
Moncabrer (1390m)

Valencia & the Costa Blanca
1st edition – May 2002

Published by
Lonely Planet Publications Pty Ltd ABN 36 005 607 983
90 Maribyrnong St, Footscray, Victoria 3011, Australia

Lonely Planet offices
Australia Locked Bag 1, Footscray, Victoria 3011
USA 150 Linden St, Oakland, CA 94607
UK 10a Spring Place, London NW5 3BH
France 1 rue du Dahomey, 75011 Paris

Photographs
Many of the images in this guide are available for licensing from
Lonely Planet Images.
Web site: www.lonelyplanetimages.com

Front cover photograph
An oblique detail of the Calatrava-designed City of Arts & Sciences,
Valencia City (Ingrid Roddis)

ISBN 1 74059 032 5

text & maps © Lonely Planet Publications Pty Ltd 2002
photos © photographers as indicated 2002

Printed by The Bookmaker International Ltd
Printed in China

Contents – Text

2 Contents – Text

NORTHERN VALENCIA   144

CENTRAL VALENCIA   174

COSTA BLANCA   196

LANGUAGE   242

GLOSSARY   249

FOOD GLOSSARY   252

INDEX   268

MAP LEGEND   back page

Contents – Maps

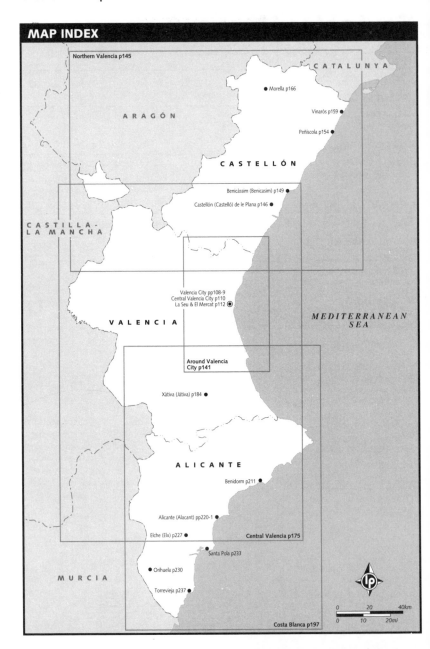

MAP INDEX

Northern Valencia p145

CATALUNYA

ARAGÓN

Morella p166 ●

Vinaròs p159 ●

Peñiscola p154 ●

CASTELLÓN

Benicàssim (Benicasim) p149 ●

Castellón (Castelló) de le Plana p146 ●

CASTILLA-
LA MANCHA

Valencia City pp108-9
Central Valencia City p110
La Seu & El Mercat p112 ◉

MEDITERRANEAN
SEA

VALENCIA

Around Valencia
City p141

Xàtiva (Játiva) p184 ●

ALICANTE

Benidorm p211 ●

Alicante (Alacant) pp220-1 ●

Elche (Elx) p227 ●   Central Valencia p175

Santa Pola p233 ●

MURCIA   ● Orihuela p230

Torrevieja p237 ●

LP

0   20   40km
0   10   20mi

Costa Blanca p197

The Author

Miles Roddis

Having been lucky enough to live and work in Spain for three years in the late '80s, Miles and his partner Ingrid bought a tatty old flat in the Barrio del Carmen, Valencia's oldest and most vibrant quarter. Now renovated, this shoe-box sized apartment is their principal home, the place to which they retreat to recover wind and write up.

Miles has contributed to Lonely Planet's *Africa on a Shoestring, West Africa, Read This First: Africa, Lonely Planet Unpacked, France, Italy, Spain, Canary Islands, Western Europe, Mediterranean Europe, Europe on a shoestring, Walking in Britain, Walking in France*, and – something that consumed five enormously satisfying months of his life – *Walking in Spain*.

FROM THE AUTHOR

Heading the list, as always, and making a huge contribution on the road and back at home, comes Ingrid.

For much general information, I drew deep from the always reliable research of fellow Lonely Planet authors Damien Simonis and John Noble, while fellow writer Derek Workman showed me the insides of La Vila Joiosa and opened my eyes to what they were keen to see in Benidorm. I very much appreciated the wise counsel of Rosa Ríos and Roc Filella on the Arts section. Thanks too to Joan Almela for invaluable help with the Language chapter and Glossary and to Dr Pep Banyuls for checking the section on Economics.

Those assiduous party people from the Rutgers University study-abroad programme shared with me some of their nocturnal experiences while Maru Viana, Raquel Ortiz and Miguel Lorente slipped me more tip-offs about Valencia after dark.

Lynda Saunders offered hospitality and hot tips about the Comunidad's hot southern tip – and also introduced me to Habaneras. Cris and Maria Luisa once again so kindly gave me the run of their apartment, whose whereabouts shall remain for ever a secret. Dra María José Santamaría provided useful information about local medical provision and José Tamarit patiently explained to me the finer points of *trinquet*. Damon guided me through the contemporary music minefield and cheerfully chased up Antipodean information. And many thanks to Owen Davies and Richard Hancock, who sent in particularly informative letters about the region.

So many tourist-office staff around the Comunidad cheerfully and enthusiastically shared their knowledge. My thanks to Beatriz López (Tuéjar), Mireya Mateo (Torrevieja), Teresa Ortuño (La Vila Joiosa), María Mercedes Lozano (Benicássim), Puri Francés (Villena), Vicen Perelló (Denia), Miguel Mata (Xábia), Salvador Bellver (Gandía) and Cristina Benito (Cullera) – and also to Juan Llantada of the Agència Valenciana de Turisme.

Some were helpful way beyond what duty required. Very special thanks go to José-Manuel Blasco (Santa Pola), Carmina Fenollosa (Castellón), Bernardo Bolumar (Segorbe), Maria-Luisa Sancho (Peñíscola) and Marcial Santos (Alicante). Also to all the team at Valencia's City's Calle Paz office, whom I incessantly pestered.

Lastly, but up front in order of priority, big *besos* to Abi Hole and Ian Stokes in Lonely Planet's London office. When I was really struggling to come in on time, both were models of calm reason and common sense.

This Book

This first edition of *Valencia* was researched and written by Miles Roddis.

From the Publisher

This book was produced in Lonely Planet's London office. Abigail Hole was the coordinating editor. Nancy Ianni and Arabella Shepherd helped with editing and proofreading, and Imogen Franks produced the index. Ian Stokes handled the design and layout and produced the maps and legend. Annika Roojun designed the cover, Lachlan Ross drew the back-cover map and Fiona Christie produced the climate chart. Fiona, Rachel Beattie, Liam Molloy and David Wenk assisted with mapping. The illustrations were drawn by Martin Harris, Kate Nolan, Jane Smith, Mick Weldon and Ian, and the photographs were provided by Lonely Planet Images. Ian also drew the decorative borders and chapter ends. Many thanks to Quentin Frayne for the benefit of his language expertise, Paul Clifton for his help with the Gay & Lesbian Travellers section, Miranda Wills for her input to the Flora & Fauna section, Hilary Rogers for her advice on Women Travellers, Emma Sangster for assisting with the Health section and Finola Collins, Tammy Fortin and Leonie Mugavin for checking the Getting There & Away chapter. *Mucho gracias* to Tim Ryder and James Timmins for all their help throughout production, and to Miles for his hard work and infectious enthusiasm.

Foreword

ABOUT LONELY PLANET GUIDEBOOKS

The story begins with a classic travel adventure: Tony and Maureen Wheeler's 1972 journey across Europe and Asia to Australia. There was no useful information about the overland trail then, so Tony and Maureen published the first Lonely Planet guidebook to meet a growing need.

From a kitchen table, Lonely Planet has grown to become the largest independent travel publisher in the world, with offices in Melbourne (Australia), Oakland (USA), London (UK) and Paris (France).

Today Lonely Planet guidebooks cover the globe. There is an ever-growing list of books and information in a variety of media. Some things haven't changed. The main aim is still to make it possible for adventurous travellers to get out there – to explore and better understand the world.

At Lonely Planet we believe travellers can make a positive contribution to the countries they visit – if they respect their host communities and spend their money wisely. Since 1986 a percentage of the income from each book has been donated to aid projects and human rights campaigns, and, more recently, to wildlife conservation.

Although inclusion in a guidebook usually implies a recommendation we cannot list every good place. Exclusion does not necessarily imply criticism. In fact there are a number of reasons why we might exclude a place – sometimes it is simply inappropriate to encourage an influx of travellers.

UPDATES & READER FEEDBACK

Things change – prices go up, schedules change, good places go bad and bad places go bankrupt. Nothing stays the same. So, if you find things better or worse, recently opened or long-since closed, please tell us and help make the next edition even more accurate and useful.

Lonely Planet thoroughly updates each guidebook as often as possible – usually every two years, although for some destinations the gap can be longer. Between editions, up-to-date information is available in our free, quarterly *Planet Talk* newsletter and monthly email bulletin *Comet*. The *Upgrades* section of our Web site (W www.lonelyplanet.com) is also regularly updated by Lonely Planet authors, and the site's *Scoop* section covers news and current affairs relevant to travellers. Lastly, the *Thorn Tree* bulletin board and *Postcards* section carry unverified, but fascinating, reports from travellers.

Tell us about it! We genuinely value your feedback. A well travelled team at Lonely Planet reads and acknowledges every email and letter we receive and ensures that every morsel of information finds its way to the relevant authors, editors and cartographers.

Everyone who writes to us will find their name listed in the next edition of the appropriate guide-book, and will receive the latest issue of *Comet* or *Planet Talk*. The very best contributions will be rewarded with a free guidebook.

We may edit, reproduce and incorporate your comments in Lonely Planet products such as guide-books, Web sites and digital products, so let us know if you don't want your comments reproduced or your name acknowledged.

How to contact Lonely Planet:
Online: e talk2us@lonelyplanet.com.au, W www.lonelyplanet.com
Australia: Locked Bag 1, Footscray, Victoria 3011
UK: 10a Spring Place, London NW5 3BH
USA: 150 Linden St, Oakland, CA 94607

Introduction

When you come to Valencia, you won't be alone. In 2000, the region received over 4.5 million overseas visitors, more than doubling its resident population. A huge majority frequent the beach resorts of the Costa del Azahar and Costa Blanca and most of these stay put, except, perhaps, for a guided outing to Valencia City. But with a little effort and cash set aside to rent a bike or car, you can leave behind the hurly burly of the narrow coastal band and explore the region's rich interior.

Valencia is both of Spain and distinct from Spain. In Muslim hands for five centuries, its Christian European history has been shaped as much by Catalunya as by Castilla. The Valencian flag bears the red and yellow stripes of Catalunya and the mother tongue of many (particularly in the hinterland) is Valenciano, a dialect of Catalan. For all that, Catalan militancy has never been as strong here as in its northern neighbour.

Despite its close language and cultural ties northwards, Valencia asserts its own regional identity. Nowadays, the region is known as the Comunidad Valenciana, the Valencian Community, but it was for many years an independent kingdom. While the Comunidad has been integrated into Spain for centuries, that sense of being different still lives on.

It's an identity reinforced by splendid local festivals. In July or August, you'll be unlucky not to find a village or town fiesta within easy reach. Biggest and noisiest is Valencia City's Las Fallas. For four days, huge effigies are erected at just about every junction – only to be burnt after midnight on 19 March. In the province of Alicante, towns re-enact the 13th-century expulsion of the Arab occupier. Moros y Cristianos parades slowly sway through town, the ladies in opulent, fanciful costumes, the men in robes and turbans, each *comparsa*, or guild, preceded by a scimitar-wielding leader, usually with a fat cigar clamped between his teeth.

The Valencia region is a land of gunpowder and fire. Whatever the pretext for the fiesta, it will almost certainly have a *castillo*, a display of aerial pyrotechnics, and most

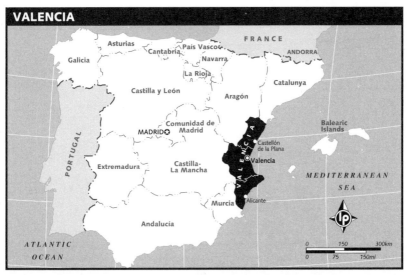

probably a *mascletá* or two, a cacophony of ear-splitting explosions.

This is the land where paella, now eaten the world over, first simmered over an open wood fire. Valencia also claims to have invented *fideuá*, a noodle-based alternative to throwing in the local short-grain rice. To accompany whichever variant you choose, there are the rapidly improving white wines from Alicante and inland Alta Turia or robust reds from Utiel-Requena.

Along the Costa Blanca, the white coast, stretch some of Spain's finest sandy beaches. You can bar-hop and party around clock and calendar in its international resorts, such as Benidorm, Torrevieja or the lively provincial capital of Alicante. Others, such as Denia, Cullera, or Vinaròs on the Costa del Azahar, still retain a much more Spanish flavour.

It would be a pity if you failed to stray from the coast. The interior, where mountains buckle and castles abound, is much less frequented. In the north, the villages of the wild Maestrazgo live to a different, rural rhythm. Morella, rising sheer from the plain, makes a splendid base for a day or two's walking. In the south, the Sierra de Mariola, recently declared a nature park, beckons hikers, while Elche's endless palm groves are a potent reminder of the region's Islamic heritage.

Valencia City, Spain's third largest after Madrid and Barcelona, is a town for all tastes. Its Ciudad de las Artes y las Ciencias is a breathtaking piece of modern architecture, and its Museo de Bellas Artes one of Spain's richest fine arts museums. If your tastes incline more towards modern works, a visit to the Instituto Valenciano de Arte Moderno (IVAM) is a must.

Fronting Valencia City's beach at Las Arenas is the world's largest concentration of paella restaurants – over 30 of them. And after dark, the city has a pub and disco scene that brings in visitors from all over Spain to party the weekend away.

Finally, a quick question of nomenclature since Valencia can be all things to all people. Valencia City is the principal town and capital of Valencia province which, in its turn, fits within Valencia region – of which Valencia City is also the capital. Confused? It's understandable, but relax. Where there's possible ambiguity in the following chapters, we spell out either Valencia City, Valencia province or Comunidad Valenciana, the usual name for the region as a whole.

Facts about Valencia

HISTORY
Early Days

Small bands of hunter-gatherers roamed the lands of present-day Valencia way back in Palaeolithic times, seeking shelter in caves from the heat of the day and the unknown of the night. Evidence so far is sparse and confined to a triangle bounded by Gandía on the coast, inland Xàtiva and Alcoy. It comes from caves – notably El Parpalló, near Gandía, whose finds top the attractions of Valencia City's Benificencia museum.

As elsewhere in Spain during the Neolithic period, itinerant bands began to settle, cultivate cereal crops and raise livestock, while continuing to use caves such as La Sarsa near Bocairent or the Cova Negra near Xàtiva. From the detritus littering their floors comes our evidence of this fundamental change in lifestyle – and also of the first use of pottery, a fairly crude style found throughout the Comunidad Valenciana. This seeking a more sedentary life was a gradual process, beginning somewhere between 5000 and 4000 BC and continuing until at least 2000 BC.

Come the Bronze Age, which lasted from about 1500 to 500 BC, and the production of threatening metal weapons, people looked for more secure, easily defendable places to live. Abandoning their often isolated caves, they sought safety in hill-top hamlets, often surrounded by simple stone walls, or at the head of steep cliffs from where aggressors could be easily repulsed.

Then, around 500 BC, two ripples of migration mildly diluted the ethnic uniformity of the Valencia region's earliest inhabitants. Bands of Celts, originally from Central Europe, crossed the Pyrenees and moved in from the north, confining themselves in the main to what is nowadays the province of Castellón. With them, they brought their knowledge of smelting iron. Richest of their legacies are the gold, silver and iron artefacts of the chance Rambla de Pandero discovery, nowadays the pride of the archaeological

museum in Villena (see the Central Valencia chapter). All the same, despite the splendour of such atypical finds, Celtic influence in the region was slight.

Greeks & Phoenicians

Much more significant was the impact of visitors from across the seas. The Phoenicians, a maritime people, began to arrive in small numbers around 1000 BC, journeying from their home base in present-day Lebanon and Syria. But, while they set up small settlements (remains have been found, for example, near Borriana on the coast north of Valencia City and inland near Orihuela, south of Alicante), contact was primarily commercial, limited to the exchange and trading of goods.

Also from across the waters came Greeks, who probably established small trading posts up and down the coast. Evidence so far for such semi-permanent structures is scant. What are much more prolific are examples of Greek pottery, discovered throughout the Comunidad, even deep inland, proving the case for a fairly profound commercial penetration.

Iberians

Though there was little intermingling of outsiders with the native Iberians, the offspin of half a millennium of trading contacts between 1000 and 500 BC was immense. It was the Phoenicians, Greeks and, later, Carthaginians who, together with isolated pockets of Celts, introduced the locals to iron. From these more advanced societies, the Iberians also adopted the concept of money, the potter's wheel and, most importantly of all, writing as a means of logging and transmitting information and ideas (the enigmatic Iberian script has still to be deciphered). The basis of the Iberian economy continued to be livestock rearing and agriculture, which became more sophisticated with the introduction of metal tools. From this era, seeds of barley, wheat and other cereals have been found, together with quantities of grinding wheels, leading

11

researchers to conclude that bread, almost certainly unleavened, was the staple element in the Iberians' diet.

Although the Romans are credited with the introduction of wine to the peninsula, it's clear that the Iberians cultivated vines – and olives too, using their oil for both cooking and illumination. While metal tools and weapons were employed for both hunting and warfare, there's no evidence of any being manufactured in the Valencia region, no doubt because iron ore just isn't found in this part of the Mediterranean world.

Carthaginians

From around the 6th century BC, Carthage, originally a Phoenician colony on the North African coast, began to flex its muscles. The Carthaginians' main interest was more than commercial. They came as conquerors, not so much interested in the land of Valencia itself as in clipping the wings of Rome, its rival for dominance of the Mediterranean, and denying the Romans access to the Iberian peninsula and Valencia's agricultural wealth. Having been severely thrashed by Rome in the First Punic War ('Punic' means Carthaginian), when they lost the islands of Sicily, Sardinia and Corsica, the Carthaginians crept around the back into peninsular Spain. Their general Hamilcar established Akra Leuke (today's Alicante). From this foothold, he set about a systematic conquest of the Iberian tribes of the area until he was killed in a skirmish near present-day Elche.

During the brief reign of his successor, Hasdrubal, Carthage won over most of the local opposition by diplomacy and strategic treaties. But it wasn't all kid gloves and sweet words. In 223 BC Hasdrubal marched into the Iberian coastal settlement of Mastia and renamed it Carthago Nova, today's Cartagena, Spain's premier naval port, just south of the Comunidad Valenciana's boundary with the region of Murcia.

His big achievement was the signing of the Ebro treaty in 226 BC, whereby the Río Ebro (today just north of the Comunidad Valenciana and in Catalunya) demarcated the limits of Roman and Carthaginian spheres of influence.

Harmony was shortlived. On Hasdrubal's death five years later, Hannibal reverted to a policy of conquest and confrontation with Rome. Still smarting from the debacle of the First Punic War and seeking a pretext to reopen hostilities on the grand scale with Rome, he attacked the pro-Roman town and stronghold of Sagunto, thus launching the Second Punic War.

Hannibal and his troops marched on northwards to eventually cross the Alps with his elephants and descend upon Italy. Yet back in Spain, the Romans' counterattack was swift, aiming to overcome all Carthage's strongholds on the Iberian peninsula. Occupied Sagunto fell to them in 212 BC, and Cartagena, three years later.

Romans

Then began nearly 700 years of Roman domination. The indigenous Iberians offered little resistance as the Valencia region was incorporated into Rome's Provincia Citerior, which stretched south of the Río Ebro and included much of contemporary Castilla. It was far from being an occupation; the Romans were few and 'conversion', a religious metaphor rather than one of war, is more appropriate. Roman civilisation sank deep roots into the fertile Valencian soil because the Iberians were receptive to its influence. Little by little, the native peoples assimilated Roman mores, customs, religions and, most importantly of all, language. For most people, Vulgar Latin became the mother tongue – and their means of access to a much larger linguistic community – during the first century AD. Gradually, the several indigenous languages and their speakers were pushed back to the remotest parts of the interior and died out.

In addition to the Pax Romana, which brought a long period of stability, other significant innovations that Rome introduced were, as elsewhere in their vast Empire, a system of taxation, Roman law, Christianity, the beginnings of an irrigation system and an excellent communications network. The famous Via Augusta, which ran from Rome to Andalucía, passed through Sagunto and Valencia before heading inland to Xàtiva and on into contemporary Murcia. The smaller arteries and veins that tapped into it helped both to reduce the isolation of many small Iberian communities and to forge trade links.

The town of Valencia was founded in AD 138, when a group of Roman legionaries were granted prime land beside the Río Turia to build themselves a retirement community.

The Romans, in addition to extending Iberian Sagunto and Elche, also established small towns such as Denia, Manises, Xàtiva and Llíria. It is from these settlements that specialists have gleaned most of what we know about the region in Roman times. But Romans come, Romans go, most people in the region would have continued to live their agricultural lives with little significant change.

Visigoths & Byzantines

In the 5th century, the Visigoths, an invading Germanic tribe, began to stream over the Pyrenees, taking advantage of Rome's slackening grip on the peninsula and establishing their capital in Toledo, far from the Valencia region. While their impact upon much of the rest of the country was considerable, upon Valencia it was negligible since in an earlier 4th-century incursion, Germanic tribes had sacked urban centres such as Elche, Manises and Sagunto and most others that were spared went into decline. Their inhabitants moved to the countryside in search of greater security – and it is from this exodus that many of the smaller towns and villages of the Comunidad Valenciana date. Consequently, when the Visigoths arrived, there was little, agricultural richness apart, to draw them towards this stretch of the Mediterranean, which they controlled only superficially.

The Roman Empire split into two in AD 330. Years later, the eastern, Byzantine emperor Justinian, ruling from Constantinople, attempted to recover from the Visigoths imperial possessions in Spain. From the middle of the 6th century, his armies occupied the southern part of the Valencia region as far as Denia, possibly incorporating Valencia City as well. For over a hundred years, they worked with a ruling elite and a people whose traditions were still strictly Roman-Iberian

and who had been touched but lightly by the Visigoth presence that had made such an impact elsewhere in the country.

The Moors

In AD 711, Tariq, the Arab governor of Tangiers in North Africa, invaded southern Spain, and within a few years the Valencia region was conquered by his mainly Berber army. The occupation was light-handed and encountered little resistance. The Arabs (in Spain more often referred to as Moros, or Moors) respected local institutions and, with many non-Muslims, such as the Berbers, among their own troops, made little or no attempt to impose Islam upon the local people.

The region was incorporated into the wider Arab land of Al-Andalus (at the time much more extensive than today's Andalucía). It was subdivided into the three provinces of Valencia, Xàtiva and Tudmir (the lands in the south around Orihuela, Villena and Alicante, previously held precariously by the Visigoth ruler Teodomiro). Each was ruled by a *wali*, or governor, appointed by the Caliph in distant Baghdad. Generally speaking, Berber tribes settled in the hilly zones of the interior, terrain akin to their own homelands across the Straits of Gibraltar. The Moors reserved for themselves the flat, fertile and more promising coastal plains with their access to the sea. To this day place names of Arab origin such as Benicàssim, Alcudia, Alcira and Benicalap are reminders of this distant colonisation.

Down south, when the Emir Abd al-Rahman declared Al-Andalus' independence from Baghdad, the distant power struggle had little impact upon the Valencia region. Later, the stability brought by the Caliphate of Córdoba (929–1031) lead to general economic prosperity from which Valencia too benefited. The Moors introduced the water wheel and throughout the region dug an elaborate network of irrigation canals, channels and ditches, many of which are still in use to this day. From the orient they introduced rice, still grown in quantity around the freshwater lagoon of La Albufera, south of Valencia City, and oranges, still the staple crop of most of the coastal plain. In Manises and Paterna to the west of Valencia City, they established a strong ceramics industry that also continues to this day, while in Xàtiva they set up Europe's first paper-making plant. Elche and Bocairent were silk-weaving centres and Denia was renowned for boat building.

Things began to fall apart on a national scale in the early 11th century, soon after the death of the Cordoban Caliph Hisham II. Pressures towards fragmentation could no longer be contained as Berbers, mercenary soldiers, Hispanoarabs and factions within factions, and groups within groups bickered for power. In 1018, as a desperate attempt to preserve unity, Abd al-Rahman IV was proclaimed Caliph in Valencia, then assassinated within months.

The Valencia region, like much of the rest of Spain, split asunder into several *taifas* – small, independent, Muslim kingdoms – dependent upon precarious alliances and bounded by fragile and constantly shifting borders. In the mid-11th century, the region was divided into three taifas with their power bases in Valencia, Denia – and Alpuente, today nothing more than a tiny inland village off the Turia valley.

Small and relatively powerless, the Valencian taifas nevertheless enjoyed prosperity. Both Valencia and Denia established schools of medicine and briefly became maritime powers that merited respect. In Valencia City, Abd al-Aziz (ruled 1021–61) planted a magnificent garden (today's Jardines del Real) and built a wall around the city, chunks of which still survive.

Looking briefly beyond Valencia's frontiers, in 1085, Toledo, the emblematic one-time capital of Visigoth Spain, long in Muslim hands, fell to Alfonso VI, king of Castilla and León. Backs to the wall, the governors of Al-Andalus sent for Yusuf bin Tasufin, chief of the Almoravids, a desert tribe that had successfully swept its way through much of North Africa. Alfonso, or rather one of his knights, the legendary El Cid, pressed on. El Cid took the city of Valencia in 1093 and, indeed, occupied the whole of the peninsula's eastern flank. When he died in 1099 his equally charismatic

widow, Jimena, held on to Valencia City for three years and nine long months of siege before capitulating to the Almoravid besiegers.

The Almohad, another desert people to surge out of North Africa, ventured to Al-Andalus not by invitation, like the Almoravids, but as conquerors. But events down south didn't impinge too much upon life in Valencia, except for the steady stream of Christian refugees who fled north, escaping the increasingly fundamentalist Almohad interpretation of Islam.

The Reconquista

As throughout Spain, the Christian Reconquista (Reconquest), far from being one long, consistent campaign, was more the result of skirmishes, pushing forward, pulling back and consolidating. You could say that, in the Valencia region, it started as early as 1117, when Alfonso I El Batallador (Alfonso the Warrior), king of Aragón, intruded into the region and, for a couple of years, occupied Morella, deep inland in the Maestrazgo. Other sorties and brief penetrations took him as far southeast as Cullera, on the coast.

Upon his death in 1137, the crowns of Catalunya and Aragón were united by royal marriage; however, while the enlarged kingdom was called El Reino de Aragón, Catalunya was always the stronger partner.

As so often, the Reconquista, when it came, was not a straight, clean victory in the field but a blend of force and skulduggery behind the scenes. In 1228, Abu Zayd, the Almohad governor of Valencia, assailed by Muslim dissidents advancing northwards from Murcia, called upon the Aragonese king Jaime I for protection. Jaime (Jaume in Catalan), known as El Conquistador (the Conqueror), saw his chance – and the protector soon became invader.

Again, it was Morella and nearby Aras that first fell to the invading Aragonese troops. Stimulated by this victory and fresh from his conquest of Mallorca in 1232, Jaime I attacked from the north taking Borriana the next year before triumphantly entering Valencia on 9 October (now celebrated as the fiesta of the Comunidad Valenciana) 1238. Continuing his push southwards, he picked off Alcira in 1242, Xàtiva two years later and had soon taken over the whole of the present-day Valencian community.

And that is why Valenciano, a variant of Catalan, is spoken in many parts of the Comunidad Valenciana today. The majority of Jaime's troops spoke Catalan. In their wake came Catalan-speaking colonisers, administrators and camp followers from Valencia's northern neighbour, many of whom stayed and settled. A smaller element of his forces from Aragón populated parts of the interior such as Segorbe and the upper Turia valley which, to this day, remain primarily Spanish speaking. However, in spite of the Christian conquest, Muslims still remained very much in the majority. Estimates suggest that in 1272 the region had around 30,000 Christians compared with some 200,000 Muslims, plus an important Jewish minority.

Perhaps Jaime I's most important legacy to Valencia City was its Fueros. These charters guaranteed the region important concessions and a considerable measure of independence from the crown of Aragón; privileges that were to remain in force for nearly five centuries.

Valencia's Golden Age

Valencia enjoyed its *siglo de oro* (golden age) in the 15th century, 200 years before the rest of Spain. It was a time of great prosperity when the capital's magnificent Lonja (commodity exchange), Generalitat, Miguelete tower and Torres de Quart were constructed. Valencia was one of the Mediterranean's strongest trading powers, exporting rice, wine, olive oil, saffron and wool to much of Europe and holding a virtual monopoly on the Mediterranean silk trade.

Valencians were bankers to the crowns of both Aragón and Castilla. Alfonso el Magnánimo of Aragón's successful campaigns to dominate Sardinia and Naples were underwritten by Valencian financiers who, later in the century, also helped to bankroll the capture of Granada and further royal campaigns in Italy. Such affluence encouraged a second, much larger wave of immigration from Catalunya. There was also a strong sense of a separate local culture; the

poet Ausias March was penning his verses in Valenciano/Catalan and in 1490 *Tirant lo Blanch*, the first Valencian epic novel, attributed to Joanot Martorell, was published. But political developments elsewhere were to have their impact...

An even more important fusion of crowns took place when, in 1469, Isabel, heir to Castilla, married Fernando (Ferdinand), heir to the kingdom of Aragón. In 1479 began the joint rule of the Reyes Católicos (Catholic Monarchs), as they were known. For Spain in general, it was a time of triumphs: the fall of Granada in 1492 and expulsion of the last of the Arab rulers; the discovery of America in that same year by Christopher Columbus; and the 1494 Treaty of Tordesillas, where Spain and Portugal as the world's superpowers coolly and presumptuously divided up the known and unknown world between themselves.

Las Germanías

In Valencia, not all was positive. The new regime made moves towards greater centralisation and, in 1483, introduced the Inquisition. More importantly, in 1492 it decreed

KATE NOLAN

Isabel I began her powerful joint rule
with Fernando II in 1469.

the expulsion of Jews from all Spanish territory, leaving Valencia bereft of many of its most important financiers, skilled artisans and water managers.

By the end of the 15th century, social unrest was stirring throughout the region. High taxes on food and textiles – the lifeblood of the Valencian economy – were imposed by a distant crown. Money invested in Fernando and Isabel's adventures by local financiers couldn't circulate locally and generate further wealth. These problems were compounded by a succession of bad wheat harvests and the constant threat of attack from the sea by Barbary pirates.

The local revolt known as Las Germanías was essentially an urban, bourgeois phenomenon as the middle classes of the city tried to wrest power from the entrenched aristocracy. They were well organised into *gremios* (guilds or trade associations) of shoemakers, wool traders, swordsmiths and so on. But the local nobility allied itself with the forces of Castilla and the outnumbered bands of the Germanías were routed in 1520 at the Battle of Alamenara. The rebels were disarmed, the city of Valencia was fined 300,000 ducats and other towns were penalised proportionately. The repression that followed was cruel and at least 800 dissidents were executed.

The Expulsion of the Moriscos

Apart from this short, unequal struggle, the 16th century was relatively uneventful. Spain's Mediterranean trade, in which Valencia participated so vigorously, was partially eclipsed by the commercial traffic between Spain and her territories in the New World, controlled through Seville. Such trouble as there was came from bandits operating in the wild lands of the Maestrazgo and around Alicante.

Between 1609 and 1614, Felipe III expelled thousands of Moriscos, Arabs who had remained in the region after the Reconquista and who had – often only nominally – converted to Christianity. It was an act of political and social intolerance whose economic repercussions were catastrophic, especially for the Valencia region, which had the highest proportion of Moriscos. In just five years an estimated 170,000 souls left by sea, most for present-day Tunisia. The region lost as much as a quarter of its inhabitants, leaving large areas of the interior severely underpopulated. Agricultural production – and therefore commerce too – plunged and a whole social layer of skilled artisans had been skimmed off. The feudal nobility lost much of its agricultural labour force. As their income dived, many could no longer service the debts they had to the financiers of the towns, so the middle classes too were affected – to such an extent that in 1613 the Banco Municipal de Valencia went bankrupt. Banditry resurged and around 1680 a new Germanías movement arose, only to be swiftly repressed.

Reeling from such blows, the Valencia region, which for two centuries had outshone Catalunya, lost a superiority that it was never again to recover.

The War of Succession (1703–13)

Barely 20 years later, the region was again in strife, caught up this time in a wider struggle for succession to the Spanish throne. The Bourbon Felipe V, nominated by the previous monarch, Carlos II, who died with no direct heir, had the nobility's support. Carlos, namesake and nephew of the old king, was championed by Archduke Charles of Austria and enjoyed the favour of the people.

Valencia's role in this pan-European rivalry, acted out on Spanish soil, was short and tragic. After the victory of the Bourbon forces at the Battle of Almansa (1707), the city surrendered unconditionally. It was deprived of the Fueros that had been its special privilege for 500 years and, with them, of the semi-autonomous status it had enjoyed since the Reconquista. From this time, the region was to remain firmly in centralist control, from Madrid, for over 250 years until a new, democratic, post-Franco Spain again looked benignly upon the principle of regional autonomy.

Felipe V sacked the town of Xàtiva, renaming it in an act of vainglory San Felipe (in partial revenge, his portrait in the town's

Bourbon Felipe V plundered and renamed Xàtiva during the tussle for the Spanish Crown.

Museo del Almudín hangs permanently upside down to this day).

In the second half of the 18th century, the region recovered much of its previous commercial muscle and its population rose by some 25%. Small industrial concerns such as those of Alcoy, Bocairent and Morella processing wool from the flocks of the highlands prospered. The silkworm farms of the interior spun the thread that was transported to Valencia for weaving. The production of ceramics, linen and cane products also flourished. The port of Alicante, at this time more important than Valencia City's, was the only one on the Mediterranean littoral authorised to trade with the Americas. But the Valencia region, its capital city apart, remained essentially agricultural. In this sphere too, output increased as cultivation was extended to the *secano*, an area of inland rain-fed agriculture, while the irrigated acreage increased significantly.

The War of Independence (1808–13)

The Bourbons ruled Spain until 1808, when once again war in the interest of others was to disrupt the region.

In Madrid, the weak monarch, Carlos IV, dominated by his chief minister – and lover of the Spanish queen – Manuel Godoy, stood by as the latter invited French troops into Catalunya and Navarra. The deal was to combine both armies in a joint invasion of Portugal but the French reneged, fanned out and occupied much of the peninsula. In 1808, as the occupiers prepared to march on Madrid, king, courtier and queen were overthrown in a popular revolt that declared Fernando, Carlos IV's son, as ruler. Contemptuously overruling the lot, the French emperor Napoleon, that less than democratically committed heir to the French Revolution, stuck his brother Joseph Bonaparte on the Spanish throne as José I.

When this news reached Valencia, the city, like other Spanish cities, rose in revolt and over 400 French citizens were murdered. Towards the end of 1808, French forces besieged the city, only to withdraw in the face of the populace's tenacious resistance. Four years were to pass before Valencia finally fell to troops of the French Marshal Suchet, who occupied all the Valencia region, except Alicante town.

It was from Alicante, where British troops landed the following year, that relief came. Harried from the south and with Napoleon's attention required more and more by his floundering Russian campaign, the French withdrew from Valencia and then, with unseemly haste, from the whole of the Iberian peninsula.

The 19th Century

The remainder of the century was a time of *pronunciamentos* (coups d'état), pronouncements of military rebellion, few of which succeeded, and of the complex Carlist Wars with pretenders and rival pretenders fighting it out for the throne. In the first one, fought between supporters of the deceased king's brother, Carlos, and of his infant daughter, Isabel (Spanish history is full of Carloses and Isabels!), Carlist troops advanced from Aragón and occupied Morella. This was the trigger for a guerrilla war in much of the Valencian region. In 1837, local Carlists under the command of Ramón Cabrera, known as El Tigre del Maestrazgo (Tiger of the Maestrazgo) reached the gates of Valencia City. But the Isabelines were victorious, the little princess became queen and the following year many Carlists were executed by firing squad in the city.

The year 1868 was one of revolt in many Spanish cities and put paid to the reign of Isabel II. In September, Valencian dissidents established a Junta Revolucionaria. Although short lived, it managed to abolish, at least temporarily, the unpopular taxes on consumer spending and, in common with the anticlerical mood of the moment, ordered the expulsion of the Jesuits and the demolition of a number of churches.

The silk industry, at its peak employing more than 25,000 workers and producing more than half of Spain's annual yield, was decimated by a combination of disease and competition from Lyons in France. All the same, the economic scene in the second half of the century was much more stable than the political and social climate. Wool continued to be processed in Alcoy and the nearby centres of Ontinyent and Bocairent and also in the Maestrazgo towns of Morella, San Mateo and Catí. In the Vall de Vinalopó, towns such as Elda, Novelda and Villena prospered from the making of *alpargatas* (*espardenyes* in Valenciano), the traditional Valencian jute sandal, preparing the way for today's shoe industry, mainstay of the valley towns' economy.

Of even greater significance for the landscape today, citrus farming gobbled up more and more of the agricultural land. This and the incipient manufacturing industries became increasingly marketable with the development of the rail network. Two years after the first short line was laid between Valencia and its port, the railway was extended in 1854 to Xàtiva, passing through the principal orange-growing terrain. Five years later, it pushed farther westwards to Almansa, linking with the Madrid–Alicante

line, although it was not until 1878 that the Comunidad had a rail link through Catalunya and on to France and northern European markets. Simultaneously and well into the 20th century, tonne upon tonne of oranges destined for France, the UK and, later, Germany was exported by sea from Valencian ports.

The Early 20th Century

The late-19th-century history of the Comunidad Valenciana very much parallels that of Spain as a whole: a couple more Carlist Wars; the First Republic, which lasted under a year; the restoration of the monarchy; and the 1898 war with the US, after which Spain lost Cuba, Puerto Rico and the Philippines.

The early 20th century was a swirl of social disorder and rising tension that an unworkable system of central government was incapable of resolving. In the cities, workers' movements increasingly gravitated towards Marxism while anarchism found fertile soil among the exploited, landless peasants. From Catalunya and the Basque country came increasingly loud calls for separatism, voices echoed by groups such as Valencia Nova and Lo Rat Penat (The Bat, symbol of Valencia City) that propounded Valencian nationalism. Strikes were frequent and often savagely repressed. In the early years of the century too, the quintessentially Valencian writer Vicente Blasco Ibañez expounded the cause of republicanism in his newspaper, *El Pueblo* (The People), and was the inspiration for Blasquismo, the revolutionary republican political movement that bore his name.

Although Spain did not participate in WWI, the Comunidad Valenciana was hit hard economically. When Germany began to blockade boats bearing oranges to enemy countries, whole orchards were ripped out and other, less viable crops planted. With austerity the rule elsewhere in Europe, sales of wine from the Comunidad slumped. Only the trade in rice, imported by all sides as a food staple, remained buoyant.

During the reign of Alfonso XIII (1902–30), there were 33 different central governments until, in 1923, General Primo de Rivera stepped in to establish a dictatorship.

This lasted until 1931 when, following elections, the king, already a negligible political player, was forced into exile and the Second Republic established.

The Second Republic (1931–36)

In the Comunidad Valenciana, the years of the Second Republic were ones of economic crisis. The impact of internal social turmoil was accentuated by the knock-on effect of the Great Depression elsewhere as importing countries put up the barriers. The US increased its tariff on onions, France, on Spanish wine, while the UK, which imported more than 50% of Valencia's annual rice harvest, did the same for cereals. In 1933 much of the citrus harvest still hung on the trees for want of buyers. While local agriculture, its produce mostly destined for export, was hit hard, industry too suffered.

The rifts in society at large split asunder the national parliament too. In the elections of 1933, power swung from the leftist coalition that had dominated the polls in 1931 to a right-wing coalition. Increasingly, republican and revolutionary sympathisers saw the solution in the streets, not in parliamentary democracy. Violence – by demonstrators from both left and right, and from a repressive police and army – was spiralling out of control.

In the February 1936 national elections, the Popular Front, a left-wing coalition with communists to the fore, narrowly defeated the right-wing National Front (results from the Valencia region were less finely balanced with 428,932 votes for the Popular Front and 379,600 for the combined right wing parties).

Civil War

Now the left feared a coup, the right a revolution. The latter came when, on 17 July 1936, General Francisco Franco led the army in his Nationalist uprising. The Comunidad Valenciana unanimously opted for the Republican cause. In many towns, popular *comités* (action committees) were established and groups of volunteers fought on the Madrid front in defence of the capital. Regional political interests focused around the Agrupació Valencianista Republicana

while, at popular level, over 350 agricultural collectives were formed, mostly in regions of intensive, export-oriented cultivation.

In November 1936, as the Nationalist noose around Madrid was tugged tighter, the Republican government – the legally elected government – moved its headquarters to Valencia City, from where it ruled the unoccupied territory until it decamped to Barcelona just under a year later. Valencia City took in numerous refugees from Nationalist occupied territory and, from 1937, was subjected to enemy bombardment.

The two decisive battles of the war took place just beyond the Comunidad's limits. In the winter of 1937–38, many Valencianos fought in the bloody battle for Teruel, in Aragón, as Republican forces fought desperately and unsuccessfully to deny the Nationalists a breakthrough to the Mediterranean. Once the latter reached the coast, entering Vinaròs in April 1938, Catalunya was split from the Valencia region and other parts of the country still in Republican hands. Victorious at the Battle of the Río Ebro, over the border in Catalunya, Franco's forces took Barcelona in January 1939 and Madrid two months later. Valencia and Alicante were the last loyal cities to be overcome.

The Franco Era (1939–75)

The victors were merciless; over a million people spent time in labour camps and there were an estimated 200,000 executions between 1939 and 1943. Spanish Communist and Republican guerrillas continued a hopeless struggle in the mountains of the Maestrazgo and other parts of rural Spain until the 1950s.

Franco kept Spain out of WWII and the country – poor and struggling to recover from its own internal war – suffered a UN-sponsored trade boycott that worsened what are known as the *años de hambre* (years of hunger). Severe frosts in both 1941 and 1946 caused huge losses for Valencia's citrus-fruit farmers and the central government's penchant for grand economic ventures provided little support for the small-scale firms that constituted most of the Valencian industrial sector.

JANE SMITH

Franco – his regime attempted to suppress
Valencian regional identity.

Franco ruled absolutely: he was commander of the army and leader of both the government and the sole political party, the Movimiento Nacional (National Movement). Army garrisons were maintained outside every large city and the jails were full of political prisoners. Church and State supported each other; most secondary schools were entrusted to the Church, divorce was made illegal and church weddings compulsory. The Movimiento was given control of press and propaganda, while unions and strikes were illegal. Control was exerted from the capital, all manifestations of a separate, Valencian identity were suppressed and the use of Valenciano was not permitted in the public sphere.

In the late 1950s, the lifting of the UN embargo and a massive injection of US aid helped a new breed of technocrats in the central government to engineer an economic boom. Only at that time did the Comunidad return to pre-Civil War economic levels. But from then on, progress was steady and swift. While there were a handful of grandiose projects such as the Altos Hornos iron foundry in Sagunto, most development was on a smaller scale. The ceramic, textile and shoemaking sectors again began to thrive, as did furniture, clothing and fertiliser manufacturing. But the greatest impact came from tourism, which altered the whole landscape of coastal Valencia and exposed its inhabitants to the sometimes bizarre habits and mores of visitors from other countries. Benidorm, the most extreme example, was transformed from a tiny coastal village into what is claimed to be the largest holiday resort in Europe.

As transitory northern European holidaymakers flocked in, a contrary and longer-lasting migration took many thousands of Valencianos northwards, seeking work in more prosperous countries such as France, Germany and Switzerland, their remittances also contributing to the economic upturn. Internally, a shorter migration route led from the interior to holiday resorts and to towns such as Elche, Alicante and Valencia, leaving much of the interior underpopulated.

The New Spain

Franco chose as his successor Prince Juan Carlos, Alfonso XIII's grandson, and the present King Juan Carlos I, who took the throne upon the dictator's death in 1975. In 1977 political parties, trade unions and strikes were all legalised, the Movimiento Nacional was abolished and the centrist party of Adolfo Suárez won nearly half the seats in the new Cortes.

Personal and social life also enjoyed a rapid liberation after Franco as contraceptives, homosexuality and divorce were all legalised.

Remember where you were on 11 September 2001 when you heard of the New York Twin Towers atrocity? In the same way, all Valencianos of sufficient age recall where *they* were on 23 February 1981 when news came in of tanks rolling through the streets of the city. This was the only act of military support throughout Spain for the failed coup, led by Lieutenant-Colonel Antonio Tejero, who took over the Cortes in Madrid and held it captive for almost 24 hours.

In 1982 Valencia, like the rest of Spain, made a final break with the past by voting the Partido Socialista Obrero Español (PSOE; Spanish Socialist Workers Party) into power in the region's Cortes. For more details see Government & Politics later in this chapter.

Four years later, again reflecting a national trend, voters elected the centre-right Partido Popular, led by the current president of the Comunidad, Eduardo Zaplana, who was re-elected in 1999.

With the death of Franco, regionalism once more became a respectable word and today the Comunidad Valenciana, like most Spanish regions, enjoys a high degree of autonomy. Since its Estatuto de Autonomía (Statute of Autonomy) became law in 1982, the Comunidad has assumed more and more control over its own affairs. The Valencian language too, for all the controversy that surrounds it, is no longer snootily regarded as socially inferior. Thanks to a regional TV station and compulsory courses at school level, it has become for many a source of regional pride. And lastly, Valencia is a region that once again has a strong sense of its identity – of Spain, yet separate from Spain, of the Catalan-speaking peoples yet distinct from them. And, after a long wait, it has a generally accepted name of its own; when leftwingers were rooting for País Valenciano (Land of Valencia) and the more traditional argued for Reino de Valencia (Kingdom of Valencia), the compromise Comunidad Valenciana (Valencian Community) won and still wins the day.

GEOGRAPHY

Historically speaking, what is known today as the Comunidad Valenciana occupies the slice of Spain that was once the Reino de Valencia, the Kingdom of Valencia, onto which were grafted in 1833 two inland areas, the Plana de Utiel and the Alto Vinalopó.

In political terms, it's composed of the three provinces of Castellón in the north, the thick wedge of Valencia in the middle and Alicante in the south, each headed by the town of the same name. It's bounded by the regions of Catalunya to the north, Aragón and Castilla-La Mancha, inland to the west, and Murcia to the south.

Reaching inland and westwards from the coast is a long, quite narrow fertile coastal plain. Known as the *huerta*, the market garden, it's green, intensively irrigated and produces, in particular, oranges. It's also where you'll find the three provincial capitals, most of the Comunidad's large towns – and where over 80% of its population live.

Rising westwards from the huerta are broad hills and modest sierras that merge into the *meseta*, Spain's high inland plateau. These pine-clad hills are known collectively as the *sécano*, where agriculture, mainly fruit and almond trees, is rain-fed. From the uplands flow a number of rivers – though river is a grand term for such relatively tiny trickles. All the same, the valleys they have cut or through which they flow are all significant geographical features and the more important ones, such as the Vinalopó, Turia and Palencia, are important communications routes. The latter two and, farther to the south, the Río Ju'car are damned for both hydro power and irrigation. Except after each year's brief yet torrential rains in the hills, when flooding is always a risk, their flow is desultory and some of the smaller streams never get as far as the sea. It wasn't always so feeble but for centuries waters have been diverted and siphoned off for agriculture.

Sea and river aren't the Comunidad's only watery manifestations. South of Valencia City, La Albufera, rich in fish and eels and a vital stopover for migratory birds, is a protected freshwater lagoon. Salt has been an important contributor to the economy of some coastal settlements and the resorts of Calpe, Santa Pola and Torrevieja are squeezed between the Mediterranean and broad *salinas* (salt pans). To their south, the land bordering the region of Murcia is arid and semi-desert.

The northerly sierras, such as the Maestrazgo, are the most easterly manifestation of the Sistema Ibérico, which runs cross country from the Rioja wine-growing district in the northwest of Spain. Ranges in the south of the Comunidad, such as the Sierra de Mariola or Aitana, are the last manifestation of the

Sistema Bético, a chain that has its origins in Andalucía. Between the two is the Meseta de Utiel-Requena, a flat upland plain, planted with hectare upon hectare of vines and source of, in particular, some robust red wines.

Some early spin doctors came up with the names Costa del Azahar (Orange Blossom Coast) and Costa Blanca (White Coast; one hopes the fee wasn't too fat for this one) for the tracts of coastline and tourist resorts north and south respectively of Valencia City. But it isn't all sand and sunshine; the sands of the Costa Blanca are modulated by wilder, less-frequented spots where the sea laps against rock. In places such as the buffer zone between Altea and Benidorm, the promontory of Cabo de la Nao or beneath Calpe's Peñon de Ifach, it beats against substantial cliffs. And beaches can vary from the magnificent deep sweep of Gandía's, Peñíscola's or Benidorm's Levante and Poniente to narrow strands no wider than a trio of sunbathing bodies laid head to toe.

Along many stretches of the some 450km of Valencian coastline, the huerta – or what's left of it after resort development over the last 50 years has eaten into traditional and highly productive agricultural land – reaches down to the shore. Take a stroll beyond the limits of Gandía or Cullera, for example, and you can still choose to walk either along the beach or through the orange orchards.

CLIMATE

The Valencia region enjoys a climate that's generally mild and healthy just about all year and pulls in visitors by the million around the calendar.

Rain may fall at any time but is negligible except in spring (March, April and May) and autumn, especially September and October. Even at these times, most days will be sunny rather than overcast. But the downpours, when they come, can be torrential and may last for several hours before the sun swiftly evaporates what hasn't been sluiced underground.

That's the broad picture, within which it's useful to distinguish three distinct yet overlapping sub-climates. The coast itself

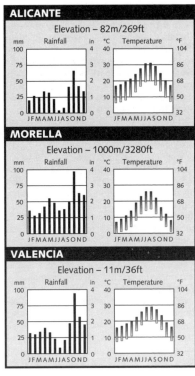

and the plain that laps up to it enjoy a Mediterranean littoral climate, where extremes are mitigated by the influence of the sea. Rainfall averages 400mm to 500mm per annum. The thermometer very rarely hits freezing point – and when it does it's a disaster for the citrus orchards that occupy so much of the plain. Winter skies are generally blue and temperatures bracing, not cold. The summer months of July and August, when average daily maximums hover just the right side of 30°C and humidity is high, can be sticky. But if you feel too sweaty, simply dunk yourself in the Mediterranean, whose average temperature is 20°C or above between June and October.

Inland, as elsewhere in Spain, the temperature variation from summer to winter is greater although differences are not as extreme as those occurring more deeply into the meseta, Spain's high inland plateau. The mean average temperature of Morella, in the Maestrazgo, is 11.5°C compared with Valencia's 17°C and Alicante's 18°C. Here, where the climate's characterised as Mediterranean mountain, verging into the continental variant typical of the meseta, winters are chillingly cold and snow lingers on the higher points (the Comunidad Valenciana even has the tiniest ski resort you've ever schussed at Virgen de la Vega). Rainfall too, at 500mm to 700mm per year, is a little higher. Summer temperatures vary from north to south. In the Maestrazgo area, they're relatively benign and draw canny local holidaymakers escaping from the humidity of the coastal towns, which they leave to tourists from the meseta and abroad. As you progress southwards and lose height (roughly speaking, from around Requena onwards), seasonal variation is even greater and summers can be scorching. What both areas have in common is a dry heat, more tolerable for many than the coastal steam bath.

Climatically, the southernmost part of the Comunidad has more in common with the dry, arid terrain of Murcia and Almería even farther south. Mild in winter and hot in summer, its rainfall low – less than 350mm per annum – and unpredictable, it engenders a semi-desert terrain, even only a kilometre or two from the coast.

ECOLOGY & ENVIRONMENT

The Comunidad Valenciana's ecological trials and triumphs tend to mirror Spain's. Since the establishment of the autonomous regional government in the early 1980s, environmental legislation with teeth has been passed through the Valencian parliament. Notable achievements are a much stricter control over high-rise coastal development and the proscription of any construction right beside what remains of untouched coastline (though images of stable doors and long bolted horses come to mind). Also, as many as 12 Parques Naturales (Nature Parks) and three offshore Parques Marinas (Marine Parks) have been created, limiting human activity and offering a real degree of protection to their wildlife (for details see

Nature Parks & Reserves under Flora & Fauna later in this chapter). Environmental pressure groups are small in number yet vocal and heard (if not always listened to).

It's invariably the activities of humankind that give rise to the environmental problems of the moment – and often the very mass tourism that brings wealth to the Comunidad is a prime contributor. Cities such as Valencia and Castellón continue to sprawl outwards, nibbling away at the prime, irreplaceable agricultural land of the huerta, while coastal resorts gobble up orchards and fields. Larger towns and coastal resorts often have satellite *urbanizaciónes* (housing estates), bulldozed from virgin or agricultural land, where a high percentage of the houses are second homes, offering owners that place in the country that the very *urbanización* is encroaching upon. The coastal plain, with 80% of the Comunidad's inhabitants and a massive upward blip in numbers during the summer, is reliant upon water that's captured in reservoirs high in the hills. Ominously, in 2001, a year when rains weren't significantly below the average, Xàbia was obliged to introduce water rationing during the summer months. In that same year, it was agreed to divert massive quantities of the Río Ebro, which both Catalunya to the north and Aragón to the west claim as their own, in order to compensate for anticipated shortfalls in the Comunidad Valenciana. Because of such issues, an increasing number of voices are calling for a significant slow down, if not total embargo, on further holiday development. But commercial interests too often manage to shout louder...

On the plus side, the driving force of the tourist euro has lead to a much cleaner shoreline. A European Union (EU) 'blue flag', indicating that a beach has met certain minimum standards of facilities and cleanliness, proudly flutters over 82 of the Comunidad's beaches.

Intensive agriculture and irrigation has, in some areas of the coastal plain, led to a lowering of the water table and increased salination. Also, fertilisers and pesticides, whether spread locally or way up in the hills, maybe even beyond the Comunidad's borders, leech out downstream. Although controls are nowadays much stricter, every so often fish and eels in the Albufera freshwater lake flop belly up because of contamination from chemicals applied to the surrounding rice paddy or more distant fields.

Two predictable media headlines every summer are forest fire and traffic deaths. Despite posted warnings and severe penalties, every year fragile forests of pine, rich in highly inflammable resin, go up in flames. (A major slice of the Parque Natural del Montgó is still blackened and dead after a fire that raged for nearly a week in 2000.) In a nation where most people are first generation car owners, the car is king and it would be political suicide to introduce legislation to control drivers' perceived right to park, drive and pollute where and when they wish.

By contrast, strict controls have been applied to that other area of untrammelled freedom so many Spanish males regard as a divine right: huntin', shootin' and fishin'. Although several species of bird and mammal have been severely depleted, many of those most at risk are now protected. This said, too much poaching and winking at the law still goes on.

FLORA & FAUNA

Although the distinction is far from rigorous, things animal and vegetable, like so much else, tend to vary from coast to hills.

Flora

The Shoreline Dunes range from a narrow, undulating strip, to which hardy, salt-tolerating, ground-hugging plants cling, to the massive piles, anchored by stands of pine around Guardamar. Onto the land's first line of defence, the most unstable and shifting sand, anchor plants such as *grama de duna*, *barrón* (European beachgrass or marram) and *algodonosa* (cottonweed or sea cudweed). Behind this barrier, in damp, salt-rich patches, *barillas* (*Salsola* sp. and *Suaeda* sp.) and hardy sea grasses survive.

The Coastal Plain On the coastal plain, the orange, first introduced and cultivated by the Arabs, is far and away the dominant tree.

Orchard upon orchard spreads across the width of the plain, especially in the provinces of Castellón and Valencia. This versatile tree can bear simultaneously both ripe fruit and the tight, white blossom. Not for nothing is the coastal strip north of Castellón, as far as the border with Catalunya, called the Costa del Azahar (Orange Blossom Coast). If the wind's blowing from the right direction, even the heart of Valencia City can be scented with its heady aroma. Lemons too hang heavy and yellow in season although grapefruit, strangely enough, has never really taken off. You may see their fat footballs growing and you *can* find them in markets but they're far from everyday fare.

Popular trees and shrubs native to the region include the kermes oak and *lentisco* (lentisk or mastic tree), which thrive at all elevations. White, or Scots pine, preferring a sandy soil, is also common near the coast. Among the cactuses and their like, the non-native, sturdy, independent prickly pear and the *Agave americana* (century plant, maguey or American aloe) are quick to occupy dry, uncultivated terrain in their adopted home.

South of Valencia, rice for paella, that gastronomically endemic Valencian dish, grows in profusion in the paddy fields near and around the Albufera lagoon. It's a round, short-grained variety of the kind you may be used to in rice pudding.

You'll see palm trees just about everywhere, usually planted for decoration and shade. In the south of the Comunidad, dates are a commercial crop. The palm groves of Elche, another legacy of the Moors, are Europe's most extensive while those of Orihuela, just down the motorway, are Spain's second largest. Similarly, the palmito (fan palm), more shrub than tree, is popular for decoration and also grows wild.

Every tight little gulch and gorge, on the plains or dropping from the sierras, will be fringed by oleander, pretty and quick to populate but poisonous.

The Inland Sierras Where the land is worked, hardy almond trees predominate together with olive trees. In the milder valleys peach, plum and apricot flourish while the

Vall de Gallinera is famous for its plump, juicy cherries.

Elsewhere, pine *encina* (holm oak) and *algarrobo* (carob) grow naturally and in profusion. Less common, yet still plentiful, are *alcornoca* (cork oak), *acebuche* (wild olive) and, especially in the higher reaches of the Maestrazgo, *quejigo* (gall oak).

The semi-scrubland known as *mattoral* or *montebajo* is quick to colonise where trees fail to take, have been logged long ago or wiped out by more recent forest fire. It can be forbidding vegetation to hack your way through but has its charm, particularly if your olfactory senses are keen. Amid the lentisco, gorse, squat juniper bushes and pink rock roses, herbs such as thyme, rosemary, lavender and sage thrive and give up their scent on hot days.

Fauna

The Coastal Plain Mediterranean shores are a vital segment of the Mediterranean migratory corridor, down which hundreds of thousands of birds pass on their twice-yearly migration, in April and May, and in late September and well into October, between Europe and Africa. Particularly good places to observe the flypast include the Albufera lake south of Valencia and the salt pans of Torrevieja and Santa Pola.

Among the more exotic species that you stand a good chance of seeing if the time's right are bee-eaters and flamingos, who, lovers of highly saline waters such as the salt pans of Torrevieja and Santa Pola, stop by to replenish their stomachs and energy.

In areas of coastal wetland such as the Albufera lake, grey herons, little egrets and cattle egrets are common year round. Here, you'll also find mallard duck and red-crested pochards bobbing their way across the water. If you're at all interested in birds, build in a visit to its Racó de l'Olla visitors centre with its hide and closed-circuit TV cameras (see Around Valencia City in the Valencia City chapter).

You'll also probably spot water rats paddling among the reeds – or their corpses, squidged all over the highway when the paddy fields are flooded in late spring.

The rare Iberian lynx is a stringently protected species.

The Inland Sierras Life is hard high inland. Birds of prey such as sparrowhawks, buzzards and white-headed eagles ride the thermals, spying for the smallest rustle in the undergrowth below. Best adapted to this harsh land are the lizards that scurry everywhere in summer. If you're *very* lucky, you might spy a wild boar, badger, red squirrel, Iberian lynx and a feral or truly wild goat. Mostly, though, it's lizards...

Endangered Species

The local Consellería de Medio Ambiente (Ministry of the Environment) is not only protecting but also actively seeking to encourage the reproduction of a couple of species of fish, once widespread but now in danger of disappearance not because they've been fished to oblivion – both types of toothcarp, they're much too tiny to be at risk from human predators – but as a result of their diminishing habitat. The *samaruc* (*Valencia hispanica*) is now limited to only a few pockets in the coastal wet zones of the Comunidad while distribution of the even more diminutive, quicksilver *fartet* (*Aphanius ibericus*) is even more limited.

Nature Parks & Reserves

If your Spanish is hot, you can get information about the Comunidad Valenciana's 12 Parques Naturales (Nature Parks) from the Consellería de Medio Ambiente (local Ministry of the Environment) on ☎ 96 386 63 50.

Parque Natural is a fairly catch-all category; most have villages and roads within their boundaries, and regulations and characteristics vary. What they have in common is an aim to arrest deterioration caused by humankind and to find that difficult equilibrium between those, be they fisherfolk, foresters or salt processors, who derive a living from the land and the need for conservation.

The 12 Parques Naturales established since the Comunidad came into being are described below, travelling from north to south. The locations of most are indicated on the regional maps sprinkled throughout this book.

Parque Natural del Prat de Cabanes y Torreblanca

Visitors Centre ☎ 908 04 84 31, Centro Experimental de Acuicultura de Torre la Sal, Ribera de Cabanes (near Benicássim). This narrow 9km strip of marshland is separated from the sea by a bank of gravel. It is rich in bird life and a breeding ground for three species of endemic fish.

Parque Natural del Desierto de las Palmas

Visitors Centre ☎ 96 476 07 27, La Bartola, Carretera Magdalena al Desert km 7.8 (near Benicássim). Above the fan palms, which give the park its name, pines and groves of cork oak flourish in the low north-south running hills.

Reserva Natural de las Islas Columbretes

Visitors Centre ☎ 964 28 29 68, Planetario de Castellón, Paseo Marítimo 1, Grao de Castellón. Boats take controlled numbers of visitors from Castellón and Peñíscola to these tiny offshore volcanic islands, which are rich in marine life.

Parque Natural de La Sierra de Espadán

Visitors Centre ☎ 964 62 91 12, Plaza Josep Sorribes Fuster 4, Ain (near Segorbe). The most recently established of the Comunidad's Parque Naturales is this pair of mountain ranges, densely clad in cork oak and pine.

Parque Natural de la Albufera

Visitors Centre ☎ 96 162 73 45, Racó de l'Olla, Carretera del Palmar s/n (near Valencia). This vast, 21,000-hectare, freshwater, reed-fringed lake is a haven for birds, with over 250 species recorded, including a huge colony of grey heron. The visitors centre is excellent.

Parque Natural de la Marjal de Pego-Oliva

Visitors Centre ☎ 96 640 02 51, Calle San Agustín 6, Pego (near Oliva). Once a freshwater lake this marshy area, with its reed beds and deeper pools, is almost permanently flooded.

Parque Natural del Montgó

Visitors Centre ☎ 96 642 32 05, Calle Ramón Ortega, Denia. Over 600 species of flora, several of them endemic, have been recorded on this magnificent 735m limestone mountain.

Parque Natural del Peñon de Ifach

Visitors Centre ☎ 96 597 20 15, Aula de Natura del Peñon de Ifach, Calle Isla de Formentera s/n, Calpe. The 45 hectares of this 332m-high slab of rock looming from the sea make it one of Europe's smallest protected areas.

Parque Natural del Carrascal de la Font Roja

Visitors Centre ☎ 96 533 76 20, Carretera de la Font Roja s/n, Alcoy. Embracing the Sierra del Menejador, this area receives protection because of the wealth and variety of its trees that differ in kind according to sunny or shady slopes.

Parque Natural del Hondo de Elche

Visitors Centre ☎ 96 667 85 15, Calle Vereda de Sendres s/n, Elche. The two large reservoirs and surrounding ponds and salt marshes at this Parque Naturale are the breeding ground for some 750 marbled ducks *(Marmaronetta angustirostris)*, 80% of the current total European population. Other species you stand a good chance of spotting include coots, shovelers, pochard, red-crested pochard and a pair of raptors, the marsh harrier and the osprey.

Parque Natural de las Salinas de Santa Pola

Visitors Centre ☎ 96 669 35 46, Museo de la Sal, Avenida Zaragoza 45, Santa Pola. Within these shallow salt pans, many of which are still worked commercially, herons and avocets nest and up to 8000 flamingos are seasonal visitors. The visitors centre and salt museum occupy an old salt mill.

Parque Natural de las Lagunas de la Mata y Torrevieja

Visitors Centre ☎ 96 692 04 04, Casa Forestal de la Mata, La Mata (near Torrevieja). These saltwater lagoons, together with the Salinas de Santa Pola and Elche's El Hondo constitute an important breeding ground and winter home for over 100 aquatic bird species.

The Comunidad also has three marine reserves, where fishing, though not access, is prohibited. These give protection to marine life in the waters around the Islas Columbretes (see the list of Parques Naturales above and Costa del Azahar in the Northern Valencia chapter), Cabo de la Nao (see Denia in the Costa Blanca chapter) and the Isla de Tabarca (see Around Santa Pola, also in the Costa Blanca chapter).

GOVERNMENT & POLITICS

In 1982 the Cortes in Madrid passed the Estatuto de Autonomía in accordance with the 1978 post-Franco constitution. From that day, the Valencia region reassumed a degree of control over its affairs that it hadn't enjoyed since 1707, when its Fueros, or special privileges, were abrogated (see The War of Succession under History earlier in this chapter). In those distant days it was the Reino de Valencia, the Kingdom of Valencia, at the receiving end. This time, the statute engendered the autonomous region of Valencia, one of the 17 that constitute the Spanish whole. It's more commonly – and certainly more easily on the tongue – called the Comunidad Valenciana.

In the following year the Partido Socialista Obrero Español (PSOE; a nominally socialist party, though these days only slightly left of, for example, the UK's New Labour) won the first Comunidad elections. Joan Lerma, its leader, was selected as Presidente of the Generalitat, the highest governing body of the Comunidad, then re-elected in both 1987 and 1991.

In the 1995 regional elections, where results reflected those of other autonomous communities and presaged that of the following year's elections at national level, the centre-right Partido Popular (PP) was victorious. Eduardo Zaplana of the PP assumed the presidency of the Generalitat, a position he continues to occupy. Both he and his party were re-confirmed in office in the subsequent 1999 elections.

The next regional elections are due to take place in 2003. Elected members take their seats in the *Cortes*, the Comunidad's parliament, a converted palace on Calle Navellos in Valencia City. At the time of writing, the composition of the Cortes is: PP 49 seats; PSOE 35 seats; and Esquerra Unida del País Valencià five seats.

There are three levels of government: the Generalitat, the *provincia* and the *municipio*.

The Generalitat governs at regional level and has wide powers over matters such as transport, education, health, trade, industry, the environment, tourism and agriculture. Its various ministries are dotted around Valencia City while the presidency and other high offices occupy the prestigious 15th-century Generalitat building and adjacent ones on Calle Caballeros.

The Comunidad (region) is divided into the three *provincias* (provinces) of Castellón, Valencia and Alicante, each named after its respective capital. The Diputación is the top provincial administrative and decision-making body (Valencia province's Diputación is on Plaza de Manises, just across the road from the Generalitat, so there's no excuse for lack of liaison!). The next level of subdivision is the *municipio* (local council), of which the Comunidad has 581, each administered by an *ayuntamiento*, or town hall.

So Valencia City has its ayuntamiento and is also the capital of both Valencia province and the Comunidad Valenciana, the entire Valencia region. Unwieldy it may be, but the system works reasonably well. However, there's a fair degree of inefficient overlap and costly duplication of functions (for example, a big city might have municipal, provincial and regional tourist offices, each with its own staff and premises and each dishing out much the same information at their respective levels).

ECONOMY

Sunshine is one of the Comunidad Valenciana's most valuable commodities. Its rays entice annually over 4.5 million visitors, most of whom home in on the coastal resorts. The euros they spend don't just go to the hotel and restaurant trade, construction industry and transport interests. There are also myriad knock-on benefits as the money generated by tourism is recycled and re-recycled, helping the Valencian economy to keep moving. The sun also kisses the crops and fruit trees that grow in profusion along the coastal plain. Agriculture represents 17% of total exports from the Comunidad. If you sink your teeth into an orange anywhere in Western Europe, it's a fair bet it grew here; Valencia's huerta produces 70% of Spain's oranges, most of which are exported.

Although annual tonnage is declining, rice, primarily from the paddy fields around the Albufera lake, is another staple export, together with fresh vegetables, a high percentage of which are also destined for northern European markets.

From the interior, where the soil is less rich, come olives, carob (used as a chocolate substitute and for animal feed), fruit – such as peaches, apricots and plums – and, above all, almonds. Livestock rearing, primarily sheep and pig farming, keeps many a rural community going. The quality of Valencian wines has also improved significantly in recent years. While its reds have for years been an anonymous but significant constituent of supermarket branded table wines, many, both red and white, can justifiably proclaim their origin with pride these days.

But there's much more to the Valencian economy than food, drink and providing for others' fun. Although the Comunidad's industrial base is not as substantial as that of Catalunya to the north, manufacturing accounts for a substantial amount of the region's wealth. Largest of the region's firms is the Ford motor company. If you drive a nifty Ka, it probably will have come from Ford's only factory in Spain, just south of Valencia City. This multinational giant apart, nearly all the Comunidad's manufacturing is undertaken by small and medium-size enterprises. Manises and Paterna, virtual suburbs of Valencia City, have been important ceramics producing centres from Arab times. Along the Costa del Azahar near Castellón, tile-making companies exploit the local clay. Spain is the second-largest tile producer in the world after Italy and the majority are fired in the Comunidad by companies such as Porcelanosa. The inland town of Alcoy produces textiles and paper while along the corridor of the Vall de Vinalopó, Elda and Novelda are famous for toy production and, together with the nearby city of Elche, for shoemaking. In the same area, the small town of Crevillent produces blankets and carpets. Furniture-making too is a significant local industry. A high percentage of all the above products is earmarked for export.

Unemployment has fallen dramatically in the last few years. Currently running at about 11%, it's some 2% below the national average and substantially lower than the figures in excess of 20% that were the norm in the mid- and late 1990s.

POPULATION & PEOPLE

The Comunidad Valenciana has just over four million inhabitants – decidedly fewer than the number of visitors it receives each year. They represent around 10% of the all-Spain total of 39.8 million and are about two million fewer than the citizens of Catalunya, to the north.

Despite the cosmopolitan atmosphere of the coastal resorts, substantial emigration in the 1950s and 1960s and Spain's presence in the EU for over 15 years, it's a very stable populace. Nearly 75% of the people were born within the Comunidad and just under 50% still live in the town or village where they were born. Indeed, it's still not uncommon to hear a Valenciano refer to someone from Madrid, Seville or elsewhere in Spain as *extranjero* (foreign)!

It's also a very homogeneous population where Spaniards still make up over 97.5% of the whole and where the largest group of non-nationals, from other countries of the EU, constitutes only 1.5%. Ah, you may be told, but the latest official figures don't yet reflect those illegal immigrants who were granted residence papers as a result of an amnesty in 2000, nor those who have arrived from the Balkans, North and sub-Saharan Africa and the Americas, especially Ecuador, since that time. True and true. However, non-European immigration still represents a very small element of Valencian society.

The average density of 173 people per sq km is substantially more than the Spanish average of 79. It varies considerably from coast to hill country; Alicante province with its intensive coastal development and medium-size inland industrial towns has 239 people per sq km whereas the province of Castellón, much less exploited, has only 70.

Valencia City, with a population of over 750,000, is Spain's third largest after Madrid and Barcelona. Way behind in second place comes Alicante with under 300,000 inhabitants. Once you've factored in Elche and Castellón, there are no more towns in the Comunidad Valenciana with a population of more than 65,000.

One of the greatest social changes since the end of the Franco era is family size. The

Comunidad figure of 1.18 children per mother parallels exactly the national average, as does the later average age when women give birth to their first baby, currently standing at just over 30.

EDUCATION

Education is compulsory from the age of six to 16. Each region in Spain administers its own education system, although overall guidelines are similar throughout the country. The Comunidad has 1427 primary schools and 1309 at secondary level, of which 28% are private, mainly church, institutions.

Upon matriculation at the end of the secondary cycle, students must also sit entrance exams if they want to study for a degree. The Comunidad has five public-sector universities with a total undergraduate enrolment of over 130,000. Most students tend to study for five or so years to first degree level, earning qualifications such as the *diploma* after three years and the *licencia* after another two, or sometimes three years' study.

ARTS
Architecture

From the Roman domination of the Valencia region, not a great deal remains intact though there's a wealth of ruins. Among the more interesting sites from an aesthetic point of view is the much adapted – and, many would say, desecrated – theatre of Sagunto and the aqueduct outside Chelva in the Turia valley.

From Muslim times, the carefully preserved chunks and hunks of Valencia's Moorish wall still clearly indicate the city limits of the era.

The 13th-century Christian reoccupation of these lands coincided with the transition in architectural style from the simplicity of the Romanesque to the more exuberant Gothic style. So, in many of the early churches, frequently established on the site of the mosque of the erstwhile rulers, a hybrid style is evident. From the earlier, Romanesque period are the rounded arches, deeply incised with geometrical or floral patterns, and also the capitals crowning supporting pillars, often intricately carved with everyday scenes of an engaging naivety.

Gothic architecture, which arrived later in Spain than in many other parts of Europe, is characterised principally by the pointed arch and, within a building, by ceilings that are cross-ribbed, often quite elaborately. A good example of such transition is Valencia's cathedral, its construction begun soon after the city was recaptured from the Moors in 1238 and finished in the middle of the 14th century. One entrance, the Puerta del Palau, the earliest, is round arched and Romanesque while the Puerta de los Apóstoles with its slender, delicately carved apostle statues snug in their niches and its soaring pointed arch is pure Gothic.

During the 14th century, a time of prosperity along Spain's Mediterranean littoral, the style known as Mediterranean Gothic flourished in Valencia, Catalunya and Mallorca, in the Balearic Islands. Building, especially ecclesiastical, was on the grand scale and the style relatively sober, relying upon the interplay of light and shade for effect. Churches tended to have a single nave bordered by side chapels. The former could accommodate the substantial congregations that would gather to worship in the larger towns. The more intimate chapels would be for rites such as funerals and marriages, and were often sponsored by trade guilds or noble families from the area. It was a style that permeated the whole region. Fine examples that remain to this day include the Iglesia de las Santas Justa and Rufina, joint patrons of Orihuela, the Real Convento de San Francisco in Morella, currently under restoration, the interior of Alicante's Iglesia de Santa María and the delightful cloister of Segorbe's cathedral.

However, Mediterranean Gothic's most exuberant flourishing was in the temporal, not spiritual, domain. Two prime examples from the 15th century in Valencia City are the Lonja de los Mercaderes, a Unesco World Heritage building, and the Palau de la Generalitat, the seat of regional government. From this time too date many of the modest yet pleasing noble palaces and wealthy merchants' residences that grace the squares and main streets of even quite small towns such as Sant Mateo, Forcall, Bocairent and

Ontinyent. Typical features are a wide, arched entrance giving onto a central patio and a stairway, often elaborately carved.

Of a more military bent, city walls were often much more than a simple line of defence against marauders. Many, such as Valencia City's, have been destroyed, often to make way for 19th-century urban expansion, but others, such as those of Morella, Peñíscola and parts of Segorbe are still fun to roam around.

The Valencia region also has an abundance of castles, many resulting from historic frontier clashes between rival kingdoms and faiths. Many, alas, are closed to the public. Among the finest and best preserved are those of Denia, Peñíscola and Alicante.

Since Valencia's links with Rome were so strong because of the Borja Popes (known in English as the infamous Borgias), the Renaissance arrived earlier here than in many parts of Spain and had its major impact in the south of the Comunidad. It manifested itself in buildings both secular and religious – the Palacio Municipal and the Iglesia de Santiago in Villena, for example, or the Colegio de Santo Domingo and Iglesia de Santiago in Orihuela.

The arrival of baroque influences in the Valencia region in the last quarter of the 17th century coincided with another period of economic wellbeing. Characteristic features of both church and civil architecture are elaborate decoration, sometimes too extravagant for northern European eyes, twisted columns known as *columnas salomónicas*, cherubs everywhere, trompe l'oeil effects in painting and decoration, gilt plastered on by the kilo and elaborately carved foliage.

Although few churches were constructed from scratch in the baroque style, many were 'improved' or extended during this period, notably by the addition of huge gilded *retablos*, or altarpieces, which often dwarf the altar itself. In Vinaròs, for example, the fine baroque facade of the parish church was grafted onto the existing building. In Valencia, the magnificent octagonal Santa Catalina tower, one of the city's symbols, soars skywards from the original Gothic

place of worship. Just up the road in Plaza de la Reina, you'll find the resplendent baroque third portal of Valencia's cathedral, recently restored to its original splendour. In civil architecture, the breathtakingly over-the-top entrance to Valencia's Palacio del Marqués de los Dos Aguas is baroque theatricality taken to its most extreme. More sober and representative, yet still elaborate, is the gracefully symmetrical facade of Alicante's town hall.

Much of the 19th century in the Valencia region was, as elsewhere in Spain and Europe, a time for the restatement of classical architectural principles and values. Popular manifestations of such a tendency are the regular, strictly symmetrical, colonnaded *plazas de toros* (bull rings), particularly Valencia's, that were constructed around the Comunidad.

At the end of the century a handful of striking public buildings were influenced by *modernismo*, an artistic movement that had its seed in Catalunya and its best known proponent in Gaudí. Characterised by the use of mosaic and decoration drawn from nature, it finds its greatest expression in Valencia City's markets, the Mercado de Colón and Mercado Central, the pleasing lines of Alicante's central market and, above all, Valencia's magnificent Estación del Norte.

Lastly, no discussion of Valencian architecture is complete without a reference to locally born, internationally renowned Santiago Calatrava, who has left his stamp upon Valencia City in the breathtaking Ciudad de las Artes y las Ciencias. For further details on the architectural achievements of the region's most famous contemporary son, see the boxed text.

Painting & Sculpture

The first known artistic manifestations in the Valencia region were a few prehistoric oxblood daubs on inland caves, highly regarded by experts but difficult of access and mostly closed to the public nowadays.

From pre-classical Iberian times, two masterpieces have come down to us; the bust of the Dama de Elche, now in Madrid's Museo Arqueológico, and, on an altogether different scale, the tiny bronze Guerrero de

Santiago Calatrava

Something of an exception among young Spaniards of his generation, Santiago Calatrava set off to study abroad, then returned, internationally renowned, to stamp his signature on the city he'd left behind.

Born in Benimámet, an undistinguished dormitory suburb of Valencia, in 1951, he qualified as an architect in Valencia and was then sent to Zurich in Switzerland for doctoral studies by his farsighted father, who had made his limited pile from agricultural exports.

You'll recognise Calatrava's structures immediately. In an age of corporate planning, financing and design, his signature is as distinctive and as easily recognised as the Coca-Cola logo. Technologically, he pushes to the limits what can balance, counter, take and impart stress in concrete, iron and steel. Yet his soaring creations, all sinuous white curves with scarcely a right angle in sight, relate more to things organic: the vast blinking eye of the Hemisféric or the filigree struts, like the veins of a leaf, of the Umbracle, a vast, shaded walkway in the Ciudad de las Artes y la Ciencias.

Not for Calatrava the discrete town house or coastal retreat of some loaded private client. From the very beginning, he shot for public projects, the biggest of canvases and structures to be experienced by thousands every single day.

In Valencia, the Puente Calatrava, nicknamed the *peineta* because it resembles the comb that women wear beneath the mantilla, spans the old Turia riverbed. Farther upstream, the Puente 9 de October, more restrained, is also his handiwork. Down south in Andalucía, he designed for Expo '92, Seville's world fair, the Alamillo bridge, a graceful 200m sweep across the Río Guadalquivir. In the Basque country, his Volantín footbridge sweeps over the Río Nervíon, complementing and by no means outclassed by Bilbao's famous Guggenheim Museum nearby.

Stations, such as his early Stadelhofen train station in Zurich or that serving Lyons' St-Exupéry airport in France are also his forte. And drop beneath Valencia's Calatrava bridge to penetrate the metro station beneath. With its soaring struts, it's like stepping into the carcass of a whale.

Still designing on the grand scale, his drawing board these days bears two transatlantic projects: the Milwaukee Art Museum on the shores of Lake Michigan and the Cathedral of Christ the Light in Oakland, California. Then one day, maybe, just maybe, backers will come forward to underwrite the US's equivalent of Barcelona's Gaudí-designed Sagrada Familia church, under constant construction since the early 1900s. His daring design for the completion of New York's Cathedral of St John the Divine, its foundations laid in 1892, is lying there, waiting to be executed...

Engineer and architect, Calatrava is also an accomplished sculptor and furniture designer, skills he brings into play in the service of his professed aim of linking more closely not only the related disciplines of architecture and engineering but also architecture and art.

Polymath and transculturalist, he maintains his principal home and studio in a lakeside villa outside Zurich but also has homes and offices in Valencia and Paris with plans afoot for a New York base too.

Moixent, the warrior of Moixent, who stands defiant in one of the showcases of Valencia's La Beneficencia cultural centre.

The Roman period is best represented artistically by it architectural legacy. One exception is the magnificent bronze statue of Apollo, also in La Beneficencia, which Valencia can rightly claim as her own. Discovered offshore by divers, it was probably cast elsewhere in the empire.

Primitivos Valencianos Valencia's first artistic flourishing came much later, in the 15th century, an era of great creativity and cultural interaction throughout Europe. This was the time of the so-called *primitivos valencianos* (Valencian primitives), individual in style, yet open to influences from both north and east. It's attested, for example, that the Florentine painter Gherardo Starnina was active in Valencia at the turn of that century.

In the reverse direction, King Alfonso el Magnánimo of Aragón (1394–1458), ruler of Valencia and a great patron of the arts, sponsored a visit to Flanders by local artist Luis Dalmau (c.1400–1450) who probably spent time at the studio of Jan van Eyck. There was considerable interplay too between the artists of the day in Valencia and their fellow painters to the north in Catalunya. The greatest cross-cultural influence, however, came from across the Mediterranean. At this time, the Crown of Aragón (Corona de Aragón) also ruled Naples and most of southern Italy. Alfonso el Magnánimo, who spent much of his time at his court in Naples, was the force behind what was to be the first of several waves of Italian cultural influence.

From the first third of the 15th century, an artistic period known as the *gótico internacional valenciano* (Valencian international Gothic), other fine Valencian artists include Miguel Alcañiz (documented 1407–47), Gonzalo Peris (active 1380–1451), Pere Nicolau (documented 1390–1408) and Lorenzo Zaragoza (documented 1363–c.1406) – Aragonese by birth and active in both Valencia and Barcelona. But there are also so many anonymous painters, known to posterity simply as *maestro* (master), responsible for such unsigned masterpieces as the vibrant Fray Bonifacio Ferrer altarpiece (named after the friar who commissioned it) displayed in Valencia City's Museo de Bellas Artes.

By the middle of the 15th century, the influence of Flemish naturalism became more marked at a time when, inspired by Italian sources, local artists had begun to apply the principle of perspective. The other great innovation owing its inspiration to the Low Countries was the gradual generalisation of oil paint upon canvas as the preferred medium rather than, as previously, water-based tempera upon wood. Prominent innovators were Jaime Baço, known as Jacomart (c.1411–61), who had spent many years painting in Naples, and the most famous of his several accomplished pupils, Joan Reixach (c.1431–86), who was also influenced by innovations spreading south from the Low Countries.

Renaissance Towards the end of the 15th century and into the 16th, artists who can more accurately be described as of the Renaissance were making their reputations around the churches and monasteries of the region. New features included a more clearly defined composition and a glorification of the human body. Typical of these were the two Osonas, Rodrigo and Francisco, father and son, with their blend of Flemish realism and Italian decorative traits, particularly in their depiction of architectural features.

This was the age when the Borgia (Borja in Spanish) family from Gandía, on the coast south of Valencia City, held sway in the Vatican. As a consequence, traffic between Rome and Valencia was once again frequent and the artistic influence of northern Italy was all the more marked. Indeed, Valencia was the first Spanish city to feel the full impact of the Italian Renaissance. Francesco Pagano, Pablo de San Leocadio and Ricardo Quatararo were contracted from Rome to work upon the decoration of Valencia's cathedral, influencing local artists such as Vicente Macip (1475–1550).

The traffic was two-way, exemplified by Hernando Yañez de la Almedina (1465–1536), who spent years practising in Florence, probably as a pupil of Leonardo da Vinci, before returning, enriched, to his homeland. Here, he continued to practise his severe, monumental style, working with Valencian artists such as Hernando de Llanos who, jointly with his namesake, Hernando Yañez, painted the magnificent altarpiece in Valencia's cathedral. Of this era, the most sensitive artist is the magnificent Juan de Juanes (c.1500–79), son of Vicente Macip, whose mannerist works, with their bright patches of colour, still decorate many a parish church in the Comunidad. Meanwhile, the Flanders tradition remained vigorous, exemplified by painters such as Bartolomé Bermejo, who had served his apprenticeship in the Low Countries.

Baroque The 17th century, when artists such as Velázquez, Murillo and Zurbarán were all active elsewhere in Spain, is generally regarded as the golden age of Spanish painting.

Religious art was fostered and patronised as a weapon of the Counter Reformation (recurrent themes are the depiction of saints, major and minor, and the celebration of the Eucharist, in both of which Catholic and Protestant dogma differ). Now painting, whether spiritual or secular, throws aside the distortions of mannerism in favour of greater naturalness. Although Valencia was no longer the innovative force it had been as the point of entry for new ideas and techniques from northern Italy, it produced two artists who stand shoulder to shoulder with the greatest painters of these productive times.

Francisco Ribalta (1564–1628), born in Lleida (Catalunya) yet painting for most of his life in Valencia, is often described as the founder of baroque Valencian painting, influencing a whole generation of artists both by the example of his canvases and through the studio and school that he established in Valencia City in 1599. The richest commissions continued to be bestowed by the Church. His altarpieces, in their portrayal of the saints in all their glory and the strong interplay of light and shade are typically baroque, exemplified in his *San Francisco abrazado al crucificado* (San Francisco embracing the crucified Jesus) in Valencia's Museo de Bellas Artes.

A little later and ploughing an independent furrow, Jerónimo Jacinto de Espinosa (1600–67) manages to blend a profound spirituality of theme with a harsh, uncompromising naturalness.

José de Ribera, born in Xàtiva in 1591 and renowned for his forceful realism, just manages to squeeze in as a scion of Valencia even though in his early twenties he moved to Rome, then Naples, at the time ruled by Spain. Here he enjoyed the patronage of the Spanish viceroy until his death in 1652 and was dubbed *il spagnoletto*, the little guy from Spain (his nickname contrasts with that of a certain Domenicos Theotocopoulos who, a generation earlier, had moved from Greece to Spain and who is today known universally as El Greco, The Greek). Like many painters of the time, he readily adopted from Italy the tenebrism of Caravaggio, selecting and counterbalancing hues from the darker end of the spectrum.

The 19th Century There then follows a fairly barren period for Valencian painting. As royal power was increasingly centred upon Madrid, the Valencia region lost its semi-independent status and its painters, like many other professionals, were increasingly drawn towards the capital. From an age when the name of Goya just about drowns out those of all other artists, José Camerón Bononat and Mariano Salvador Maella, who painted for the monarch, Valencianos by birth, still receive recognition for their works.

Neoclassicism, a reaction against the overwrought excesses of the baroque and its even more embellished offshoot, rococo, was the inspiration for some of the Comunidad's most commanding public buildings yet failed to fire its painters. Two artists from this era who enjoy minor fame are Vicente López (1772–1850), official artist to the court of Fernando VII and remembered in the main for his portrait work, and Antonio Gisbert (1834–1901), who specialised in capturing on canvas dramatic, evocative moments from Spanish history.

The second half of the 19th century saw what is sometimes called, with more than a touch of overstatement, *el nuevo siglo de oro de la pintura valenciana* (the new golden age of Valencian painting). The artists who inspire such a label all received their initial training in the Academia de San Carlos in Valencia City. Then a farsighted local government gave each a scholarship to undertake further study in Paris or Rome. And all, after being exposed to and assimilating wider European artistic trends of the day, returned to the Valencia region. Working at speed, they rapidly filled their canvases, whether with a multitude of dots and small brush strokes or by applying broad swathes of colour. Themes vary enormously but, since they worked very much to commission and to satisfy their bourgeois patrons, they are generally safe and not contentious: portraits that flatter, peasants and folk customs viewed through a somewhat romantic eye and landscapes.

Oldest of this quartet of near contemporaries – and least celebrated nowadays – is Francisco Domingo Marqués (1842–1920), who was the first to apply the new techniques associated with the Valencian school. He is paradoxically now remembered more for his large canvases with religious themes that hark back clearly to baroque times. The lasting reputation of Ignacio Pinazo (1849–1916) rests upon his vivid feel for colour and sensitivity to light. Esteemed mainly for his portraiture, especially of children, he succeeds in capturing with broad brushstrokes the essence of a subject's character.

José Benlliure Gil (1855–1937) is a source of inspiration for students of social history as well as for artists. He captures on his canvas popular traditions and defunct or half-remembered customs – a farm worker in workday clothing puffing at a pipe, worshippers at Mass or a peasant with his flask of wine. You can visit his studio and museum in Valencia City (closed at the time of writing for renovations).

Joaquín Sorolla (1863–1923), the most famous of the four, also dug deep into the daily life of everyday folk for much of his inspiration. He too eked out his official stipend as an aspiring artist, managing to live in both Italy and France from where he returned invigorated and inspired. A supremely Mediterranean artist by both birth and instinct, he was inspired by the sea lapping almost at his doorstep; known as 'the painter of light', in painting after painting he portrays its transient flicker upon waves, people and natural objects and captures too its contrary, the play of shadow. He also did his share of portraits for hard cash, fixing for ever on canvas prominent personalities from the Valencian society of the day. He lived for many years in Madrid, where he was inundated with commissions. His house in the capital at Paseo General Martínez Campos 37, now a museum, has the largest number of his canvases of any museum in Spain, the majority of them depicting Valencian scenes. He spent the latter years of his life in the US, working upon the huge – seriously huge at 60m long and 3.5m high – mural for the Hispanic Society of New York.

The 20th Century & Beyond In the field of sculpture, Mariano Benlliure (1886–1947), brother of the painter José Benlliure, has left his traces around the Comunidad in the form of statues, fountains, well rounded cherubs and busts of the famous and not so famous.

In the second half of the 20th century, when Spain once more opened herself to external artistic influences and the demand for art in public places was on the increase, a number of sculptors chiselled their mark. Oldest of these is Antonio Sacramento, who worked in stainless steel on a grand scale. Also using steel and iron as a primary medium is Valenciano Amadeo Gabino, who produced much of his work in exile in the United States, to which he first travelled thanks to a scholarship from the Ford Foundation. Andreu Alfaro, initially attracted, like Amadeo Gabino, to constructivism, imbued his abstract shapes with a firm social and political import, evident in many of their titles such as *Els Camins de la Llibertat* (Freedom's Ways) or his *Bon Dia Llibertat* (Good Morning Freedom), sculpted in 1975, the year of Franco's death.

Even more socially committed was the primarily graphic artist José Renau (1907–1982). Prolific during the Spanish Civil War (1936–9), he created murals, photomontages and – the main reason for which he is remembered today – revolutionary posters for the Republican cause. He too accomplished most of his later work in exile, firstly in Mexico and then in the German Democratic Republic.

Returning to the latter half of the 20th century, in 1957, a nucleus of young painters, dissatisfied with what they regarded as compromising, unquestioning 'official' art, formed the Grupo Parpalló. Members such as the sculptor Andreu Alfaro (see earlier in this section), Joaquín Michavila and Eusebio Sempere produced some of the most exciting abstract painting of the period.

Simultaneously, other artists, notably Juan Genovés with his juxtaposed and manipulated photos, were adopting a more political stance, often ironic and caustic. In the 1960s Equipo Crónica, a neoexpressionist group, later reduced to a couple of members who continued to collaborate, practised Pop

Art. This movement was also embraced by another Valencian artist, still painting to this day, 'Anzo' (José Iranzo). Equipo Realidad was a similar collaborative pair, uniting Jorge Ballester and Juan Cardells. Also deeply influenced by Pop Art, they used primarily photomontage and, like Equipo Crónica, signed their canvases with the name of the collective.

Eusebio Sempere, the most famous Valenciano artist of this period, exploited the illusions of Op Art in both his sculpture and painting. The latter, although executed with mathematical precision, are much more than visual tricks. Much less brash than most art that falls within this label, his sensitive paintings employ soft, mild colours, gradually blending from one to another.

You'll see examples of the works of most of the noncontemporary painters we mention – plus, of course, artists from elsewhere in Spain and beyond her frontiers – in the Museos de Bellas Artes of Alicante, Castellón and, especially, Valencia City. Excellent too for religious art is the Museo Diocesano attached to the cathedral in Segorbe. For contemporary art, the Instituto Valenciano de Arte Moderno (IVAM) in Valencia is a must and a visit to Castellón's brand new Museo de Bellas Artes is well worthwhile. Make an effort too to get off the beaten track and call by the contemporary painting and sculpture museum in Villafamés, inland and north of Castellón. Its quality and importance are out of all proportion to the tiny village in which it's established.

Pottery

Pottery, tilework and ceramics have been important crafts – and latterly industries – in Valencia since medieval times and it's no coincidence that the Museo Nacional de Cerámica (National Ceramics Museum) is in Valencia. Manises and Paterna, both important production centres to this day, each have a ceramics museum and plenty of outlets offering factory prices.

Literature

It's not easy to talk of a specifically Valencian literature. Its men of letters – and, so far,

those who have made their reputation have been almost exclusively male – write and have written either in Spanish (or Castilian, as it is often called) or in Catalan and its regional variant, Valenciano.

The first truly Valencian literary figure, writing in Catalan, was the poet Ausias March (1397–1459). His verses were strongly influenced by the medieval conceit of courtly love and he, in his turn, was a major influence upon poetry written in Spanish over the next two centuries.

Tirant lo Blanch, which first appeared around 1490, is generally recognised to be the first Valencian epic novel. Two years later, the philosopher and humanist Luis Vives (1492–1540), son of Jews converted to Christianity, was born in Valencia. When the Inquisition began to show a menacing interest in his family, he set out on his literary travels, which were to take him to the Universities of Paris, Louvain in Belgium, and Rotterdam in Holland, where he knew Erasmus. He also spent time in England, lecturing and writing at the University of Oxford, enjoying the protection of Catherine of Aragón, the first of Henry VIII's many wives, and engaging in debate with Sir Thomas More. Regarded as the Comunidad's most influential philosopher, his statue sits at the heart of the main courtyard of the University of Valencia.

Writing in the Golden Age of Spanish literature, Guillén de Castro (1569–1631), a popular dramatist born in Valencia, was strongly influenced by Lope de Vega. Among the most enduring of his plays are *Los Mocedades del Cid* (Youth of El Cid) and *Los Malcasados de Valencia* (Unhappily Married of Valencia).

Without doubt Valencia's most famous literary figure, at least within Spain, is the novelist Vicente Blasco Ibañez (1867–1928), who was also an active politician and militant for the twin causes of republicanism and Valencian autonomy, propounded through *El Pueblo*, the newspaper that he founded and edited. Many of his novels are set in the countryside around Valencia and describe in particular the life of the rural poor. Several of his works have been translated into English.

Among the most often read are *Entre Naranjos* (Among the Oranges), *Sangre y Arena* (Blood and Sand) and *Los Cuatro Jinetes del Apocalipsis* (Four Horsemen of the Apocalypse). You can visit his summer house, now a museum in his honour, at Malvarrosa, just north of Valencia City's port (See Other Museums in the Valencia City chapter).

Joan Fuster (1922–92), born in Sueca just south of Valencia City, was primarily but far from exclusively a political writer who had great influence upon dissidents active in the latter years of the Franco dictatorship. Writing in Catalan at a time when the language was semi-suppressed, his works (indeed 'his' – the name Joan is the Catalan form of Juan, or John) include *El Descrèdit de la Realitat* (Denying Reality) and *País Valenciano Per Què* (Case for a Land of Valencia).

Gabriel Miró (1879–1930) hailed from Alicante. His writing is characterised by its rich vocabulary and the freshness of his images. Miguel Hernández (1910–42) was another Valencian writer with provincial origins. A poet born in Orihuela and committed supporter of the Republican cause, he was active both politically and in literary terms before and during the Civil War. Imprisoned by the victorious nationalists, he died of tuberculosis while still in jail.

José Martínez Ruiz, known as Azorín (1873–1967), born in Monóvar, Alicante province, was a key member of what is known as the Generation of 1898. This was a group of artists and writers active after 1898, a disastrous year for Spain in which defeat by the US led to the loss of Cuba and the Philippines and an economic crisis at home. Something of a literary jack of all trades, he turned his hand to playwriting, novels and journalism (many of the books published under his nom de plume are compilations of articles).

Music
Classical Music Remember *Rodrigo's Guitar Concerto*, originally composed for guitar and orchestra and subsequently adapted in just about every possible musical mode? Known in Spain as the *Concierto de Aranjuez*, it was composed by Joaquín Rodrigo (1901–99), born in Sagunto and the Valencia region's most famous musical son. Blind since childhood because of diphtheria, the loss of one sense accentuated his aural sensitivity. Despite his infirmity, he studied in Paris (1927–32), supported by a scholarship.

The Concierto de Aranjuez was inspired by the gardens of Aranjuez, near Madrid, which are today the venue for an annual summer music festival. It's but one, if the most famous, element in a prolific output that includes other pieces of distinction such as his *Concierto Heróoica, Invocación y Danza* and *Fantasía Para un Gentilhombre*, all of which received prestigious awards.

Rodrigo served as head of music broadcasts for Radio Nacional de España and also held the Manuel de Falla chair of music at the University of Madrid. He was also appointed head of the Organización Nacional de Ciegos de España and, in later life, received a sheaf of honorary doctorates from, among others, the Universities of Salamanca, Southern California and Exeter (UK). In 1992 King Juan Carlos appointed him, appropriately, Marqués del los Jardines de Aranjuez (Marquis of the Gardens of Aranjuez).

Folk & Pop Raimon – always known simply as Raimon – is difficult to categorise and sits a little uncomfortably in the company of this section. As much poet as singer, he's been active since he gave his first concert in 1961 to a rapturous audience at the University of Valencia while still a student. In the latter days of the dictatorship, he became a symbol of democracy and regional pride for his contemporaries, his song *Al Vent* (To the Wind) becoming almost an informal anthem for the young dissidents of that era.

It may seem strange to read a paragraph about a musical instrument, but nothing on Valencian folk music (true folk music rather than some gritty ditty composed last week in a bar) is complete without reference to the *dulzaina*. This translates into English as 'shawm', a small fact that may leave you little the wiser but which Shakespeare and his contemporaries would have understood. Made of wood, it's like a stubby clarinet with a flat, circular mouthpiece against which the lips rest as you blow over a double reed. No

Listen to the Banda

If you're around the Comunidad in summertime, it's unlikely that you'll head home without having heard the oompah of a Valencian *banda*, a good old-fashioned band, predominantly brass but also often with wind instruments such as clarinets, flutes and even saxophones. The quality varies from alarmingly wheezy to very professional indeed and just about every town and village boasts one. Each banda has its uniform, most of them about as exciting as a bus driver's, which serves to stamp a common identity.

The tradition began in the 18th century and far from it being an urban phenomenon, the bandas, some of them with a history going back over 150 years, first came together in the villages of the interior.

Bandas couldn't be more democratic as the school teacher, the farm worker and the baker are brought together by a common love of music and of playing it in company. And generations of young people have come to read and appreciate music by playing in the local banda. Often, its headquarters vies with the *casa fallera* (falla house) as the focal point of a village's social life. Bandas participate in any street parade, are an essential element of Moros y Cristianos (Moors and Christians) celebrations and belt out their very best when the home town is *en fiesta*. And a banda accompanies every single one (OK, so some of them turn up three or four times but it's still impressive!) of the more than 350 fallas that, on 17 and 18 March, parade through Valencia's Plaza de la Virgen to offer flowers to the Virgin.

It's all good fun – but there's a keen and competitive side too. The folk of Llíria in Valencia province will tell you of the family-splitting rivalry between the town's two highly regarded bands, the Banda Primitiva and the Unión Musical de Llíria. And every year as part of Valencia City's summer festival, there's an annual competition, held in the bullring with finalists progressing to the prestigious Palau de la Música, a venue which normally resounds to the strains of top classical orchestras.

---

street procession, popular gathering or even wedding worth the name is complete without its piercing tones, often accompanied by a side drum and, during fallas, loud bangers.

Bacalao, sometimes written 'bakalao', with its pounding, technobeat originated in Valencia. It still brings in ravers from Madrid, Seville and Barcelona, intent upon an intensive weekend's partying, following *la ruta del bakalao* from bar to disco and back again. Popular local groups who've achieved national and, among the cognoscenti, international fame include Revolver, Seguridad Social and Presuntos Implicados.

Dance

In the field of classical and modern ballet, Valencia's most famous son is Nacho Duarte, director since 1990 of Spain's Compañia Nacional de Danza (National Dance Company). In addition to dancing his way around the globe with some of the world's most presti-gious corps de ballet, he has choreographed works for, among many others, the Nederlands Dans Theater, with whom he spent several years as principal dancer, the UK's Royal Ballet, the Australian Ballet and, in the US, the Washington Ballet and American Ballet Theater, New York.

SOCIETY & CONDUCT

Most Valencianos take great pride in their local culture and are proud of their reputation as the most fun-loving of Spaniards with an unrivalled capacity to party.

No-one really expects you to speak Valenciano and you can more than get by in coastal resorts without even a smattering of Spanish. This said, if you can stumble along good-humouredly in Spanish in shops and other basic situations you'll generally meet with a friendly response.

Codes of good manners differ the world over and what can sometimes seem brusque treatment to Anglos is not intended as anything of the sort. Many speakers of English lard their conversation with 'pleases' and 'thank yous' whereas your average Valenciano is more economical with the 'por favors', preferring the more direct approach, saying simply 'give me' whatever it might be. But they stand on ceremony in other ways. It's fairly common to wish all and sundry *buenos días/bon día* when entering a shop or bar and to leave with an *adiós*. Similarly, if you're eating in a restaurant, others may well wish you *que aprovecheis* or, in Valenciano *bon profit* (enjoy your food) as they enter or leave.

Socialising tends to be very much a public activity with friends meeting up in cafes, bars and restaurants. You can know people very well yet never have passed beyond their front door. By contrast, the family continues to assume, for many, an important part of their social life.

The standard form of greeting between women and between men and women (even when meeting for the first time) is a kiss on each cheek. A light peck will do the job. Manly handshakes tend to be optional on informal occasions but remain pretty much standard in a business context.

Treatment of Animals

Bulls apart – and they get a *really* rough deal – the average dog, cat or other animal probably has as good a life beside the Mediterranean as anywhere else in Europe. The myth of the Spaniard, callous to dumb animals' suffering, is one perpetrated by the tabloid press.

Bedtime

In summer, Valencianos tend to stay up late. Even with a working day in front of them, many will enjoy the relative cool of the night until 2am or later. And Friday or Saturday nights year round barely begin until midnight for those doing the rounds of bars and discos.

Siesta

Contrary to what many non-Spaniards believe, most people in the Comunidad Valenciana, as elsewhere in the country, don't

take an afternoon snooze. The relatively long breaks between morning and afternoon working sessions are filled by a lingering lunch and relaxed conversation. Then again, if you've been out until 6am...

RELIGION

The Comunidad Valenciana, like the rest of Spain, is largely Catholic – at least in name. However, the number actively practising the faith has fallen dramatically since the near-mandatory Franco days and the dominant element in most congregations is elderly women.

As in France and elsewhere in Spain, there can be quite a strong anticlerical streak. Nothing so strong, of course, as during the Civil War when many nuns and priests were assassinated but the memory of the Franco era, when Church and State were hand in glove, lingers on.

LANGUAGE

The Comunidad Valenciana is officially bilingual. Everyone can understand Spanish, which is often called Castellano, meaning literally, the language of Castilla, the Spanish heartland up on the central plateau. And just about everyone is at home speaking the language.

Valenciano, the second official language is, according to strictly linguistic criteria, a dialect of Catalan, as is the mother tongue of many in Andorra, the Balearic Islands and even parts of Sardinia, where Alghero, a form of Catalan clings on from the distant days when it belonged to Catalunya.

But the linguistic dimension is only one of many and there's nothing like a good language issue to rouse the emotions. For the right and the folkloric wing of the political spectrum, Valenciano is a separate language with its own norms, rules and literature while those on the left are content to regard it as a dialect, on equal terms, with Catalan.

You're unlikely to get drawn into such parish-pump debating but if you are, pull back since many take their passion for Valenciano to the extreme. For example, a farcical situation arose when the king was about to open a new metro station and it came to light that – shock, horror – what was a perceived Catalanism, the word *amb*, meaning 'with', had been used on the bronze explanatory plaques. So someone – that's someone official, not a casual vandal – went round scratching out the offensive word. The language issue can also lead to irritating vandalism whereby small bands of obsessives splash black paint on traffic signs, altering them to reflect the Valenciano rather than Spanish version of a place name – or (and here's where it can become *really* parochial), the Valenciano, rather than a perceived Catalan form.

Sometimes the issue runs deeper. Not long ago, there was a standoff between the local Ministry of Culture and Education and the University of Valencia when the Ministry deliberately excluded a clause, drafted by the university for its revised statutes, obliging all newly appointed staff to sit examinations in both Spanish and Valenciano. It went all the way to the Tribunal Superior de Justicia (High Court), who ruled in the university's favour. Discrimination in employment, some would argue, limiting equality of employment and particularly inappropriate in an institution of higher learning, which should be actively looking outwards. Just a means of ensuring that the most appropriate lecturers are directed towards classes given in Valenciano, says the university. 'Oh yeah?' ask many, sceptically.

Facts for the Visitor

If you're here for the **beaches**, among the best are the long strands of Gandía's, Peñíscola's, Benidorm's Levante – and the much less-frequented sands of Guardamar, backed by huge dunes.

If **museums and galleries** are your scene, be sure to take in Valencia's Museo de Bellas Artes, its fine arts museum, and the Instituto Valenciano de Arte Moderno (IVAM). Try too to take a detour to the excellent contemporary arts museum in tiny Vilafamés, inland from Castellón.

For **diving and snorkelling**, drift through the protected offshore marine reserves of the Islas Columbretes and Isla de Tabarca or explore the waters off the craggy coastline around Alcossebre.

Opportunities for **walking** are infinite and many towns have developed their own signed trails. Favourite areas are the Maestrazgo in the north and the Sierra de Mariola down south. Two spectacular walks from coastal resorts are the Peñon de Ifach, looming above Calpe, and Montgó, the mountain that rears between Denia and Xàbea.

For **fiestas**, Valencia City's Las Fallas celebrations in mid-March are enough in themselves to justify a visit (but be sure to reserve your accommodation months in advance) while most major towns to the south have spectacular Moros y Cristianos parades, celebrating the distant Christian expulsion of the Arab occupiers.

Valencia City's wild **nightlife** brings in revellers from all over Spain, while the summertime discos of Benidorm can rival anything Ibiza throws up. On a smaller scale, but just as wild, is Alicante's way of banishing darkness, whether in the old town or along the freshly developed Paseo del Puerto.

And if the crowds and frenzy of the coastal resorts begin to pall, simply head **inland** for only a few kilometres to another, completely different Spain. Here, there's space, spectacular mountain scenery, rich cuisine, small, friendly villages and a fascinating variety of rural accommodation. In fact, why not follow in the footsteps of more and more Spaniards and make rural, inland Valencia the focus of your holiday…?

SUGGESTED ITINERARIES

The majority of visitors to the Comunidad Valenciana have one or at most two weeks at their disposal. Many come to the Costa Blanca on an all-inclusive package. Or perhaps you're including the Comunidad within a wider sweep through Spain? Whatever your constraints of time and place, by applying only a little initiative you can sample much of what the region has to offer.

Although the temptations of lounging on the beach by day and living it up by night are seductive, it would be a shame if you limited yourself – as millions do – to the coastal belt and the resort in which you have landed up.

Wherever you may be based, Valencia City merits at the very least a day of your life and ideally two or three. Train and bus communications are good from any point in the Comunidad and many package tour operators arrange a day visit to the regional capital.

Public transport to the more offbeat destinations of the interior is less impressive, although inland towns such as Requena, Xàtiva (Játiva), Elche (Elx) and Orihuela are well served. The suggestions that follow aren't dependent upon your having a vehicle, but wheels, whether two and self-propelled or four and hired, will widen your range of possibilities significantly.

If you're around for a **week**, you'll probably want to dig your heels in at your resort for at least half the time and allow a day for Valencia City.

If staying on the **Costa del Azahar**, north of the regional capital, you could profitably fill in the other days by describing a two- to four-day circuit embracing the wild Maestrazgo and the Palencia valley. Take in Morella and San Mateo, both of which make good overnight stops. Of the mountain villages we describe, be sure to include Mirambel, just over the border into the Aragonese Maestrazgo. There are some invigorating trails for walkers in this area, while art lovers might prefer to call by the bijou contemporary painting and sculpture museum in the village of Villafamés. You can then snake through the hills via the spa town of Montanejos and descend to the coast down the Palencia valley, stopping off briefly in Segorbe and allowing yourself an hour or two to explore the provincial capital of Castellón.

If you're based on the **Costa Blanca**, allow a day for Alicante, a pleasant provincial capital that gets better every time we visit it. To explore other coastal resorts, consider taking the *trenet*, the narrow gauge train that regularly runs the scenic route between Denia to Alicante, in preference to a car journey. On the other hand, a car allows you to sally into the hinterland. From Denia or Xàbea (Jávea), you can head up the underpopulated Vall de Gallinera, returning along the Vall de Guadalest, calling in at Guadalest itself. From Benidorm or La Vila Joiosa (Villajoyosa), you can make the same journey in reverse.

Alternatively, head out up that same Guadalest valley to Alcoy (Alcoi) and return to the coast along the mountain road that passes through Jijona (Xixona), pausing to pick up a packet or two of *turrón*, a particularly lipsmacking variant of nougat.

For a day of culture and monument visiting, head up the Vinalopó valley to visit Elda and its shoe museum, Novelda, with its Art Nouveau treasures, and stylish Villena while perhaps slipping in an extra castle or two, in which the region abounds. Fit in the monuments and palm groves of Elche, and, time allowing, push on to Orihuela, rich in baroque buildings.

Each route is possible within one day, or you can take them at a more relaxed pace, overnighting in Alcoy, Villena or Elche.

With **two weeks** at your disposal, you can combine most of the above and allow Valencia City the couple of days or more that it so richly deserves. To really get way off the tourist trail, think too of basing yourself for a night or two in Xàtiva. This allows you to take in the provincial towns of Albaida, Ontinyent and Bocairent and also spend a day exploring the riches of the Vall de Ayora.

Alternatively and equally off the tourist track, make your way up the Turia valley, where there are plenty of opportunities for gentle walking, or head up the Madrid road, which leads to Requena, interesting in its own right and main town of the Utiel-Requena wine-growing region.

With even more time in hand, as many long-term winter visitors have, you can mix and match from these suggestions – and still come back the following year to explore what you've had to omit.

PLANNING
When to Go

The best time to visit coastal Comunidad Valenciana is between April and June. The only exception is Semana Santa (Holy Week), unless you're coming specifically to enjoy its Easter week parades and ceremonies, since the whole country seems to be on the move as Good Friday approaches. Or else pick the autumn, a delightfully refreshing season, once the heat of summer has abated and the tourist tide turned. September, October, even early November – all are wonderful, though October usually brings a day or two of downpour. During these months, you can chill out on the beach and the water temperature makes for a pleasant dip in the sea.

Inland, where spring bursts later and winter bites earlier, mid-April to July plus September and October are ideal in the north, though the sierras of Alicante province can be sticky by June.

If you can, avoid the coast during the second half of July and August simply because so many millions of others don't. During this slice of high summer, prices are inflated, accommodation is at a premium, the sun at its hottest and coastal humidity at its highest. More and more people who are obliged to take their holidays at this time opt for inland and the Maestrazgo or upper Turia valley precisely because they're cooler and less crowded than the coast. Since rural tourism is becoming more popular by the year, it's wise to reserve accommodation in advance in high summer.

Winter in the Maestrazgo (roughly November to March) is best avoided unless you're one of those – and there are many of them – who enjoy bracing cold-climate walking. During this season, a good clear day in the sierras of Alicante and inland Valencia province, where winters are much milder, can mark you for life, even if you're not a particularly hardy soul.

On the coast, really any time is tourist time and major resorts such as Benidorm, Benicàssim. or Torrevieja have a year-round influx of visitors. Winters are mild with average temperatures around 18°C. They attract in particular long-stay northern European third-age visitors, who are escaping a more rigorous climate back home.

In July and, particularly, August, just about every town in the land has its fiesta, usually commemorating its patron saint or the expulsion of the Moors (or, neatly and economically, both) with parades, fireworks and, often, bull running. Just ask at the nearest tourist office and you've a very good chance of taking one in.

For dates of the Comunidad's major festivals, around which you might want to plan a vacation, consult the Public Holidays & Special Events section later in this chapter.

What Kind of Trip

A very high proportion of overseas visitors to the Comunidad Valenciana arrive by air and stay at coastal resorts on package-tour terms. But this doesn't mean that you have to be confined to wherever the coach from the airport dumps you. Car, scooter and bicycle hire is relatively cheap and the temptations of the hinterland are great. So perhaps budget for a day or two in the inland hills.

If you're travelling independently, you might want to mix sand and sierra, spending, say, half your time on the coast and the rest exploring the interior. A third option, which really requires your own wheels if you're to get about to the full, is to plan a whole visit around the interior of the Comunidad.

Wherever you're based, you should build in a minimum of a day and ideally at least one night in Valencia City, savouring its museums, monuments, restaurants and through-the-night life.

Maps

Road Atlases Several road atlases cover not only the Comunidad Valenciana but also the rest of Spain and include plans of major towns. Among the most reliable is the Mapa Oficial de Carreteras (€15.65) produced by the Ministerio de Fomento. Another, available in and outside Spain, is Michelin's *Motoring Atlas: Spain & Portugal*. In Spain it's called *Atlas de Carreteras y Turístico: España y Portugal* (€15.60). You can find them at most decent bookshops and some petrol stations in Spain.

Regional & Provincial Maps The Instituto Geográfico Nacional (IGN) produces a map (€6) of the whole of the Comunidad at 1:250,000. An alternative is Alonso Editor's *Mapa de les Carreteres Valencianes* (€4.50) at 1:333,333. Irritatingly, it gives place names only in Valenciano but it's reliable enough and has a useful table of distances.

Other reliable maps for general orientation are those at 1:200,000 produced by the IGN. There's one for each of the Valencia region's three provinces, Valencia, Alicante and Castellón, and they retail for €5 each. They're fine for travellers who don't want the cost or bulk of a pan-Spain road atlas.

Walking Maps The Institut Cartogràfic Valencia produces a series of good walking maps (€7.50) at 1:15,000 covering most of the Comunidad's Parques Naturales (Nature Parks). Each has useful illustrative and background information (in Spanish).

The Centro Nacional de Informacíon Geográfica (CNIG), the publication arm of the Instituto Geográfico Nacional (IGN) covers practically all of the Comunidad Valenciana in 1:25,000 sheets, most of which are recent. The CNIG and the Servicio Geográfico del

Ejército (SGE; Army Geographic Service) each publish a 1:50,000 series; the SGE's at this scale tend to be more up to date but they're not so readily available.

Specialist Map Shops In Valencia City, Librería Patagonia (☎/fax 96 391 52 47), Calle Guillem de Castro 106, keeps a large range and Indice-La Casa del Mapa, the local CNIG retail outlet, at Calle Avellanas 14, stocks all IGN sheets.

What to Bring

Bring as little as possible. Everything you bring, you have to carry. Unless you're really out in the sticks, you can buy just about anything you might need in the Comunidad Valenciana anyway.

Luggage If you'll be doing any walking with your luggage, even just to and from stations and hotels, a backpack is often the best answer. One whose straps and openings can be zipped inside a flap is most secure. If you'll be using taxis or your own car, take whatever luggage is easiest to stow away, open and shut, unpack and pack. You may find that several smaller pieces are easier to store and manipulate than a couple of monsters. However you travel, a small day pack is a useful addition.

Writing your name and address on the inside of your luggage, as well as labelling it on the outside, increases your chances of getting it back if it's lost or stolen. Packing things in plastic bags inside your backpack or suitcase will keep them organised and, if there's a downpour, dry.

Clothes & Shoes In high summer you won't need more than one layer of clothing, even at 4am. At cooler times, layers of thin clothing, which trap warm air and can be peeled off if necessary, are better than a single thick layer. See Climate in the Facts about Valencia chapter for the kind of temperatures and rainfall you can expect. It's a good idea to pack a set of neat clothes for smart restaurants and some discos.

You'll probably need a pair of strong shoes, even strong trainers, no matter what type of trip you're making. You'll probably also sometimes appreciate having a lighter pair. Smarter clubs and restaurants might look askance at your trainers, however designer cool they may be.

Useful Items Apart from any special personal needs, or things such as camping gear and hiking boots you might require for particular kinds of trips, consider the following:

- an under-the-clothes money belt or shoulder wallet, useful for protecting your money and documents in cities
- a towel, soap and sink plug, often lacking in cheap accommodation
- sunscreen lotion
- a small Spanish dictionary and/or phrasebook
- books in English, which aren't easy to find outside main cities and tourist resorts
- photocopies of your important documents, kept separate from the originals
- a Swiss army knife
- minimal unbreakable cooking, eating and drinking gear if you plan to prepare your own food and drinks
- a medical kit (see Health later in this chapter)
- a padlock or two to secure your luggage to racks and to secure hostel lockers
- a sleeping sheet to save on sheet rental costs if you're using youth hostels (a sleeping bag is only really useful if you're camping)
- an adapter plug for electrical appliances
- a torch (flashlight)
- an alarm clock
- sunglasses and sun hat
- binoculars, if you plan to do any wildlife-spotting

RESPONSIBLE TOURISM

Travelling responsibly in Spain means much the same as journeying responsibly in any first world country, including your own. Dos and don'ts that come naturally to aware travellers include not clambering over monuments or daubing them with graffiti and making sure you pick up every single scrap of your litter – even though the locals can be deficient in this area – especially on beaches and in fragile mountain areas.

Don't use a flash when photographing artworks in museums and churches. The burst of light damages the art. Never light a fire in areas of coastal and inland pine. If nicotine's your scene, there can be smoke without fire, but be especially careful where and how you stub out your dog-ends. In summer, the risk of forest fire is very high indeed. Thousands of hectares are destroyed every single year as a result of negligence or, worse, because fires are deliberately lit.

If you've just left a drizzly airport in northern Europe, water conservation won't be uppermost in your mind. But water – or rather the lack of it – and the annually increasing consumption in coastal resorts are more and more important issues. Fact: incredible as it may seem, a luxury hotel consumes around 600 litres of water per day for every single guest on the register. So do turn off every dripping tap, ask for your towels to be changed less regularly than every day and take a shower rather than a bath. Fact: by replacing fresh water showers with low taps dispensing seawater so you can wash the sand off your feet, the Valencian government reckons that it saved about 96 million litres in a single summer. And the fact that they hope to provide about 25% of the Costa Blanca's water from desalination plants by 2003 is no cause for complacency; the process is costly – and what will they do with all that salt?

The Spanish are on the whole a gregarious, tolerant people with over half a century's experience in coping with the odd ways of foreign visitors. Short of blatantly insulting someone, you're unlikely to give offence. This said, while most Spaniards like a tipple or two, you rarely see legless, loudmouthed drunks and even more rarely come across a brawl. The packs of northern European lager louts known to bay and rampage through popular resorts are regarded at best with disdain and more often simply as barbarians. So, out of consideration for the locals and maybe for the reputation of your fellow countryfolk, hold your ale. If you can't, at least do everyone a favour by getting pissed quietly and unaggressively.

TOURIST OFFICES
Local Tourist Offices

Cities in the Comunidad Valenciana and many smaller towns too have an *oficina de turismo* or *oficina de información turística*. Look out for the white '*i*' for information

logo on a dark blue background or the word 'Turinfo'.

Of Valencia City's four tourist offices, the most useful is the one on Calle Paz, which has a regional remit. The one in the Teatro Principal covers Valencia province and there are similar provincial information offices in the other two regional capitals, Castellón and Alicante. You'll find contact details for these and municipal tourist information offices under Information within each town's entry.

There's also a nationwide tourist information line, which might come in handy if you're planning to visit other regions of Spain. Call Turespaña on ☎ 901 30 06 00 (€0.25 per minute) between 9am and 6pm daily for basic information in Spanish, English or French.

Tourist Offices Abroad

You can get information from any of 29 Spanish national tourist offices in 22 countries. These include:

Canada
(☎ 416-961 3131, [e] toronto@tourspain.es)
2 Bloor St W, 34th floor, Toronto M4W 3E2
France
(☎ 01 45 03 82 57, [e] paris@tourspain.es)
43 rue Decamps, 75784 Paris, Cedex 16
Germany
Berlin: (☎ 030-882 65 43, [e] berlin@tourspain
.es) Kurfürstendamm 180, 10707 Berlin
Düsseldorf: (☎ 0211-680 39 80)
Frankfurt-am-Main: (☎ 069-72 50 33)
Munich: (☎ 089-530 74 60)
Italy
Rome: (☎ 06 678 31 06, [e] roma@tourspain
.es) Piazza di Spagna 55, 00187 Rome
Milan: (☎ 02 72 00 46 12)
Japan
(☎ 03-3432 6141, [e] tokio@tourspain.es)
Daini Toranomon Denki Bldg 4f, 3-1-10
Toranomon, Minato-ku, Tokyo 105
Netherlands
(☎ 070-346 59 00, [e] lahaya@tourspain.es)
Laan Van Meerdervoort 8a, 2517 AJ The Hague
Portugal
(☎ 213 54 19 92, [e] lisboa@tourspain.es)
Avenida Sidónio Pais 28, 3° Dto, 1050 Lisbon
UK
(☎ 020-7486 8077, brochure request ☎ 09063 640630 at 60p per min, [e] londres@tourspain
.es) 22-23 Manchester Square, London
W1M 3PX

USA
New York: (☎ 212-265 8822, e nyork@
tourspain.es) 666 Fifth Ave, 35th floor, New
York, NY 10103
Chicago: (☎ 312-642 1992)
Los Angeles: (☎ 323-658 7188)
Miami: (☎ 305-358 1992)

VISAS & DOCUMENTS
Passport
Citizens of the 15 European Union (EU)
member states and Switzerland can travel
to Spain on simply their national identity
card. EU countries are Belgium, Denmark,
Finland, France, Germany, Greece, Ireland,
Italy, Luxembourg, the Netherlands, Portugal, Spain, Sweden and the UK.

If you're from an EU country – such as the
UK – that doesn't issue ID cards, you must
carry a full valid passport (UK visitor passports are not acceptable). All other nationalities must have a full valid passport.

Check that your passport's expiry date is at
least some months away, otherwise you may
not be granted a visa, should you need one.

By law you are supposed to have your
passport or ID card with you at all times in
Spain. It's unlikely to happen but, should
you be asked by the police to flash your
documentation, it could be embarrassing if
you don't have it with you. You will usually
be asked to produce one of these documents
when you take a hotel room or register at a
camp site. It's also useful to memorise your
passport number.

Visas
There are no entry requirements or restrictions on EU nationals. Citizens of Australia,
Canada, Israel, Japan, New Zealand and the
USA do not need visas to visit Spain as
tourists for up to three months. Except for
people from a few other European countries
(such as Switzerland), everyone else must
have a Schengen Visa.

This visa is named after the Schengen
Agreement that has abolished passport controls between all EU countries (except Ireland and the UK), plus Iceland and Norway.
A visa for any of these countries should in
theory be valid throughout the area, but it
pays to double-check with the embassy or

consulate of each country you intend to
visit. Residency status in any of the Schengen countries negates the need for a visa,
whatever your nationality.

Tourist (Schengen) visas are valid for up
to 90 days. You must apply for the visa *in
person* at the Spanish consulate or embassy
in your country of residence. Postal applica-
tions are not accepted. You'll need a valid
passport and sufficient funds to finance your
stay. Fees vary depending on your nationality and the visa does not guarantee entry.

You can apply for no more than two visas
in any 12-month period and you can't renew
once inside Spain.

Visa Extensions & Residence Cards
Schengen visas cannot be extended. In practice, nationals of EU countries, Norway and
Iceland can virtually (if not according to the
rule book) enter and leave Spain at will.
Those wanting to stay in Spain longer than
90 days are supposed to apply during their
first month for a *tarjeta de residencia* (resident's card). This is a lengthy bureaucratic
procedure: if you intend to subject yourself
to it, get advice from a Spanish consulate before you go to Spain as you will need to take
certain documents with you.

People of other nationalities who want to
stay in Spain longer than 90 days are also
supposed to get a resident's card, and for
them it's a truly nightmarish process, starting with a residence visa issued by a Spanish consulate in your country of residence.
Start the process light years in advance.

Non-EU spouses of EU citizens resident
in Spain can apply for residency too. The
process is lengthy and those needing to
travel in and out of the country in the mean-
time could ask for an *exención de visado* –
a visa exemption. In most cases, spouses are
obliged to make the formal application in
their country of residence. A real pain.

Travel Insurance
Insurance to cover theft, loss of luggage or
tickets, medical problems and perhaps can-
cellation or delays in your travel arrangements, is a good idea (see Health later in the
chapter for more on medical insurance).

A wide variety of policies is available and your travel agent will be able to make recommendations. The international student travel policies handled by STA Travel or other student travel organisations are usually good. Check the small print:

- Does the policy exclude 'dangerous activities', which can include scuba diving, motorcycling and even trekking?
- Is there a surcharge for expensive photo equipment and the like?
- Does the policy cover ambulances or an emergency flight home?
- Does the policy require you to pay up front for medical expenses, then to claim from the insurance company afterwards, showing receipts? You might prefer one where the insurance company pays the doctor or hospital directly.

Paying for your ticket with a credit card often provides limited travel accident and delay insurance and you may be able to reclaim payment if the operator fails to deliver. Look at the small print on your credit card terms and conditions document.

Insurance papers and the international medical aid numbers that generally accompany them are valuable documents, so treat them like air tickets and passports. Keep the details (photocopies or handwritten) in a separate part of your luggage.

Driving Licence

All EU member states' driving licences (pink or pink and green) are recognised. In principle you should get a Spanish licence if you stay in the country for more than a year, but many foreign residents ignore this requirement. The old-style UK green licence is not accepted.

Other foreign licences are supposed to be accompanied by an International Driving Permit. In practice, your national licence will suffice for renting cars or dealing with traffic police. The International Driving Permit is available from automobile clubs in your country and is valid for 12 months.

For information on vehicle papers and insurance see under Car & Motorcycle within the Land section of the Getting There & Away chapter.

Hostel Cards

There are 11 youth hostels in the Comunidad Valenciana and many more throughout Spain. At most of them, you'll need a valid HI (Hostelling International) card or youth hostel card from your home country. If you don't already have one, you can pay in instalments of €1.80 for each night you spend in a hostel. Once you've dropped €10.85, you're entitled to a full card (people legally resident in Spain for at least a year can get a Spanish hostel card for €6). Membership cards are also available from offices of Turivaj (see Useful Organisations later in this chapter) in the three provincial capitals, Valencia, Alicante and Castellón.

Student, Teacher & Youth Cards

These cards can get you worthwhile discounts on travel and reduced prices at some museums, sights and entertainment venues.

The International Student Identity Card (ISIC), for full-time students (€4.25 in Spain), and the International Teacher Identity Card (ITIC), for full-time teachers and professors (€6 in Spain), are issued by over 5000 organisations worldwide. Anyone under 26 can get a GO25 card (€4.25 in Spain) or a EuroGT26 card. Both of these give similar discounts to the ISIC one and are issued by most of the same organisations. The EuroGT26 has a variety of names including the Under 26 Card in England and Wales and the Carnet Joven Europeo (€6.40 in Spain). In the UK, you can contact Under 26 (for information ☎ 0870 240 1010). You'll need to call by in person at 52 Grosvenor Gardens, London SW1W 0AG to pick up a card. In the Comunidad Valenciana, places that issue the ISIC card also sell the Carnet Joven Europeo (for which you don't have to be Spanish to be eligible). In the Comunidad Valenciana, all the above cards are issued at Turivaj offices.

As an example of the sort of discounts you can expect, the better things on offer for EuroGT26 card holders include 20% or 25% off most 2nd-class train fares, 10% or 20% off many Trasmediterránea ferries and some bus fares, as well as discounts at some museums.

Copies

Before you leave home, you'd do well to photocopy all important documents (passport data page and visa page, credit cards, travel insurance policy, air/bus/train tickets, driving licence etc) – twice. Leave one copy with someone at home and keep another with you, separate from the originals.

Lonely Planet's online Travel Vault is another option for storing details of your vital travel documents before you leave. Keeping details of your important documents in the vault is even surer than carrying photocopies. It's the best option if you travel in a country with easy Internet access. Your password-protected travel vault is accessible online at anytime. You can create your own travel vault for free at **W** www.ekno.lonelyplanet.com.

EMBASSIES & CONSULATES
Your Own Embassy

It's important to realise what your own embassy – the embassy of the country of which you are a citizen – can and can't do to help you if you get into trouble. Generally speaking, it won't be much help in emergencies if the trouble you're in is remotely your own fault. Remember that you are bound by the laws of the country you are in. Your embassy will not be sympathetic if you end up in jail after committing a crime locally, even if such actions are legal in your own country.

In genuine emergencies you might get some assistance, but only if other channels have been exhausted. For example, if you need to get home urgently, a free ticket home is exceedingly unlikely – the embassy would expect you to have insurance. If you have all your money and documents stolen, it might assist with getting a new passport, but a loan for onward travel is out of the question.

Spanish Embassies & Consulates

Among the many Spanish embassies and consulates abroad are:

Australia
(☎ 02-6273 3555, **e** embespau@mail.mae.es) 15 Arkana St, Yarralumla, Canberra, ACT 2600
Consulate in Melbourne: (☎ 03-9347 1966)
Consulate in Sydney: (☎ 02-9261 2433)

Canada
(☎ 613-747 2252, **e** spain@docuweb.ca) 74 Stanley Ave, Ottawa, Ontario K1M 1P4
Consulate in Montreal: (☎ 514-935 5235)
Consulate in Toronto: (☎ 416-977 1661)

France
(☎ 01 44 43 18 00, **e** ambespfr@mail.mae.es) 22 ave Marceau, 75008 Paris, Cedex 08
Consulate in Bayonne: (☎ 05 59 59 38 91)
Consulate in Bordeaux: (☎ 05 56 52 80 20)
Consulate in Strasbourg: (☎ 03 88 32 67 27)
Consulate in Lille: (☎ 03 20 57 70 05)
Consulate in Lyons: (☎ 04 78 89 64 15)
Consulate in Marseilles: (☎ 04 91 00 32 70)
Consulate in Montpellier: (☎ 04 67 58 20 21)

Germany
(☎ 030-254 00 70, **e** embesde@mail.mae.es) Schoneberger Ufer 89, 6th floor, 10785 Berlin (moving to Lichtensteinallee 1, 10787 Berlin in 2003)
Consulate in Düsseldorf: (☎ 0211-43 90 80)
Consulate in Frankfurt-am-Main: (☎ 069-959 16 60)
Consulate in Hamburg: (☎ 040-414 64 60)
Consulate in Hanover: (☎ 0511-31 10 85)
Consulate in Munich: (☎ 089-998 47 90)
Consulate in Stuttgart: (☎ 0711-226 20 01)

Ireland
(☎ 01-269 1640) 17A Merlyn Park, Ballsbridge, Dublin 4

Japan
(☎ 03-3583 8533, **e** embesjpj@mail.mae.es) 1-3-29 Roppongi, Minato-ku, Tokyo 106

Netherlands
(☎ 070-302 49 99, **e** embespnl@mail.mae.es) Lange Voorhout 50, 2514 EG The Hague
Consulate in Amsterdam: (☎ 020-620 38 11)

New Zealand
Covered from Australia (see above)

Portugal
(☎ 01-347 2381, **e** embesppt@mail.mae.es) Rua do Salitre 1, 1250 Lisbon

UK
(☎ 020-7235 5555, **e** empespuk@mail.mae.es) 39 Chesham Place, London SW1X 8SB
Consulate in London: (☎ 020-7589 8989) 20 Draycott Place, London SW3 2RZ
Consulate in Edinburgh: (☎ 0131-220 1843)
Consulate in Manchester: (☎ 0161-236 1233)

USA
(☎ 202-452 0100) 2375 Pennsylvania Ave NW, Washington, DC 20037
Consulate in Boston: (☎ 617-536 2506)
Consulate in Chicago: (☎ 312-782 4588)
Consulate in Houston: (☎ 713-783 6200)
Consulate in Los Angeles: (☎ 213-938 0158)
Consulate in Miami: (☎ 305-446 5511)

Consulate in New Orleans: (☎ 504-525 4951)
Consulate in New York: (☎ 212-355 4080)
Consulate in San Francisco: (☎ 415-922 2995)

Embassies & Consulates in Spain

Embassies are all located in Madrid. Some countries also maintain consulates in major cities. Embassies and consulates in Madrid include:

Australia (☎ 91 441 93 00) Plaza del Descubridor Diego de Ordás 3-2, Edificio Santa Engrácia 120
Canada (☎ 91 423 32 50) Calle de Núñez de Balboa 35
France (☎ 91 700 78 00) Calle del Marqués Ensenada 10
Germany (☎ 91 557 90 00) Calle Fortuny 8
Ireland (☎ 91 436 40 93) Paseo de la Castellana 46
Netherlands (☎ 91 353 75 00) Avenida del Comandante Franco 32
New Zealand (☎ 91 523 02 26) Plaza de la Lealtad 2
Portugal (☎ 91 782 49 60) Calle Pinar 1
Consulate: (☎ 91 577 35 38) Calle Lagasca 88-40
UK (☎ 91 700 82 00) Calle Fernando el Santo 16
Consulate: (☎ 91 308 52 01) Calle del Marqués Ensenada 16
USA (☎ 91 587 22 00) Calle Serrano 75

Consulates in the Comunidad Valenciana A few countries have consulates in the Valencia region.

Germany (☎ 96 521 70 60) Plaza Calvo Sotelo 1, Alicante
Netherlands (☎ 96 521 21 75) Calle Castaños 29, Alicante
UK (☎ 96 521 60 22, 96 521 61 90) Plaza Calvo Sotelo 1, Alicante
USA (☎ 96 351 69 73) Calle Doctor Romagosa 1, 2nd floor, Valencia

CUSTOMS

For duty-paid items bought in one EU country and taken into another, the guidelines are up to 90L of wine, 10L of spirits, unlimited quantities of perfume and 800 cigarettes (or 200 cigars or 800g of tobacco). Customs officers stress that these amounts are guidelines rather than permitted maxima. VAT-free shopping is available in the duty-free shops at airports for people travelling between EU countries. However, since taxes on booze and tobacco remain relatively low in Spain, you'll normally find that it's cheaper to buy these from a local shop or supermarket.

Visitors entering Spain from outside the EU can bring in duty-free 1L of spirits or 2L of fortified wine, sparkling wine or other liqueurs, 2L of still table wine, 60mL of perfume and 200 cigarettes (or 50 cigars or 250g of tobacco).

MONEY

You can get by easily enough with a single credit or debit card that lets you withdraw euros from Automatic Teller Machines (ATMs, cash machines), but it's also sensible to take some travellers cheques and a second card (if you have one). This combination gives you a fallback if you lose a card or it lets you down.

Exchange Rates

With the introduction of the euro, you need never again worry about leftover notes in your pocket or hustling for the best exchange rate when travelling between EU countries (except the out-of-it-all northern fringe of Denmark, Sweden and the UK). Rates between euro zone and non-euro zone currencies, of course, remain variable.

country	unit		euros
Australia	A$1	=	€0.59
Canada	C$1	=	€0.72
Japan	¥100	=	€0.85
New Zealand	NZ$1	=	€0.48
UK	£1	=	€1.63
USA	US$1	=	€1.14

Exchanging Money

You can change major first-world currency notes at most banks and exchange offices (though the New Zealand dollar tends to be greeted with a blank gaze). A minority of places may be sniffy about travellers cheques or demand an exorbitant commission for accepting them. In this case, just walk on to the next. Many banks have ATMs. Both Valencia and Alicante airports have an exchange office and ATM.

Adios Peseta, Hola Euro

The euro is now the sole currency in Spain and 12 of the 15 EU countries (the three footdraggers are Denmark, Sweden and the UK). It's divided into 100 cents (called *céntimos* in Spain). Coin denominations are one, two, five, 10, 20 and 50 cents, €1 and €2. The notes are €5, €10, €20, €50, €100, €200 and €500.

All euro coins across the EU are identical on the side showing their value but there are 12 different obverses, each representing one of the 12 euro zone countries. All euro notes of each denomination are identical on both sides. *All* euro coins and notes are legal tender throughout the euro zone.

A small warning: some of the research for this book took place during the very last months of life of the peseta, when, even though the euro was looming, many places had still not established their prices in the new currency. So, in addition to the inflation that normally occurs within the lifetime of a book, you may notice some small fluctuation (almost certainly upwards!) in the prices we quote.

Banks tend to offer slightly better exchange rates. They're common in cities, and even small villages often have one. They usually open from about 8.30am to 2pm Monday to Friday and 9am to 1pm Saturday. Many don't open on Saturday in summer while main branches may open longer hours during the week.

Exchange offices – usually indicated by the word *cambio* (exchange) – exist mainly in tourist resorts and other places that attract high numbers of foreigners. Generally they offer longer opening hours and quicker service than banks, but worse exchange rates. In some exchange offices, the more money you change, the better the exchange rate you'll get.

Wherever you change, ask from the outset about how much will be deducted in commission, if this isn't displayed, and confirm that exchange rates are as posted (it may well have been a day or two since the board was updated). Typical commissions range from 1% to 3%, with a minimum of €2 to €3, but there are lots of places that demand a minimum of €6 or more. Those that advertise 'no commission' usually enhance their cut by offering poorer exchange rates or imposing, not always transparently, a 'service charge'.

Cash You might want to bring a float with you. Keep the amount you carry in readies modest, both on arrival and when travelling around. Theft isn't rife in the Comunidad Valenciana but if you're unlucky enough to be rolled, most insurance companies have a low ceiling for reimbursing cash losses.

Travellers Cheques These protect your money because they can be replaced if they are lost or stolen. In the Comunidad Valenciana they can be cashed at many banks and exchange offices and usually attract a slightly higher exchange rate than cash. Very few places allow you to use them like money and make purchases. American Express (AmEx) and Thomas Cook are widely accepted brands with efficient replacement policies. For AmEx travellers cheque refunds, call ☎ 900 99 44 26, a Spain-wide number.

Get most of your cheques in fairly large denominations (the equivalent of €50 or higher) to save on any per-cheque commission charges. It's vital to keep your initial receipt, and a running record of your cheque numbers and the ones you have used, separate from the cheques themselves.

ATMs & Plastic Money Carrying plastic (whether a credit or debit card) is the simplest way to organise your funds. You don't have large amounts of cash or cheques to lose, you can get money after hours and at weekends and the exchange rate is good if not always the absolute best. Credit cards (such as MasterCard and Visa) can be used more widely than a straight debit card (such as one with the Maestro or Cirrus logo). In addition to direct purchases, you can flash a credit card for an over-the-counter euro advance from a bank and insert it into an ATM to withdraw cash.

The advantage of some debit cards, such as those in the Cirrus and Maestro networks, is that you can access money in your home bank account from Spain without any cash-advance fee.

All major credit/debit cards are widely accepted. They can be used for many purchases (including at petrol stations, larger shops and supermarkets, who sometimes ask to see some form of ID) and in hotels and restaurants (although smaller establishments tend to accept cash only).

Very many Spanish banks, even in small towns and some villages, have an ATM *(cajero automático)* that will dispense cash round the clock if you have the right piece of plastic.

If you can, take more than one card and keep them separate in case one gets lost or stolen. AmEx cards tend to be the easiest to replace; others may not be replaceable until you get home. Report a lost or stolen card immediately:

Visa	☎ 900 97 44 45
MasterCard/EuroCard	☎ 900 97 12 31
AmEx	☎ 902 37 56 37
Diners Club	☎ 91 547 40 00

International Transfers It's very rarely worth the hassle, but if you do run low on funds and ATMs start to spit back your plastic, this is the deal.

You need to organise someone back home to send it to you, through a bank there or – much more rapidly – via a money-transfer service such as Western Union. And you'll have to specify a local bank or money-transfer agent where you can collect it. If there's money in your bank account at home, you may be able to instruct the bank yourself.

For information on Western Union services, call free on ☎ 900 63 36 33, or visit online at Ⓦ www.westernunion.com.

To set up a transfer through a bank, either get advice from your bank at home on a suitable pick-up bank in the Comunidad Valenciana, or check with a local bank on how to organise it. You'll need to let the sender have precise details of the Spanish bank branch –

its name, full address, city and any contact or code numbers required. A bank-to-bank telegraphic transfer typically costs around US$20 to US$30 and can take as much as a week to clear.

It's also possible to have money sent quickly by AmEx.

Security

Your money, in whatever form, is at risk unless you look after it. Carry only a limited amount of cash and keep the bulk in more easily replaceable forms such as travellers cheques or the promise of plastic. If your accommodation has a safe, use it. If you must leave money in your room, divide it into several stashes and hide them in different places.

For carrying money on the street the safest thing is a money belt or wallet that you can strap on under your clothes. External money belts call attention to you and the strap can easily be slashed with a sharp knife.

Keep the little cash you're carrying in your *front pockets* and beware of any stranger who touches you or seems to be getting unnecessarily close – there is an infinite number of tricks used by teams of delinquents, whereby one distracts your attention and another deftly empties your pockets.

Costs

Daily living expenses in the Comunidad Valenciana are generally lower than those in most countries of Western Europe. If you are extremely frugal, it's possible to scrape by on €30 a day if sharing a room in the cheapest budget accommodation, avoiding restaurants except for an inexpensive set lunch, minimising your visits to museums and bars and moving around very little.

A more comfortable budget if you're one element of a travelling pair would be €40 to €60 a day. This could allow you €15 to €20 for accommodation, €2.50 for breakfast (coffee and a pastry), €7 to €15 for lunch or dinner, €3 to €6 for another light snack or sandwich, €3 to €6 for admission fees, and a bit of slack for a drink or two and travel.

If you've got €120 to €150 a day you can stay in excellent accommodation, rent a car and eat at some of the region's finest restaurants.

Cost-Savers Your cost of living won't vary much between cities, such as Valencia or Alicante, coastal resorts or the inland sierras. Two people can live more cheaply (per person) than one by sharing rooms. In fact, in many of the cheapest *pensiónes* you are charged for a double room even if you're all alone in your bed. You can also save by avoiding high season rates, particularly for accommodation, which many places slap on at Christmas/New Year, Easter week and from mid-July to early September.

A student or youth card, or a document such as a passport proving you're over 60, may bring worthwhile savings on travel costs and admission to some museums and sights. Some public-sector museums and sights are cheaper, or even free, for EU passport holders.

You'll find more information on overnight, eating and travel costs in the Accommodation and Food & Drink sections later in this chapter and also in the Getting Around chapter.

Tipping & Bargaining

Tipping is a matter of personal choice. Most people leave some small change if they're satisfied: 5% would normally be adequate and 10% generous. Many locals leave a couple of coins at bar or cafe tables. Porters will generally be happy with €1, and most won't turn their noses up at €0.75. Taxi drivers don't have to be tipped but a little rounding up won't go amiss.

Bargaining is rare and you risk being regarded as a skinflint. The only exceptions might be budget accommodation, where you could try negotiating a reduction if you're staying for a few days, and markets – though here too fixed prices are the norm.

Taxes & Refunds

In Spain, value-added tax (VAT) is known as IVA (pronounced ee-ba; *impuesto sobre el valor añadido*). On accommodation and meals, it's 7%. In restaurants and modest accommodation, it's usually included in quoted prices. Medium and top-range hotels frequently slap it on as a separate item. On retail goods and car hire, IVA is 16%. To ask 'Is IVA included?', say *'¿Está incluido el IVA?'*

Visitors are entitled to a refund of the 16% IVA on purchases costing more than €95 from any shop if they're taking them out of the EU within three months. Ask the shop for an invoice showing the price and IVA paid for each item and identifying the vendor and purchaser. Then, if you're leaving by air, present the invoice to the customs booth for IVA refunds when you leave Spain. The officer will stamp the invoice and you hand it in at a bank in the airport for the reimbursement. This will only work if you're flying from Madrid or Barcelona; there's no such facility at Valencia or Alicante airports, which serve only European destinations.

POST & COMMUNICATIONS
Post
Postal Rates A postcard or letter weighing up to 20g costs €0.25 within Spain, €0.50 to other European countries and €0.75 to the rest of the world. Corresponding prices for letters between 20g and 50g are €0.38, €1.16 and €1.63. Three regular-weight A4 sheets in an air-mail envelope weigh between 15g and 20g.

A letter sent *certificado* (registered mail) costs an extra €1.10 for international mail. *Urgente* service, which means your letter may arrive two or three days more quickly, costs an extra €2.10 for international mail. Pay an extra €1.50 and your letter goes both urgente and certificado.

Postal Exprés, sometimes called Express Mail Service (EMS), usually works out a day or two quicker than urgente mail. Packages weighing up to 1kg cost €33.05 to European destinations, €45.10 to North America and €54.10 to Australia or New Zealand. It's a heck of a lot more expensive than urgente mail but still significantly cheaper than private courier services.

Sending Mail Post your mail in a yellow street postbox *(buzón)* or at a post office.

Stamps are sold at every post office *(oficina de correos* or *correos)*, most *estancos* (tobacconist shops: look for the yellow-on-brown 'Tabacos' sign) and some newsagents. Even quite small villages have a post office, though its opening hours may be very restricted. Main post offices in cities and towns are usually open from about 8.30am to 8.30pm Monday to Friday and around 9am to 1.30pm Saturday. Estancos usually open during normal shop hours.

Delivery times are a disgrace: mail to other EU countries routinely takes up to a week; to North America up to 10 days; to Australia or New Zealand as long as two weeks.

Receiving Mail Delivery times are similar to those for outbound mail. All Spanish addresses have five-digit postcodes, use of which will help your mail arrive a bit less slowly. One abbreviation you may come across – and which we use quite frequently in this book – is 's/n', short for *sin número*, meaning that a place has no street number. Another, often used in rural addresses, is 'km' followed by a number – the distance of the location from the nearest place specified.

Poste restante mail can be addressed to you at poste restante (or better, *lista de correos*, the Spanish name for it) anywhere in the Valencia region that has a post office. If a town has more than one post office, your mail will fetch up at the main one unless another is specified in the address. Take your passport when you pick up mail. It helps if people writing to you capitalise or underline your surname and include the postcode. A typical lista de correos address looks like this:

> Sam BROWN
> Lista de Correos
> 46001 Valencia
> Spain

AmEx card or travellers cheque holders can use the free client mail-holding service at AmEx offices in Spain. For a list of these, contact any AmEx office.

Telephone

Pay phones are blue, distinctive, abundant and easy to use for both domestic and international calls. You have the option of using coins, a phonecard *(tarjeta telefónica)* issued by the national phone company Telefónica, or, in some cases, a credit card. Phonecards come in denominations of €6 and €12. Like postage stamps, they're sold at post offices and estancos.

Coin pay phones inside bars and cafes normally cost a little more than street pay phones. Phones in hotel rooms are frequently a good deal more expensive.

An alternative in some larger towns and popular resorts is the telephone centre, whether belonging to Telefónica or a small shop that often doubles up with fax and Internet facilities. It usually has a number of booths where you do your own dialling; you pay at a desk after your call.

Costs Calls from pay phones using coins or a slot-in card cost about a third more than calls from private lines. This table shows the approximate cost of a three-minute, payphone call at peak times. However competition has, at long last, begun to bite. As a result, Telefónica has found itself obliged to reduce its bloated charges, which may well be even lower by the time you read this.

call to	cost
Number starting with 900	free
Local area	€0.15
Number starting with 901	€0.15
Same province	€0.45
Number starting with 902	€0.45
Other province	€0.65
Other EU country (all day)	€1.00
North America	€1.00
Spanish mobile phone (any number starting with 6)	€1.20
Australia	€4.35

Calls except those to mobile phones are cheaper between 8pm and 8am (6pm to 8am for local calls), and all day Saturday and Sunday. Calls to mobile phones cost €0.65 from 10pm to 8am Monday to Friday, 2pm to midnight Saturday and all day Sunday. To fixed phones, off-peak discounts are around 50% for provincial and interprovincial calls and around 10% for local and international ones (other than the EU and US, where the tariff is constant).

A variety of discount cards is available. These can cut costs significantly, especially for international calls – see Phonecards and eKno Communication Service later in this section.

Domestic Calls Spanish numbers have nine digits. Dial all of them, wherever in the country you are calling.

Dial ☎ 1009 to speak to a domestic operator, including for a domestic reverse-charge (collect) call *(una llamada por cobro revertido)*. For directory enquiries within Spain dial ☎ 1003; calls cost €0.30 from a private phone but are free from pay phones.

The Yellow Pages (Páginas Amarillas) are online at W www.paginas-amarillas.es (Spanish only). For emergency numbers, see the Emergencies section later in this chapter.

International Calls To make an international call, dial the international access code (☎ 00), wait for a new dialling tone, then dial the country code, area code and number you want.

For international reverse-charge (collect) calls, dial ☎ 900 99 00, followed by the usual code for the country you're calling (for example ☎ 33 for France, ☎ 44 for the UK and ☎ 61 for Australia). Among the few exceptions are ☎ 15 for Canada and, for the USA, ☎ 11 to get AT&T or ☎ 14 for MCI.

For international directory enquiries dial ☎ 025 and be ready to pay about €1.

Mobile Phones As in many places, mobile phone *(teléfono móvil)* use has mushroomed. Spain uses GSM 900/1800, compatible with the rest of Europe and Australia but not with the North American GSM 1900 or the totally different system in Japan (this said, some North American GSM 1900/900 phones do work here). If you have a GSM phone, check with your service provider about using it in Spain and beware of calls being routed internationally (very expensive for a 'local' call). Larger towns have mobile phone shops. There are several networks with varying price plans. You can buy phones for as

little as €60, generally with around €25 of calls thrown in.

Calling Spain from Other Countries
Spain's country code is ☎ 34. Follow this with the full nine-digit number that you are calling.

Phonecards In Valencia, Alicante and the larger coastal resorts you'll find quite a few local and international discount phonecards on sale, not all of which are the seductive bargain they'd have you believe. Most, however, work out considerably cheaper than Telefónica for international calls.

eKno Communication Service Lonely Planet's eKno global communication service provides low-cost international calls – for local calls you're usually better off with a local phonecard. eKno also offers free messaging services, email, travel information and an online travel vault, where you can securely store all your important documents. You can join on-line at W www.ekno.lonely planet.com, where you will find the local-access numbers for the 24-hour customer-service centre. Once you have joined, check the eKno Web site every so often for each country's latest access numbers and updates on new features.

Fax
Most main post offices have fax services. The first page and subsequent pages cost €1.90/0.60 within Spain, €5.80/1.45 to elsewhere in Europe and €11.15/3 to other countries. You'll often find cheaper rates at shops or offices showing 'Fax' signs.

Email & Internet Access
By far the simplest way to access the Internet and email while you're on the road is through cybercafes and other public access points. You'll find several in coastal resorts and larger towns. The local tourist office will have details. Charges for an hour online average about €3.

If you plan to carry your notebook or palmtop computer with you, check that the power supply in the Comunidad Valenciana is the same as at home; if not, you risk meltdown. A universal AC adapter for your appliance will let you plug it in anywhere without frying the innards. Most phones in Spain use the standard US RJ-11 telephone jack.

An easy option for collecting mail through cybercafes is to open a free eKno Web-based email account online at Ⓦ www.ekno.lonely planet.com. You can then access your mail from anywhere in the world from any net-connected machine running a standard Web browser. Popular alternatives include Yahoo (Ⓦ www.yahoo.com) and Hotmail (Ⓦ www .hotmail.com).

DIGITAL RESOURCES

The World Wide Web is a rich resource for travellers. You can research your trip, hunt down bargain air fares, book hotels, check on weather conditions or chat with locals and other travellers about the best places to visit (or avoid!).

There's no better place to start your Web explorations than the Lonely Planet Web site (Ⓦ www.lonelyplanet.com). Here you'll find succinct summaries on travelling to Spain, postcards from other travellers and the Thorn Tree bulletin board, where you can ask questions before you go or dispense advice when you get back. You can also find travel news and updates to many of our most popular guidebooks. The subWWWay section links you to the most useful travel resources elsewhere on the Web.

The following sites have an English version, except where we indicate otherwise. You'll find other useful ones mentioned under a town's entry later in the book.

You can draw upon the following sites for pan-Spain information and click your way through the links for material particularly relevant to the Comunidad Valenciana:

Turespaña This, the Spanish tourist office's official site, has lots of general information about the country, lists of Spanish embassies and overseas tourist offices plus some interesting links.
Ⓦ www.tourspain.es
All about Spain A varied site with information on everything from fiestas to hotels via a Yellow Pages guide to tour operators around the world that do trips in Spain.

Ⓦ www.red2000.com
Renfe Timetables, tickets and special offers for Spain's national rail network.
Ⓦ www.renfe.es
BBC Spanish The BBC has an excellent selection of Spanish courses at all levels that you can access online. If you're an absolute beginner, you'll have fun working through *Talk Spanish*, which is based upon Valencia City. Even if you already have some Spanish, take a trip to the site and browse through a videoclip or two to give yourself an idea of the city.
Ⓦ www.bbc.co.uk/education/languages/ spanish/talk

You may also find these Valencia-specific sites useful:

Agència Valenciana de Turismo This, the site of the Comunidad-wide official tourism body, is packed with information, both permanent and ephemeral.
Ⓦ www.comunidad-valenciana.com
Terra i Mar This is another official site, covering the province of Valencia. Not as rich as the Agència Valenciana de Turisme site, it nevertheless harbours lots of useful information.
Ⓦ www.valenciaterraimar.org
Turisvalencia Maintained by the Turismo Valencia Convention Bureau, this site carries information about Valencia City of interest to both business folk and general visitors.
Ⓦ www.turisvalencia.es
Generalitat Valenciana Most of the site of the Generalitat, the regional government of Valencia, is in Spanish or Valenciano only. It has links to municipalities throughout the Comunidad, many of which include tourist information within their pages.
Ⓦ www.gva.es
Fallas The site of the Junta Central Fallera (Fallas Central Committee), gives a good idea in words and pictures of Valencia City's March Fallas festival. During the festivities, with web cameras, video and almost hourly updates, it explodes with info – literally so since you can click on a recording of every day's *mascletá*, over five minutes of ear-drum-shattering explosions. Remove your earphones first...
Ⓦ www.fallas.com

BOOKS

Most books are published in different editions by different publishers in different countries. As a result, a book might be a hardcover rarity in one country while it's readily available in paperback in another. Fortunately, bookshops and libraries search by title or author so your local bookshop or library is best placed to advise you on the availability of the following recommendations.

Although there's a veritable libraryful of books in English on just about every aspect of Spain and the Spanish, little has been written specifically about the Comunidad Valenciana. There's considerably more in Spanish and Catalan/Valenciano but it's difficult to get at such sources until you arrive in Spain.

In the UK, Stanfords bookshop (☎ 020-7836 1321, W www.stanfords.co.uk), 12–14 Long Acre, London WC2E 9LP, 150 years in business, is the world's largest map and guidebook store.

Books on Spain (☎ 020-8898 7789, fax 8898 8812, W www.books-on-spain.com), PO Box 207, Twickenham TW2 5BQ, UK, is an excellent mail-order service specialising in out-of-print and rare titles on Spain.

Lonely Planet

Lonely Planet publishes a language-packed yet practical and pocket-size *Spanish phrasebook*. *World Food: Spain* takes you through the menu, from tapas (bar snacks) to *postres*, guides you through the wine list and has a comprehensive culinary dictionary. *Walking in Spain* has detailed walk descriptions for all the major hiking areas, including the offshore Balearic Islands, and a whole chapter describing walks and treks in the Comunidad Valenciana.

If you're planning to travel more widely in Spain, you might also want to arm yourself with *Spain*, which includes the Balearic Islands, east of the Valencian coast. In addition, we publish more detailed regional guides, like this one, to *Catalunya & the Costa Brava*, *Andalucía* and the *Canary Islands* plus city guides to *Madrid* and *Barcelona*. There is also a *Barcelona Condensed* guide.

If your ambit is even wider and you're on a grand European tour, consider our *Mediterranean Europe*, *Western Europe* or – written with budget travellers in mind and covering the whole continent – *Europe on a shoestring*.

Travel Photography: A Guide to Taking Better Pictures is written by internationally renowned travel photographer, Richard I'Anson. It's full colour throughout and designed to take on the road.

Guidebooks

Although every pan-Spain guidebook devotes considerable space to the Comunidad, there's very little in English written exclusively about the region.

One partial exception is outdoor activity books. If you're a climber, arm yourself in advance with *Costa Blanca Climbs*, by the appropriately surnamed Chris Craggs. For day walks inland from the Costa Blanca, pick up the *Mountain Walks on the Costa Blanca*, by Bob Stansfield. *Landscapes of the Costa Blanca*, by Christine and John Oldfield, describes both walks and car tours in the area. Locally published *Excursions in Eastern Spain*, by Nick Inman and Clara Villanueva, offers 30 excursions by car in and around the Comunidad.

If you're planning to tour around, consider the official *Guía de Hoteles*. It's a mite heavy to stick in a backpack but this official, comprehensive multilingual listing of accommodation throughout Spain can pay back the modest investment (€9) in just a couple of nights. An accompanying booklet has multicolour street plans of all Spain's major towns and cities, including Alicante, Benidorm and Valencia. If you're aiming to camp, the slimmer official *Guía de Campings* (€6), while weighing and costing less, is no less comprehensive. Both titles are updated annually.

History, Politics & Society

If you want to familiarise yourself with the wider context of Spanish history and the Comunidad Valenciana's place within it, *The Story of Spain*, by Mark Williams, offers a colourful but thorough and fairly succinct overview. Also concise and worthwhile is Juan Lalaguna's *A Traveller's History of Spain*.

The Civil War is said to be the second most written-about conflict in history (after WWII) and has spawned some wonderful books. *The Spanish Civil War*, by Hugh Thomas, is probably the classic account of the conflict in any language: long and dense with detail yet readable, even-handed and humane. Raymond Carr's more succinct *The Spanish Tragedy* is another well written and respected account. Great reads also are George Orwell's compelling *Homage to Catalonia*, the story of his involvement in the Civil War (he fought on the Republican side), and Ernest Hemingway's powerful and terse novel, inspired by his experiences as a foreign correspondent during the war, *For Whom the Bell Tolls*.

Paul Preston's *Franco* is the big biography of one of history's little dictators.

The New Spaniards, by John Hooper, is an informed, highly entertaining introduction to contemporary, post-Franco Spain by the former Madrid correspondent of the British *Guardian* daily newspaper. For another contemporary, personal and at times controversial introduction to modern Spain, go to *Fire in the Blood*, by Ian Gibson, based upon his British TV series.

Flora & Fauna

Wildlife Travelling Companion: Spain, by John Measures, is a good traveller's guide, focusing on 150 of the best sites throughout the country for viewing flora and fauna, with details of how to reach them and what you can hope to see.

The single best guide to flowers and shrubs in Spain is *Flowers of South-West Europe, A Field Guide*, by Oleg Polunin & BE Smythies.

For books on bird-watching, see the Activities section later in this chapter.

FILMS

Even though you won't glean a thing about contemporary Valencia or its history, borrow from the video shop *El Cid*, the 1961 grand epic starring Charlton Heston and Sophia Loren as the hero's legendary lover, Chimene. Despite some witless acting and a fanciful plot, it's fun for the splendid action sequences, in particular the capture of Valencia City (in fact filmed in Peñíscola on the Costa del Azahar).

NEWSPAPERS & MAGAZINES
Local Press

The two best-selling local Spanish dailies with Comunidad-wide distribution and coverage are *El Levante* and, sitting considerably further to the right of the political spectrum, *Las Provincias*. *El Diario de Valencia*, which claims to cover the Comunidad, is much thinner fare and its coverage is largely restricted to Valencia City.

English-Language English language publications in the Comunidad Valenciana are based on the Costa Blanca. The weekly *Costa Blanca News* (W www.costablanca-news .com), although targeted more towards longterm Anglophone residents, has useful what's on information and TV listings (both land and satellite) and carries budget car hire and flight advertisements. Its letters page gives a fascinating glimpse into what's bugging resident crusties up and down the coast. Readily on sale along the Costa Blanca, it's available in Valencia City only from the kiosk on the corner of Plaza del Ayuntamiento and Calle en Llop. Its tabloid format sister paper, the *Weekly Post* (W www.cbweeklypost.com) is very much the same – even down to the same fonts and format. *The Entertainer*, a fat freebie, is less complete in its listings. All are very expat-oriented.

Valencia Life (W www.valencialife.net) is a glossy quarterly. It too is pitched more towards an expat readership but carries interesting articles about the Comunidad.

National Press

The main Spanish dailies can be identified along roughly political lines. The old-fashioned *ABC* represents the conservative right, *El País* identifies with the PSOE (Spain's centre-left, nominally socialist party), while *El Mundo*, a paper that prides itself on breaking political scandals, is the liveliest of the big three.

For a good spread of national and international news, *El País* is the pick. One of the best-selling dailies is *Marca*, which is devoted exclusively to sport.

Spain has three excellent monthly travel magazines. *Península* covers general places of interest while *Aire Libre* and *Grandes Espacios* are directed primarily at outdoor activities enthusiasts.

International Foreign-Language Press

In coastal resorts and Valencia City's Plaza del Ayuntamiento, you'll find rack upon rack of newspapers from all over Western Europe. They're normally on sale within a day of publication. In such places, you'll also come across US/International publications such as *Time*, *Newsweek* and the *International Herald Tribune* (which has a daily *El País* supplement in English, an excellent resource for knowing what are the local issues of the moment if your Spanish reading skills aren't so hot). Several British newspapers have editions published in Madrid.

RADIO

You can pick up BBC World Service broadcasts on a variety of frequencies. Broadcasts are directed at Western Europe on, among others, 648kHz, 7325kHz, 9410kHz and 12,095kHz (short wave). Voice of America can be found on various short-wave frequencies, including 1197kHz, 9700kHz, 9760kHz, 15,205kHz and 15,255kHz, depending on the time of day. The BBC and VOA broadcast around the clock, jumping from wavelength to wavelength. The quality of reception varies considerably.

The Spanish national network Radio Nacional de España (RNE) has several stations. RNE 1 has general interest and current affairs programmes, RNE 2 plays classical music, RNE 3 has a decent range of pop and rock music and RNE 5 is a round-the-clock news station. Among the most listened-to rock and pop stations are 40 Principales, Onda Cero and Cadena 100.

On the Costa Blanca, Onda Cero Internacional (try 94.6FM, 95.9FM or 97.3FM) beams out mainly in English around the clock and carries BBC World Service news.

TV

The main local TV channel is Canal 9. Heavily subsidised by the Valencian government, it broadcasts in both Valenciano and Spanish, offering, in the main, a dismal diet of noisy chat shows, bought-in variety spectaculars and karaoke. The general dreariness is now and again mitigated by some good films and documentaries.

In many parts of the Comunidad, you can also pick up the altogether more worthwhile Catalunya regional government station, TV-3, and Canal 33, another Catalan channel.

There are four main terrestrial channels with national coverage – two from Spain's state-run Televisión Española (TVE1 and La 2) and two independent (Antena 3 and Tele 5). Many TVs in bars and hotels also pick up Canal Plus, a mainly subscription channel.

News programmes are generally decent, if longwinded, and you can occasionally catch an interesting documentary or film. Canal Plus and La 2 stand out and, in general, offer fairly serious fare. Otherwise the staple diet is soaps (many from Latin America), an exhausting amount of sport, endless talk shows and naff variety shows.

More and more quite ordinary hotels now have satellite TV carrying foreign stations such as BBC World, BBC Prime, CNN, Eurosport, Sky and the German SAT 1.

VIDEO SYSTEMS

Most prerecorded videos on sale throughout Spain use the PAL (phase alternation line) system common to most of Western Europe and Australia. France uses the incompatible SECAM system, and North America and Japan use the equally incompatible NTSC.

PHOTOGRAPHY
Film & Equipment

Most major brands of film are widely available, though you may have to visit more than one shop to find your favourite make of slide film. Processing is fast and generally efficient. A roll of print film (36 exposures, ISO 100) normally costs €3.50 to €4 and can be processed for €6 to €7.50 (dearer for same-day service), although there are often better deals if you have two or three rolls developed together. The equivalent in slide *(diapositiva)* film is €4 to €5 plus €3.50 to €4 for processing, which may take longer than for print.

Airport Security

Your camera and film will be routinely passed through airport x-ray machines. Make sure that your camera and films are in your hand baggage. Although the x-ray machine for hand baggage shouldn't damage film, you can ask for inspection by hand if you're worried. Lead pouches for film are another solution if you're a really serious photo buff.

TIME

The Comunidad Valenciana, like the rest of Spain and most of Europe, is on GMT/UTC plus one hour during winter and GMT/UTC plus two hours during the daylight-saving period, from the last Sunday in March to the last Sunday in October. Britain, Ireland and Portugal are one hour behind.

Spanish time is normally USA Eastern Time plus six hours and USA Pacific Time plus nine hours. In the Australian winter (Spanish summer), subtract eight hours from Australian Eastern Standard Time to get Spanish time; in the Australian summer subtract 10 hours. The difference is nine hours for a few weeks in March.

ELECTRICITY

The electric current throughout Spain is 220V, 50Hz. Plugs have two round pins, as in the rest of mainland Europe. Some countries outside Europe (such as the USA and Canada) use 60Hz, which means that appliances from those countries with electric motors (such as some CD and tape players) may perform poorly.

WEIGHTS & MEASURES

Spain uses the metric system. You'll find conversion tables at the back of this book. Like other mainland Europeans, the Spanish indicate decimals with commas and thousands with points.

LAUNDRY

Self-service laundrettes are rare. Small laundries *(lavanderías)* are fairly common; staff will usually wash, dry and fold a load for €6 to €9. Some youth hostels and a few *hostales* (budget hotels) have washing machines for guests' use.

TOILETS

Public toilets are rare and rarely inviting. The easiest option is to wander into a bar or cafe and use its facilities. The polite thing to do is to have a drink or something at the place, but you're unlikely to raise too many eyebrows if you don't. Some curmudgeonly places in popular tourist areas post notices saying that their toilets are for clients only – such mean-spirited venues are best boycotted.

The cautious carry some toilet paper with them when out and about as many toilets lack it. If there's a bin beside the loo, put paper and so on in it – it's probably there because the local sewage system has trouble coping. Here and there, though less frequently every year, you may find yourself astride a pair of giant's footsteps squat toilets.

HEALTH

Most visitors to the Comunidad Valenciana experience no medical problems; in fact the climate is positively healthy. The worst many visitors pick up is an extended hangover from too much partying in the resorts. Other potential risks are sunburn, dehydration, insect bites or mild gut problems, usually due to a change in diet.

Predeparture Planning

Immunisations No jabs are mandatory for a visit to Spain. Although there is no risk of yellow fever in Europe, if you are arriving from a yellow-fever infected area (most of sub-Saharan Africa and parts of South America) you'll need proof of yellow fever vaccination before you will be allowed to enter the country.

Health Insurance Make sure that you have adequate health insurance. For more information, see Travel Insurance under Visas & Documents earlier in this chapter.

Visitors from other EU countries and Norway are entitled to free emergency medical care in the Comunidad Valenciana under the Spanish national health system on production of an E111 form, which you must get in your home country before you arrive.

In the UK, E111s are issued free by post offices; all you need to supply is your name,

Everyday Health

Normal body temperature is up to 37°C (98.6°F). More than 2°C (4°F) above this indicates a high fever. The normal adult pulse rate is 60 to 100 per minute (children 80 to 100, babies 100 to 140). As a general rule the pulse increases about 20 beats per minute for each 1°C (2°F) rise in fever.

Breathing rate is also an indicator of illness. Between 12 and 20 breaths per minute is normal for adults and older children (up to 30 for younger children, 40 for babies). People with a high fever or serious respiratory illness breathe more quickly than normal.

address, date of birth and National Insurance number. In other EU countries ask your doctor or health service how to get the form.

Though armed with an E111, you will still have to pay for medicines bought from pharmacies, even if prescribed, and perhaps for a few tests and procedures. Your own national health system may reimburse some of these costs.

An E111 is no good for private medical consultations and treatment; this includes virtually all dentists, some of the better clinics and surgeries and emergency flights home. To avoid paying for these, ensure that adequate medical insurance is included within your travel policy.

Most but not all US health insurance policies stay in effect, at least for a limited period, if you travel abroad. On the other hand, most other non-European national health plans (including Australia's Medicare) don't, so you need to take out special medical as well as theft and loss insurance.

Travel Health Guides Lonely Planet's *Travel with Children* offers advice on travel health that is particularly relevant for younger children.

Other Preparations If you wear glasses or contact lenses, pack a spare pair and, if you're ultracautious, your prescription too. If you pop a special medicine take enough

with you as it may not be available locally. Take the packet too; if it shows the generic name, and not just the brand, this will make getting replacements easier. It's a good idea to have a legible prescription or letter from your doctor to show that you use the medication legally.

Medical Kit Pharmacies abound and medicines are easily available; quite a few items that would normally require a prescription in other countries can be obtained easily over the counter.

Basic Rules

Water Domestic, hotel and restaurant tap water is safe to drink throughout the Comunidad. Ask *'¿Es potable el agua?'* if you're in any doubt. Water from public spouts and fountains is not necessarily reliable unless it has a sign saying 'Agua Potable'. Safe bottled water is available for about €0.50 per 1.5L bottle in shops and supermarkets.

Medical Treatment

If you need an ambulance anywhere in the Comunidad, call the general, pan-European emergency number ☎ 112.

For serious medical problems and emergencies, the local public-health service provides care to rival that of anywhere in the world. Larger resorts such as Benidorm or Torrevieja have private clinics, catering in the main to tourists, where English is spoken. Elsewhere, seeing a doctor about more mundane problems may be a frustrating business because of queues and a haphazard appointments system. If you want to see one quickly or need emergency dental treatment, even quite small towns in the Comunidad have a *centro de salud* (health centre) with an *urgencias* (emergency) section. Failing this, ask for the nearest *ambulatorio* (local clinic) or the urgencias section of the nearest hospital. All are public sector.

The expense of a private clinic or surgery is often worth the saving in time and frustration. A consultation at such a place typically costs somewhere between €25 and €40 (not counting medicines). If you have

Medical Kit Check List

Here's a practical list of things that you might like to tuck into your toilet bag.

- ☐ **Aspirin or paracetamol (acetaminophen in the USA)** – for pain or fever
- ☐ **Antihistamine** – for allergies (eg, hay fever), to ease the itch from insect bites or stings and to prevent motion sickness
- ☐ **Cold and flu tablets, throat lozenges and nasal decongestant**
- ☐ **Loperamide or diphenoxylate** –'blockers' for diarrhoea
- ☐ **Calamine lotion, sting relief spray or aloe vera** – to ease irritation from sunburn and insect bites or stings
- ☐ **Insect repellent, sunscreen, lip balm and eye drops**
- ☐ **Antiseptic cream** – for cuts and grazes
- ☐ **Bandages, plasters (Band-Aids) and other wound dressings**

travel insurance you may well be covered wholly or in part for this expense. All dental practices are private.

A pharmacy *(farmacia)* can help with many minor ailments. A system of duty pharmacies *(farmacias de guardia)* operates so that each town or district of a city has at least one open all the time (although often only for dispensing prescriptions). When a pharmacy is closed, it posts the name of the nearest open one(s) on the door. Lists of farmacias de guardia are also often given in local papers.

Environmental Hazards

Heat Exhaustion & Prickly Heat Dehydration and salt deficiency can cause heat exhaustion. Take time to acclimatise to high temperatures, drink litres of liquids and don't overexert yourself in the first few days. Salt deficiency leads to fatigue, lethargy, headaches, giddiness and muscle cramps. Salt tablets can help – or simply lace your food with extra salt.

Prickly heat is an itchy rash caused by excessive perspiration trapped under the skin. It usually strikes people who have just flown in. Keeping cool, bathing often, drying the skin and using a mild talcum or prickly heat powder, or even resorting to air-conditioning may help.

Heatstroke This serious, occasionally fatal, condition can occur if the body's heat-regulating mechanism breaks down and the body temperature rises to dangerous levels. Long, continuous periods of exposure to high temperatures and insufficient fluids can leave you vulnerable to heatstroke.

The symptoms are feeling unwell, not sweating very much (or at all) and a high body temperature (39° to 41°C or 102° to 106°F). Where sweating has ceased, the skin becomes flushed and red. Severe, throbbing headaches and lack of coordination will also occur, and the sufferer may be confused or aggressive. If untreated, severe cases will eventually become delirious or convulse. Hospitalisation is essential, but in the interim get victims out of the sun, remove their clothing, cover them with a wet sheet or towel and then fan continually. Give fluids if they are conscious.

Sunburn Out on the beach or up in the hills you can get sunburned surprisingly quickly, even through cloud. Use a sunscreen, hat and barrier cream for your nose and lips. Calamine lotion or a commercial after-sun preparation is good for mild sunburn. Protect your eyes with good-quality sunglasses, particularly when you're near water or sand.

Infectious Diseases

Diarrhoea Simple things such as a change of water, food or climate can all cause a mild bout of diarrhoea but a few rushed toilet trips with no other symptoms aren't indicative of a major problem. Weak black tea with a little sugar, soda water or soft drinks allowed to go flat and diluted 50% with water are all good for replacing the fluids you've lost. Urine is the best guide to whether you've been topped up again – if your pee is still brightly coloured and just a dribble, you need to drink more. Keep drinking small amounts often, and stick to a bland diet as you recover.

Hepatitis This is a general term for inflammation of the liver. The symptoms are similar in all forms of the illness, and include fever, chills, headache, fatigue, feelings of weakness and aches and pains, followed by loss of appetite, nausea, vomiting, abdominal pain, dark urine, light-coloured faeces, jaundiced (yellow) skin and yellowing of the whites of the eyes. People who have had hepatitis should avoid alcohol for some time after the illness, as the liver needs time to recover.

Hepatitis A is transmitted by contaminated food and drinking water. You should seek medical advice, but there is not much you can do apart from resting, drinking lots of fluids, eating lightly and avoiding fatty foods. Hepatitis E is transmitted in the same way as hepatitis A; it can be particularly serious in pregnant women.

Hepatitis B is spread through contact with infected blood, blood products or body fluids, for example through sexual contact, unsterilised needles or contact with blood via small breaks in the skin. Other risk situations include having a shave, tattoo or body piercing with contaminated equipment. The symptoms of hepatitis B may be more severe than type A and the disease can lead to long-term problems such as chronic liver damage, liver cancer or a long-term carrier state. Hepatitis C and D are spread in the same way as hepatitis B and can also lead to long-term complications.

HIV & AIDS Infection with the human immunodeficiency virus (HIV) may lead to acquired immune deficiency syndrome (AIDS), which is a fatal disease. Any exposure to blood, blood products or body fluids may put the individual at risk. The disease is often transmitted through sexual contact or dirty needles – vaccinations, acupuncture, tattooing and body piercing can be potentially as dangerous as intravenous drug use. Blood used for transfusions in European hospitals is screened for HIV and should be safe.

A few years ago Spain had the highest AIDS rate in Europe, the major reason being intravenous drug use. But the number of new cases is now half what it was in the mid-1990s.

HIV and AIDS are VIH and *sida*, respectively, in Spanish. The Fundación Anti-Sida España has a free information line (☎ 900 11 10 00) and a Web site at 🆆 www.fase.es (Spanish only).

Sexually Transmitted Infections (STIs)

HIV/AIDS and hepatitis B can be transmitted through sexual contact. Other STIs include gonorrhoea, herpes and syphilis; sores, blisters or rashes around the genitals and discharges or pain when urinating are common symptoms. In some STIs, such as wart virus or chlamydia, symptoms may be less marked or not observed at all, especially in women. Chlamydia infection can cause infertility in men and women before any symptoms have been noticed. Syphilis symptoms eventually disappear completely but the disease continues and can cause severe problems in later years. While abstinence from sexual contact is the only 100% effective prevention, using condoms is also effective.

Bites & Stings

None of the mosquitoes in Spain carry malaria. You can reduce the risk of bites by covering your skin and using an insect repellent. Bee and wasp stings are usually painful rather than dangerous. Calamine lotion or a sting relief spray or cream should ease the irritation while ice packs will reduce the pain and swelling. However, people who are allergic to them may experience severe breathing difficulties and require urgent medical care.

In forested areas, watch out for the hairy, reddish-brown caterpillars of the pine processionary moth. They live in silvery nests up in the pine trees and, come spring, leave the nest to march in long lines (hence the name). Touching the caterpillars' hairs sets off a severely irritating allergic skin reaction.

Ticks Check your body for ticks if you've been walking where sheep and goats graze. If you find one, smother it in cooking oil or something similar. Once suffocated, it's easy to pick off.

WOMEN TRAVELLERS

Harassment is much less frequent than the stereotypes of Spain would have you believe. Any unpleasantness you might encounter is more likely to come from drunken northern European yobs in the big resorts than from the Valencianos themselves.

In towns, you may get the occasional unwelcome stare, catcall or unnecessary comment, to which the best (and most galling) response is indifference. Don't get paranoid about what's being called out; the *piropo* – or harmless, mildly flirty compliment – is deeply ingrained in Spanish society and, if well delivered, even considered gallant.

It's inadvisable for a woman to hitchhike alone – and not a great idea even for two women together.

Topless bathing and skimpy clothes are generally OK at the coastal resorts and at swimming pools. Elsewhere, a little more modesty is the norm. Many local young women feel no compunction about dressing to kill, but equally feel absolutely no obligation to respond to any male interest this arouses.

If you want to touch base with a local women's organisation, contact the Institut de la Dona, which has a base in each provincial capital.

Valencia (☎ 96 398 56 00), Calle Naquera 9, Valencia 46003
Alicante (☎ 96 592 05 74), Calle García Andreu 12, Alicante 03007
Castellón (☎ 964 22 80 14), Calle Ensenyament 10, Castellón 12001

Each has a comprehensive list of women's associations throughout the Comunidad.

Recommended reading is the *Handbook for Women Travellers,* by M & G Moss.

GAY & LESBIAN TRAVELLERS

Gay and lesbian sex are both legal throughout Spain. The age of consent is 16, as for heterosexuals. Lesbians and gay men generally keep a fairly low profile but can be more open in Valencia City and major coastal resorts.

Gay magazines in Spanish, on sale at some newsstands, include the monthly *Mensual*

(€3.60; W www.mensual.com), which includes listings for gay bars, clubs and so on throughout Spain and *Zero* (€3.60; W www.zero-web.com), a monthly gay glossy. *Entiendes*, a free broadsheet available in gay haunts, also has nationwide listings. *Nosotras* is a bi-monthly lesbian review. GINS also provides listings throughout Spain at W www.gayinspain.com.

There are a few Spanish queer sites on the Web. There are nationwide listings of bars, clubs, accommodation and the like that include options in Comunidad at W www.chueca.com.

A useful local association for lesbians and gays is Colectiva Lambda, ☎ 96 391 20 84, e lambda@arrakis.es, W www.arrakis.es/~lambda, Calle San Dionisio 8, 1st floor, 46003 Valencia.

You'll find some pointers to gay venues under Valencia City, Benidorm and Alicante.

DISABLED TRAVELLERS

Some Spanish tourist offices in other countries can provide a basic information sheet with useful addresses for disabled travellers and give details of accessible accommodation in specific places.

You'll find some accessible accommodation in main centres but it's rarely in the budget category. Many hotels that claim to be accessible retain problem features. In the UK, Holiday Care (☎ 01293-774535), 2nd floor, Imperial Buildings, Victoria Rd, Horley, Surrey RH6 7PZ, produces an information pack on Spain for physically disabled people. This lists hotels with disabled access (though do contact the hotel or tour operator directly since, as Holiday Care stresses, information, culled from the Spanish National Tourist Office's official hotel guide, is only as good as what the hotel told the publisher). The pack also has details of, for example, where you can hire equipment and tour operators dealing with the disabled.

Federació ECOM (☎ 93 451 55 50, fax 93 451 69 04), Spain's federation of private organisations for the physically disabled, is at Gran Via de les Corts Catalanes 562, 08011 Barcelona. They can provide information on accommodation throughout Spain with disabled people's facilities. Their Web site, W www.ecom.es, gives links to other useful sites in Spain.

Le Ro (☎ 902 158329, W www.lero.net) rents out specialised equipment including wheelchairs, scooters and walking frames along the Costa Blanca.

SENIOR TRAVELLERS

Depending on the place, there may be reduced prices for people aged over 60, 63 (how's that for an arbitrary cut-off?) or 65 at some museums and attractions and occasionally on transport (see the Getting There & Away and Getting Around chapters). You usually need to provide ID proof of age. The top-end chain of public-sector *parador* hotels (see Accommodation later in this chapter) offers attractive discounts for people aged over 60 and their partners. It's also worth rooting out, through senior citizens' organisations and travel agents in your own country, information on travel packages and discounts for senior travellers.

TRAVEL WITH CHILDREN

The Spanish as a rule are very friendly to children. Accompanied children are welcome at all kinds of accommodation and in virtually every cafe, bar and restaurant. In fact, having children with you can often open doors to contact with local people who you otherwise may not have the opportunity to meet.

Many bars and cafes have outside tables, allowing grown-ups to indulge in their favourite tipple while the young ones run around and play – a good sign of a comparatively child-friendly society. Local kids are quite used to staying up late and at fiestas it's commonplace to see even tiny ones toddling the streets at 2am or 3am. Visiting kids like this idea too but often can't cope with it – or the next day – quite so readily.

Travelling with children usually implies taking a different approach to your holiday. Constant moving around can be fascinating for adults, but knee-high visitors may fail to appreciate the joys of the road. Most young children don't like moving around too much but are happier if they can settle into places

and make new friends. It's easier on parents too if you don't have to pack up and move on every day or two. Children are also likely to need extra time to acclimatise and extra care to avoid sunburn. Be prepared for minor health problems, brought on by change of diet or water or disrupted sleeping patterns.

Once the beach begins to pall – if it ever does – younger children can have lots of fun running around and trying out the slides and swings in municipal parks and playgrounds where even quite small places, on the coast or inland, offer fun for free. Far from free but spectacular of its kind, Terra Mítica theme park (see Benidorm in the Costa Blanca chapter) can easily exhaust a whole day. On a different theme (park), if you're staying at one of the northern resorts on the Costa del Azahar, you might all want to hop on the train and visit Port Aventura, over the border in Catalunya and west of Tarragona. Many of the larger resorts such as Benidorm, Cullera and Benicàssim have aquaparks. You might also want to take the kids on a boat journey to, for example, the Isla de Tabarca, accessible from Alicante, Santa Pola and Torrevieja, or the Isla de Benidorm, just off the coast. The Islas Columbretes (see Costa del Azahar in the Northern Valencia chapter) are nearly three hours from the shore and the sea can be quite rough.

You might not want to cover the whole of the narrow-gauge railway running between Alicante and Denia but it's easy to hop on and off at one of the intervening stations, have a fun journey and give yourselves a day out in another of the Costa Blanca's resorts.

As a counterpoint to all the fun of the unfamiliar, bring along some of the children's favourite toys, games and books and let them have time to enjoy some of the activities they are used to back home.

Most children are fascinated by the street-corner *kioscos*, selling sweets and *gusanitos* (corn puffs; literally little maggots or grubs – tell them that and it triples the thrill) for a coin or two. The magnetism of these places often overcomes children's inhibitions enough for them to carry out their own first Spanish transactions.

There are no particular health precautions you need to take with your children. That said, kids tend to be more affected than adults by unaccustomed heat, changes in diet and sleeping patterns, and just being in a strange place.

Nappies (diapers), creams, lotions, baby foods and so on are all as easily available in the Comunidad Valenciana as in any other western country but if there's some particular brand you swear by, it's best to bring it with you. Calpol (a paracetamol preparation for children), for instance, isn't easily found.

Children benefit from cut-price or free entry at many sights and museums. Those under four travel free on Spanish trains and those aged four to 11 normally pay 60% of the adult fare.

Lonely Planet's *Travel with Children* has lots of practical advice and first-hand stories from Lonely Planet author-parents and others.

USEFUL ORGANISATIONS

Turivaj, a branch of the Institut Valenciá de la Joventut (IVAJ), is a public-sector youth and student travel organisation. Good for reduced-price youth and student tickets, it also issues various useful documents such as GO25, ISIC, and HI youth hostel cards (see Visas & Documents earlier in this chapter). The Comunidad Valenciana version of the national TIVE organisation for under-25s, it has an office in each of the Comunidad's three provincial capitals:

Turivaj Valencia (☎ 96 386 99 52, @ turivaj@ ivaj.gva.es) Calle Hospital 11, 46001 Valencia
Turivaj Alicante (☎ 96 593 67 21) Plaza San Cristóbal, 03002 Alicante
Turivaj Castellón (☎ 96 435 79 99) Calle Orfebres Santalinea 2, 12005 Castellón

If you're a walker holidaying on the Costa Blanca and want to hook up with others, contact the Costa Blanca Mountain Walkers. This splendid informal group of mostly expats has been exploring the area for over 15 years. They walk on Wednesdays and Saturdays between September and May. For walk details, check their weekly posting in the General section of the *Costa Blanca News*' small ads.

DANGERS & ANNOYANCES

The Comunidad Valenciana is, in general, a very secure place to be and the vast majority of visitors risk little more than sunburn and maybe GBH (grievous bodily hangover). The warnings below apply particularly to Valencia and Alicante cities and the larger coastal resorts. Inland Valencia, if you except the slight risk of robbery from your vehicle, must rank as among the safest areas in Europe.

For some specific hints about looking after your luggage and money and on safety for women, see the Planning, Money and Women Travellers sections earlier in this chapter.

Theft & Loss

The risk of theft is highest in the larger coastal resorts and the cities of Valencia and Alicante, particularly around the bus and train stations. You're most at risk when you first arrive in a new place and may be off your guard, disoriented or unaware of danger signs. Pickpockets and bag snatchers are the main worry, along with theft from cars. Carry valuables under your clothes if possible – certainly not in a back pocket, a day pack or anything that could be snatched away easily – and keep your eyes open for people who get unnecessarily close to you. Be cautious also with people who come up to offer or ask you something (like the time or directions) or start talking to you for no obviously good reason. These could be attempts to distract you and make you an easier victim. Don't leave baggage unattended and avoid crushes.

Anything left lying on the beach can be whisked away when your back is turned. At night, avoid dingy, empty city alleys and back streets – or anywhere that just doesn't feel 100% safe. Don't leave anything valuable lying around your room and use a safe if one's available.

Theft from cars, especially those with foreign plates or which are clearly hired, is all too common. And it can happen in broad daylight even if you leave the car unattended for just a short while. Never leave anything visible in your vehicle – it's an open invitation to break in. Remove the radio and, if possible, don't even leave anything valuable in the boot (trunk). Always keep an eye on your car if you stop at one of the A-7 motorway service stations. Thieves can empty it in a flash and be up and away before you've downed your coffee.

If anything valuable is stolen or lost, you must report it to the police and get a copy of the report if you want to make an insurance claim. If your passport has gone, contact your embassy or consulate for help in issuing a replacement.

Annoyances

Apart from one or two aspects of Valencia City – which fully merit their own brief Annoyances section in that chapter– there isn't that much to get worked up about. Throughout the Comunidad, most things generally work well, service is fairly prompt and people courteous. The only persistent indigenous irritation in towns and resorts is noise; of traffic, whining scooters, late night bars, blaring TVs in bars when all you're after is a drink and a chat – and simple everyday conversation, which takes place at a higher decibel level than in most other parts of Europe. Not for nothing does Spain bear the dubious title of the world's second-noisiest country!

Loud and drunken louts ferried in on charter flights from northern Europe can be a pain in seaside resorts favoured by package tour operators. A sad and rather shaming holiday resort statistic is that the bulk of those who end up in the local slammer are foreigners who couldn't hold their liquor.

Terrorism

Basque ETA terrorists are a particularly vicious bunch who realise that by targeting tourist interests they can inflict economic damage and raise their profile outside Spain. In 2001 an ETA terrorist blew herself up in an apartment in Torrevieja while handling a bomb intended for others and a bomb exploded without loss of life in Salou, over in Catalunya. To put these incidents in perspective, of Spain's over 40 million visitors that

year, a hundred or so were inconvenienced. Yes, there's always that minimal risk – as there is when crossing the road, eating fish with bones or walking under a ladder – but you'd have to be very unlucky indeed to find yourself directly involved. It certainly should not be a factor in your decision whether or not to take a holiday in the Comunidad.

EMERGENCIES

The best combination to remember is ☎ 112, the pan-European emergency telephone number. It's the one to dial if you need urgent medical assistance, the ambulance service, police or fire.

If you're seriously ill or injured, someone should let your embassy or consulate know (see the Embassies & Consulates section earlier in this chapter for telephone numbers).

LEGAL MATTERS

Should you be arrested, you will be allotted the free services of a duty solicitor (abogado de oficio), who may speak only Spanish. You're also entitled to make a phone call. If you use this to contact your embassy or consulate, it will probably be able to do no more than refer you to a lawyer who speaks your language. If you end up in court, the authorities are obliged to provide a translator.

Drugs

The only legal drug is cannabis and it's only legal in amounts for personal use, which means very little. In the occasional bar people smoke the stuff openly, but the more liberal days of the late '80s are long gone and discretion is now the better part of valour.

BUSINESS HOURS

Generally, Valencianos work from about 9am to 2pm and then again from 4.30pm or 5pm for another three hours, Monday to Friday. Shops and travel agencies are usually open these hours on Saturday too, although some may skip the evening session. In summer, many people work a jornada intensiva (intensive working day), starting as early as 7am and finishing by 2pm.

Big supermarkets and department stores generally stay open from about 9am to 9pm without a break, Monday to Saturday. A lot of government offices don't bother with afternoon opening any day of the year. For bank and post office hours respectively, see Money and Post & Communications earlier in this chapter.

We indicate each museum's opening hours since there's no regular pattern. Major ones tend to open for something like normal Spanish business hours (with or without the afternoon break) and many close on Monday.

PUBLIC HOLIDAYS & SPECIAL EVENTS

There are two main periods when any self-respecting Spaniard is on the move: Semana Santa (the week leading up to Easter Sunday) and, especially, the second half of July and the month of August, when millions head down to Valencian seaside resorts from the *meseta*, Spain's high inland plain. On key summer weekends the Comunidad's main roads can be a nightmare of departing and returning holidaymakers.

Public Holidays

The Comunidad Valenciana observes around 14 official holidays a year. When one falls close to a weekend, locals like to make a *puente* (bridge) – meaning they take the intervening day off too. On occasion, when a couple of holidays fall close to the same weekend, the puente becomes an *acueducto* (aqueduct)!

Holidays observed throughout Spain (though the authorities seem to change their minds about some of these from year to year) are:

Año Nuevo (New Year's Day) 1 January
Epifanía (Epiphany) or **Día de los Reyes Magos (Three Kings' Day)** 6 January – when children traditionally receive presents
Viernes Santo (Good Friday) March/April
Fiesta del Trabajo (Labour Day) 1 May
Corpus Cristi June – observed on the ninth Sunday after Easter, an occasion for processions in many parts of Spain, including the Comunidad Valenciana.
La Asunción de la Virgen (Feast of the Asumption) 15 August

Día de la Hispanidad (National Day) 12 October
Todos los Santos (All Saints' Day) 1 November
Día de la Constitución (Constitution Day) 6 December
La Inmaculada Concepción (Feast of the Immaculate Conception) 8 December
Navidad (Christmas) 25 December

The Comunidad's own special holidays are:

Día de la Comunidad (Valencian Regional Day) 9 October
San Vicente Martir (Valencia City only) 22 January
San Vicente Ferrer March/April – eight days after Easter Sunday
San José 19 March

In addition, many a town and village will tag on another day in honour of its own patron saint.

Special Events

See the special section 'Fiestas' for details of special events in the region.

ACTIVITIES
Walking

The Comunidad offers some excellent walking, especially inland. You might want to arm yourself with a copy of Lonely Planet's *Walking in Spain*, which has a chapter devoted to the region. Star destinations include the Sierra Mariola and Sierra Aitana, both easily accessible from Costa Blanca resorts. Serious walkers might even want to consider a whole walking holiday in the area with recommended environmentally and socially committed Terra Ferma (see Organised Tours in the Getting Around chapter). *Mountain Walks on the Costa Blanca*, by Bob Stansfield, published by Cicerone, is a good guide to walks in the south of the Comunidad.

In the north and deeper inland, much of the Maestrazgo offers fine trekking; see the Northern Valencia chapter for further information on walking in the area.

Cycling

If you intend to cycle tour, bring your own machine. In a region that's ideal for biking, there are surprisingly few rental opportunities

(Valencia City, for example, pancake flat, fairly well endowed with bike lanes and with a wonderful Paseo Marítimo, has just one option). If, on the other hand, you're happy pootling along the front or around town, you'll find hire shops in, for example, Peñíscola, Benidorm and Torrevieja.

Horse Riding

On the Costa Blanca, Hípica Los Robles in Denia organises rides along the beach and salt flats. Inland, Equitación Mariola, just outside Bocairent, conducts scenic equestrian outings in the Sierra Mariola. On the Costa del Azahar, Masía del Rull, based outside Alcossebre, offers gentle riding along the coastal plain.

Up the Vall de Turia in Villar del Arzobispo, you can hire a horse or, if you prefer something inanimate and easier to handle, a mountain bike at Granja-Escuela La Serranía, a working farm.

Climbing

Climbing is essentially an inland activity. Chulilla in the Turia valley entices climbers from all over Europe. In summer, Elsports in Morella offers guided climbing, plus canoeing and mountain biking. Avensport, operating from Venta del Moro near Utiel has in its repertoire canyon clambering as well as rock climbing – and canoeing too.

On the coast, Calpe's Peñon de Ifach is a popular challenge – but strictly for the intermediate to advanced climber.

Rafting & Canoeing

These too are essentially inland sports, exploiting the swifter spate of the Comunidad's few rivers of any consequence as they tumble down towards the coastal plain.

JANE SMITH

A favourite is the Río Cabriel, where three companies – Avensport, Kalahari and Ozono – operating from the village of Venta del Moro, offer canoeing and/or rafting.

For a gentler paddle, go with Aventuria, based beside the lake at Benagéber. Here, you can also windsurf and enjoy other water sports, including sailing.

Diving & Snorkelling

Diving is at its best around the Islas Columbretes, off the Costa del Azahar, and Isla de Tabarca, off the Costa Blanca. Barracuda in Alcossebre does courses and organises visits to the former, as does Aqua Sub in Vinaròs. Down south, you can take the plunge with, for example, Diving Center Mores in Santa Pola and Tevere or Diving Mediterraneo, both based in Torrevieja.

Sailing

The Comunidad Valenciana has nearly 500km of coastline. Add to this soft yet reliable breezes, the offshore Islas Columbretes and, farther out in the Mediterranean, Ibiza and its sister Balearic Islands (but an overnight's sail away), and you're in for a satisfying sailing holiday.

For the most spectacular coastal views, beat parallel with the Sierra de Irta, running from Peñíscola to Alcossebre before perhaps setting the sails for the Islas Columbretes. On the Costa Blanca, views landwards are at their best between Denia, dominated by the mountain of Montgó, and the Isla de Benidorm, conveniently beyond hailing distance of the coast's busiest resort, leaving in your wake the spectacular craggy headlands of Cabo de San Antonio and Cabo de la Nao.

You can learn to sail in most of the major resorts though language will be an impediment unless your nautical Spanish is ship-shape. Benicàssim has a school and in most other coastal resorts there's a Club Náutico that gives courses.

Surfing & Windsurfing

For an inland venue, skim along the man-made lake of Benagéber (see Rafting & Canoeing earlier). With your own board, you can scud the sea's waves at will. However, not many resorts hire equipment or offer tuition. Among those that do are Santa Pola and Benicàssim. Cullera, with its gentle waves, is particularly suitable for first-timers.

Bird-Watching

Freshwater La Albufera lake, just south of Valencia City, is a twitcher's dream. With migratory flamingos and one of Spain's largest heron colonies, it's interesting for everyone, not just ornithologists, and has an excellent nature centre. Other salinated marshy areas along the coast, many of them also one-time sweetwater lakes, are a regular haunt of aquatic birds. Don't neglect the large man-made pools and salt pans of, for example, Santa Pola and Torrevieja; the birds certainly don't.

Collins Field Guide to the Birds of Britain and Europe or their handier *Pocket Guide* will help you to identify anything feathered that you're likely to see. *A Birdwatching Guide to the Costa Blanca,* by Malcolm Palmer, is a slim yet informative guide to the species you're most likely to spot.

Golf

Throughout the Comunidad, there are no fewer than 20 18-hole golf courses – an impressive provision, say golfers, a profligate waste of increasingly scarce water, say environmentalists: every fairway and green in a land where green is not the natural hue needs to be soaked and squirted liberally. Among the most renowned courses is El Saler (☎ 96 112 73 66), recently ranked third in Europe and just squeezing into the world's top 30 courses. Around 20km south of Valencia, it's a frequent venue for the Spanish Open.

COURSES
Learning Spanish

Outside Spain, the Instituto Cervantes, with branches in over 30 cities around the world, promotes the Spanish language and culture. It's mainly involved in Spanish teaching and library and information services. The library at the London branch (☎ 020-7235 0353), 102 Eaton Square, London SW1W 9AN, has a wide range of reference books, literature, books on history and the arts, periodicals,

over 1000 videos including feature films, language-teaching material, electronic databases and music CDs. In New York, the institute (☎ 212-689 4232) is at 122 East 42nd St, Suite 807, New York, NY 10168. You can find further addresses on the institute's Web site at **W** www.cervantes.es.

Another way to get stuck into Spanish before you travel is to work through one of the BBC's excellent courses for all levels. *Talk Spanish*, pitched at absolute beginners, is all about Valencia City. For it and others, go **W** www.bbc.co.uk/education/languages/spanish.

If you're planning to be in the Comunidad for some time, a language course is a great way not only to get a grip on Spanish but also to meet locals and other foreign students. The provincial capitals of Alicante, Castellón and Valencia have a public sector Escuela Oficial de Idiomas, as do Gandía and Torrevieja on the coast. It's certainly the cheapest option and, if you get a good teacher, as good as anywhere. To register, you'll need to be around in September or February. Bring your wallet, ID and huge reserves of patience; the bureaucracy will have you climbing up the wall.

For shorter and more flexible courses, you're better off with a private school or a teacher who really knows how Spanish works (an informant who simply speaks the language well can be a disaster). We recommend some schools for Valencia City (see the Valencia City & Around chapter for details). Elsewhere, tourist offices can usually advise.

WORK

Although it's dropping steadily, Spain's unemployment rate remains among the EU's highest. With a ready pool of North Africans and ex-Yugoslavs for construction, factory and fruit-picking labour, competition's tough and the work ill paid and scarcely worthwhile unless you're seriously unflush.

Nationals of EU countries, Norway and Iceland may work throughout Spain without a visa but for stays of more than three months they are supposed to apply within the first month for a *tarjeta de residencia* (residence card). For information on this laborious process, see Visas & Documents earlier in the chapter.

Virtually everyone else is supposed to get a work permit from a Spanish consulate in their country of residence and, if they plan to stay more than 90 days, a residence visa. These procedures are well nigh impossible unless you have a job contract lined up before you begin the long haul. In any case you should start the paper chase a long time before you aim to go to Spain. All this said, quite a few people do work, discreetly, without bothering to tangle with the arcane bureaucracy.

Language Teaching

This is the most obvious option but don't kid yourself that, just because you speak English, you'll fall into a job. Competition's tough; the Comunidad Valenciana's a cosy place to hunker down and the better language schools get inundated with requests for employment from English native speakers, ranging from speculative no-hopers to qualified and experienced teachers. To enhance your chances, work for some formal qualification, at least to the level of the RSA Certificate for the Teaching of English as a Foreign Language (TEFL). Giving private lessons is another avenue, although unlikely to bring you a living wage straight away.

Tourist Resorts

Fairly ill-paid work, especially in high summer and in a large resort, is another possibility, especially if you arrive early in the season and are prepared to stay a while. In places such as Benidorm and, to a lesser extent, Torrevieja and its ilk, quite a lot of bars, restaurants and other businesses are run by foreigners.

Busking

A few travellers earn a crust (and not much more) busking in the resorts.

ACCOMMODATION

During Semana Santa (Holy Week – the week leading up to Easter) and between mid-July and early September, it's prudent to reserve accommodation anywhere along the coast. If you plan to arrive after 7pm, make this clear as you book. And if you're delayed en route, ring in; many are the travellers who've arrived late to discover that the room they reserved has been re-let.

Even in high summer, a camp site can often squeeze space for a small bivouac tent – and maybe for a family tent too.

Camping

Camp sites *(campings)* liberally dot the full length of the Valencian coastline but are much rarer inland. All can be very crowded and often noisy late into the night in high summer. Many pitches within ones that are an easy drive from Valencia, Alicante and Elche are occupied by families who install their tents, caravans, plants, tarps and TVs year round, so fewer are available for short-term campers.

Few camping grounds are near town centres and many are inconvenient if you're reliant on public transport. There are also *zonas de acampada libre*, free camping areas, usually run by the local municipality, that have few or minimal facilities. In rural areas, they're sometimes splendid. Near towns, in high summer or after a public holiday, some could easily double up as pigsties.

Facilities range from reasonable to very good. Most camp sites these days offer hot showers and electrical hook-ups. Many have a cafeteria and a 'supermarket' (for most, read 'small shop'). The best ones have heated swimming pools, restaurants, a laundry service, children's playgrounds and even tennis courts. Sizes range from a capacity of fewer than 20 tents to more than 2000.

Camping grounds usually charge per person, per tent and per vehicle – anywhere between €3 and €6 for each, with an average of around €3.50. Some places charge by the *parcela* or pitch, a price which includes your car and tent space. To this you need to add the fee per person. Children usually pay a bit less than adults. Some sites are open all year but quite a few close from around October to Easter. Many have significantly lower charges outside July and August.

The annual official *Guía de Campings* (€6), updated annually, is an invaluable resource if you're planning to camp around. Otherwise, tourist offices can always direct you to the nearest camping ground.

With certain significant exceptions – such as most beaches, all environmentally protected areas and a few municipalities that ban it – it is legal to camp outside camping grounds (although not within 1km of official ones!). Signs usually indicate where wild camping is not allowed. You'll need permission to camp on private land.

Camping Gaz and Coleman are the only common brands of camping gas; screw-on canisters are hard to find.

Youth Hostels

There are 11 youth hostels in the Comunidad Valenciana, the majority of them affiliated to Hostelling International. Several, open to all in July and August, are student dormitories during the academic year. You can reserve either by phoning or emailing the hostel itself or via a central booking number (☎ 96 398 59 00, fax 96 398 59 14). See also Hostel Cards in the Visa & Documents section earlier.

They usually represent the cheapest option for lone travellers though a couple might come across a basic double room for an equivalent price. Many are heavily booked by school and community groups so it's always wise to reserve.

All have the same price structure. For people aged under 25, a bed costs €4.80, B&B €5.40 and lunch or dinner €4.20. Equivalent rates for those aged over 25 are €6.60/8.40/4.80.

Hostales, Pensiónes & Hotels

Prices, as normally expressed by hotels and the like and as quoted in this book, are net. Mid-range and top-end hotels add on separately a 7% value-added tax (IVA; *impuesto sobre el valor añadido*). Most budget places subsume IVA, if they pay it, within the prices they quote. To be sure where you stand, ask '¿*Está incluido el IVA?*' (Is IVA included?).

For budget hotels, we indicate whether rooms are basic (many basic rooms these days have at least a wash basin), come with a shower (but not toilet) or have full bathroom (shower and/or bath plus toilet). All rooms in mid-range and top-end hotels have full bathroom facilities, which usually include a bidet and often a hair dryer and other accoutrements.

The lone traveller has a tougher time. Some places, especially pensiónes and hostales, rent by the room. Many others may have only one or two single rooms on their books. Truly budget options are also on the decline as more and more places upgrade and install bathrooms throughout, leaving one basic room as an enticement in guidebooks and listings.

The official multilingual *Guía de Hoteles* (€9) lists accommodation throughout Spain and can repay the modest investment in just a couple of nights.

The Guía and many tourist office listings reflect the grading of hotels from one to five stars, hostales between one and three and pensiónes with one or two. These star ratings refer to specific amenities offered rather than overall quality. In practice, they aren't a very useful indicator of quality; the more stars a place has, the more tax it pays so many worthwhile establishments deliberately choose to keep their star rating low.

A *pensión* is basically a small private hotel, often family run. At the cheaper end, some only have communal bathroom facilities in the corridor. Others provide a mix or, increasingly, full bathroom. At the worst, rooms will be bare and basic and sometimes tiny. They are, however, usually clean. Hostales are generally similar and tend towards the more comfortable, the majority offering a private bathroom and, increasingly, TV.

Hotels range from simple places, where a double room could cost as little as €35, up to wildly luxurious, five-star places where you could pay €360 or more. Even the cheapest rooms will probably have an attached bathroom and there'll probably be a restaurant and/or bar.

Paradores de Turismo A *parador de turismo* is one of a state-run chain of quality hotels, often set in magnificent castles or mansions. Offers include their five-night card at €66 per night and a 35% reduction for people aged over 60 and their partners.

The region's three paradores – in El Saler, just south of Valencia, Xàbia and Benicarló – are in modern buildings, tastefully decorated yet short on history. You can book via the Central de Reservas (Reservation Centre; ☎ 91 516 66 66, fax 91 516 66 57), or online at Ⓦ www.parador.es.

Casas Rurales

The Comunidad Valencia is energetically promoting rural tourism in an effort to encourage visitors to explore the interior once they've toned up their tans on the coast. Typical prices are from €12 to €15 per person per night in casas rurales (village or country houses). The accommodation varies between a *refugio* (mountain refuge or simple hut) and a *masía* (whole farmhouse). Some offer only accommodation while others can provide B&B or even full board.

Organisations include:

Asociación de Casas Rurales de la Comunidad Valenciana (Ⓦ www.casasrurales-cv.com)
Agrotur (☎ 902 11 53 56, fax 96 392 44 79, Ⓦ www.agrotour.org) Calle Caballeros 26, Valencia
Asociación de Alojamientos Rurales de la Montaña Alicantina (☎/fax 96 552 90 39, Ⓦ www.cederaitana.com – Spanish only) Masía del Pinet, 03459 Alfafara
Turistrat (Cooperativa Agroturística de L'Alt Maestrat; ☎ 96 442 84 32, fax 96 442 83 58) Plaça Gaspar Fuster 13, 12140 Albocasser
Altretur (☎ 96 425 60 52, fax 96 425 56 75) Plaza Real 10, 12001 Castellón

Alternatively, get hold of a copy of the excellent *Guía de Alojamiento Rural* (Guide to Rural Accommodation), a free, comprehensive booklet produced by the regional tourist agency, available at major tourist offices.

Apartments & Villas

In many places, especially along the coast, you can rent self-catering apartments, or even houses and villas. Tourist offices can normally supply lists. Average starting rates are about €30 per night for two or three people in a simple one-bedroom apartment. Many demand a minimum stay of from three days to one week.

Apartments are worth considering if you plan to stay several days, in which case there will usually be discounts from the daily rate.

FOOD
Regional Cuisine

Paella Think Spanish food and your first thought may well be *paella*. Now truly international, paella, named after the wide, shallow pan in which it simmers, originated in Valencia. Although locals wouldn't dream of picking at a panful at anytime other than lunchtime, you'll also find it dished up for dinner in holiday resorts. There are two main varieties: *de carne* (with chicken and rabbit; see the boxed text) and *de marisco* (with

---

Paella with Rabbit & Chicken

Ingredients (4 servings)
125g oil
400g round grain rice (as for risotto or rice pudding)
400g butter beans (soak overnight and precook until almost tender)
800g runner beans
4 small chicken pieces
4 small rabbit pieces
1 handful of snails (optional)
1 pinch of saffron (roast gently in a pan until it changes colour then crumble into water)
2 teaspoons salt
1 ladle tomato puree
2–4 teaspoons paprika
2L water

Method
Heat oil and add salt. Fry chicken pieces for 5 minutes. Add rabbit and fry for 15 minutes. Add the vegetables and a little water. Add the tomato puree and paprika. Add the remaining water; when this boils add the saffron. Once the water has reduced, top up to the original level and add the rice in an even layer. Once the rice is added, cooking takes about 20 minutes. Boil fast, reducing heat for the last few minutes. Turn off heat and allow to stand uncovered for 10 minutes.

seafood). Some restaurants will serve individual portions from a large, communal pan while others, especially more upmarket joints, require a minimum order of two.

Other Rice Dishes Rice was introduced into Spain by the Moors (indeed one of the several speculative etymologies of the word paella is that it's a hispanified version of the Arabic *al baqiya*, the remainder, meaning here the 'leftovers' that were tossed into the pan). Cultivated around the Albufera lake and in Alicante province, it's the staple of many other Valencian dishes such as *arroz a banda* (rice cooked in a fish stock), *arroz negro* (rice with squid, including its ink) or *arroz al horno* (rice baked in the oven). *Arròs amb fesols i naps* is rice with haricot beans and turnip. It's several times tastier than the mundane ingredients might suggest. Rice dishes are often accompanied by a dish of *all i oli*, very garlicky mayonnaise. When you can't face another grain, go for *fideuá*, a paella made with noodles instead of rice.

Fish & Seafood As befits a land overlooking the Mediterranean, fish and (on more special occasions; it doesn't come cheap) shellfish figure large on the diet. Behind many a bar, you'll see a dish of *boquerones* (fresh anchovies), ready to be served as a tapa (bar snack). Although available all over Spain, most are landed in Valencian ports. Juicy, raw and pickled in vinegar, they're quite different from the salty, thirst-inducing variety in tiny tins. A freshwater favourite, especially in Valencia province is *all-i-pebre*, hunks of eel in a peppery sauce. As you travel beside the Albufera lake, you'll see the eel traps, set for the next wriggling victim. Another favourite starter is *escarrat*, strips of salted cod and roasted red pepper bathed in olive oil.

Fish and shellfish are at their freshest in those towns – such as Vinaròs on the Costa del Azahar, Torrevieja on the Costa Blanca or Valencia City – where a fishing fleet still survives.

The Interior Inland, traditional cooking owes more to the *meseta*. Gazpacho, not the

cold, sloppy Andalucian kind but *gazpacho manchego*, steaming and rich in pasta and gobs of meat, keeps out the winter chill. Much of the protein in the inland diet comes from lamb and, especially in the Maestrazgo, pork. Try its popular *tombet*, which brims with both, or *puchero*, a slow simmering of meat, potato, onions, green beans and chard or *cabrito al horno* (roast kid – of the four-legged variety!). The most frequent come-hither sign is *carnes a la brasa*, grilled meat. Nothing comes more tender than a plate of sizzling *chuletas de cordero* (lamb chops). The gun was the other provider of nourishment; to this day and, if the season's right, you'll find some kind of game on the menu of even a modest inland restaurant.

Fruit & Veg In the Comunidad Valenciana, you'll have some of the freshest vegetables you're ever likely to taste. The artichokes of Benicarló on the Costa del Azahar are so prized that they've been awarded a *denomi-*

Fresh Fruit

If you travel through the huerta by train or along the A-7 *autopista*, what will probably strike you more than the mathematically straight lines of artichokes, lettuces, beans, peppers, tomatoes, aubergines, carrots, courgettes, potatoes, onions, cabbages, cauliflower and the like is the forest upon forest of citrus fruit trees. Valencian oranges, lemons, grapefruit and mandarins are exported all over the EU and a freshly squeezed juice is one of the day's great starters. You'll also find the more exotic *nispera* (medlar or loquat in English: it's yellowy-orange like an apricot, and about the same size; the flesh is juicy like a sweet plum and at its heart there's a smooth shiny stone), originally planted around orange orchards as a wind break, and soft, squishy *caquis* (persimmons).

Inland, where it's cooler, fat, juicy cherries grow in and around the Vall de Gallinera. From Alicante province too come sweet white table grapes while Elche is renowned for its dates.

nación de origen (see Alcoholic Drinks later in this section), just like a good wine! The extensive fertile coastal agricultural plain that extends almost from the border with Catalunya and well into Alicante province is called the *huerta*. Intensively cultivated under a benign sun, its rich soil yields more than one crop a year.

Ensalada Valenciana, which turns up on most menus, is a salad of lettuce, tomato, onion, olives and tuna.

Turrón This Spanish variant upon – improvement upon, many would say – nougat is a speciality of the mountain town of Jijona in Alicante province. Traditionally eaten only around Christmas time, it's a treat at any time of the year. It's also a compact, nutritious, and above all delicious, item to slip into your backpack if you're off walking. There are two main kinds: Turrón de Jijona, which is soft and fudge-like, and Turrón de Alicante, crispier and crunchier. For more details, see the boxed text 'Turrón, the Finger Lickin' Fudge' in the Central chapter.

When to Eat

Valencianos reckon they can fit in seven feeds a day. Not every day or there'd be little time left for work or play and they'd have difficulty getting through the average door. But it's comforting to know the possibility's there if you suddenly turn peckish.

Breakfast *(desayuno)* is nothing more than a coffee and a *tostada* (slice of toast with jam or some such) or *bollo* (roll), accompanied in season by a *zumo de naranja* (fresh orange juice), grabbed at a bar on the way to work.

Almuerzo is a particularly Valencian daily ritual. Taken at a more leisurely pace about a couple of hours after breakfast (and therefore coinciding with what the British term 'elevenses'), it's a time when bars are packed with customers tucking into *bocadillos* (French-bread sandwiches), picking at tapas and washing them down with a glass of beer or wine, chased by a coffee.

Unsurprisingly, given this mid-morning pick-you-up, lunch *(comida)*, the main meal of the day for most people, is taken much later than in other countries. Restaurants

---

Turrón for Softies

We ourselves go for the soft, tooth-wrecking Turrón de Jijona every time. To replicate it on a kitchen-stove scale, try this recipe:

Ingredients
250g sugar
250g white honey
500g toasted almonds
5 egg whites

Method
Whirr the nuts in a food processor until they're a smooth paste. Then beat the egg whites stiffly and add them to the paste. Put the sugar and honey in a saucepan and bring to the boil. Add the paste to the honey mixture. Mix constantly with a wooden spatula over a low heat for 10 minutes. Remove from the heat and put into moulds lined with rice paper. Leave to cool. Enjoy!

---

don't usually start serving until 2pm, continuing until 4pm, even 5pm. But committed trencherfolk manage to fit in the *aperitivo*, nibbling away at a tapa or two before lunch.

Between lunch and dinner, many a Valenciano will take a *merienda*, usually consisting of a hot drink and some sweet cake or pastry or another bocadillo.

Dinner *(cena)* is often a lighter meal, beginning at the earliest about 9pm, though most locals don't drift in until at least 10pm. Like lunch, the evening meal can easily last two or three hours – a leisurely and highly social affair.

Lastly, and particularly if the night has been a long one, some will head for bed after a *resopón*, a nightcap snack.

This punishing schedule doesn't mean that you're obliged to alter your gastronomic clock or return home significantly heavier. All seven stages are, of course, optional. And in popular tourist areas, restaurants begin to serve lunch and dinner much earlier.

Where & What to Eat

Cafes & Bars The distinction between cafes and bars is negligible; coffee and alcohol are

Fresh seafood is worth shelling out for
on the Mediterranean coast.

almost always available in both. Bars take
several different forms, including *cerve-
cerías* (beer bars). *Tabernas* (taverns) and
bodegas (old-style wine bars) sometimes
serve a decent meal too.

Many cafes and bars also offer food,
ranging from bocadillos and tapas via
raciones (literally 'ration', a copious tapa)
to a full meal. Eating at the bar rather than
sitting down usually saves you 10% to 20%
of the bill.

You can't really give an average price for
a night out picking at tapas since it all depends what and how many you select. It's a
convivial and fun way to experience lots of
different flavours that usually works out more
expensive than selecting from a set menu.

The meal prices that we quote in a town's
Places to Eat section reflect the typical cost
of a three-course meal *without drink* since
your tipple, whether a bottle of plain mineral water or a celebratory bottle of Catalan
champagne, can skew the cost significantly.

The menu, which is often posted outside a
restaurant, should indicate whether IVA (7%
value-added) is included in prices quoted or
added to your bill. Similarly, it should show
whether a service charge is slapped on or not.

Restaurants *Restaurantes* generally open
for lunch and dinner. Those with an attached bar may stay open throughout the
day. Most display a menu *(carta)*, usually
with prices, out the front. Any taxes and
service charges should also be advertised,
but quite often are not.

Variations on the theme include the
mesón (traditionally a place for simple home
cooking, although this is often no longer the
case), *comedor* (a dining room, usually attached to a bar or hotel), *venta* (roadside
inn) and *marisquería* (seafood specialist).

The traveller's friend is the *menú del día*,
a set meal available at most restaurants for
lunch, and occasionally in the evening too.
Usually you get a starter or side dish, a main
dish, a simple dessert and a drink for a modest price – around €5 in budget establishments, rising to over €12 at smarter places.

Another budget option is the *plato combinado*. Literally 'combined plate', it's usually on offer at both lunch and dinnertime.
The combos are often illustrated by fading
photos, each with a number, which makes
ordering easy if you don't speak Spanish.

Vegetarian Food

There are few strictly vegetarian restaurants.
Elsewhere, even if a waiter tells you that
there's, say, vegetable stew on offer, it's
quite possible that it simmered in a meat
stock. You're in meat and fish-eating country, so you will find your choices (unless you
cater for yourself) rather limited. Salads are
OK (but remember that ensalada Valenciana
contains tuna), and you will come across
various side dishes such as *champiñones*
(mushrooms, usually lightly fried in olive
oil and garlic). Other possibilities include
berenjenas (aubergines), *menestra* (vegetable stew), *espárragos* (asparagus), *lentejas* (lentils; take care though, they're often
cooked in a ham stock) and other vegetables
that are sometimes cooked as side dishes.

Self-Catering

Spain is as rich in chain supermarkets as
anywhere in the EU. It's much more fun to
buy from a town's *mercado*, its produce
market. Buy your bread from a *panadería*.

Some hostels and a very few pensiones
and hostales have facilities for cooking.

DRINKS
Nonalcoholic Drinks
Coffee In Spain coffee is strong and slightly
bitter. A *café con leche* is about 50% coffee,

50% hot milk. A *café solo* is an espresso, short and black; this is what you'll be served if you simply ask for *un café*. *Café cortado* (or just *cortado*) is an espresso with a splash of milk. If you prefer your coffee piping hot, ask for any of the above to be *caliente*.

For iced coffee, ask for *café con hielo* or *café del tiempo*: you'll get a glass of ice and a hot espresso that you trickle over the ice.

Tea Valencianos generally prefer coffee but most cafes and bars can rustle up a tea. You normally get a cup with a tea bag so you can make it swamp-water strong or weak as gnat's urine. Locals drink it black. If you want milk *(leche)*, ask for it to be separate *(a parte)*; otherwise, you'll end up with a cup of milky water with a tea bag floating dismally in it. Most places also offer *infusiones* (herbal teas) such as camomile *(manzanilla)* and mint *(poleo)*, also served in sachets.

Chocolate Spaniards brought chocolate back from the New World and adopted it enthusiastically. Generally a breakfast drink or winter almuerzo drink, it's served thick and often taken with *churros*, deep-fried batter fingers.

Nuts to You, Your Highness

One sultry summer day in 1238, as King Jaume I was preparing to relieve the city of Valencia from Moorish occupation, a young farm girl offered him a glass of cool, milky liquid. '*Aixo es or, xata*', exclaimed the king in Catalan, wiping the driblets from his beard: 'This is gold, lass'.

Such, according to dubious legend, is the origin of *orxata* (*horchata* in Spanish), a cloudy white drink, as Valencian as paella, that's made from crushed *chufa* (tiger nuts), sweetened with sugar and served icy cold. You can have it *líquido* (cold and natural) or *granizado* (a slush puppy; literally, 'like hail'). Order with it half a dozen *fartons*, long finger-shaped buns that you dunk in the divine fluid. Both name and taste are to savour.

Soft Drinks *Refrescos* (soft drinks) include the usual international brands, local ones such as Kas, and more expensive *granizado* (iced fruit crush).

You can drink clear, cold water from a public fountain or tap – but first check that it's *potable*. In restaurants, for tapwater, ask for *agua del grifo*. Bottled water *(agua mineral)* comes in several brands, either fizzy *(con gas)* or still *(sin gas)*.

A *batido* is a flavoured milk drink or milk shake; the bottled variety is usually oversugared and sickly. And, of course, as we've already had occasion to mention, supplement your vitamin C intake with a *zumo de naranja* (orange juice), freshly squeezed from a handful of the region's finest fruit.

Alcoholic Drinks

Wine Leaving Valencia on the A-7 towards Barcelona, you'll notice on your right a cluster of huge silos. In them is wine, cheap, red and of the kind you take to and leave at strangers' parties. Much is used for blending within Spain. A lot too makes its way to northern Europe, where it's also blended and sold as ordinary table wine, often under a major supermarket's brand name. Wine producing is big business in the Comunidad Valenciana – and by no means all the output merits such an anonymous end.

It was the Romans who introduced the vine to Valencian soil, where it readily took root. Soon, trade was reversed as shiploads of amphoras, filled with local wine, sailed for the capital of the Empire.

Within the Comunidad, over 100,000 hectares are given over to wine production. There are three recognised DOs (regions meriting a *denominación de origen*, roughly the equivalent of the French *appellation controlée*); Alicante, Valencia and Utiel-Requena.

Most Alicante wine comes from the basin of the Río Vinalopó while the Marina Alta area inland from Denia produces *mistela*, a sweet muscatel dessert wine. Like Alicante wines, those of Valencia are named after the province, not the capital city. The reds are mostly robust but undistinguished. Subtler are the dry whites of the upper Turia, the

.lto Turia. Utiel-Requena produces the Comunidad's finest red wines while Bodega Torre Oria produces a sparkling wine, traditionally fermented, that can hold its own with the more famous *cavas* of Catalunya.

Vino comes in white *(blanco)*, red *(tinto)* or rosé *(rosado)*. Prices vary considerably. In general, you get what you pay for and can pick up a really good tipple for under €4. If it's kick not quality you're after, a bottle of raw plonk need cost no more than €1.50. In restaurants, you can, if you wish, order the house wine *(vino de la casa)*, the cheapest option, which varies from very drinkable to one up on vinegar.

Cava is a sparkling wine produced by the *méthode champenoise*, where the wine continues to ferment in the bottle. The vast bulk of cava is produced in Catalunya – indeed it's popularly known as Catalan champagne, a phrase that tends to make many a Frenchman apoplectic. However one or two Valencian bodegas, especially in the Utiel-Requena wine-producing area, are now turning their hand to cava – and turning their bottles too, for every single one has to be turned several times during fermentation.

Beer The most common way to order a beer *(cerveza)* is to ask for a *caña*, which is a small draught beer *(cerveza de barril)*. The next size up, *un tubo* (literally 'tube', served in a tall, straight glass) is usually called a *doble* around the Valencia region. A

jarra holds roughly a pint. If you just ask for a cerveza you may get bottled beer, which is more expensive than draught. A *clara* is a shandy, a beer with lemonade.

Other Alcoholic Drinks *Agua de Valencia* (Valencia water) is a popular summer drink. For this belter of a Buck's Fizz, just add two glasses of orange juice to a bottle of cava (Catalan champagne) and spike it with a healthy slug of vodka. Sometimes other spirits such as vermouth or gin feature but their flavour tends to dominate the divine mix.

Sangría is a wine and fruit punch, usually laced with spirits. It's refreshing going down but can leave you with a sore head. *Tinto de verano* is a mix of wine and Casera, a brand of fizzy lemonade.

Coñac (Spanish brandy) is cheap and palatable. Many international brands such as Bacardi, Beefeater and Gordons are distilled in Spain and retail considerably cheaper than in countries with high liquor taxes. Most bars also stock the grape-based *aguardiente* (like schnapps or grappa) and a whole rack of other enticing *licores* (liqueurs).

ENTERTAINMENT
Simply sitting over a coffee or a glass of wine on a cafe terrace and watching life go by can be entertainment enough in itself. The innumerable fiestas (see the Fiestas special section) that spatter the local calendar provide heaps of colourful spectacle.

Local papers often carry entertainment listings. On the Costa Blanca, pick up the *Weekly Post* or *Costa Blanca News* (though both are very expat-oriented in their listings). In Valencia City, the weekly *Turia* is an excellent Spanish-language guide to what's on, while *24-7 Valencia* is a monthly freebie in English.

Bars, Pubs & Discos
Valencia and the coastal resorts have plenty to keep you busy. In July and August, you can rave nightly at coastal discos. During the rest of the year, bars normally open throughout the week while most discos crank up only at weekends; many coastal ones shut their doors until the next summer comes round.

Sangría – refreshing and certainly packing a punch

Mind Your Language!

The Spanish normally use the full word *discoteca*, not the abridged form *disco*. And since the word 'club' for many Spaniards is a synonym for brothel, banish it from your vocabulary or you could be in for an awkward misunderstanding!

Most locals don't head for bars until 10pm or later. As these start closing from 2am onwards, night owls drift on to clubs, active from about 3am until dawn. The big ones work out expensive and some won't let you in wearing jeans or trainers.

Inland, the tempo is very much slower, although you should be able to find the occasional bar open until about 2am.

Gay & Lesbian Venues

Valencia, Benidorm and Alicante all have an active gay scene. For sources of information, see the Gay & Lesbian Travellers section earlier in this chapter.

Music

Rock, Pop & Jazz The home-grown Spanish rock, pop and jazz scene is large and lively. Benicàssim's *Mulabe* is a feast of Latin American music and its Festival Internacional de Benicàssim (FIB) is one of Europe's top outdoor music fests. Valencia City (year round) and major coastal resorts (in summer) attract big names. Jazz also gets a decent run in the capital.

Classical Music, Dance & Theatre Valencia, followed at some distance by Alicante, are the main scenes for theatre, classical music, opera and so on. Plays are almost always in Spanish.

Cinemas

Cinemas abound. A visit costs around €4.50 unless you pick the cinema's weekly cheap day, or *día del espectador*, when it will cost about €3. Foreign films are usually dubbed into Spanish. Only in Valencia do you have a fair choice of films in their original language with Spanish subtitles; they tend to be art house genre. Look for the letters 'v.o.' *(versión original)* in listings.

SPECTATOR SPORTS
Football

Fútbol is as much a preoccupation in the Comunidad Valenciana as elsewhere in Spain. Interest has, if anything, been boosted by the performance of Valencia who, in both 2000 and 2001, were European Champions League finalists. Vila Real is the other club from the Comunidad to play in the first division. Elsewhere, Elche, Hercules (from Alicante) and Castellón have all had a brief spell in the top flight before sinking to the Segunda División.

Bullfighting

Call it sport, call it art, call it – as an increasing number of Spaniards do – barbarity, bullfighting remains a part of the national psyche. Valencia City has a splendid arena that attracts star matadors while even quite small places such as Bocairent and Utiel can boast a *plaza de toros*. Bullfights are only held on a few days in the year, often to coincide with a local festival.

Trinquet

For details of this very Valencian game, a cross between fives, squash and royal tennis, see the boxed text 'Pelota Valenciana' in the Valencia City & Around chapter.

SHOPPING

In Valencia City, you'll find everything from chic designer boutiques to stalls specialising in lace and buttons. Check the Shopping section in the Valencia City chapter. Elsewhere, every town of any consequence will have its weekly market, supplementing what the shops can offer.

Regional specialities to look for include ceramics (from Paterna and Manises), shoes (manufactured in and around Elche and the towns of the Vall de Vinalopó) and leather goods in general. An original souvenir is a pair of *alpargatas*, the traditional Valencia peasant footwear with a sole of woven fibre and tapes to tie, cross-garter. Artisans in

Elche produce intricate items, woven and shaped from palm fronds – everything from things for the mantelpiece to boughs used in Palm Sunday processions. OK, so it may be only one up on a straw donkey, but don't reject the idea of a fan, practical in the heat and, if you're prepared to spend a bit, stylish and hand painted; in Valencia and in Albaida, the craft still continues, despite killer competition from mass manufacturers.

Getting There & Away

As befits one of Europe's top holiday destinations, Valencia and the Costa Blanca are well linked to the rest of Spain and other European countries by air, rail and road. Even if your budget is tight, don't discount air travel. Travel from elsewhere in Europe on one of the cheap, 'no-frills' airlines or on an excursion ticket, normally valid for up to 28 days and requiring you to spend a Saturday night in Spain, will probably work out less expensive than an equivalent journey by car, bus or train. It will certainly save you a couple of days or more in travelling time.

Most visitors from North America, Australia or New Zealand take in the Comunidad Valenciana as part of a wider visit to Europe. If you're one of the minority of visitors from outside Europe whose main destination is the Comunidad, you'll probably find that it's less expensive to fly long haul to a major European hub such as London, Amsterdam, Milan or Frankfurt, then make the relatively short hop to Valencia or Alicante by scheduled airline or charter. Choosing Madrid and Barcelona brings you nearer but rarely works out to be cheaper.

Car and passenger ferries link the Balearic Islands of Ibiza, Mallorca and Menorca with Valencia City and also run between Ibiza and Denia. There are also frequent flights from both Valencia and Alicante to Ibiza and Mallorca.

See under Visas & Documents and Health in the Facts for the Visitor chapter for hints on travel insurance – something you should always consider.

AIR

If you're on a charter flight, it's essential to reconfirm your onward flight or return booking at least 72 hours before departure. Charter times and take-off slots are notoriously subject to change and if you don't reconfirm you risk missing your flight because it was rescheduled or you've been classified as a 'no-show'. For most scheduled European flights you no longer need to reconfirm your reservation but if it gives you peace of mind, go ahead and do it; no-one will criticise you for being overcautious.

Airports & Airlines

The Comunidad Valenciana has two international airports: Valencia's Aeropuerto de Manises and El Altet, which serves Alicante and the bulk of the Costa Blanca. The high season for flights to both destinations is July and August plus Easter and Christmas/New Year. Peak prices also operate on charter flights from the UK during school mid-term holidays.

Some Spanish and several European and international carriers compete with the country's largest national airline, Iberia.

Buying Tickets

Despite the Twin Towers horror, world aviation remains competitive. But you have to research your options to get the best deal. Increasingly, travellers are turning to the Web to hunt for flights and book tickets; most airlines and many travel agencies now operate interactive Web sites.

Full-time students and those aged under 26 have access to better deals than other travellers. You have to show a document proving your date of birth or a valid International Student Identity Card (ISIC) when buying your ticket and, sometimes, when checking in.

Generally, there is nothing to be gained by buying a ticket direct from the airline (this said, a commercial airline's Web site may offer deals that are well worth considering). Airlines release discounted tickets to selected travel agencies and specialist discount agencies, and these are usually the cheapest deals going.

One exception to this rule is the expanding number of no-frills carriers, which mostly only sell direct to travellers. Unlike the 'full-service' airlines, no-frills carriers often have one-way tickets at about half the return fare, meaning that it is easy to put together an open-jaw ticket when you fly to one place but leave from another.

The other exception is booking on the Internet. Many airlines, full service and no frills, offer some excellent fares to Web surfers. Lots of travel agencies also have Web sites, making the Internet a quick and easy way to compare prices. Increasingly there are more and more agencies who only operate online.

You may find the cheapest flights are advertised by obscure agencies. Most of these firms are honest and solvent, but there are some rogue fly-by-night outfits around. Paying by credit card generally offers you protection as most card issuers provide refunds if you can prove you didn't get what you paid for. You get similar protection by buying a ticket from a bonded agency, such as one covered by the Air Travel Organiser's Licence (ATOL; W www.atol.org.uk) scheme in the UK. Agencies who only accept cash should hand over the tickets straight away and not tell you to 'come back tomorrow'. If you have made a booking or paid your deposit and have the least grounds for suspicion, call the airline and confirm that the booking was indeed made.

If you're contemplating the possibility of changing your route or timing, think carefully before you buy a ticket which is not easily refunded or where a change incurs a heavy service charge.

Once you have your ticket, write its number down, together with the flight number and other details, and keep the information somewhere separate. If the ticket is lost or stolen, this will help you get a replacement.

Travellers with Special Needs

If airlines are warned early enough, they can often make special arrangements for travellers who require, for example, wheelchair assistance at airports or vegetarian meals on the flight. Children under two years travel for 10% of the standard fare (or free on some airlines) as long as they don't occupy a seat. They don't get a baggage allowance. 'Skycots', baby food and nappies should be provided by the airline if requested in advance. Children aged between two and 12 can usually occupy a seat for half to two-thirds of the full fare, and do get a baggage allowance.

Guide dogs for the blind usually have to travel in a specially pressurised baggage compartment with other animals. All guide dogs will be subject to the same quarantine procedures (which may include a period in isolation) as any other animal when entering or returning to countries currently free of rabies, such as Britain or Australia.

Travellers with a hearing impairment can ask for airport and in-flight announcements to be written down for them.

The disability-friendly Web site W www.everybody.co.uk has an airline directory that provides information on the facilities offered by various airlines.

Departure Tax

Airport taxes are factored into ticket prices, but a travel agency will generally quote fares without taxes factored in. These can range from €15 to as much as €65 depending on your destination. Travel agencies will normally tell you what taxes will be imposed as they quote the air fare. If not, ask; they could tip the balance in favour of

Air Travel Glossary

Alliances Many of the world's leading airlines are now intimately involved with each other, sharing everything from reservations systems and check-in to aircraft and frequent-flyer schemes. Opponents say that alliances restrict competition. Whatever the arguments, there is no doubt that big alliances are the way of the future.

Cancelling or Changing Tickets If you have to cancel or change a ticket, you need to contact the original travel agency who sold you the ticket. Airlines only issue refunds to the purchaser of a ticket – usually the travel agency who bought the ticket on your behalf. There are often heavy penalties involved; insurance can sometimes be taken out against these penalties.

Fares Airlines traditionally offer 1st class (coded F), business class (coded J) and economy class (coded Y) tickets. These days there are so many promotional and discounted fares available that few passengers pay full fare.

Lost Tickets If you lose your airline ticket, an airline will usually treat it like a travellers cheque and, after inquiries, issue you with another one. Legally, however, an airline is entitled to treat it like cash and if you lose it then it's gone forever. Take very good care of your tickets.

Open-Jaw Tickets These are return tickets where you fly out to one place but return from another. If available, this can save you backtracking to your arrival point.

Overbooking Since every flight has some passengers who fail to show up, airlines often book more passengers than they have seats. Usually excess passengers make up for the no-shows, but occasionally somebody gets 'bumped' onto the next available flight. Guess who it is most likely to be? The passengers who check in late. If you do get 'bumped', you are normally offered some form of compensation.

Reconfirmation Some airlines require you to reconfirm your flight at least 72 hours prior to departure. Check your travel documents to see if this is the case

Restrictions Discounted tickets often have various restrictions on them – such as needing to be paid for in advance and incurring a penalty to be altered or cancelled. Others are restrictions on the minimum and maximum period you must be away.

Ticketless Travel Airlines are gradually waking up to the realisation that paper tickets are unnecessary encumbrances. On simple one-way or return trips, reservations details can be held on computer and the passenger merely shows ID to claim their seat.

Transferred Tickets Airline tickets cannot be transferred from one person to another. Travellers sometimes try to sell the return half of their ticket, but officials can ask you to prove that you are the person named on the ticket. On an international flight, tickets are compared with passports.

---

an alternative route if price is your main consideration.

Other Parts of Spain

Flying within peninsular Spain is generally not economical unless you're really pushed for time. The exceptions are the Canary Islands, off the coast of North Africa, where a plane journey is effectively the only option, and the Balearic Islands, to the east of the Comunidad Valenciana, where flying from Valencia or Alicante rather than taking a boat can save a day in each direction.

Iberia (☎ 902 400500) and its small franchise subsidiaries Iberia Regional-Air Nostrum and Binter Mediterráneo (under threat and probably soon to be gobbled up) cover all destinations. For information on any of the three – maybe two – dial ☎ 902 400500. You receive about 25% off flights departing after 11pm (there are only a few of these). People under 22 or over 63 get 25% off return flights and another 20% off night flights. Iberia's Alicante town office (☎ 96 521 86 13) is at Calle Doctor Gadea 12. Its Valencia branch (☎ 96 352 85 52) is at Calle Paz 14.

A standard one-way fare between Madrid and Valencia or Alicante with the Iberia consortium costs €132. The equivalent return fare without restrictions is €265. A cheaper return option on this and all Iberia internal routes is their Estrella scheme. If you reserve your seat a minimum of 48 hours in advance and your stay doesn't exceed 14 days and includes a Saturday night, the return fair for Madrid–Alicante is €147.25 while Madrid–Valencia costs €143.30. Iberia also has three flights daily from both airports to the Balearic Island of Ibiza.

Competing with Iberia on some internal and international routes are Spanair (☎ 902 131415, W www.spanair.com) and Air Europa (☎ 902 401501, W www.aireuropa .com). Air Europa is the bigger of the two, with several direct daily flights from Valencia and Alicante to Madrid and Palma de Mallorca in the Balearic Islands, plus a host of mainland Spanish destinations, usually connecting in Madrid or Palma.

Single fares on Air Europa to Madrid–Valencia or Madrid–Alicante vary between €99 and €132 while a return flight costs from €100 right up to €260. A typical price is around €165. Fares from both Valencia and Alicante to Palma de Mallorca are similar in that there's a huge variation. A typical single fare costs about €125, while return fares range from €115 to €268 and average about €165.

The UK & Ireland

Discount air travel is big business in London. Advertisements for many travel agencies appear in the travel pages of the weekend broadsheet newspapers, in *Time Out*, the *Evening Standard* as well as the free magazine *TNT*.

For students or travellers under 26 years, the popular UK-based STA Travel (☎ 020-7361 6161 Europe line, W www.statravel .co.uk) has an office at 86 Old Brompton Rd, London SW7 3LQ, as well as branches across the country. STA sells tickets to all travellers but caters particularly for young people and students.

Other recommended travel agencies for all age groups include:

Flight Centre (☎ 020-8543 9070, W www .flightcentre.com) 34 The Broadway, London SW19 1PS
Flightbookers (☎ 020-7757 2000, W www .ebookers.com) 177–178 Tottenham Court Rd, London W1P 0LX
Quest Travel (☎ 020-8547 3123, W www .questtravel.com) 10 Richmond Rd, Kingston-upon-Thames, Surrey KT2 5HL
Spanish Travel Services (STS; ☎ 020-7387 5337) 138 Eversholt St, London NW1 1BL
Trailfinders (☎ 020-7937 1234 Europe line, W www.trailfinders.co.uk) 194–196 Kensington High St, London W8 7RG

All of these agencies deal in scheduled British Airways and Iberia flights to Valencia and Alicante. In addition, Flightbookers sells seats on the charter airlines Air 2000 and Monarch.

Most British travel agencies are registered with ABTA (Association of British Travel Agents) and all agencies that sell flights in the UK must hold an Air Travel Organiser's Licence (ATOL). If you have paid for your flight with an ABTA-registered or ATOL agency who then goes bust, the Civil Aviation Authority will guarantee a refund or an alternative under the ATOL scheme. Unregistered travel agencies are riskier but sometimes a little cheaper.

The two flagship airlines linking the UK and Spain are British Airways (BA; ☎ 0845 773 3377, W www.british-airways.com), 156 Regent St, London W1R 5TA, and Spain's Iberia (☎ 0845 601 2854, W www.iberia .com), Venture House, 27–29 Glasshouse St, London W1R 6JU. Iberia has one daily flight between Valencia and London (Heathrow) and one daily flight from Alicante into London (Heathrow) and another to London

(Gatwick). BA's daily flights to Valencia and Alicante leave from London (Gatwick).

For contact details for Iberia airlines within Spain, see Other Parts of Spain earlier in this section. Typical prices from London to both Alicante and Valencia at the time of writing were £140 for a single fare and £220 for return. A few seats on each flight during the low season retail for around £120.

Of the two airlines, BA is more likely to have special deals. British Airways flights to the Comunidad Valenciana are run by its affiliate, GB Airways. Within Spain, call ☎ 902 111333 for reservations, ☎ 96 152 40 26 for the Valencia airport office and ☎ 96 691 94 72 for the Alicante equivalent. Typical excursion fares to and from both destinations vary between £110 and £170 return, are valid for up to a month and encompass a Saturday night. For a few seats on a low-season flight, the price can drop to as low as £95 return, a rate that is competitive with anything that a charter company might offer.

Of the budget airlines Go (W www.go-fly .com) flies from London (Stansted) to Alicante. Reserve via the Web for a £10 discount, or ring ☎ 0870 607 6543 (☎ 901 333500 within Spain). Return fares swing between £80 and £280, averaging £120 to £130. Both Britannia and Monarch Airlines run charter flights between Alicante and several UK destinations. Monarch (☎ 0870 040 50 40 in the UK, ☎ 96 691 94 47 in Alicante, W www.fly-crown.com) also operates scheduled daily flights to/from London (Luton) and to/from Manchester (four weekly).

Valencia itself is one of the few significant cities in Western Europe that's still not served by a no-frills carrier. If your budget is tight, you can take advantage of a cheap flight into Alicante and continue your journey to Valencia by bus, train or hire car. If you're planning to visit Valencia City and/or the northern part of the Comunidad, an alternative is to do the same via Barcelona, which is served by Go and also easyJet (☎ 0870 600 0000, W www .easyjet.com) from London (Luton). Easy-Jet's number within Spain is ☎ 902 299992.

Charter flights operate from Ireland to Alicante in summer only. For a scheduled flight to either Valencia or Alicante, the most convenient option is to make a connection in London, Barcelona or Madrid.

Mainland Europe

You can often find fares that will beat overland alternatives in regards to cost.

Belgium Whether SN Brussels Airlines, the successor to the bankrupt national carrier Sabena, will establish flights to Valencia remains to be seen. The low-cost airline Virgin Express (☎ 02 752 05 05, W www .virgin-express.com) has its European hub in Brussels. Up to seven flights a day connect Brussels with Bar-celona and Madrid, from where land communications to the Comunidad Valenciana are excellent. One-way fares range from about €95 to €130.

Travel agencies worth consulting include:

Air Stop (☎ 070 233 188, W www.airstop.be) 28 rue Fossé-aux-Loups, 1000 Brussels
Nouvelles Frontières (☎ 02 547 44 44, W www .nouvelles-frontieres.be) 2 blvd Maurice Lemmonier, 1000 Brussels. This French chain also has branches in Anvers, Bruges, Liège and Gand.

France Air France (☎ 0820 820 820 in France, ☎ 901 112266 in Spain) and Iberia each have two flights a day between Paris and Valencia.

The student travel agency OTU Voyages (☎ 01 40 29 12 22, W www.otu.fr) has a central Paris office at 39 av Georges-Bernanos and branches around the country. STA Travel's Paris agency is Voyages Wasteels (☎ 08 03 88 70 04, W www.wasteels.fr) at 11 rue Dupuytren. Nouvelles Frontières (☎ 01 45 68 70 00, W www.nouvelles-frontieres.fr) has its main Paris branch at 87 blvd de Grenelle as well as others around the country.

Germany At the time of writing, Lufthansa (☎ 01803 803 803 in Germany, ☎ 902 220101 in Spain) had dropped both of its direct flights between Frankfurt and Valencia and travellers needed to change flights or mode of transport in Barcelona or Madrid.

In Berlin you could try STA Travel (☎ 030-311 09 50, W www.statravel.de), Goethestrasse 73. They also have offices in

Frankfurt-am-Main, including one at Bockenheimer Landstrasse 133 (☎ 069-70 30 35), and in 16 other cities across the country.

Italy Alitalia (☎ 8488 65642 in Italy, ☎ 902 100323 in Spain) flies twice daily between Milan and Valencia.

Just about the best place to look for cheap fares is Centro Turistico Studentesco (CTS), which has branches countrywide. In Rome it is at Corso Vittorio Emanuele II 297 (☎ 06 687 26 72). It has three offices in Milan, including one office (☎ 02 58 47 51) at via San Antonio 2, just south of the cathedral.

Netherlands At the time of writing, KLM-Royal Dutch Airlines had suspended its direct flights to Valencia. Plenty of charters run into Alicante from Amsterdam.

The student travel agency MyTravel Reiswinkel (☎ 020-692 7788, **W** www.my travel.nl – Dutch only), Linnaeusstraat 28, offers reliable and reasonably low fares. Compare their prices with what's on offer in the discount flight centres along Rokin before deciding. MyTravel has branches throughout the city. Another budget place worth sounding out is Holland International (☎ 070-307 6307), which has offices in most cities.

Portugal Portugalia (☎ 21 842 55 59 in Lisbon, ☎ 902 100145 in Spain) flies Sunday to Friday between Lisbon and Valencia for around €254 return.

In Lisbon, Tagus (☎ 311 30 37) is worth a visit. It has a branch at Rua Camilo Castelo Branco 20 and other offices all over the city.

Switzerland Crossair (☎ 0848 85 20 00 in Switzerland, ☎ 901 116712 in Spain, **W** www.crossair.com), an affiliate of the late Swissair, has a daily flight from Valencia to both Zurich and Basel.

SSR (☎ 022-818 02 02, **W** www.ssr.ch) specialises in student, youth and budget fares. It has a branch at 8 rue de la Rive, Geneva, and others throughout the country. Nouvelles Frontières (☎ 022-906 80 80), 10 rue Chante Poulet, also in Geneva, is another good source of budget fares.

The USA

There are no scheduled flights from the USA to Valencia. Several airlines fly to Madrid and Barcelona, from where you can travel on by plane, train or bus. If you're contemplating the onward flight option, you can often save money by flying into another European hub and making the short-haul flight to Valencia City or Alicante from there. Prices are fickle and the best options vary. At the time of writing the cheapest option was to take a transatlantic Alitalia flight to Milan then backtrack westwards on one of the airline's two daily flights between Milan and Valencia.

Standard fares can be expensive. Discount and rock-bottom options from the USA include charter flights and stand-by. Discount travel agencies in the USA are known as consolidators (although you won't see a sign on the door saying 'Consolidator'). San Francisco is the ticket consolidator capital of America, although some good deals can be found in Los Angeles, New York and other big cities. Consolidators can be found through the *Yellow Pages* or the major daily newspapers. The *New York Times*, the *Los Angeles Times*, the *Chicago Tribune* and the *San Francisco Examiner* all produce weekly travel sections carrying a number of travel agency ads. Ticket Planet is a leading ticket consolidator in the USA. Visit its Web site at **W** www.ticketplanet.com.

Council Travel, America's largest student travel organisation, has around 60 offices in the USA. Its head office (☎ 800 226 8624) is at 205 E 42 St, New York, NY 10017. Call it to find out the office nearest you or visit its Web site at **W** www.counciltravel .org. STA Travel (☎ 800 777 0112) has offices in most major cities. Call the freephone 800 number for office locations or visit its Web site at **W** www.statravel.com.

For flights to Madrid or Barcelona, the best-value low-season (November to December) fares from the east coast (New York) hover around US$575 return. From Los Angeles you pay around US$200 more. In the high season (June to August) you are looking at around US$950 and US$1300 respectively. Plenty of flights leave from other cities, usually connecting through New York. Fares from Chicago, for example, are comparable to those from Los Angeles.

Single stand-by fares, allowing you to travel on a regular, scheduled flight, are often sold at 60% of the normal one-way price. Whole Earth Travel (☎ 212-864 2000, ☎ 800 326 2009 freephone), 325 W 38th St, Suite 1509, New York, NY 10025, is a specialist. One-way flights from the USA to Europe cost from US$550 (east coast) to US$900 (west coast), plus taxes. In Europe it operates offices in Prague, Madrid and Rotterdam. Destiny Travel, based in LA, also supplies stand-by fares (☎ 800 397 1098).

If you can't find a good deal, consider a cheap transatlantic hop to London and stalk the discount flight centres there.

Canada

As is the case with the US, there are no direct flights from Canada to the Comunidad Valenciana. Again, your options are to fly into Madrid or Barcelona and continue by land or internal flight from a major European hub such as London, Frankfurt or Milan and pick up a connection to Valencia.

Canadian discount air ticket sellers are also known as consolidators. Their air fares tend to be about 10% higher than those sold in the USA. Scan the travel agency ads in the *Globe & Mail*, *Toronto Star* and *Vancouver Sun*.

Travel CUTS (☎ 800 667 2887, W www .travelcuts.com), known as Voyages Campus in Quebec, is Canada's national student travel agency. It has offices in all major cities, including Toronto (☎ 416-977 0441), 74 Gerrard St E, and Montreal (☎ 514-398 0647), Université McGill, 3480 rue McTavish.

Australia

There are no direct flights from Australia to Spain, let alone Valencia. You will have to fly to another European city via Asia or the US and change flights (and possibly sairlines). A low season return fare with KLM via Kuala Lumpur and Amsterdam will set you back around A$2306; Alitalia charges A$2400 for a flight via Mumbai and Rome.

Two well known agents for cheap fares are STA Travel and Flight Centre. STA Travel (☎ 1300 360 960 Australiawide, W www .statravel.com.au) has its main office at 224 Faraday St, Carlton, Vic 3053. It maintains offices in all major cities and on many university campuses. Visit its Web site for the location of your nearest branch. Flight Centre (☎ 133 133 Australiawide, W www.flight centre.com.au) has a central office at 82 Elizabeth St, Sydney, NSW 2000 and dozens of others throughout Australia.

On the other hand, you may have to search no further than your local travel agency to find heavily discounted fares. Or take a look at the Saturday editions of the Melbourne *Age* and the *Sydney Morning Herald*. Both carry many advertisements offering cheap fares to Europe.

New Zealand

As with Australia, STA Travel and Flight Centre are popular agencies. Flight Centre (☎ 09-309 6171) has a large central office in Auckland at National Bank Towers (corner Queen & Darby Sts) and many branches throughout the country. STA Travel (☎ 09-309 0458, W www.statravel.co.nz) has an office at 182 Queen Street, Auckland plus other offices in Auckland as well as in Hamilton, Palmerston North, Wellington, Christchurch and Dunedin. A round-the-world ticket can be good value from New Zealand as it may well prove cheaper than a return, especially in the high season. The *New Zealand Herald* has a travel section in which travel agencies advertise fares.

Sample fares include Lufthansa via Los Angeles and Frankfurt for NZ$2499, and Alitalia via Bangkok and Rome for NZ$2790.

LAND

There are plenty of options for reaching the Comunidad Valenciana by train, bus or private vehicle. Bus is generally the cheapest option but over long distances services can be less frequent and considerably less comfortable than the train.

Bus

Other Parts of Spain You can take a bus to most large Spanish cities from Valencia, Alicante and – especially during the summer

– major coastal resorts (see the boxed text below for details).

For long-distance destinations such as Madrid and Barcelona, if you simply want to travel between two points as quickly as possible, be sure to catch a bus that may be described variously as *directo, por autopista* (motorway) or *exprés*. On the other hand, if you want to see a bit more of Spain – and stopping services, if cash counts, are often a little cheaper – take the less direct option.

The major long-distance company, in Valencia as well as throughout Spain, is Alsa, which continues to gobble up smaller companies. You may find some routes described as still being operated by Enatcar or, even further into the past, Ubesa. To check Alsa/Enatcar schedules, call ☎ 902 422242 or visit W www.alsa.es. For more bus operators, check the destination table in the Getting Around chapter.

Europe If you're planning to travel around Spain or, more widely, Western Europe, you might want to consider Busabout (☎ 020-7950 1661, W www.busabout.com), a UK-based hop-on, hop-off bus service aimed at younger travellers and based in London at 258 Vauxhall Bridge Rd. One option is their 'consecutive' pass, allowing unlimited travel within a specified period. Typical prices are £170 for two weeks and £310 for a month. Perhaps more useful is their 'flexipass', allowing you a number of travelling

days within the period you opt for. So, for example, 10 days of travel within two months costs £260 and there's a discount if you have an international student card. Bear in mind that, beyond the Busabout network, you'll have to use local alternatives (which is no great trauma). You can buy passes direct from the company, online or from suppliers such as STA Travel.

All standard international routes passing through the Comunidad Valenciana originate and terminate in Murcia, capital city of the region to its south. Both Eurolines and, within the Comunidad, the Spanish company, Linebus, sell tickets at identical prices for the routes described (we use the name Eurolines here as it is the one that is internationally recognised).

The UK The company Eurolines (☎ 0870 514 3219, W www.gobycoach.com in the UK, ☎ 96 349 68 55 within Spain, W www .eurolines.es – Spanish only) runs two buses a week from London, calling in at Castellón and Valencia (£63), and Benidorm and Alicante (£67). Buses depart from Alicante every Monday and Saturday at 7.30am and pull into London's Victoria coach station at 4.30pm the next day. In July and August there's a third run from Alicante departing Wednesday.

France Eurolines also has offices in several French cities, including the Paris bus station

Bussing Around Spain

Destinations elsewhere in Spain served from Valencia bus station include:

destination	fare (€)	hours	daily frequency	bus company
Barcelona (direct)	23.55	4¼	10	Alsa/Enatcar
Barcelona (stopping)	21.07	5	9	Alsa/Enatcar
Bilbao	22.75	9	2-4	Bilman Bus
Córdoba	32.50	8¾	4	Alsa/Enatcar
Madrid	20.90	4	13	Auto Res
Seville	40.50	10¾	4	Alsa/Enatcar
Teruel	7.30	2	5	Autocares Samar
Zaragoza	13	2¾	4	Autobuses Jiménez

(☎ 01 49 72 51 51, W www.eurolines.com), 28 av Général de Gaulle. It has another more central office (☎ 01 43 54 11 99) at rue St Jacques 55, off blvd St Michel. UK passengers may have to change buses in Paris.

A Eurolines bus runs three times a week (four in high summer), linking Alicante and intermediate stops in the Comunidad to Toulouse (€70.10) and continuing to Bordeaux (€83.25). There's also a service to and from Paris (€115.85) via Lyons (€91.65) that operates Monday to Saturday.

Germany For German destinations, Eurolines runs four times a week between Alicante and Frankfurt (€100), three times weekly to and from Dortmund (€125) via Cologne and Düsseldorf (both €114) and twice to and from Munich (€114) and Hamburg (€125).

Train

The *Thomas Cook European Timetable* is the trainophile's bible, giving a complete listing of train schedules, supplements and reservations information. Updated monthly, it's available from Thomas Cook offices and agencies worldwide. In the USA, call ☎ 800 367 7984.

Two main train lines serve the Comunidad Valenciana. One line runs north-south to/from France and Catalunya, keeping more or less parallel to the coast and at times affording spectacular views. From Valencia, it snakes inland to Xàtiva then curls around through Villena and Elda to Alicante. From Alicante, trains run southwards to Murcia and, ultimately, Granada. The other line branches westwards beyond Xàtiva and heads for Madrid, via Albacete.

Information It is always advisable, and sometimes compulsory, to reserve in advance on most domestic or international long-distance trains. On overnight hauls you can book a *cama turista* (bunk). The price depends upon how many kilometres you're travelling, rather than being a standard supplement. As an indication, a journey between Valencia and Malaga on the Costa del Sol will set you back €60 with a bunk and €43 without.

For information on all national Red Nacional de los Ferrocarriles Españoles (Renfe) train services call ☎ 902 240202. You can also make reservations via this number – and avoid long booking office queues at peak periods – by quoting your credit card details. Renfe will send the tickets to any address within Spain or you can pick them up from your departure station. Alternatively, visit the Web site at W www.renfe.es. It will give you prices and timetables and you can also book long-distance tickets online.

Train timetables are posted at the main stations. Impending arrivals *(llegadas)* and departures *(salidas)* appear on big electronic boards and TV screens. Timetables for specific lines are generally available free.

Eurail, Inter-Rail, Europass and Flexipass tickets are valid on the Renfe network throughout Spain.

Types of Train in Spain Spain has a bewildering variety of different kinds of train. In general the main principle to remember is that the faster the train goes, the more you'll be paying. If time isn't too important, you can make a significant savings coup by taking a slower option.

No train in and out of the Comunidad Valenciana is all that swift compared with norms elsewhere in Europe. Journeys are comfortable, relaxed and agreeable but the overall speed won't set the adrenaline flowing. It will remain so until the high-speed track, approved and under construction, is laid from Valencia and Alicante to both Madrid and Barcelona.

Most long-distance *(largo recorrido)* trains have 1st and 2nd classes. Sleek *Euromed* trains glide between Barcelona, Valencia and Alicante. The equivalent on the Madrid–Valencia line is called the *Alarís*. A less-expensive option on the former route is the *Arco* or *Talgo*, which takes only 30 minutes more on the Barcelona–Valencia stretch and has an almost comparable level of comfort.

Cheapest and by far the slowest of the intercity alternatives are the *regionales*, which generally stop at all stations within one region (although a few travel between regions). If your train is a *regional exprés* it will make fewer stops but it will still be fairly lumbering.

Train Passes It's not worth investing in a Eurail or Inter-Rail pass if you're travelling just within the Comunidad Valenciana, or even if you only intend to go further afield within Spain, since train fares are reasonably cheap. On the other hand, several national passes are available from Renfe in Spain.

An ExploreRail card offers you unlimited travel on 2nd-class trains anywhere in Spain. The only exceptions are the *AVE* (the high-speed train that bullets between Madrid and Seville) and the *Euromed* (the swankiest, but by no means only, option between Barcelona, Valencia and Alicante). Valid for seven, 15 or 30 days, an ExploreRail card costs €115/139/ 180 respectively – a real bargain for anyone contemplating serious train travel in Spain. You can graft on *rodalías/cercanías* trains (local networks around main cities) by paying €132.50/169/223 respectively.

The Tarjeta Dorada is a senior citizens' pass issued by Renfe. To qualify, you must be over 60 and a resident in Spain. The card entitles you to 25% off train fares from Friday to Sunday and up to 40% off during the week.

Renfe also issues a Tarjeta Turística (Spain Flexipass). Strictly for non-European residents, it's valid for three to 10 days' travel in a two-month period on all Spanish trains. A 2nd-class three/10-day pass costs US$155/ 365. The Flexipass is sold by travel agencies outside of Europe and at a few main stations as well as Renfe offices in Spain.

Railing Around Spain

The variety of possible fares is truly bewildering. The ones we quote below are for a one-way journey from Valencia:

to	one way (€)	duration (hours)	daily frequency
Alicante	20.50	1½ to 2	7
Barcelona	28.25 to 31.25	3 to 3½	10+
Granada	31.25 to 38.50	6¾ to 8¾	2
Madrid	35	3½	10
Seville	33.75	8½	1

Destinations within the Comunidad Valenciana linked to Valencia City include:

to	one way (€)	duration (hours)	daily frequency
Alcoy	5.80	1¾	2
Benicarló/Peñíscola	6.90	1½	8
Benicàssim	4.10	1	7
Buñol	2.05	1	hourly
Castellón	3.16	1	every 30 mins
Cullera	2.10	30 mins	every 30 mins
Gandía	3.16	55 mins	every 30 mins
Moixent	3.16	1¼	9
Requena	3.16	1¼	7
Segorbe	3.16	1¼ (change in Sagunto)	3
Sagunto	2.05	30 mins	every 30 mins
Utiel	3.16	1½	7
Vinaròs	6.90	1¾	8
Xàtiva	2.43	45 mins	20+

If you buy a return ticket you can get a 20% discount (25% if the return is on the same day). Children aged under four travel free (those aged four to 11 get 40% off). If you flash your Euro<26 pass (called a Carnet Jove in the Comunidad Valenciana), a GO25 or ISIC student card, you can get a discount of around 20% on most train tickets.

Car & Motorcycle

From the UK and with your foot flat on the floor through France, you may save a little time travelling by vehicle over a ferry to Spain (see below). Whether or not it is cheaper depends on how long you spend on French toll roads, how thirsty your vehicle is and how many overnight stops you fit in.

For information on car ferries from the UK, see under Sea later in this chapter.

Spain has invested massively in highways over the last two decades and roads are generally very good, if sometimes overcrowded. The main motorway link to the Comunidad Valenciana from the north is the A-7 *autopista* (toll road), which crosses the Pyrenees from France south of Perpignan, trails through Catalunya, bypassing Barcelona and Tarragona and enters the Valencia region just north of Vinaròs. From Valencia it continues down to Alicante, then onto Murcia. Your alternative is the parallel, heavily used and more dangerous N-340.

Coming from the ports of Bilbao or Santander, you'll arrive inland, passing by Zaragoza and taking the N-330 and N-234 to enter the Comunidad via Teruel, or the N-232 via Alcañiz, hitting the coast and joining the A-7 motorway near Vinaròs.

Westwards, the A-3/N-III links Madrid and Valencia. The N-330 and N-301, much of the route motorway (superhighway) standard, runs between Madrid and Alicante. Both these latter routes, and the A-7, too, give access to the Costa Blanca.

If heading for Andalucía, the A-7 to Murcia then the A-92 onto Granada will guarantee motorway driving for the whole journey. A more interesting, lightly trafficked alternative from Valencia City is to take the four-lane N-430, then fork onto the N-344 and cut southwest via Yecla, Caravaca and Baza.

A Web site loaded with advice for people planning to drive in Europe is W www .ideamerge.com/motoeuropa. If you would like some help with route planning, try out W www.euroshell.com.

For information on Spanish road rules, see the Getting Around chapter.

Paperwork & Preparations When driving in the Comunidad Valenciana, always carry proof that the vehicle is yours. This means, the Vehicle Registration Document for UK-registered cars or the car-hire document, if you're renting.

Third-party motor insurance is a minimum requirement. If your vehicle is registered outside of Spain, you also need a Green Card, which is an internationally recognised proof of insurance that your insurer should supply at no extra cost. Ask your insurer for a European accident statement form, which can simplify matters if you should have an accident. Never sign statements you can't read or understand: insist on a translation and only sign it if it's acceptable.

A European breakdown assistance policy, such as the AA Five Star Service or RAC Eurocover Motoring Assistance, is a good investment.

Every vehicle travelling across an international border should in theory display a nationality plate of its country of registration. Two warning triangles (to be used in the event of a breakdown) are compulsory in Spain. Other recommended accessories are a first-aid kit, a spare bulb kit and a fire extinguisher. In the UK, useful sources of information are the RAC (☎ 0870 572 2722) and the AA (☎ 0870 600 0371).

SEA

Regular ferries run between Valencia and Denia and the Balearic Islands. The number of sailings varies according to season.

From Valencia, Trasmediterranea (☎ 902 454645, W www.trasmediterranea.com) runs a daily fast car and passenger ferry to Ibiza (3¼ hours) and onto Palma de Mallorca (6¼ hours) in July and August. Another ferry leaves for Palma (7¼ hours) and continues to Mahón (Menorca; 13¾ hours), Monday to

Saturday. During the rest of the year, there's normally at least one sailing daily for Palma, but few ferries put in at Ibiza and Mahón receives as little as one ferry a week. The fare is standard, whatever your destination: from €24.25 for a *butaca* (an airline-type seat) and from €39.50 for a cabin berth.

From Denia, ferries run to Palma de Mallorca, Ibiza City and San Antonio, Ibiza island. For details, see Getting Around under Denia in the Costa Blanca chapter.

From Alicante, there's a twice-weekly ferry connection (☎ 96 514 15 09) to Oran (Algeria), but until things calm down over the water, you'd be mad to get aboard.

If travelling by vehicle from the UK, you can opt for P&O European Ferries (☎ 0870 242 4999, ⓦ www.poferries.com) from Portsmouth to Bilbao, or a Brittany Ferries (☎ 0870 536 0360, ⓦ www.brittanyferries .co.uk) vessel from Plymouth to Santander. Sailings are generally a couple of times a week and take 24 to 30 hours. From your port of arrival in Spain, you'll reach the Comunidad Valenciana in seven to nine hours of driving on good roads.

ORGANISED TOURS
The UK
You don't need our help to sign on with one of the multitude of package tour companies that offer vacations on the Costa Blanca and Costa del Azahar. Just step into any travel agency and pick up a pile of brochures.

Walking Holidays Destinations can change as regularly as the seasons. At the time of writing, Alternative Travel Group (ATG; ☎ 01865-315 678, fax 315 678, ⓦ www .atg-oxford.co.uk), 69–71 Banbury Rd, Oxford OX2 6PE, offered a one-week walking tour in the Maestrazgo – wild, walking country inland in Castellón province. Exodus (☎ 020-8675 5550, fax 8673 0779, ⓦ www .exodustravels.co.uk), 9 Weir Rd, London SW12 0LT, does a five-day walking holiday in the Sierra de Aetana, inland from the Costa Blanca. Both Waymark Holidays (☎ 01753-516 477, ☎ 691 404 brochures, ⓦ www .waymarkholidays.co.uk), 44 Windsor Rd, Slough SL1 2EJ, and Headwater (☎ 01606-

813 333, fax 813 334), Freepost, Northwich, Cheshire CW9 5BR, offer one-week walking tours based upon the tiny village of Quatretondeta, near Alcoy in Alicante province.

You might also like to check out other UK walking tour operators such as Explore Worldwide (☎ 01252-760 000, fax 760 001, ⓦ www.exploreworldwide.com), 1 Frederick St, Aldershot, Hants GU11 1LQ, and the daddy of them all, Ramblers Holidays (☎ 01707-331 133, fax 333 276, ⓦ www. ramblersholidays.co.uk). Neither organisation, though active elsewhere in Spain, offered the Comunidad Valenciana as a destination at the time of writing but both are continually adding venues to their repertoire.

For information on walking tour operators within the Comunidad Valenciana, see Organised Tours in the Getting Around chapter.

The USA
Plenty of operators run tours from the USA. Spanish Heritage Tours (☎ 800 456 5050), 116–47 Queens Blvd, Forest Hills, NY 11375, is a reputable mainstream operator that can organise a broad array of tour options.

Escapade Vacations (☎ 800 223 7460), 630 Third Avenue, New York, NY 10017, offers a range of tours, from coach trips staying in *paradores* (state-owned hotels; see Accommodation in the Facts for the Visitor chapter), to more flexible 'plan-it-yourself' packages.

Alta Tours (☎ 800 338 4191, ⓦ www.alta tours.com), 870 Market St, Suite 784, San Francisco, CA 94102, specialises in customised itineraries for individuals and groups. Saranjan Tours (☎ 800 858 9594), PO Box 292, Kirkland, WA 98033, does everything from city breaks to walking trips in the Pyrenees.

Australia
You can organise tours of Spain through Victoria-based Ibertours Travel (☎ 03-9670 8388, ⓦ www.ibertours.com.au), 1st floor, 84 William St, Melbourne, Vic 3000, and Spanish Tourism (☎ 03-9670 7755, ⓔ sales@ spanishtourism.com.au), Level 2, 221 Queen St, Melbourne, Vic 3000.

FIESTAS

Fire and gunpowder, flames and explosions, usually supplemented by a few running bulls – these are the essential ingredients of an authentic Valencian fiesta. Nearly every single celebration has a religious origin, often honouring a pueblo's patron saint, even if the spiritual element is not always very evident these days.

Las Fallas

Las Fallas de San José – an exuberant, anarchic swirl of fireworks, music, explosions, festive bonfires, eating paella in the street and far too much drinking – is a time for all-night partying. If you're anywhere in Spain between 15 and 19 March, just let your eyes and ears direct you towards Valencia City and the flickering explosions on the horizon.

This wild fiesta honours San José (St Joseph), father of Jesus and in his time, as we know, a carpenter by trade. Tradition has it that the origins of the festival go back to the time when carpenters' apprentices, once Spring was in the air, gathered up Winter's cut-offs, end bits and shavings, piled them up high and burnt them in the street to honour their patron, the Greatest Carpenter of All.

The *fallas* themselves are huge sculptures of papier-mâché stuck onto wooden laths, increasingly with environmentally damaging polystyrene. Each *falla* is built by a team of local artists and artisans, of whom the most famous command respect and a very fat fee indeed.

Each neighbourhood sponsors its own falla. When the town wakes to the *plantà* (overnight construction of the fallas) on the morning of the 16 March, over 350 have popped up overnight on just about every street corner. Reaching up to 15m in height, the most expensive costs over €120,000 (oh yes, we've got those eurozeros right!). These grotesque, colourful, kitsch, quite tasteless and quite wonderful effigies satirise celebrities, current affairs and local customs. So, for example, popular themes at the moment are the euro, street delinquency, how

Title page: Solemnity reigns at the Fiesta de Moros y Cristianos. (photograph: Hannah Levy)

Left: Traditionally dressed women await the start of Las Fallas.

HANNAH LEVY

Madrid and Spain's centre screw the brave Comunidad Valenciana and – as ever and every year – the fortunes and misfortunes of Valencia Club de Fútbol.

Round-the-clock festivities include street parties, paella-cooking competitions, parades, open-air concerts, bullfights and nightly free firework displays.

Justifiably, Valencia considers itself to be the pyrotechnic capital of the world. Each day from 1 to 19 March starting at 2pm on the dot, a *mascletà*, over five minutes of deafening thumps and explosions, shakes the window panes of the Plaza del Ayuntamiento. Presiding from the town hall balcony and surrounded by her court of honour is the Fallera Mayor, the 'queen' of that year's Fallas. In fact, queen of queens, chosen by that year's organising committee from over 350 rivals, each one representing her falla. After 19 days of bombardment, it's a wonder that she and her retinue aren't stone deaf by the end of the last and loudest one.

Just after midnight on 19 March, every single falla goes up in flames, except, that is, for one small *ninot* (figurine) elected by popular vote, which is saved for display in the city's Museo Fallero.

Fallas, behind all the fun and razamatazz, also performs an important social function, breaking down a city of over ¾ million souls into smaller, human-scale communities. The focal point of each falla is its *casa fallera*, the 'falla house', a social centre in the town where the folk of the neighbourhood (or at least those who've coughed up their dues!) meet and relate to each other. And, once all the fire and fun are over and when the embers of the neighbourhood falla are scarcely cool, in every one of Valencia's *casas falleras* the annual cycle begins again...

Moros y Cristianos

Top: A ninot dominates Plaza del Ayuntamiento during Las Fallas.

More than 80 towns and villages in the south of the Comunidad Valenciana hold their own Fiesta de Moros y Cristianos (Moors and Christians festival) to celebrate the Reconquista, the region's liberation from Arab

HANNAH LEVY

rule. Each one features a colourful parade and probably a mock battle between cross and crescent, Muslim and Christian forces. Backstage, there's usually more competition to be an Arab soldier or damsel than a Christian one as the Moors' costumes are always more spectacular and exotic, This festival takes place despite the fact that the forces of Islam always finish up with a no-hard-feelings, good-natured drubbing, a stylised re-enactment whose political correctness no-one would dream of questioning even in these sensitive times.

The biggest and best-known Moros y Cristianos festival is that of **Alcoy**, which hosts the Comunidad's most colourful event after Valencia City's Fallas. Between 22 and 24 April, bracketing the Día de San Jorge (St George's day), hundreds of locals dress up in elaborate costumes representing different 'factions' – Muslim and Christian soldiers, slaves, guild groups, town criers, heralds and bands among them – and march through the streets in spectacular and colourful processions engaging in mock battles.

A wooden fortress is erected in the main plaza, on which the various processions converge from different directions. Tradition dictates who goes where and when, but, as you stand in the crowd it feels as though processions are coming at you from every direction.

It's an exhilarating spectacle of sights and sounds: soldiers in shining armour, white-cloaked Muslim warriors carrying scimitars and shields, turban-topped Arabs, scantily clad wenches, brass bands, exploding blunderbusses, fireworks displays and confetti showering down on the crowds from above.

Most other Moros y Cristianos fiestas and parades are based upon this same theme, steeped in traditions that allude to the events of the Reconquista, often enriched by local, sometimes fanciful, variants. In the fiestas of **Bocairent**, for example, held from 1 to 5 February, poor old prophet Mohammed finishes up, like Britain's Guy Fawkes, atop a bonfire. At those of **Ontinyent** (held at the end August), the fez is the headware of choice as the town commemorates the battle of Lepanto (1571) when the Turks were sent packing. On the Costa Blanca, **La Vila Joiosa** holds a week-long fiesta at the end of July, recalling the distant 16th-century invasion and repulsion of Barbary and Turkish pirates. Other major Moros y Cristianos fiestas include those of **Biar** (10 to 13 May), **Villena** (5 to 9 September) and **Guardamar** (late July).

San Antonio

San Antonio Abad, also known as Sant Antoni del Porquet (San Antonio of the Piglet), was an obscure 3rd-century anchorite who saw out his life in the deserts of Egypt where he reputedly lived to be 105

Top: Exquisite traditional finery is a common sight at Valencia's festivals.

years old. In mid-January, many villages of the interior celebrate the special day of this patron saint of shepherds, cowherds and farmers with – need we say it – fire.

In the village of **Canals**, near Xàtiva, the tallest pine in the neighbourhood is felled and its trunk re-erected before the parish church to form the heart of a huge conical bonfire. Taking a couple of weeks to construct, the pyre is over 17m high, more than 10m in diameter and weighs in at some 150 tonnes. Late on 16 January, the village priest lights the candles of the faithful, who then leads a procession from the church to the pyre and sets light to what's the biggest bonfire you're ever likely to see.

The tower of fresh-cut pine towering over the main square of the small Maestrazgo village of **Forcall** may not be able to match these dimensions but the heat from the bonfire is still enough to make you back off – or not. A tunnel is left at the base of the pyre and the youth of the village run a gauntlet of fire through it. Forcall's festival of *Sant-antonà* also features a re-enactment around the village streets of the life of the good saint and the conflict between good and evil.

A more gentle dimension to the fiesta of San Antonio is the blessing of the animals, where bulls, sheep, dogs, even pet hamsters are brought to the priest to be blessed. It's a moving ceremony, but for some, not entirely in the spirit of the gentler St Francis of Assisi who smiles upon creatures furry and feathery. *Sant Anton, sant ditxós, fes que els porquets siguen grossos i menjadors* (St Anthony make our piglets fat and hungry) goes one folk saying, while another goes *El baconet beneirem i després el menjarem* (We'll bless the little porker, then eat him up).

San Juan & Midsummer

The night of 23 June, just beyond the summer solstice or midsummer and the longest day of the year, has been celebrated well before Christianity first reached Spain. Onto it was grafted the feast of San Juan (St John), marked by fires, both big and small. Most splendid of all the midsummer festivals and fired up for several days, is Alicante's **Las Hogueras**, which is replicated in several towns on the Costa Blanca including Xàbia, Benidorm and Torrevieja. In essence, the fiestas are similar to a summertime Fallas, a time for feasting and fun, when *barracas*, or wooden huts, are set up in the streets which are closed to all traffic. *Hogueras*, effigies like Valencia's fallas, yet more innovative, less kitsch and less bound by convention, sprout up at every major junction. Then, at precisely midnight on the Noche de San Juan (St John's Night), flames lick around the base of every *hoguera* and, all over town, the effigies go up in flames.

Other pueblos have their own midsummer night's dreams. Massamagrell, a village just north of Valencia, risks burning itself off the map every Día de San Juan (St John's Day). The *correfoc* (fire running) takes place all along the main street of the town as devil figures, clad in fireproof costumes and bearing swirling catherine wheels atop pitchforks, hurtle through the crowd with sparks flying. A bike, spurting flames in every direction, wobbles down the Calle Mayor, followed by a bobbing, swaying fire-breathing dragon. If you turn up to join in the fun, wear old clothes and cover your hair.

In honour of San Juan, the youth of Altea, a town just north of Benidorm on the Costa Blanca, go in search of (you'll notice that an awful lot of this folklore is fairly phallic) the tallest, thickest poplar they can find. A procession winds its way from sea level up through the old town for the erection of the poplar in the Plaza de la Iglesia, the church square, followed by a splendid bonfire.

The Comunidad also greets the longest day of the year in more modest ways. Many folk from Valencia City simply head for the coast, especially the Playa de la Malvarrosa, light a campfire on the beach, and cleanse themselves by washing their feet in the sea and writing their sins of the moment on a piece of paper and casting it into the embers of the fire. Instant absolution and a good night out for all…

Corpus Cristi

Corpus Cristi, observed on the ninth Sunday after Easter, is another good excuse for a street spectacle. With its roots in the 14th century, Valencia's huge procession is headed by eight giant heads that are out of all proportion to the puny human legs that bear them. Behind follow characters from the old and new testaments – Jacob and his 12 sons, Abraham, the apostles, the saints, cherubs – as well as other characters that are more apocryphal, such as the Queen of Saba (or Sheba) and La Moma, who receives the loudest applause. The role of La Moma, this haunting, veiled lady in white (in fact played by a man), her dress rich in lace and embroidery and on her head a crown of flowers, is to drive away sin.

Spain has many a Corpus Cristi procession, but only Valencia City has La Moma and Las Rocas – huge allegorical carriages, the oldest dating back to the early 16th century. Creaking and with their paintwork darkened with age, the carriages are pulled from their home in the Barrio del Carmen and into the Plaza de la Virgen, heart of the celebrations, to be given a public airing. Nearby the plaza on a specially erected stage, young people enact *misteris*, short mystery plays or sketches.

La Magdalena

Castellón de la Plana's La Magdalena pilgrimage celebrates the day when, liberated from the Moors by Jaime I, the townspeople came down from a nearby hill to settle on the plain (La Plana), which is crowned today by the chapel of La Magdalena. The evening before the third Sunday of Lent, the fiesta begins with the **Pregó**, a procession depicting the town's long history.

The next morning in the Romería de les Canyes, the crowd assembles in the Plaza Mayor. Pilgrims, wearing a black blouson and a kerchief slung around the neck, each bear a staff with a twist of green ribbon to help them up the hill to La Magdalena.

What follows the pilgrimage that same evening must be unique in Valencian revelry. **Les Gaiates** are, goes the saying, *un esclat de llum sense*

Over 350 grotesque giants – up to 15m high – parade through Valencia City during the fabulously wild Las Fallas de San José. There are explosions of fireworks at 2pm daily for most of March.

MICHAEL TAYLOR

MICHAEL TAYLOR

MICHAEL TAYLOR

MICHAEL TAYLOR

MICHAEL TAYLOR

Fiestas de Moros y Cristianos (Moors and Christians Festival): more than 80 Valencian towns and villages hold celebrations to mark the region's liberation from Arab rule.

foc ni fum (a burst of light without fire and without smoke). Recalling that first descent from the hills, at night and illuminated by lanterns, Les Gaiates turns the Castellón night into bright day as 19 large, brilliantly lit floats, one from each area of town, converge in a single parade through the town.

Morella's Sexenni

What distinguishes Morella's Sexenni from other fiestas is that, as its name in Valenciano implies, it only happens every six years (the next one is due in August 2006). But this mountain town deep in the Maestrazgo makes up in sheer colour for the fiesta's irregularity. Tonnes of brightly coloured tissue paper, tens of thousands of pieces each no bigger than the size of a leaf, decorate balconies, form elaborate tapestries, giant birds and flowers, and transform workaday tractors and farm carts into exotic vehicles. There are processions and fire, of course, all in honour of the Virgen de la Vallivana, Morella's patron who, back in the Middle Ages, saved the town from the plague.

But, strangely, the effigy of the virgin – a tiny beauty, encrusted with jewels – doesn't reside in Morella. Her home is in Vallivana, some 24km eastwards of Morella (see the Northern Valencia chapter for more details). Every six years, though, she returns to the scene of her miracle for the Sexenni and remains in the town for a couple of months before being returned to Vallivana.

Fiestas with a Difference

Valencia has a few more fiestas that merit a mention for their originality.

Algemesí, a small town midway between Valencia and Xàtiva, is famous for its **Muixeranga**, a day of festivities in early September. This fiesta showcases a strange dance, peculiar to the town, performed by husky men in white dresses and tights, and mystery playlets in Valenciano on themes such as the temptation of Adam and Eve or Abraham's near-sacrifice of his son Isaac. And, in something that's much more suited to Catalunya than Valencia, men, wearing distinctive blue, red and white striped outfits like pyjamas, build tall human towers up which clambers some tiny mite to top things off like the fairy on the Christmas tree.

Les Danses, held in Peñíscola on 8 and 9 September, manages to include a Moros y Cristianos re-enactment as well as a mix of both Algemesí's special elements. A very special dance is performed where men, in this variation wearing sky-blue skirts, also build human towers albeit of more modest proportions.

Tiny Zorita in the Maestrazgo has less than 150 inhabitants, yet each 8 September, it puts on the **Lucha Entre el Diablo y el Ángel** (Fight Between the Devil and the Angel). As the procession of pilgrims winds its way from the village towards the Santuario de La Balma (see Around Forcall in the Northern Valencia chapter) the very devil of a man leaps out and bars their way. Clad in a costume adorned with lizards and snakes, his face blackened and his arms stained red, brandishing a trident and wearing a hat that imitates some fearsome beast, he's guaranteed to make the smaller pilgrims shudder. But out steps the angel, clad in silk, his shield and sword painted deep purple and, after a duel of words and a brief struggle, Satan is exorcised for yet another year...

Another commonly observed fiesta in fishing communities along the coast is 16 July, day of the **Virgen del Carmen**, patron of fisherfolk. In some communities, such as Santa Pola and Torrevieja, her image is carried out to sea or borne amid a flotilla of small boats.

No resumé of Valencian fiestas can be complete without reference to La Tomatina, Buñol's 60 minutes of sticky, red mayhem where participants hurl literally tonnes of tomatoes at each other. For details, see the boxed text 'La Tomatina' in the Central Valencia chapter. And the **Misteri d'Elx** couldn't be more different. To learn more about this haunting medieval-mystery play, see the boxed text in the the Costa Blanca chapter.

A Load of Bulls

We need one more ingredient to make a truly typical Valencian fiesta: a bull or two, which even the smallest of pueblos usually manages to rustle up. The spectacle's a far cry from the plaza de toros (bullring) with its formal pageant, matadors in fancy dress and death in the afternoon. In the villages, they go for what's termed *bou al carrer* (bull in the street) or *bou per la vila* (bull in the old quarter). And that's just what happens. A square or street in the old part of town is cordoned off with stepped wooden barriers that double as seating for spectators. A bull (sometimes two) is led in. It's not your usual bullring heavyweight but a young steer, lean, fast and sharp-horned all the same. The youth of the village venturing out from a protective cage, proceed to taunt the bewildered beast. A popular nocturnal variant is the *bou embolat*, where a pair of lighted torches are fixed to the hapless animal's horns.

MARK WELDON

Getting Around

AIR

There are no direct flights between the cities within the Comunidad Valenciana. The only possibility would be between Valencia City and Alicante, and even then, the journey would prove much quicker by train or road anyway.

BUS

Unless you have your own wheels, bus is the only way to get around large tracts of inland Valencia. Except on a few major routes, bus services are likely to be limited on weekdays and they might even be restricted to an early morning and early evening run, getting workers and school kids into and out of the nearest town of con-

sequence. For the coastal resorts south of Alicante, bus is likewise your only option. Services in this area are more frequent and operate daily.

It's advisable that you check the timetable carefully before travelling at the weekend. Even a fairly frequent weekday service can trickle down to just a few departures on Saturday, or, as is often the case, none at all on Sunday.

Larger towns have an *estación de autobuses*, a bus station (which in some cases, such as in Denia or Orihuela, is integrated with the train station) where both local and longer distance buses will pull in. In villages and smaller towns, buses usually terminate on a particular street or square, often

Bussing Around Valencia

Destinations within the Comunidad Valenciana served from Valencia bus station include:

destination	fare (€)	duration (hours)	daily frequency	bus company
Alcoy	6.15	2¼	6	Travicoi
Alicante	12.35	2¼ to 2½	up to 12	Alsa/Enatcar
Benidorm	9.50	1¾	9	Alsa/Enatcar
Bocairent	6.10	1¾	2	Autobuses La Concepción
Buñol	2.50	1	hourly	Autobuses Buñol
Carcaixent	2.55	1½	7	Autobuses Buñol
Castellón	3.90	1¼	up to 5	Autocares Hife
Chelva	4.70	1½	3	Hispano Chelvana
Chiva	2	3	4	Autobuses Buñol
Cullera	2.45	1¼	9	Alsa/Enatcar
Denia	6.50	1½	up to 9	Alsa/Enatcar
Xàbea	7.10	2¼	up to 7	Alsa/Enatcar
Ontinyent	5.50	1½	5	Autobuses La Concepción
Requena	3.65	1	up to 14	Autolineas Alsina
Sagunto	1.75	3/4	every 30 mins	Autobuses AVSA
Segorbe	3.80	1¼	8	Autocares Herca
Tavernes de la Valldigna	3.85	1½	5	Autobuses Buñol
Utiel	4	1¼	8	Auto-Lineas Alsina
Villena	8.20	2¼	2	Autobuses La Concepción

For destinations beyond the Comunidad, see the table in the Getting There & Away chapter.

halting beside a cafe, which acts as an informal ticket office for the buses as well as source of information about timetables and routes.

There's no fixed rule about whether you pay on the bus or in advance. It's well worth asking while you're waiting around since a minority of drivers can get quite snotty if you proffer your money instead of a prepaid ticket. Some may even have little compunction about driving off without you as you scuttle around to the ticket office to organise things.

Among the veritable fleet of companies operating services linking Valencia City, the region and cities beyond it, the major players and the destinations they travel to are:

Alsa/Enatcar (☎ 902 42 22 42, W www.alsa.es) Links major towns within the Comunidad and beyond

Auto Res (☎ 902 02 09 99 reservations, ☎ 96 349 22 30 in Valencia, W www.auto-res.net) Madrid

Autobuses Buñol (☎ 96 349 14 25) Chiva and Buñol

Autobuses La Concepción (☎ 96 349 99 49) Ontinyent, Bocairent and Villena

Autocares Herca (☎ 96 349 12 50) Sagunto and Segorbe

Autocares Hife (☎ 902 11 98 14) Castellón and Costa del Azahar

Autocares Samar (☎ 91 723 05 06) Teruel and Madrid

Autolineas Alsina (☎ 96 349 72 30) Utiel and Requena

Autos Mediterraneo (☎ 964 22 00 54) Castellón, the Maestrazgo and Costa del Azahar

AVSA (☎ 96 469 97 900) Sagunto, Castellón, Segorbe and Vall d'Uixó

Bilman Bus (☎ 96 347 89 89) Basque country

Hispano Chelvana (☎ 96 198 50 09) Vall del Turia

Travicoi (☎ 96 347 04 27) Alcoy

TRAIN

Train is the easiest way to move yourself northwards from Valencia to Castellón, travelling along the Costa del Azahar as far as Vinaròs and onto the border with Catalunya. In the other direction, the main train line loops inland from Valencia City, passes through Xàtiva, then drops down the Vall de Vinalopó, serving towns such as Villena,

Elda and Novelda, to meet the coast again at Alicante.

Prices can vary quite substantially according to the category of train you catch. If time isn't a consideration, you can take a *regional* train, which stop at just about every station en route, between Valencia and Alicante for as little as €8.60. To sink back into a plush seat on the smart *Euromed*, which covers just about the same route, you'll need to lay out €18.65. If you aren't in a hurry, a *regional* train is the most pleasant way to linger over and savour the train line north of Castellón, where it hugs the coast for quite long stretches.

Cercanía trains (*rodalia* in Valenciano; local trains operating around Alicante and Valencia) radiate out from Valencia to such destinations as Castellón, Gandía, Utiel and Requena. From Alicante, they serve places such as Elche and Orihuela. Most run fairly regularly (at least hourly and often more frequently). Operating using a very reasonable fixed-fare, zonal system, the trains are usually a practical alternative to the bus (if there's an option between the two) and are unlikely to take longer, even though they also stop at every last station.

All the above services are operated by Renfe (Red Nacional de los Ferrocarriles Españoles), the national train network. For information and prices, visit their Web site at W www.renfe.es or call ☎ 902 2402021 or ☎ 96 352 02 02.

South of Valencia, Renfe doesn't serve destinations between Gandía and Alicante. Much of the gap is covered by the splendid *trenet* (little train), the clanking, narrow-gauge railway operated by Ferrocarriles de la Generalitat Valenciana (FGV). It runs between Alicante and Denia through, at times, quite stunning coastal scenery. Typical single fares are Alicante–Benidorm €2.85 and Alicante–Denia €6.35.

CAR & MOTORCYCLE

If you bring your own car to Valencia, remember to have your insurance and other papers in order (see Paperwork & Preparations under Car & Motorcycle in the Getting There & Away chapter).

ROAD DISTANCES (KM)

	Alicante	Benidorm	Castellòn	Denia	Elche (Elx)	Xàtiva (Játiva)	Morella	Requena	Valencia City	Vinaròs	Madrid	Barcelona
Alicante	---											
Benidorm	55	---										
Castellòn	231	192	---									
Denia	96	57	166	---								
Elche (Elx)	19	64	250	115	---							
Xàtiva (Játiva)	103	111	127	74	127	---						
Morella	336	318	105	271	335	232	---					
Requena	180	225	137	173	171	114	242	---				
Valencia City	166	148	65	101	185	38	170	72	---			
Vinaròs	298	314	67	233	317	194	64	204	166	---		
Madrid	419	458	409	515	411	357	551	285	347	615	---	
Barcelona	535	498	286	458	554	395	260	429	357	199	618	---

1 mile = 1.61km

Road Maps & Atlases

See under Maps in the Facts for the Visitor chapter for information on road maps.

The table below gives distances between the Comunidad's major towns.

Road Rules

In built-up areas the speed limit is 50km/h. This rises to 100km/h on major roads and up to 120km/h on *autovías* and *autopistas* (toll-free and tolled dual-lane highways respectively). Cars towing caravans are restricted to a maximum speed of 80km/h. The minimum driving age is 18.

Motorcyclists must use headlights at all times and wear a crash helmet. The minimum age for riding bikes and scooters of 80cc and over is 16, and for those 50cc and under it's 14. Whatever the size of the engine, the bike needs a licence.

One common road signal might confuse you. Spanish truck drivers often have the courtesy to turn on their right indicator to show that the way ahead of them is clear for overtaking (and the left one if it is not and you are attempting this manoeuvre). On the other hand, they may indeed be about to turn right or left so bide your time until their intention is clear.

Vehicles already on roundabouts have right of way.

The blood-alcohol limit is 0.05% (0.03% for drivers with less than two years' experience and professional drivers) and breathalysing is occasionally carried out. If fitted, rear seat belts – standard on more modern cars – must be worn. Fines for many traffic offences, including driving under the influence of alcohol, range from €300 to €600.

Nonresident foreigners can be fined up to €300 on the spot – the minor compensation is that they get 20% off normal fines if they settle it immediately. You can contest the fine in writing (and in English) within 10 days, but don't hold your breath for a favourable result.

Roadside Assistance

The head office of the Real Automóvil Club de España (RACE; ☎ 900 20 00 93) is at Calle José Abascal 10 in Madrid. It also has a branch (☎ 96 334 55 22) in Valencia City at Gran Vía Marqués de Turia 79. For the RACE's 24-hour, nationwide emergency

Road Numbers

Most secondary and tertiary roads in the Comunidad Valenciana have recently been allotted completely new numbers, beginning with the letters CV, indicating that the road is a *comarcal Valenciana* (Valencian local road). These replace older numbers, which started with V or VV.

We've quoted the new label both on maps and in the text. However, if you're working from an older map, you may well find that a road bears its previous number. Similarly, numbers on the ground may cause confusion until old roadside markers are uprooted or get a new lick of paint and stencilling. So, for example, what features as the CV-390 on recent maps was still signed as the V-622 at the time of research, while the CV-452 remains the VV-8108 on a fairly recent road map.

breakdown assistance, you can try calling ☎ 900 11 22 22.

The Comunidad Valenciana's equivalent of RACE is – just as you might expect – the Real Automóvil Club de Valencia (RACV, ☎ 96 333 94 05), which has its headquarters at Avenida Antic Regne de Valencia 64.

As a rule, holders of motoring insurance with foreign organisations such as the RAC, AA (both UK) or AAA (USA) will be provided with an emergency assistance number to use while travelling in Spain, so, in general, you shouldn't need the above numbers.

City Driving & Parking

Driving in crowded urban environments such as Valencia can be nerve-racking at first. Road rules and traffic lights are generally respected but the pace and jostling may take a little getting used to. On other occasions, it's the slow crawl along overcrowded urban arteries that can fray the nerves. The quietest time is between about 2pm and 5pm, when most locals are either eating or snoozing. The most dangerous time is the early hours of the morning when far too many drivers have been hitting the bottle.

Finding a cranny to park can be a frustrating exercise. Where possible, avoid leaving luggage and valuables in unattended vehicles. If you must leave luggage in your vehicle, you might be safer in a paying car park (costs average about €1.20 per hour).

All the main town centres operate a restricted parking system (look for the blue lines painted on the roadway). Although many locals simply ignore fines, you risk your car being towed away if you double-park or leave your vehicle in a designated no-parking zone. Recovering it can cost as much as €100. Fines for overstaying your welcome in a designated parking bay begin at €30. However, many towns have a system whereby, if you're not too late back, you can annul the fine by paying €2.50 into the nearest meter. You then enclose the receipt it spits out within the envelope that was tucked under your windscreen together with the penalty form and pop it into the special slot on the parking metre.

Tollways

Spain has two kinds of motorways. There are paying autopistas, such as the A-7, which runs north-south through the Comunidad along the coastal plain. Rates are fairly steep, which is why all too often you'll see a delightfully traffic-free A-7 snaking almost parallel to the N-340 main road that is choked with trucks and other traffic. You can pay tolls in cash or by credit card. In an effort to encourage greater use of the latter, the company running the A-7 gives a small discount to payers using plastic.

Autovías, such as the A-3, which heads west towards Madrid, are free of charge. At least four lanes wide, they're of much the same standard as the autopistas.

Petrol

In Spain, petrol *(gasolina)*, although pricey, generally comes cheaper than in many other European Union (EU) countries (including France, Germany, Italy and the UK). About 30 companies, including several foreign operators, run petrol stations in Spain, but the two biggest are the home-grown Repsol and Cepsa.

Prices vary slightly between different service stations *(gasolineras)*, and fluctuate rather more according to changes in oil tariffs and tax policy. At the time of writing, diesel *(gasóleo)* cost €0.69 to €0.72 per litre. Lead-free *(sin plomo*; 95 octane) was €0.77 to €0.85 per litre and a 98-octane variant (also lead-free) that goes by various names, cost up to €0.92 per litre.

You can pay with major credit cards at most service stations.

Rental

Many smaller inland destinations have no bus services so, if you're planning to break out from one of the coastal tourist resorts, budget for at least a day or two of car hire. Even in the high season, rates at the main resorts are substantially cheaper than in many European countries.

If you're travelling independently, you can pick up a vehicle at either Valencia or Alicante airport.

Reliable local car-hire companies, operating from both Valencia and Alicante airports, are normally substantially cheaper than the multinationals. They include:

Javea Cars (☎ 96 579 3312, fax 96 579 60 52, **W** www.javeacars.com)
Solmar (☎ 96 646 10 00, fax 96 646 01 09, **W** www.solmar.es)
Victoria Cars (☎ 96 579 27 61, fax 96 583 20 00, **W** www.victoriacars.com)

Of the big boys, multinationals Hertz, Europcar and Avis, plus pan-Spain National/Atesa and Centauro, are also represented at Valencia and Alicante airports.

No matter where or from whom you rent, make sure you understand what is included in the price (features such as unlimited kilometres, tax, insurance, collision-damage waiver and so on) and what your liabilities are. The minimum rental age in Spain is 21 years. A credit card is usually required.

Purchase

Only people legally residing in Spain may buy vehicles there. One way around this is to have a friend who is a resident put the ownership papers in their name.

People wishing to buy a car in Spain need a reasonable knowledge of Spanish to get through paperwork and understand dealers' patter. Trawling around showrooms or looking through classifieds can turn up second-hand small cars in good condition from around €1800. The annual cost of third-party insurance on such a car, with theft and fire cover and national breakdown assistance, comes in at between €250 and €300 (with annual reductions if you make no claims).

Vehicles of five years and older must be submitted for a roadworthiness check, known as the Inspección Técnica de Vehículos (ITV). If the car passes the test, you get a sticker for two years. After its 10th birthday, a car is checked annually. If you're buying such a vehicle, check that it's been through the test, which costs about €25.

You can pick up a second-hand 50cc *moto* (motorcycle) for anything from €250 to €600.

Warning

If you drive a foreign or manifestly rented car, take extra care at A-7 motorway service areas, where several travellers have reported thefts from their cars. Never leave anything of value in view and try to park close to the building. Ideally, take a window seat and keep an eye on your car while you sip your coffee. In Valencia City, the threat is lower but still there – car radios are particularly at risk.

BICYCLE

Bicycle rental, except in some coastal resorts, is quite rare. For example, although it is pancake flat, has several bike lanes and a perfect cycling climate for three out of the four seasons, the whole of Valencia City has only one rental outlet. A mountain bike – *bici de montaña* or *bici todo terreno* (BTT; pronounced 'bay-tay-tay') – is the most popular kind, although some places where the going's easy may also stock *bicis de ciudad* (city bikes).

If you're flying and plan to bring your own bike, check with the airline about any hidden costs and whether you will have to disassemble or pack it for the flight.

You should travel light on a cycle tour but bring tools and some spare parts, including a puncture-repair kit and a spare inner tube. Panniers are essential to balance your possessions on either side of the bike frame. A bike helmet is a good idea, as is a solid bike lock and chain to prevent theft.

Fill all your water bottles before you set out since it can be hot on the open road. Springs and fountains are sparse and more often than not you won't find anything between villages, especially in the interior.

Outside the heat of summer, the inland hills and valleys make great cycling territory – and even the summer heat is lower and less sticky here than on the coastal plain.

UK-based cyclists planning to cycletour in the Comunidad might want to contact the Cyclists' Touring Club (CTC; ☎ 01483-417217), Cotterell House, 69 Meadrow, Godalming, Surrey GU7 3HS, UK. It can supply information to members on cycling conditions and itineraries in the Comunidad and offers cheap insurance. UK membership costs £25 per annum.

It's not that easy to heave your bike onto a train if you get tired of pedalling. Absurdly, for a long inter-regional journey it can normally only be sent separately as a parcel. Some regional trains allocate space for bicycles, others don't. Ask before buying a ticket. Bikes are permitted on most cercanía trains although there may be restrictions during peak hours. It's often possible to take your bike on a bus (usually you'll just be asked to remove the front wheel).

European Bike Express (☎ UK 01642-251440, fax 232209, 🛱 www.bike-express .co.uk) is a bus service that enables cyclists to travel with their bikes. It leaves north-east England every Wednesday and Saturday between May and October with pick-up and drop-off points en route. Its final destination is Empuriabrava in Catalunya, from where you can travel south to the Comunidad. The one-way/return fare costs £99/179 (£169 return for CTC members).

HITCHING

Hitching is never entirely safe and we don't recommend it. If you decide to hitch, you should understand that you're taking a small but potentially serious risk. If you do plan *el autostop*, you'll be safer if you travel as one of a pair, the downside being that you reduce the chances of being picked up. It's always wise to let someone know where you're heading for.

Hitching on autopistas and autovías is illegal and it is unlikely anyone will stop for you. Heavily trafficked major roads such as the N-340 are your best bet. You're wasting your time trying to hitch from town centres. Take local transport to the outskirts and, to enhance your chances, make yourself a temporary sign, indicating your destination in Spanish. On the smaller provincial roads of the interior, traffic can be scarce and drivers may be reluctant to pick you up. This said, many young locals hitch inland as often it's the only way to get around if you haven't got your own wheels.

BOAT

Boats run to the three sets of islands off the coast of the Comunidad Valenciana. For seasonal sailings to the Islas Columbretes, see the sections on Castellón, Alcossebre, Peñíscola and Vinaròs in the Northern Valencia chapter. Regular boats ply between Benidorm and the Isla de Benidorm and you can reach the Isla de Tabarca from Alicante, Santa Pola and Torrevieja. For more information, see the Costa Blanca chapter, where you'll also find details of services between Benidorm and Calpe via Altea and information about boats that shuttle between Calpe and Denia via Xàbia.

LOCAL TRANSPORT

Valencia City has an impressive integrated public transport system where bus, metro (most of it above ground) and high-speed tram all come into play. Alicante and other major towns have a reasonable local bus service. Generally though you won't need to use town buses. While the suburbs of conurbations such as Elche or Castellón seem to sprawl on forever, the 'action' part of town is compact, with sights, hotels, restaurants and long-distance transport stations within walking distance of each other.

Buses connect both Alicante and Valencia City with their airports. For the latter, a cercanía train from Estación del Norte is a faster option. In Valencia, both will be superseded by the metro extension as far as the airport, its construction about to begin at the time of writing.

Under the Getting Around section of all major towns, you'll find the number to call if you need a taxi.

ORGANISED TOURS

The highly recommended Terra Ferma (☎/fax 965 89 03 92, **W** www.terraferma .net, Calle Lepanto 13) is a small, environmentally committed walking and climbing outfit. Closely involved with local communities, they also participate in other activities such as footpath signing and mam. They can arrange anything from a one break in the hills to a week of trekking in the Sierra Aitana and the team speaks excellent English.

Brian and Pat Fagg, a British couple who have long resided in the tiny village of Quatretondeta, can arrange customised walking tours for individuals or groups; their delightful hotel is a base. For details see Around Alcoy in the Central Valencia chapter.

Several British-based companies organise all-inclusive walking holidays within the Comunidad in association with local operators (such as the aforementioned Terra Ferma and Brian Fagg). You'll find the details under Organised Tours in the Getting There & Away chapter.

a City & Around

a City

postcode 46003 • pop 753,500

Valencia, home to paella and the Holy Grail, is blessed with great weather and serves up the mid-March festival of Las Fallas, Spain's – even Europe's – wildest street party.

If you've followed the excellent BBC TV series for beginners, *Talk Spanish* (see Language Courses, later in this chapter), you'll already have something of a feel for this dynamic city. It's a vibrant, friendly, mildly chaotic place that boasts an outstanding fine arts museum, an accessible old quarter rich in restaurants and bars, Europe's newest cultural and scientific complex – and one of Spain's most exciting nightlife scenes.

Valencia is Spain's third city after Madrid and Barcelona according to population and just about any other criterion you care to name. Equidistant and about 350km from each of its bigger brothers, it's also an excellent jumping off point for the Balearic Islands that lie directly east over the water. Regular flights and ferries link it with the larger islands of Ibiza and Mallorca.

ITINERARIES

The city merits a week of your life but few visitors can afford such luxury. If you've only a day at your disposal, we suggest beginning with the bustle of the Mercado Central (Central Market), visiting the Ciudad de las Artes y las Ciencias, then indulging in a paella lunch at Las Arenas (see Places to Eat later) followed by a stroll along the Paseo Marítimo (Seafront Promenade) to shake it all down. Resume the trail by calling in on the cathedral and the Nuestra Señora Virgen de los Desamparados and some of the other monuments around the Plaza del la Virgen. Come dusk, dine in one of the many restaurants in the Barrio del Carmen district then, round about midnight and if you've got the stamina, award yourself a nightcap at one of the bars on or around Calle Caballeros.

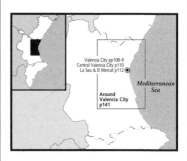

Valencia City pp108-9
Central Valencia City p110
La Seu & El Mercat p112 ⊙

Mediterranean Sea

Around
Valencia City
p141

If you tag on another day, you could fit in a visit to the Museo de Bellas Artes, the fine arts museum and a must for serious art lovers, then take a stroll westwards along the Jardines del Turia, Valencia's landscaped former riverbed. This will lead you to, by way of complete contrast, the Instituto Valenciano de Arte Moderno (IVAM) on the south side. Here, you can take in one or more of its excellent temporary contemporary art exhibitions. For more on the history of the town, sign on for the audiovisual presentation at the Cripta de la Cárcel de San Vicente Mártir. Alternatively, to know more about Las Fallas,

Valencia's week-long Spring bacchanal, visit the Museo Fallero.

Beach bugs can just chill – or rather sweat – out on the Playa de la Malvarrosa. For somewhere quieter (except at weekends), take a bus ride to Playa El Saler, some 10km south of town.

Art lovers will enjoy, too, the Museo Nacional de Cerámica, the national ceramics museum with its splendid way-over-the-top main portal, and the small yet richly endowed museum of the Colegio del Patriarca.

In between times, and if you're in need of a little peace and quiet, relax in one of the city's several green spaces – anywhere along the 7km-long swath of the Jardines del Turia, the Jardín Botánico, Spain's oldest and most mature botanical gardens, or the bijou Jardín de Montforte.

Night owls can roost for a week or more in the Barrio del Carmen but, if you want to ring the changes, head for the areas circling the Mercado de Abastos or around the university. In summer, you'll find the action in the throbbing bars of Malvarrosa, just back from the beach.

HISTORY

It was pensioned-off Roman legionaries who founded 'Valentia' on the banks of the Río Turia in 138 BC and who first developed irrigation for the surrounding regions.

As Rome collapsed, the Visigoths moved in, only to be expelled by Muslim cohorts in AD 711. The Arabs made Valencia a rich agricultural and industrial centre, establishing ceramics, paper, silk and leather industries and extending the network of irrigation canals in the rich agricultural hinterland.

Muslim rule was briefly interrupted in 1094 by the triumphant rampage of the legendary Castilian knight El Cid. The Christians definitively retook the city in 1238, when Jaime I incorporated the area into his burgeoning Catalan kingdom.

Valencia's Golden Age was in the 15th and 16th centuries, when it was one of the Mediterranean's strongest trading centres. Like Catalunya, Valencia backed the wrong horse in the War of the Spanish Succession and in retribution the victorious Bourbon

king Felipe V abolished Valencia's Fueros, the autonomous privileges the city had enjoyed. The Spanish Civil War proved similarly unlucky; Valencia's siding with the Republicans (and acting as seat of the Republican government from November 1936 until October 1937) did not endear the city to General Franco.

The fueros may not have been restored, but benefiting from the decentralisation that followed Franco's death, Valencia and its region today enjoy a high degree of autonomy.

ORIENTATION

The 'action' part of the city is an oval area bounded by the old course of the Río Turia and the sickle-shaped inner ring road of Calles Colón, Xàtiva and Guillem de Castro. These trace the walls of the old city, demolished in 1865 as a job-creation project when Valencia was expanding.

Within the oval are three major squares: Plazas del Ayuntamiento, de la Reina (also known as Plaza de Zaragoza) and de la Virgen. The oldest quarter of the city, the Barrio del Carmen (or El Carmé), is delimited by the Plaza de la Virgen, the Quart and Serranos towers and the Turia riverbed.

The train station, Estación del Norte, is 250m south of Plaza del Ayuntamiento. The main bus station is on the north side of the riverbed on Avenida Menéndez Pidal.

Maps

The newest – and therefore the most up-to-date – of several decent competing large-scale maps of town is the *Plano de Valencia* (€4.50) published by Alonso Editores at a scale of 1:10,000. Good alternatives are Editorial Everest's *Valencia: Plano Callejero* (€3) at 1:13,000 and the *Gran Plano de Valencia* (€5.70) published by Bayarri at a scale of 1:9000 (make sure you buy this one rather than the more expensive versions that come with tourist information in Spanish only). Bayarri also produces a hardback street guide (€5.70). All, particularly the Bayarri street guide, are useful if you're staying in town for some time. If your visit's a short one, the free town plans provided by Valencia's tourist office should be more than adequate.

VALENCIA CITY

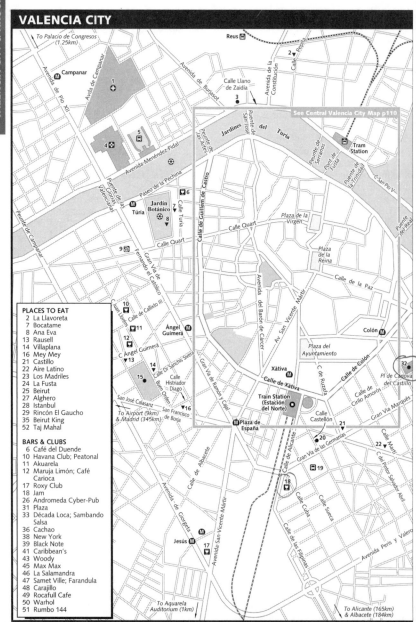

To Palacio de Congresos
(1.25km)

Reus

Campanar

Avda de Campanar

Avenida de Pío XII

Avenida de Burjasot

Avenida de la Constitución

Calle Sagunto

Calle Llano
de Zaidía

3

See Central Valencia City Map p110

Jardines   del   Turia

Puente de
San José

Puente de
Serranos

Puente de
la Trinidad

Tram
Station

Avenida Menéndez Pidal

C San Pío V

Paseo de la Pechina

Puente de las
Glorias
Valencianas

6

Jardín
Botánico

7
Calle Turia
8

Calle Quart

Calle Quart

Plaza de la
Virgen

Puente
del Real

Puente de campanar

Calle de Guillem de Castro

Túria

9

Calle Quart

Plaza
de la
Reina

Calle de la Paz

Gran Vía de Fernando el Católico

Juan Llorens

10
Calle de Callito III
11

Ángel
Guimerá

Colón

Avenida del Barón de Cárcer

12
C Ángel Guimerá

13

14
Calle Dr Sanchis Sivera

15
Calle Baja Ocean

Calle
Histriador
Diago

Xàtiva

Plaza del
Ayuntamiento

Pl de Cánova
del Castillo

32

San José Calasanz

San Francisco
de Borja

To Airport (9km)
& Madrid (345km)

16

Gran Vía de Ramón y Cajal

Calle de Xàtiva

Train Station
(Estación
del Norte)

Av. San Vicente Mártir

C de Ruzafa

C de Colón

Calle de
Cirilo Amorós

Gran Vía Marqués

Calle Martí

Plaza de
España

Calle de Alicante

Calle
Castellón

21

Gran Vía de las Germanías

20

22
C del Pintor Salvador Abril

Avenida de Albacete

Avenida San Vicente Mártir

18

19

Calle Cuba

Calle Sueca

Calle de las Filipinas

Jesús

17

Avenida de Giorgeta

Avenida Perís y Valero

To Aquarela
Auditorium (1km)

To Alicante (165km)
& Albacete (184km)

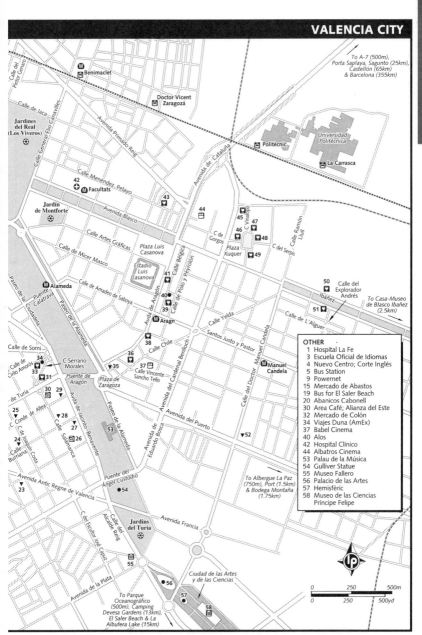

VALENCIA CITY

To A-7 (500m),
Porta Saplaya, Sagunto (25km),
Castellón (65km)
& Barcelona (355km)

Calle del Pintor Genaro

Ⓜ Benimaclet

Doctor Vicent
Zaragozá

Jardines
del Real
(Los Viveros)

Calle de Jaca

Calle General Elio Cabanilles

Avenida Primado Reig

Universidad
Politécnica

Avenida de Cataluña

Ⓜ Politècnic

La Carrasca

Calle Menéndez Pelayo

42 ✚ Ⓜ Facultats

43

44

45

47

Calle Ramón Llull

Jardín
de Montforte

Avenida Blasco

Calle Artes Gráficas

Plaza Luis
Casanova

Calle de Micer Masco

C de
Gorgos

C Vinalopo

46

48

Plaza
Xuquer

49

C del Serpis

Estadio
Luis
Casanova

41

Calle Bélgica

Ⓜ Alameda

Puente
Calatrava

Calle de Amadéo de Saboya

40
39

50

Calle del
Explorador
Andrés

Paseo de la Ciudadela

Paseo de la Alameda

Avda. de Aragón

Calle de Polo y Peyrolón

Ⓜ Aragn

51

Ibáñez

To Casa-Museo
de Blasco Ibáñez
(2.5km)

Calle de Sorni

Calle Yelda

Calle de L'Alguer

38

Calle Chile

Santos Justo y Pastor

Calle de
Cirilo Amorós

34
33

C Serrano
Morales

31

Puente de
Aragón

36

35

37

Calle Vincente
Sancho Tello

Calle del Cardenal Benlloch

Avenida del Doctor Manuel Candela

Ⓜ Manuel
Candela

30
29

Plaza de
Zaragoza

25

28

27

26

C Conde de Altea

Avda. de Jacinto Benavente

53

Avenida del Puerto

Avenida de Eduardo Boca

52

24

Calle
Salamanca

Calle
Burriana

Calle de Joaquin Costa

Puente del
Ángel Custodio

Avenida Antic Regne de Valencia

23

54

To Albergue La Paz
(750m), Port (1.5km)
& Bodega Montaña
(1.75km)

Puente del
Ángel Custodio

Jardins
del Turia

Avenida Francia

Calle del
Escultor José Capuz

Calle del
Alcalde Reig

55

56

Ciudad de las Artes
y de las Ciencias

57

58

Avenida de la Plata

To Parque
Oceanográfico
(500m), Camping
Devesa Gardens (13km),
El Saler Beach & La
Albufera Lake (15km)

OTHER
1 Hospital La Fe
3 Escuela Oficial de Idiomas
4 Nuevo Centro; Corte Inglés
5 Bus Station
9 Powernet
15 Mercado de Abastos
19 Bus for El Saler Beach
20 Abanicos Cabonell
30 Area Café; Alianza del Este
32 Mercado de Colón
34 Viajes Duna (AmEx)
37 Babel Cinema
40 Alos
42 Hospital Clínico
44 Albatros Cinema
53 Palau de la Música
54 Gulliver Statue
55 Museo Fallero
56 Palacio de las Artes
57 Hemisfèric
58 Museo de las Ciencias
    Príncipe Felipe

0   250   500m
0   250   500yd

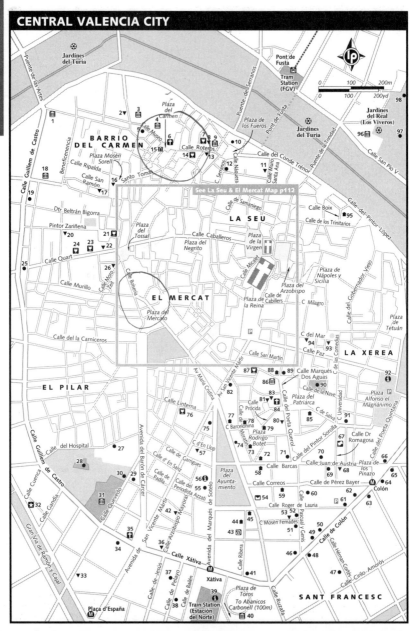

CENTRAL VALENCIA CITY

Jardines del Turia

Pont de Fusta

Tram Station (FGV)

Jardines del Real (Los Viveros)

Plaza del Carmen

BARRIO DEL CARMEN

Beneficencia

Plaza Mosén Sorell

Calle Ripalda

Calle San Ramón

Calle Santo Tomás

Calle Museo

Calle Roteros

Plaza de los Fueros

Jardines del Turia

Calle del Conde Trénor

Calle San Pío V

Calle del Pintor López

See La Seu & El Mercat Map p112

Dtr. Beltrán Bigorra

Pintor Zariñena

Calle Quart

Calle Murillo

Plaza del Tossal

Calle Caballeros

Plaza del Negrito

LA SEU

Calle de Samaniego

Calle Boix

Calle de los Trinitarios

Plaza de la Virgen

Plaza de Nápoles y Sicilia

Plaza del Arzobispo

EL MERCAT

Plaza del Mercado

Plaza de Cabillers

Plaza de la Reina

C Milagro

Plaza de Tetuán

Calle de la Carniceros

Calle San Martín

Calle Paz

C del Mar

LA XEREA

EL PILAR

Calle Linterna

Av María Cristina

Calle San Vicente Mártir

Calle Marqués Dos Aguas

Calle de la Nave

Plaza Alfonso el Magnánimo

Calle del Hospital

Calle Bolsería

Calle Prócida

Plaza del Patriarca

C de Salvá

C Universidad

Calle de Garrigues

C Barcelonina

Plaza Rodrigo Botet

Calle del Poeta Querol

Calle Dr Romagosa

Calle Guillem de Castro

Gran Vía de Ramón y Cajal

Calle Cuenca

Calle Gandía

Calle Quevedo

Calle d'En Llop

Calle de Fadilla

Avenida del Barón de Cárcer

Avenida del Marqués de Sotelo

Plaza del Ayuntamiento

Calle Barcas

Calle Correos

Calle de Pérez Bayer

Calle Juan de Austria

Plaza de los Pinazo

Colón

Calle de Colón

Calle Hernán Cortés

Calle Cirilo Amorós

Calle Ribera

Calle Xàtiva

Avenida de Jesús

Calle-de-Pelayo

Calle de Bailén

Plaça d'Espanya

Xàtiva

Train Station (Estación del Norte)

Plaza de Toros

To Abanicos Carbonell (100m)

SANT FRANCESC

Plaza del Pintor Sorolla

Pascual y Genís

Calle Roger de Lauria

C Mosén Femades

CENTRAL VALENCIA CITY

PLACES TO STAY
44 Hostal-Residencia Alicante
45 Hostal Castelar
58 Hotel Reina Victoria
59 Hotel Continental
72 Hostal-Residencia
   Universal
73 Hostal Moratín
77 Hotel Londres
78 Hotel Excelsior
79 Hotel Astoria Palace
85 Pensión París
88 Hotel Inglés
95 Hotel Ad Hoc; Restaurante
   Chust Godoy

PLACES TO EAT
2 La Bottega dell'Ozio
8 El Forcat
11 Stortini
13 Herboristería del Carmen
16 La Carmé
17 La Lluna
20 Suchi Cru
22 El Tossal
26 Bar Pilar
33 Tasca Jesús
36 Las Añadas de España
42 Navarro
53 Palacio de la Bellota
57 Pizzería La Vita é Bella
68 Villanueva
80 La Tienda del Astoria
81 La Utielana
83 Ñam Ñam
93 Turangalila
94 Al Pomodoro

BARS AND CLUBS
7 Records de l'Avenir
14 Santa Companya

21 Café Sant Miguel
23 Venial
24 La Goulue
76 La Linterna Jazz Café
87 Cervecería Madrid

SHOPPING
29 Artesanía Fidela
30 Casa de los Falleros
41 Albero
46 Massimo Dutti
48 Zara
49 Camper
50 Purificación García
51 Max Mara
60 Spaghetti & Co
61 Corte Inglés
62 Mango
63 Adolfo Domínguez
64 Calzados Beguer
65 Cortefiel
66 Corte Inglés
69 Massimo Dutti
70 Mango
82 Rosalén
89 Loewe
91 Valencia Football Club Shop

OTHER
1 Instituto Valenciano de Arte
   Moderno (IVAM)
3 Centro del Carmen (IVAM)
4 Museo del Siglo XIX
5 Ergobike
6 Iglesia del Carmen
9 Casa de las Rocas
10 Torres de Serranos
12 Institut de la Dona
15 Palacio de Pineda
   (Universidad Menéndez
   y Pelayo)

18 La Beneficencia;
   Museo de la Prehistoria
19 Librería Patagonia
25 Torres de Quart
27 Turivaj
28 Casa de la Cultura &
   Municipal Library
31 Museo Valenciano de la
   Ilustración y la Modernidad
   (MUVIM)
32 Police Station
34 FNAC
35 Iglesia de San Agustín
37 Bar Trinquet Pelayo
38 Laundrette
39 Tourist Office
40 Museo Taurino
43 www.confederacion.com
   (Internet)
47 Eurollibre
52 English Book Centre
54 Post Office
55 Town Hall; Museo Histórico
   Municipal
56 Municipal Tourist Office
67 US Consulate
71 Teatro Principal; Municipal
   Tourist Office
74 Filmoteca & Teatro Rialto
75 Intereuropa
84 Iglesia de San Juan
   de la Cruz
86 Palacio del Marqués de Dos
   Aguas; Museo Nacional de
   Cerámica
90 Colegio del Patriarca
92 Regional Tourist Office
96 Museo de Bellas Artes
97 Museo de Ciencias
   Naturales
98 Jardín Zoológico

INFORMATION

To get a grip on what's happening around town, buy one of the 'what's-on' guides. *La Turia* and *Que y Donde*, are both published weekly in Spanish and are available for €1.20 from newsstands. The publication *24-7 Valencia*, a monthly freebie in English, is available at places where foreigners tend to congregate.

Tourist Offices

The main, regional tourist office is at Calle Paz 48 (☎ 96 398 64 22, fax 96 398 64 21).

It's open 10am to 6.30pm Monday to Friday and 10am to 2pm on Saturday. Three smaller municipal offices are at the train station (☎ 96 352 85 73), Calle Xàtiva, town hall (☎ 96 352 58 12), Plaza del Ayuntamiento, and Teatro Principal (☎ 96 351 49 07), Calle Poeta Querol s/n. All are well endowed with information in English.

Money

There's no shortage of ATMs (cashpoints) around town, and both the airport and Estación del Norte train station have one.

PLACES TO STAY
26 Hostal El Rincón
27 Hospedería del Pilar
32 Hôme
33 Hôme Lonja
36 Hostal Antigua Morellana

PLACES TO EAT
5 Las Cuevas
6 Seu-Xerea; S'Horabaixa
14 Restaurante El Generalife
35 Maramao
37 No Solo Pasta
38 Horchatería de Santa Catalina
44 Horchatería el Siglo
47 Tapinería
48 La Pappardella

BARS AND CLUBS
1 John Silver
2 Jimmy Glass
3 Dona Dona
4 Café de las Horas
16 Café-Bar Negrito
17 Cava del Negret
18 Fox Congo
20 Johnny Maracas
21 Hanax
22 San Jaume
24 Café Infanta
25 Café Bolsería
34 The Lounge; Tasca Ángel
43 Finnegan's

OTHER
7 Palacio de Benicarló (Cortes)
8 Almudín
9 Palacio del Marqués de Campo (Museo de la Ciudad)
10 Cripta de la Cárcel de San Vicente Mártir
11 La Almoina
12 Cathedral
13 Nuestra Señora de los Desamparados
15 Palau de la Generalitat
23 Agrotur
23 Galería del Tossal
28 Lavandería El Mercat (Laundrette)
29 Iglesia de los Santos Juanes
30 Mercado Central (Food Market)
31 La Lonja
39 Nela
40 Guantes Camps
41 Iglesia de San Martín
42 Iberia Office
45 Iglesia de Santa Catalina
46 Bus Turístico; Horse-Drawn Carriages

American Express (AmEx) is represented by Viajes Duna (☎ 96 374 15 62), Calle Cirilo Amorós 88.

Post
The neobaroque main post office *(correos)* building is on Plaza del Ayuntamiento. The poste restante section is on the 1st floor.

Email & Internet Access
The noisy, 48-terminal www.confederacion .com (yes, that's the name) at Calle Ribera 8, is just off Plaza del Ayuntamiento. Its advantages are that it couldn't be more central and is open 11am to 10pm daily. It charges €3 per hour.

If you're a bedtime reader or just fancy clicking on with a *copa* (drink), visit the friendly Andromeda Cyber-Pub, at Calle Salamanca 37, open 6pm to at least 2.30am. A drink entitles you to 15 minutes' free Internet access. Buy a round for three mates and you've earned yourself a free hour (normally €2.40)!

On the same street at No 5, Area Cafe's hourly rate is also €2.40. It opens 11am to 2am Monday to Thursday, 4pm to 2am on Saturday and 4pm to midnight on Sunday. You can log on for free between 4pm and 5pm. Next door at No 3, Alianza del Este has 42 machines.

Powernet, Calle Quart 112 at the junction with Gran Vía de Fernando el Católico, charges €2.40 per hour and opens 11am to 10pm Monday to Saturday, and 4pm to 10pm on Sunday.

Travel Agencies
Turivaj (☎ 96 386 9952), Calle Hospital 11, the local organisation specialising in youth travel, can point you towards travel discounts for under-25s. Also see Useful Organisations in the Facts for the Visitor chapter.

Bookshops
There are two good predominantly English-language bookshops in Valencia: the English Book Centre, Calle Pascual y Genís 16, and Eurollibre, Calle Hernán Cortés 18.

Librería Patagonia (☎/fax 96 391 52 47), Calle Guillem de Castro 106, is excellent

for maps and also carries a number of travel guides in English, including various Lonely Planet titles.

The large FNAC department store (☎ 96 353 90 00), Calle Guillem de Castro 9, has a small section of books in English.

Laundry
There are two central laundrettes. Lavandería El Mercat (☎ 96 391 20 10) at Plaza Mercado 12, close to the covered market, charges €9 per load, which you can either spin yourself or collect within the hour. There's another at Calle Pelayo 11, near the train station.

Medical Services & Emergency
Whatever the nature of the emergency, dial ☎ 112, the pan-European number, where you have the greatest chance of finding a speaker of English. The Policía Nacional answer to ☎ 091. Their main office (☎ 96 351 08 62) is at Gran Vía de Ramón y Cajal 40. Dialling ☎ 092 will get you through to the local police.

To find your nearest all-night pharmacy, call ☎ 900 16 11 61 (toll free).

The two best public-sector hospitals are La Fe (☎ 96 386 27 00), Avenida de Campanar 21, and the Hospital Clínico (☎ 96 386 26 00), Avenida de Blasco Ibáñez 17.

Dangers & Annoyances
There are two downsides to this otherwise wonderful city. Many of the narrow streets, of the old city in particular, are slick with dog mess. And then there's the traffic... The private car is as dear to a Valenciano (we're being deliberately sexist here as the problem is primarily of male making) as his partner. Despite the generous provision of paying car parks, anarchy rules. In the Barrio del Carmen, nothing can stop illegal, intrusive, stick-the-vehicle-anywhere parking: certainly not the lines of ugly metal poles – potential kneecappers bolted into the footpath so that you can't walk two abreast or force through a pram – nor the giant flowerpots against which the dogs (see above) pee or worse.

If you have to bring your vehicle into town and manage to find a legitimate streetside

Dial Me a Monument

Valencia Museo Abierto (Valencia: An Open Air Museum) is a novel joint initiative of the town hall and Movistar, Spain's largest mobile phone company.

Beside every major and quite a lot of minor sites, you'll see a numbered sign. Switch on your mobile phone, programme in ☎ 650 800 200 followed by the number of the attraction in front of you, select 'English' and a husky voice will whisper what's important about it into your ear.

In all, there are 11 routes, such as Muslim Valencia, Seaside Valencia or Valencia in the Third Millennium. Pick up a brochure – which lists the routes but gives little additional information – from any tourist office.

We also recommend that you check first with your mobile phone provider the cost per call within Spain; an informative morning could do major damage to your credit card.

space, you'll probably be assailed by a self-appointed parking attendant, rushing out from nowhere and guiding you into the empty space you'd already spotted, or – even more galling – standing at your door, hand outstretched, when you're already squarely parked. The going rate is €0.60. It's worth coughing up for the peace of mind.

CIUDAD DE LAS ARTES Y DE LAS CIENCIAS ✓

The aesthetically stunning City of Arts & Sciences (☎ 96 352 55 07, Calle Arzobispo Mayoral 14) occupies a huge swath of the old Turia riverbed, south-east of the city centre. Although elements are still under construction, it has already become Valencia's premier tourist attraction. Its daring 21st-century architecture, largely designed by local architect Santiago Calatrava (see the boxed text under Arts in the Facts about Valencia chapter), is rivalled only by Frank Gehry's Museo Guggenheim in Bilbao. The number of visitors each year – already approaching four million – are exceeded only by those of the Prado museum in Madrid. And one superlative that can't be challenged:

covering 350,000 sq m, it's Europe's largest urban complex. You can take a virtual tour at ⓦ www.cac.es.

Two elements of this complex are already up and running: the **Hemisfèric** (info & reservations ☎ 902 100 031; adult/child €6.60/ 4.80; regular projections noon-9.30pm Mon-Thur & Sun, noon-11pm Fri & Sat) broods like a huge, heavy-lidded eye over the shallow lake that surrounds it. It's at once a planetarium, IMAX cinema and laser show and you can select from one of four languages, including English.

The shell of the **Museo de las Ciencias Príncipe Felipe** (information & reservations ☎ 902 100 031; adult/child €6/4.20; open 10am-8pm Mon-Thur, 10am-9pm Fri-Sun) recalls the skeleton of a huge whale. Each section of this interactive science museum has a pamphlet in English summarising its contents.

You can buy a combined ticket for both the Hemisfèric and Science Museum for €9/7.20 per adult/child.

Still under construction at the time of writing were the **Palacio de las Artes**, a multifunctional arts complex with three auditoriums and the **Parque Oceanógrafico**, a series of aquaria, lagoons and islets illustrating coastal marine life – plus what the advance publicity tantalisingly and paradoxically describes as a 'floating underwater restaurant'. Bring your flippers...

To get there jump on bus No 13, 14, 15, 35 or 95.

CENTRO HISTÓRICO – PLAZA DE LA VIRGEN & AROUND ✓
Plaza de la Virgen

The Plaza de la Virgen occupies what was once the forum of Roman Valencia and the very spot where its main north-south and east-west highways intersected. From 1302 until 1860, the town's Casa Consistorial or town hall was situated here – until it was made redundant by the construction of today's Ayuntamiento. Nowadays, apart from being home to as many pigeons as London's Trafalgar Square, it's a pleasant spot for a lingering drink on one of the square's terraces, surrounded by fine buildings. You may think it's crowded, but numbers are nothing compared to the morning of the second Sunday in May. Then the Virgin in her finery makes the journey, all of 200m but lasting over 20 minutes, from her basilica and into the cathedral's baroque door, pressed on all sides by hysterical crowds fighting and pushing to touch her robes.

On 17 and 18 March, over 20,000 *falleros* and *falleras* process through the square, bringing bouquets and huge mounted displays of flowers as an offering to the Virgin Mary, who gives her name to the square.

The handsome reclining figure in the square's central fountain represents the Río Turia, while the eight maidens with their gushing pots symbolise the main irrigation canals flowing from the river.

After dark, the square's smooth flagstones are a favourite spot for skateboarders and rollerbladers doing their stunts.

Cathedral

The cathedral (☎ 96 391 81 27; open 7.30am-1pm & 5pm-8.30pm daily) was begun in 1262, shortly after the reconquest of Valencia City from the Moors. It was built on the site of Valencia's main mosque, which was reduced to rubble, as a symbol of the new temporal as well as spiritual power. Added to and modified over the centuries, it's a microcosm of the city's architectural history: the Puerta del Palau is Romanesque; the dome, tower and Puerta de los Apóstoles giving onto the Plaza de la Virgen are Gothic; the presbytery and main entrance on Plaza de la Reina are baroque; and there are a couple of Renaissance chapels inside.

In the flamboyant Gothic Capilla del Santo Cáliz, right of the main entrance, is what's claimed to be the **Holy Grail**, the chalice from which Christ sipped during the Last Supper and one of a dozen or more rival claimants around the world. Beyond it is the **museum** (admission €1.20; open 10am-1pm & 4.30pm-7pm Mon-Sat Mar-Nov, 4.30pm-6pm Mon-Sat Dec-Feb). The next chapel south, La Capilla de San Francisco de Borja, has a pair of particularly subtle Goyas.

Left of the main portal is the entrance to the octagonal **Miguelete bell tower** (admis-

sion €1.20; open 10am-12.30pm & 4.30pm-6.30pm Tues-Sun). Clamber up the 207 steps of its spiral staircase for great 360-degree views of the city and skyline from its upper balcony, 70m above ground level.

As for the past thousand years, the **Tribunal de las Aguas** (Water Court) meets every Thursday on the dot of noon outside the cathedral's Plaza de la Virgen doorway. Here, local farmers' irrigation disputes are settled, in Valenciano.

You can hire an English-language audioguide (€3) to the cathedral from the shop just inside the baroque (south) portal, but only – and absurdly – from 10.15am to noon or 5pm to 6pm.

Nuestra Señora de los Desamparados

The church (☎ 96 391 86 11; Plaza de la Virgen; open 7am-2pm & 4-9pm daily), or basilica, of Nuestra Señora de los Desamparados (Our Lady of the Abandoned), which was begun in 1652, is on the eastern side of the square, immediately north of the cathedral. Above the altar is a highly venerated 15th-century statue of the Virgin, patroness of the city. If you arrive after hours,

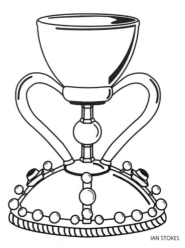

IAN STOKES

End your quest for the Holy Grail at Valencia cathedral.

VALENCIA CITY & AROUND

peer in through the grilles on the southern, cathedral side, and push your nose against its bars, which have been worn smooth over the years by tens of thousands of supplicants.

Palau de la Generalitat

Stretching from the square's north-western corner and giving onto Plaza de Manises is the handsome late-Gothic Palau de la Generalitat, seat of government for the Valencia region. It's closed to the public, but you can admire its massive presence from the exterior. Although it doesn't detract from the building's harmony it's interesting to note that the present pleasing symmetry goes back well under a hundred years. Building began in 1421 while the Renaissance tower – the one facing Plaza de la Virgen – was completed almost a hundred years later in 1519. The second tower, which perfectly matches its partner, had to wait over 400 years and dates back no further than 1940.

Cripta de la Cárcel de San Vicente Mártir

About 100m east of Plaza de la Virgen is the crypt of a Visigoth funerary chapel *(☎ 96 394 14 17, Plaza del Arzobispo; admission free; open 9.30am-2pm & 5.30pm-8pm Tues-Sat & 9.30am-2pm Sun; multimedia show 10am, 11.30am, 1pm, 6pm & 7pm Mon-Sat, 10.30am, 11.30am, 12.30pm & 1.30pm Sun)*, which was reputedly a prison to the 4th-century martyr San Vicente. Although the crypt itself isn't memorable for its own sake, it's well worth taking in the free 25-minute multimedia show that presents Valencia's history and the life and gory death of the saint. Make reservations either by phone or at the Palacio del Marqués de Campo (Museo de la Ciudad) just opposite the crypt and ask for a showing in English.

Palacio del Marqués de Campo (Museo de la Ciudad)

Something of a misnomer since most of the museum material has now been transferred to the Ayuntamiendo (see Plaza del Ayuntamiendo & Around, later), the Palacio del Marqués de Campo these days functions as a **gallery** *(☎ 96 352 54 78 ext 4126, Plaza del Arzobispo; admission free; open 9.30am-2pm & 5.30pm-8pm Tues-Sat Oct-Mar, 9.30am-2pm & 4.30pm-9pm Tues-Sat Apr-Sept, 9.30am-2pm Sun year round)* whose ground floor is used for temporary exhibitions. The 1st floor displays a collection of religious paintings, which compare unfavourably with those of the Bellas Artes and Patriarca collections, plus 19th-century works. The second floor has a vast, if less than riveting, collection of weights and measures.

La Almoina

Immediately north of the crypt is the large archaeological site of La Almoina *(Plaza del Arzobispo; admission free; overlooking catwalk open 10am-2pm Tues-Sun May-Sept, 10am-1pm Tues-Sun Oct-Apr)*, the heart of 'Valentia', the Roman town. Excavated almost continuously since 1985, it has been of enormous importance for interpreting the history of the city. For the visitor, however, it's something of a jumble, the confusion dispelled in part by the introductory pamphlet and information panels, both of which have versions in English. You can also watch a free 15-minute video (in Spanish), projected four to six times each day. Choose an evening showing since in bright daylight the screen scarcely shows any detail.

Almudín

Now used as an art gallery for exhibitions of the larger kind, the Almudín *(☎ 96 352 54 78 ext 4521, Calle Almudín 3; admission free; opening hours as per Palacio del Marques de Campo)* derives its name from the Arabic word for a measure of grain. It was built in the early 15th century to serve as the city's granary where wheat, brought in from the surrounding countryside, was stored. Notice the writing high up on the interior walls, indicating the levels that various harvests had reached and where the grain had come from.

Palacio de Benicarló

This late Gothic 15th-century palace *(☎ 96 387 61 00, Plaza de San Lorenzo 4)*, now restored and stripped back to its original state after some infelicitous 19th-century 'improvements', was once the family home of the Borjas (known in English as the infamous Borgia popes, who had their power base in Gandía, down the coast). Nowadays, it's the seat of the Cortes, the parliament of the Valencia region.

Barrio del Carmen
The Barrio del Carmen forms a near-square, bounded on its south side by Calles Caballeros and Quart, the old city's main thoroughfare, Calle Guillem de Castro to the west and Calle Serranos on its eastern flank. The curve of the old Río Turia riverbed to the north completes the pattern.

Torres de Serranos & Torres de Quart
Two imposing, twin-towered stone gates are all that remain of the old Christian-era city walls, demolished – to provide room for the city to expand – as part of a work-creation project in the mid-19th century when unemployment was high. Once the main exit to Barcelona and the north, the well preserved, 14th-century Torres de Serranos *(☎ 96 391 90 70, Plaza de los Fueros; admission free; open 9.45am-1.45pm Tues-Sun, 4.30pm-7.45pm Tues-Sat)* overlook the bed of the Río Turia. For a full 300 years, between 1586 and 1887, the towers also served as a lockup for wealthier prisoners. From their battlements you get a good panoramic view of the old quarter for less input than the long slog up the stairs of the Miguelete tower (see under Cathedral, earlier). From the towers in the lead up to Las Fallas, the Fallera Mayor (the 'queen' of that year's festivities) proclaims the *crida*, the invitation to participate to the thousands of chanting *falleros* below, followed by the first of the season's spectacular firework displays. Although admission is free, the attendant may brazenly beg a tip.

At the western extremity of the old city, the Torres de Quart *(Calle Guillem de Castro 92)*, constructed a century later, look towards Madrid and the setting sun. Designed to resemble the towers of the Castel Nuovo in Naples (which at the time belonged to Spain), this solid structure has also served as

a prison over the years. High up on the walls facing Calle Guillem de Castro, you can still see the pockmarks caused by French cannonballs during the 19th-century War of Independence, when Napoleonic troops invaded the city.

Calle Caballeros ✓
Running between the Torres de Quart and the Plaza de la Virgen, this thoroughfare (called Calle Quart at its western end) was Valencia's main highway from Roman times until the demolition of the old city walls and expansion of the city in the second half of the 19th century. Nowadays it's the nucleus of the old quarter's nightlife (see Entertainment, later), but by day it merits a stroll, and, if you're lucky and the massive doors are open, a peek into one or two of the fine patios of the large bourgeois mansions and minipalaces that flank the street.

Halfway along the Calle Caballeros is the **Galería del Tossal** *(☎ 96 398 18 03, Plaza del Tossal s/n; admission free; open 9.30am-2pm & 5pm-8pm Tues-Sat, 9.30am-2pm Sun)*, which merits a quick browse. Beneath Plaza Tossal, a swath of the wall demarcates the limits of the Moorish city and there's a small display of recently recovered artefacts, representative of Valencia's history.

La Beneficencia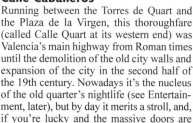
In addition to temporary exhibitions, these large premises house the **Museo de la Prehistoria** *(☎ 96 388 35 65, Calle Corona 36; admission free; open 10am-9pm daily)*. The first floor covers the Palaeolithic period to the Bronze Age. Particularly interesting are the rich deposits from the Cueva de Parpalló near Gandía, including tools, jewellery, human and animal bones and, most important of all to archaeologists, but unexciting to the lay person – over 5000 fragments of limestone bearing scoring, incisions and traces of paint.

On the second floor are artefacts from Iberian times including the famous 4th-century BC miniature plumed warrior on horseback, the Guerrero de Moixent and finds from the Tossal de Sant Miquel near Llíria. Sadly, exhibits from the Beneficencia's other permanent exhibition, the Museo de la Etnología (Folk Museum), which gave an excellent introduction to local crafts and rural and coastal lifestyles, are currently in crates, their future undecided.

Instituto Valenciano de Arte Moderno (IVAM)

The city's museum of contemporary art (☎ 96 386 30 00, Calle Guillem de Castro 118; adult/student €2.10/1.05, free Sun; open 10am-7pm Tues-Sun) lies beside the new Puente de las Artes bridge at the northwestern limit of the Barrio del Carmen. IVAM (pronounced **ee**-bam) houses an impressive permanent collection of 20th-century Spanish art, which includes a whole gallery devoted to Julio Gonzalez, the prominent Catalan metal sculptor. It also hosts excellent temporary exhibitions. Beneath it, in a gallery reserved for temporary exhibitions is a hefty length of the old Moorish city wall.

IVAM also has a second gallery, the **Centro del Carmen** (☎ 96 391 26 93, Calle Museo 2; admission free except for some special exhibitions; open 10am-2.15pm & 4pm-7.30pm Tues-Sat, 10am-9pm Sun), which puts on temporary exhibitions of contemporary art.

Plaza del Carmen

The Plaza del Carmen, an architecturally pleasing, pedestrianised square is, alas, something of a haunt for dropouts and, by night, dope dealers. On its north side is the massive 17th-century baroque facade of the **Iglesia del Carmen**. The large former convent that it once served is now occupied by two art galleries: the Museo del Siglo XIX and Centro del Carmen (see under the Museo de Bellas Artes and IVAM, respectively). The church's rundown interior has little interest except for one illuminating detail from recent Spanish history: look for a portly Generalísimo Franco, kneeling among the saints in the huge wall painting behind the altar.

Facing the church is the less flamboyant but no less impressive frontage of the **Palacio de Pineda**, built in 1728 and now a branch of the Universidad Menéndez y Pelayo, a university with its headquarters in the Basque country.

Casa de las Rocas

From the Plaza del Carmen, a short, 150m walk eastwards along Calle Roteros brings you to what is essentially a garage for carts (☎ 96 392 23 26, Calle de las Rocas 3; admission free; open 10am-2pm Mon-Fri). But las Rocas are no ordinary carts. Huge structures, the earliest dating back to the early 16th century, the paintwork darkened with age, they're wheeled out for Valencia's Corpus Christi festival in June and transported to the Plaza de la Virgen. If you speak Spanish, don't reveal the fact to the engagingly enthusiastic custodian unless you want your ear bent with detail.

PLAZA DEL AYUNTAMIENTO & AROUND
Plaza del Ayuntamiento

If the Plaza de la Virgen is the centre of Valencia City's spiritual life, the Plaza del Ayuntamiento is its temporal equivalent. It has a long history. During Moorish times, it was the palace of the local ruler, Abu Zeid. Much later it was the site of the convent of San Francisco, which had extensive market gardens. Dominating its western flank today is the Ayuntamiento (Town Hall) itself. Parts of it date from the 18th century but the majority, including its main glory, the imposing facade, was constructed in the early 20th century.

Within the town-hall building is the **Museo Histórico Municipal** (☎ 96 352 54 78; admission free; open 9am-2.30pm Mon-Fri). It houses stack upon stack of significant documents from the city's long history; a superb Medusa-headed mosaic from Roman times; the sword that Jaime I the Conqueror is reputed to have brandished as he sent the Muslims packing; and a fascinating early map of Valencia, drafted by Padre Tosca in 1704. The museum has, at the time of writing, two sections: one on the first floor, reached via the main entrance and a walk up the Ayuntamiento's main, resplendent marble stairway (well worth the effort even if you never penetrate the museum); the other approached from the building's rear, south-west corner on Calle Arzobispo Mayoral (these entry points may change during the lifetime of this book). It's complex, we grant you, but make the effort; you won't be disappointed.

Staring the Ayuntamiento in the face from the opposite, eastern perimeter is Correos, Valencia's resplendent neoclassical main post office dating from the 1920s, the winged angels on its roof would perhaps be more able to get letters swiftly to their destination than today's slow-coach service.

It's a wonder they and their fellow buildings are still standing. From 1 March until the climax of Las Fallas on 19 March, the day of San José, bang (and we mean 'bang') on the dot of 2pm (firework displays and bullfights are about the only events in town guaranteed to start on time), windows tremble to the *mascletá*, some five minutes of constant, eardrum-shattering explosions from the heart of the square.

Like a frame around the heart of the action are lines of stalls, rich with flowers. Even if you don't purchase, stroll by, gaze and sniff.

Estación del Norte

A short walk from the square down Avenida Marqués de Sotelo, or a more relaxing and pleasant one along parallel, pedestrianised Calle Ribera to its east, brings you to the Estación del Norte, no ordinary train station. Inaugurated in 1917, it's a jewel of Valencian *modernismo*, rich in decorative touches that you rarely find in what's only a functional site for mass transportation. Illustrative of Valencia's industry and the *huerta*, its surrounding market garden, the ceramic mosaics depict cheery peasant ladies in traditional costume with naked, frolicking children at their skirts, cornucopias brimming with fruit, bouquets of roses and friezes of oranges. In the main hall, a delight of mosaic and stained wood, 'bon voyage' is picked out in gold leaf in all the major European languages. 'Pleasant Journey', it wishes the anglophone passer-by.

Museo Taurino

Down a covered passageway behind the mid-19th century **Plaza de Toros** (bullring) is Valencia's small museum of bullfighting

memorabilia *(☎ 96 388 37 38, Pasaje Doctor Serra 10; admission free; open 10am-2pm Mon-Sun, 4pm-8pm Tues-Sun)*. It merits a visit if images of strutting machomen in sequinned tights and funny hats appeal. Seriously – and, wow, the bullfighting fraternity takes itself seriously – there's a good 15-minute commentary-less video shown on the half hour (in principle, but times sometimes slip), portraying a bull's life on the range all the way up to its tortured death in the ring. You can also prance out into the very heart of the bullring itself, sink to one knee and slowly drag your daysack in the sand. Dream on...

Museo Valenciano de la Ilustración y la Modernidad

The high point of Valencia's Museum of the Enlightenment *(MUVIM; ☎ 96 388 37 30, Calle Guillem de Castro 8; admission free; open 10am-2pm Tues-Sun, 4pm-8pm Tues-Sat)*, a trawl through the last 300 years inaugurated in 2001, has to be its permanent, multimedia exhibition **La Aventura del Conocimiento** (Adventure of Thought). It's an odd concept: the history of ideas and thought presented through images, dioramas and dialogue. The English commentary is sometimes muffled and drowned by background music and ambient sound, but just go with the flow of the images. Hour-long visits start every half hour. On arrival, ask for the English version of the audio or, to avoid hanging around, phone in advance to reserve a slot.

Museo Nacional de Cerámica (Palacio del Marqués de Dos Aguas)

Originally constructed in the 15th century, this palace *(☎ 96 351 63 92, Calle Poeta Querol 2; admission €2.40, free Sat afternoon & Sun morning; open 10am-2pm Tues-Sun, 4pm-8pm Tues-Sat)*, was elaborately modified in the mid-18th century, when the main doorway was added. The alabaster door surround was designed by Hipólito Rovira, a local sculptor who later went insane and committed suicide. With only a pinch of imagination, you can see the makings of madness in its over-the-top whorls of vegetation, twists of water and sinuous pair of Herculean caryatids propping up the whole. One of the finest examples of extravagant rococo sculpture in Spain, it's not to be missed, even if you simply walk by. Inside is the Museo Nacional de Cerámica which displays ceramics from around the world – and especially the renowned local production centres of Manises, Alcora and Paterna.

Colegio del Patriarca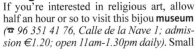

If you're interested in religious art, allow half an hour or so to visit this bijou **museum** (☎ 96 351 41 76, Calle de la Nave 1; admission €1.20; open 11am-1.30pm daily). Small

but strong, especially on both Spanish and Flemish Renaissance painting, it has a number of canvases by both Juan de Juanes and Ribalta and a trio of El Grecos. You'll find it on the first floor, off a tranquil and porticoed internal patio. As you leave, poke your head into the patio of the adjacent church. Above the door is a desiccated, centuries-old alligator, originally a gift from South America. It's hung there as an exhortation to silence since the alligator, unlike the church's more garrulous parishioners, has no tongue.

Trinquet

To see this very Valencian ball game, played with the bare hands, visit **Bar Trinquet Pelayo** (☎ 96 357 07 56, Calle Pelayo 6), near

---

Pelota Valenciana

So you thought pelota was the preserve of the Basques? In its several forms Pelota Valenciana has been played ever since it was first recorded in the 14th century. In 1391, a proclamation, symbolically rescinded in 1991, 600 years later, banned it from the streets because of the inconvenience to passers by.

Whereas the Basques hurl the ball from a curved basket, Valencian variants of the game are played with bare hands, which are taped to reduce the impact of the small, hard leather ball, and the scoring system has more in common with tennis.

The most popular form is *trinquet*, played on a court of the same name that's often affiliated to a bar. It's an all-in game played over a narrow net. Everything counts – the rear walls, side walls and even the raked seating where spectators sit. As in the Basque game, men (the audience tends to be exclusively male) eagerly place side bets at popular sessions and it's not rare for quite large wads of euros to pass from hand to hand.

All around the Comunidad, you'll see high-walled, three-sided courts for *frontón*, a game akin to squash. This other popular and peculiarly Valencian game is usually played with a short-handled racquet but the hard men pit themselves against each other bare handed.

You may come across regional variants. *Llargues*, more popular in Alicante province, is usually played in the street. *Galotxa*, too, is a street sport, usually contested between teams of three. A playing area similar to that of a very deep tennis court is staked out and a net slung across the middle. *Raspall*, much the same, is also more popular in the south of the Comunidad.

MARTIN HARRIS

Among some of the 50 other towns in the Comunidad that boast a trinquet court are Gandía, Llíria, Sagunto and Castellón. If you want to delve more into the game, contact the Federación Valenciana de Pelota (☎ 96 374 95 58), Calle Centelles 9-11, 46006 Valencia.

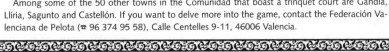

Estación del Norte. Matches begin around 5.30pm, Wednesday to Saturday and admission costs from €3 to €5 according to the calibre of the players that day.

PLAZA MERCADO

Facing each other across Plaza Mercado are a pair of magnificent buildings, each a masterpiece of its era.

Mercado Central

Set aside time to prowl Valencia's *modernista* covered market (☎ *96 382 91 01, Plaza Mercado 6; open 8am-2.30pm Mon-Sat)* and visit some of the over 900 stalls there (see also Self-Catering under Places to Eat). Completed in 1928, the market is a swirl of smells, movement and colour. The fish market, in an annex on its northern side, has everything from eels, still slithering, to swordfish. Most colourful of all are the stalls brimming with shellfish.

An even finer *modernista* building, the **Mercado de Colón** on Calle Cirilo Amorós is no longer, alas, used as a market. It was being renovated at the time of writing and has yet to discover a new role.

La Lonja

Fifteenth-century Gothic La Lonja (☎ *96 352 54 78, Plaza Mercado s/n, admission free; open 9.15am-2pm & 4.30pm-8pm Mon-Sat, 9.15am-1.30pm Sun)* was founded in 1498 as an early Valencian commodity exchange and meeting place for the merchant classes. A Unesco World Heritage site, its clinical, sweeping lines are the perfect antidote if you're suffering from a twinge of indigestion at the rich baroque around town. The rib-vaulted ceiling of the main colonnaded hall is supported by what the experts call helicoidal columns – wonderful, slim, twisted pillars curling up high like sticks of barley sugar. The Consulat del Mar (closed for renovations at the time of writing), a side room that was once a separate building, has a stunning *artesonado* (moulded ceiling). Between 9.30am and 1.30pm on Sunday, the Lonja resumes its trading role, albeit on a small scale, when it's the meeting place for coin and stamp collectors.

Watch the Birdie

Before you go into the Mercado Central, step back and look at the cockatoo (or could it be a budgie?), green with verdigris, on its roof. According to legend, desperate fathers from the poverty-stricken villages of inland Aragón would bring to the big city a son the family could no longer afford to feed. 'Here, look at that strange green bird up there', the father would say. Then, as the child gazed upwards, Dad would slip away into the crowd. And the boy, a de facto orphan, would find work as a market porter or day labourer – if luck was on his side.

Iglesia de Santa Catalina & Plaza Redonda

A brief walk along Calle Mantas brings you to the Iglesia de Santa Catalina *(Calle Zapatería)*. The church itself, badly knocked about in the civil war, is starkly impressive inside. Its tall, 17th-century hexagonal baroque bell tower is one of the city's best-known landmarks. Nearby, stalls in the small circular Plaza Redonda sell bits and bobs, buttons and bows, clothes, and locally made crafts and ceramics. If you pass by between 10am and 1pm on Friday, you can see lacemakers at work. On Sunday, the square trills with the song of caged birds as it and surrounding streets become a flea and pet market, specialising in mournful kittens and puppies.

NORTH OF THE TURIA RIVERBED

Museo de Bellas Artes

On the north side of the former riverbed of the Río Turia, Valencia's Fine Arts Museum (☎ *96 360 57 93, Calle San Pío V 9; admission free; open 10am-2.15pm & 4pm-7.30pm Tues-Sat, 10am-7.30pm Sun)* ranks among Spain's best. Within it you'll find works by greats such as El Greco, Goya and Velázquez. It's also well endowed with canvases from Valencia's first golden age of painting, including works by internationally recognised artists such as Ribera, Ribalta and Juan de Juanes. You'll also find what is referred to as the Valencian impressionist school and works by its leading exponents, Sorolla and Pinazo. To get here take bus No 6, 8, 16, 26, 29, 36 or 79 from the Plaza del Ayuntamiento.

Right next door to IVAM's offshoot, the Centro del Carmen, and interconnecting with it, the Museo de Bellas Artes has a second gallery of its own, the **Museo del Siglo XIX** (☎ 96 369 30 88, Calle Museo 2; admission free; open as per the Centro del Carmen). Although its name translates as the 'Museum of the 19th Century', its temporary exhibitions are by no means confined to this epoch.

Museo de Ciencias Naturales

The main section of this relatively small natural science museum (☎ 96 352 54 78 ext 4313, Jardines del Real, Calle San Pio V s/n; admission free; open 9.30am-2pm & 5.30pm-9pm Tues-Sun) has an ambitious theme: the history of life. It has some spectacular local and international fossils and shells. The high spot – literally; it must be nearly 10m tall – is the skeleton of a huge megathere, a prehistoric beast to rival the dinosaur. Like the fossils of more modest extinct animals that prowl at its feet, it was found in Argentina.

Implanted within the Jardines del Real (see Parks & Gardens later in this chapter), it makes a stimulating afternoon for children (exhibits are also captioned in English), particularly if you combine it with a visit to the zoo next door.

Jardín Zoológico

Among the highlights of Valencia's small zoo (☎ 96 360 08 22, Jardines del Real, Calle San Pio V s/n; adult/child €3.60/1.80; open 10am-sunset daily) are a rhino, a pair of somnolent hippos and a drop-dead gorgeous orang-utan called Boris. At a date as yet unspecified, the museum will be moving to new premises at the western end of the old Turia riverbed. Let's hope they leave behind the dreamy new-age piped music that intrudes everywhere.

OTHER MUSEUMS
Museo Fallero

This museum (☎ 96 352 17 30, Plaza Monteolivete s/n; adult/child €1.80/0.60; open 9.15am-1.30pm & 4.30pm-7.30pm Tues-Sat, 9.15am-1.30pm Sun) is dedicated to the festival of Las Fallas (see Special Events later in this chapter and the special section 'Fiestas'). Ninots are near-life-size figurines that strut and pose at the base of each falla. The ninot indultat ('reprieved' or 'exempted' and selected by popular vote) is the only one from among thousands of ninots to be saved from the flames each year. After visiting the nearby Ciudad de las Artes y las Ciencias, you could pop in here for a touch of a more traditional Valencia.

Casa-Museo de Blasco Ibáñez

This small, sparse museum (☎ 96 356 47 85, Calle Isabel Villena 156; admission free; open 9.15am-2pm Tues-Sun, 4.15pm-8pm Tues-Sat) was the summer residence of Blasco Ibáñez, Valencia's most famous literary son and author of, among many other works, The Four Horsemen of the Apocalypse, which was twice made into a Hollywood film, the original version starring Rudolf Valentino. It houses many of his personal belongings and furniture of the period.

CONTEMPORARY ARCHITECTURE

Valencia isn't all Gothic, baroque and 19th-century revival. The most exciting contemporary development is the Ciudad de las Artes y las Ciencias (see earlier). A visit to the site is a must if you enjoy daring construction, even if you only view the complex from the outside. On a more modest scale, the Puente Calatrava, nicknamed the peineta because it resembles the comb that women wear beneath the mantilla, spans the Turia riverbed and is another bold and relatively recent addition to the urban skyline. North of the riverbed, 2km along Avenida Pio XII, is the **Palacio de Congresos**, designed by British architect Sir Norman Foster, whose many other imprints upon cities of the world include the dramatic glass dome topping the Reichstag – the parliament building in Berlin. Nicknamed the pez varado (beached fish), its slender columns, which harmonise with the vertical lines of the fountains playing in the forecourt, and shimmering aluminium, topped by the trowel-shaped roof, take the breath away. To get there, take Metro Line 4 or bus No 62 or 63. Alternatively, experience a virtual visit at W www .palcongres-vlc.com and save yourself the busfare.

PARKS & GARDENS
Jardines del Turia
The Jardines del Turia, in the former riverbed, are a 7km-long lung of green, and a glorious mix of cycling, jogging and walking paths, playing fields, trees, fountains, lawns and playgrounds – see Lilliputian kids scrambling over a magnificent, ever-patient **Gulliver** *(open 10am-8pm; admission free)* east of the Palau de la Música. If you're heading for the Ciudad de las Artes y las Ciencias, which occupy their eastern end, it's a very pleasant way to get there.

Jardines del Real
Reaching down to the Jardines del Turia are the Jardines del Real *(Royal Gardens; open 7.30am-9.30pm daily Apr-Sept, 7.30am-8.30pm daily Oct-Mar)*, more commonly called Los Viveros. Popular with Valencianos, especially on Sunday morning when you almost have to elbow your way through the throng, the gardens another lovely spot for a stroll and a drink at one of the several cafe terraces. Within these gardens are the **Museo de Ciencias Naturales**, the Natural Science Museum, and the **Jardín Zoológico** a small zoo (see earlier for details).

Jardín de Montforte
Altogether more intimate than Jardines del Real, this garden *(Calle Monforte s/n; open 10.30am-sunset daily)*, a little haven of tranquillity, is laid out on formal, classical lines. It's a favourite spot for bridal photos, both for those who tie the knot in the small pavilion in its north-east corner and also for others coming from further afield to enjoy its charm. There's not a more pleasant place in town to munch your sandwiches, catch up on the newspaper or grab a quick nap.

Jardín Botánico
The Botanical Gardens *(☎ 96 315 68 00, Calle Quart 80; admission €0.30; open*

10am-6pm Tues-Sun), established in 1802 and nowadays administered by the University of Valencia, was the first botanical garden to be established in Spain. With its mature trees and plants and an extensive cactus garden, it too is a shady place to relax. You'll enjoy the clean lines of its recently restored 19th-century shade house, which has a small pond at its heart.

BEACHES
Valencia City's beach is the broad **Playa de la Malvarrosa**, east of the town centre. It's bordered by the **Paseo Marítimo** (promenade) and a string of restaurants. Those restaurants at the southern end, nearer the port, in Las Arenas, are famous for their paella. One block back, lively bars and discos thump out the beat in summer. For a selection of the best, see Entertainment later.

A veritable fleet of buses service the port and beach – a total of eight routes, including No 19 from Plaza del Ayuntamiento, and Nos 1 and 2 from outside the bus station or on the Gran Vías. Bus Nos 22 and 23 are special additional summer services. Another, swifter option is the high-speed tram, best picked up at Pont de Fusta or the Benimaclet Metro junction.

For another good beach, scarcely a half-hour bus ride away, see Playa El Saler under Around Valencia City.

LANGUAGE COURSES
One way to get stuck into a little Spanish before you travel is to work through the BBC's excellent course for absolute beginners, *Talk Spanish*. It's based upon Valencia and, as you follow it, you'll meet a range of locals and get a feel for the city before you even leave home. British readers can pick it up on BBC2's The Learning Zone, where it's repeated regularly. Wherever you are in the world, you can access the course and its accompanying video snippets, plus a whole range of other Spanish courses suitable for all levels, at W www.bbc.co.uk/education/ languages/spanish/talk.

In town, *Intereuropa (☎ 96 394 49 95, W www.ctv.es/intereuropa, Plaza del Ayuntamiento 5, 1st floor)* has classes ranging from the hyperintensive to a more leisurely twice weekly commitment. They're strong on student outings and extracurricular activities and can arrange accommodation with Spanish families or in a shared apartment. *Alos (☎ 96 393 13 14, e alos@terra.es, Calle Po-lo y Peyrolón 23)* is also excellent for individual or small group tuition. If you're planning to be in town for some months the public-sector *Escuela Oficial de Idiomas (☎ 96 348 77 55, Calle Llano de la Zaidía 19)* is another option, although it's much less flexible in the courses it offers. To register, you'll need to be around in September or in February. Bring your money, your ID and ample reserves of patience; the cumbersome bureaucracy will have you climbing up the wall.

ORGANISED TOURS

Valencia Bus Turístico (☎ 96 342 02 85) Fares €7.80. This company runs 90-minute city tours with a recorded commentary in eight languages. Its double-decker buses depart half-hourly from 10.30am to 9.30pm. It's fastidious, too: 'for sanitary reasons it will be given a new set of earphones to every single person', proclaims its pamphlet in charming not-quite-English.

The same company has also introduced a similar multilingual tour of La Albufera (€9.65; two hours including a half-hour boat trip on the Albufera lake; see Around Valencia City later in this chapter for details). Regular times and dates were still to be established at the time of writing. The company hoped to sustain four runs per day, leaving at 10.30am, 1pm, 4.30pm and 7pm, Monday to Saturday.

Both services leave from Plaza de la Reina. Look for their fluorescent orange, hard-to-miss buses.

A cheaper, although much less comprehensive, option is *EMT* bus No 5, El Interior, which will take you around the circumference of the town's inner oval (see Orientation, earlier) for the standard €0.80 fare. It too bills itself as a *bus turístico* and its TV monitors (not available on all buses) indicate major sights as you pass them. Alternatively, and for the same standard price,

take a trip on the No 5B, a gas-powered minibus that meanders its way around the *centro histórico* and gives you a good overall orientation of the city.

If you're in a group, a half-hour ride around the centre of town in a *horse-drawn carriage* (€30), leaving from Plaza de la Reina, is a pleasant way to see the main sights.

Ergobike (see Bicycle under Getting Around later in this chapter) organises friendly one- to three-hour tours around town on recumbent bikes – an easily acquired skill if you can ride a normal bicycle – at the perfect pace for assimilating things.

Every weekend between February and December, buses sponsored by the Diputación, the provincial governing body, take off to explore the farther flung and less well known gems of the province. A full day out, beginning at the antisocial hour of 8am and including transport, guide services and an agreeably drawn-out lunch based upon local specialities, costs €23. It's a great day out even if your Spanish is limited. Ask for the brochure *Ven de Excursión con la Diputación* at larger travel agencies, where you can book, or at any tourist office.

SPECIAL EVENTS

On 22 January, when people have scarcely recovered from the festivities of Christmas, which led into New Year, which in turn led into Los Reyes (Día de los Reyes Magos; see Public Holidays in the Facts for the Visitor chapter), the city sets the tone for the year by celebrating the feast day of San Vicente Mártir. Or rather, some of the city does. San Vicente Mártir is associated with the heart of town, '*cruces por dentro*', and is celebrated within the bounds of the old city crosses. This means children from the heart of town can thumb their noses that day at friends farther out, for whom it's just another school day.

Valencia's festival par excellence and one which is unrivalled anywhere else in Spain, is Las Fallas, a week of street revelry leading up to the feast of San José on 19 March. For details, see the special section 'Fiestas'.

The seaside suburb of La Malvarrosa celebrates Semana Santa (Holy Week) with elaborate processions. On the second Sunday after Easter, the Fiesta de San Vicente Ferrer (quite different from his namesake, San Vicente Mártir) sees colourful parades and miracle plays performed around town. The following day, all the Comunidad Valenciana observes a holiday in honour of San Vicente Ferrer, its patron saint.

On the second Sunday in May, the effigy of the Virgen de los Desamparados, patron of the city, makes the short journey across the Plaza de la Virgen to the cathedral's southern door, hemmed in by fervent believers struggling to touch her.

The festival of Corpus Christi, held in June, is the occasion for a major procession and for the Rocas (giant carriages; see Casa de las Rocas, earlier) to be trundled into the Plaza de la Virgen, where teenagers enact religious playlets.

On 24 June each year, the day of San Juan, which coincides with pre-Christian midsummer's day, thousands spend the evening on the Playa de la Malvarrosa, picnicking around campfires in the sand. They take part in a traditional act of cleansing where you wash your feet in the ocean and write your bad habits on a piece of paper, which you then throw into the embers.

Valencia's Feria de Julio (July Fair) features a packed, month-long programme of performing arts, brass-band competitions, a jazz festival, free concerts, bullfights and fireworks. Among the most colourful events is the *batalla de flores* (battle of the flowers), when decorated, horse-drawn floats parade down the Paseo de la Alameda while their occupants and spectators pelt each other with tens of thousands of orange marigolds.

Every October, Valencia hosts a festival of Mediterranean cinema. The 9 October marks the Día de la Comunidad, a holiday throughout the region to commemorate the city's liberation from the Arabs in 1238. In Valencia City, it's celebrated in style on the stroke of midnight on the 8th by an unmissable fireworks display, the Gran Festival de Pirotécnia, where an internationally renowned foreign manufacturer is pitted against the best that the locals can offer. The day itself is also marked by a parade of Moros and Cristianos.

PLACES TO STAY

You'll generally be able to squeeze yourself into a budget bed at any time of year. Mid-range and top-end accommodation, however, can sometimes be a problem. Valencia is a popular fair and conference venue and when one or another is in full swing, a spare bed can be hard to come by. Paradoxically, many hotels offer healthy discounts both at weekends and during the latter half of July and August, when most of Spain is on holiday and accommodation along the coast is bursting at the seams. If you intend to visit the city during the week leading up to Las Fallas, you should reserve months in advance otherwise you'll find yourself sleeping under one of the bridges spanning the former riverbed.

PLACES TO STAY – BUDGET
Camping
Devesa Gardens (☎ 96 161 11 36, fax 96 161 11 05, e *campingdevesagardens@ctv.es, Carretera el Saler)* €3/3.60/3 per person/tent/car. This place, the nearest camping ground to Valencia, lies 15km south of town. Open year round, it's a 15-minute walk from El Saler beach. Take the toll-free motorway that begins beside the Ciudad de las Artes y las Ciencias.

Apartments
An attractive option if you're planning to visit Valencia for a few days is to hire an apartment in Port Saplaya. The apartments are 4.5km up the Barcelona motorway, the first coastal resort to the north of Valencia and 15 minutes' away by car or taxi. The minimum stay during July and August is one week and prices rise to about €90/100/110 per night for apartments catering for 4/6/8 guests. For the rest of the year, you can book in for as little as two nights, paying no more than €37/47/63. Buses run at least hourly and a taxi to or from the heart of town costs about €9. Two agencies among the several in Port Saplaya are Saplaya (☎ 96 371 36 11, fax 96 371 41 13), Avenida de la Huerta 2, Port Saplaya, 46120 Valencia, and Serviplaya (☎ 96 372 3798, fax 96 372 36 69), Plaza Mayor 9.

Hostels

Hôme (☎ 96 392 40 63, Calle Cadirers 11) and *Hôme Lonja* (☎ 96 391 62 29, Calle Lonja 4) Dorm beds/singles/doubles/triples/quads €13.85/20.50/29.50/54.10/43.30. We warmly recommend these two recently opened, private hostels. The decor's cheery and there's a cosy living room with TV, video and small library, cooking facilities, corridor bathrooms, Internet access and a washing machine (€3.60 per load). They'll store your backpack for €0.60 per day. Reserve a room at either on Ⓦ www.likeathome.net. A true *hôme* from home.

Albergue Las Arenas (☎/fax 96 356 42 88, Calle Eugenia Viñes 24) Dorm beds Adult/child €10.25/7.20. Albergue Las Arenas is a fairly tatty place but it's friendly; they have campfires in summer and offer free Internet access plus – a neat touch, this – free Spanish lessons. It's also a pebble's throw from the beach and within earshot of La Malvarrosa's wild, summer nightlife. Open year round, it has a small kitchen area for guest use. Bus No 32 from Plaza del Ayuntamiento pulls up right outside. Ask for the Las Arenas stop. From the Gran Vía or bus station, take No 1 or 2 and ask the driver to indicate the Virgen del Sufragio stop.

Albergue La Paz (☎ 96 369 01 52, fax 96 360 70 02, Ⓔ j.badenas@valenciamail.net, Avenida del Puerto 69) Adult/child B&B €12/9.65. A student hostel during the academic year, this place is open to everyone between July and September. Take bus No 19 from Plaza del Ayuntamiento or No 2 from the bus station.

Hostales & Pensiones

There are a few scruffy *hostales* (budget hotels) around the western side of the train station, but the budget options in the Barrio del Carmen or around Plaza del Ayuntamiento are better value.

Barrio del Carmen *Hospedería del Pilar* (☎ 96 391 66 00, Plaza Mercado 19) Basic singles/doubles/triples €9.65/18/23.50, with shower €13/23.25/29. This rather rambling place has clean, pleasant rooms.

Hostal El Rincón (☎ 96 391 79 98, Calle Carda 11) Basic singles/doubles €10/18, with bathroom €13/24. The basic rooms here are rather small and dim yet quite acceptable. By contrast, its 11 renovated rooms with bathroom and air-con/heating represent excellent value.

Around Plaza del Ayuntamiento *Pensión París* (☎/fax 96 352 67 66, Calle Salvá 12, 1st & 3rd floors) Basic singles/doubles/triples €16.25/25.25/36, doubles/triples with shower €29/36, doubles with bathroom €31.25. The centrally heated rooms and corridor bathrooms are spotless at this tranquil place.

Hostal-Residencia Universal (☎/fax 96 351 53 84, Calle Barcas 5, 2nd-4th floors) Basic singles/doubles/triples €16.25/25.25/36, doubles with shower €29. The Universal is run by the same family as Pensión París to a similar high standard.

Hostal Castelar (☎/fax 96 351 31 99, Calle de Ribera 1, 3rd floor) Singles/doubles €15/27, with shower €18/30. Add €3 for high-season rates. All the basic rooms here have a TV. Ask for a room at the front for an excellent view of the Plaza del Ayuntamiento.

Hostal-Residencia Alicante (☎/fax 96 351 22 96, Calle de Ribera 8, 2nd floor) Singles/doubles with shower €18/26, with bathroom €24/33. Across the road from Hostal Castelar, the colourfully tiled hallways of this welcoming place lead to pleasant rooms, all of which have heating and TV. Some doubles with bathroom have air-con, for which you pay a small supplement.

PLACES TO STAY – MID-RANGE

Hostal Antigua Morellana (☎/fax 96 391 57 73, Calle En Bou 2) Singles/doubles with air-con & heating €29/42. This friendly, warmly recommended family-run hotel occupies a recently renovated 18th-century building and is excellent value for money.

Hostal Moratín (☎/fax 96 352 12 20, Calle de Moratín 15, 4th & 5th floors). Singles/doubles/triples with shower €26.50/33.10/49.60, with bathroom €36/45.25/67.75. This is a quiet, welcoming place on a traffic-free street in the heart of town.

Hotel Londres (☎ *96 351 22 44, fax 96 352 15 08, Calle Barcelonina 1)* Singles with shower €29, singles/doubles/triples/ quads with bathroom €32.25/54.10/64.50/ 80.50. The uppermost rooms of Hotel Londres offer fine views of the Plaza del Ayuntamiento. The hotel has been recently refurbished and all rooms have satellite TV, air-con and central heating.

Hotel Continental (☎ *96 353 52 82, fax 96 353 11 13,* W *www.contitel.es, Calle Correos 8)* Singles/doubles €40.60/63.25, rooms €54.10 July & Aug. All rooms in this modern, friendly place have air-con, heating and satellite TV. Prices also include breakfast.

PLACES TO STAY – TOP END

Since Valencia is a business centre, the more up-market hotels struggle to fill rooms at weekends. Many offer fat discounts of up to one-third at weekends and throughout the second half of July and August. We quote the normal, weekday tariff. There are five good choices in the heart of town.

Hotel Reina Victoria (☎ *96 352 04 87, fax 96 352 27 21,* e *hreinavictoriavalencia@ husa.es, Calle Barcas 4)* Singles/doubles/ triples €73.35/88.05/112.70. This grand old place, although comprehensively renovated and equipped to the most demanding standards, has preserved its good old-fashioned charm.

Hotel Excelsior (☎ *96 351 46 12, fax 96 352 34 78,* e *cataloni@hotels-catalonia .es, Calle Barcelonina 5)* Singles/doubles €96/120. Just along the street from Hotel Londres, this 81-room hotel has also undergone a recent fundamental overhaul. Attractively furnished rooms come equipped with air-con, satellite TV, safe, minibar and – an advantage in the heart of town – double-glazed windows.

Hotel Inglés (☎ *96 351 64 26, fax 96 394 02 51,* e *melia.confort.ingles@solmelia .es, Calle Marqués Dos Aguas 6)* Singles/ doubles €93.35/119. Now part of the Melia chain, Hotel Inglés offers a discounted weekend and high-summer doubles rate of €72, including breakfast that's particularly good value for money.

Hotel Ad Hoc (☎ *96 391 91 40, fax 96 391 36 67,* e *adhoc@nexo.net, Calle Boix 4)* Singles/doubles €87.25/119.60. Established relatively recently, this small 28-room hotel, in a quiet side street has quickly and justifiably established a reputation for itself.

Hotel Astoria Palace (☎ *96 398 10 00, fax 96 398 10 10,* W *www.hotel-astoria -palace.com, Plaza Rodrigo Botet 5)* Singles/ doubles €193.50/235. Self-consciously modern, and at the tip-top end, the Astoria Palace is a favourite with visiting dignitaries. Don't leave without visiting the roof-garden terrace, which offers a fine view over the heart of town.

PLACES TO EAT

Valencia is the capital of *la huerta,* a fertile coastal agricultural plain which supplies the city with delightfully fresh fruit and vegetables. It's a fishing port as well so the bounty of the sea also comes fresh to your table.

Restaurants – Budget

La Utielana (☎ *96 352 94 14, Plaza Picadero dos Aguas 3)* Meals €10. Open Mon-Sat lunch. Not easy to track down and tucked away just off Calle Prócida, La Utielana, which is excellent value and unpretentious, merits a few minutes' sleuthing.

Cervecería-Restaurante Pema (☎ *96 352 66 50, Calle Mosén Femades 3)* Also just off Plaza del Ayuntamiento, here you can have anything from a simple tapa to a full-blown meal. Its weekday lunch *menú* at €7.25, including a drink and coffee, ranks among central Valencia's best deals.

Restaurante El Generalife (☎ *96 391 78 99, Calle Caballeros 5)* Menú €8. The *menú del día* at El Generalife, just off Plaza de la Virgen, is considerably more imaginative than most. For this reason, it's so popular that you'll probably have to wait to be served unless you arrive early.

Los Madriles (☎ *96 374 23 35, Avenida Antic Regne de Valencia 50)* Meals €12-15. Open Tues-Sun. This tiny, family-run place does excellent home-style cooking based upon the freshest of ingredients.

Tasca Jesús (☎ *96 351 13 22, Calle de Jesús 22)* Open Mon-Fri & Sat eve. Meals from €12. Sides of ham like Sumo wrestlers' legs festoon the bar and walls of this always packed, award-winning restaurant. Their lunch menú at €6 is exceptional value.

La Fusta (☎ 96 334 59 96, Calle de Joaquín Costa 26) Mains €5-7. Open Mon-Fri & Sat eve. Preceded by an agreeable small bar, this small restaurant with its high ceiling and natural wooden beams, typical of Valencia City's traditional architecture, does an excellent-value midday menú for only €7.50.

La Carmé (☎ 96 392 25 32, Plaza Mosén Sorell) Open Tues-Sat. Set meals €15. Except for seasonal variations, La Carmé's menú – and they keep things simple and only do a set meal – has scarcely changed in the last 15 years. Why should it when, with its pleasing decor of wood and bare brick and friendly service, the place offers such superb value?

Tapinería (☎ 96 391 54 40, Calle Tapinería 16) Menú €15. Open Mon-Fri & Sat eve. Since it's so small, it's wise to make a reservation at this intimate split-level, reliable place, especially for dinner.

Restaurants – Mid-Range & Top End

Seu-Xerea (☎ 96 392 40 00, Calle Conde Almodóvar 4, ⓦ www.seuxerea.tdv.net) Meals around €25. Open Mon-Fri & Sat eve. This welcoming place has an inventive a-la-carte menu, with dishes that are both international and rooted in Spain, and it keeps an even more impressive wine cellar. It does a warmly recommended lunch menú for €15.

El Tossal (☎ 96 391 59 13, Calle Quart 6) Mains €7.50-11.50, menú based upon rice dishes €10. Open Mon-Fri & Sat eve. Closed Aug. Just off bustling Plaza del Tossal, this airy restaurant has a short, simple menu. The food is so attractively presented that it's almost a shame to tuck in and destroy the composition.

Restaurante Chust Godoy (☎ 96 391 38 15, Calle Boix 6) Mains €14.50-19. Next door to Hotel Ad Hoc, the Chust Godoy isn't

large white triangular or square platters, is delicious and inventive.

Calle Mosén Femades, a pedestrian street one block south-east of Plaza del Ayuntamiento, has a cluster of superb upmarket seafood restaurants. Take your credit card; the quality comes at a price. Perhaps the one with the best reputation is *Palacio de la Bellota (☎ 96 351 53 61, Calle Mosén Femades 7)* open Monday to Saturday. For a full seafood splurge, budget about €50 to €60 per head.

Paella, Rice & Fish

Valencianos normally eat rice only at lunchtime. Then locals by the hundred head for Las Arenas, just north of the port, where there's a long line of restaurants, all serving up the real stuff. They're all much the same and, for less than €12, you can enjoy a three-course meal overlooking the beach.

La Pepica (☎ 96 371 03 66, Paseo Neptuno 6) The food at La Pepica, last of the line of restaurants and more expensive than its competitors, is less impressive than its reputation as a place where Ernest Hemingway, among other luminaries, once strutted.

The other traditional place for a lunchtime paella or other rice concoction is the village of El Palmar, beside the Albufera lake (see Around Valencia City, later in this chapter).

La Lonja del Pescado Frito (☎ 96 355 35 35, Calle Eugenia Viñes 243) Meals around €12. Open 8.30pm-11pm Tues-Sun, 8.30pm-11pm & 1.30pm-4pm Sat & Sun (open weekends only Nov-Feb). One block back from the beach at Malvarrosa and occupying an unadorned shed right beside the Eugenia Viñes tram stop, this bustling place is unbeatable value for fresh fish. Grab an order form as you enter and fill it in at your table.

El Forcat (☎ 96 391 12 13, Calle Roteros 12) 2 mains & dessert €11. If you don't want to slog out to the beach, El Forcat, in the Barrio del Carmen, does a wide range of rice dishes and serves by the portion.

Tapas

Rausell (☎ 96 384 31 93, Calle Ángel Guimerá 61) Open Wed-Mon. Rausell, excellent for tapas, also does takeaway, anything

Valencia's low-key neoclassical post office, complete with angels

The colours of the Comunidad

The cathedral gets the blues.

Romanesque Puerto del Palau: part of the city's eclectic cathedral

Museo de las Ciencias Príncipe Felipe – a sci-fi whale's ribcage

The reptilian Hemisfèric, hunched over its glassy pool, houses a planetarium and IMAX cinema.

Valencia City's vibrant old quarter, packed with historic buildings

Inner-city awnings

Soak up the sangria with some *churros, buñuelos y chocolate*.

from a ración of Russian salad to a paella for eight. It's justifiably popular for both lunch and dinner and reservations are essential at the weekend, even for takeaway.

Villaplana (☎ *96 385 06 13, Calle Doctor Sanchis Sivera 24)* Open Tues-Sun. Handy, like Rausell, for tapas before a roustabout night around the Mercado de Abastos (see Entertainment), this is another popular spot where tables come at a premium unless you arrive early.

Las Cuevas (☎ *96 391 71 96, Calle Samaniego 9)* Aptly named 'The Caves', this low-ceilinged, semi-basement place carries a huge range of tapas. Pick from the splendours displayed on or behind the bar or, if you can handle Spanish at a machine-gun pace, ask the owner to rattle off the menu. It's a real *tour de force*.

Bodega Montaña (☎ *96 367 23 14, Calle José Benlliure 69)* Around €20 for a good selection of tapas. Open Tues-Sat & Sun lunch. Serving wines and tapas ever since 1836, Bodega Montaña with its marble bar, barrels and yellowing posters is a Valencian institution. It carries a good wine list. It's in the Cabañal district.

If the sound and scent of fresh, boned sardines sizzling on the griddle drives you wild, call by *Tasca Ángel* (☎ *96 391 78 35, Calle Purísima 2)*, established in 1946 and something of a Valencian institution. Half a dozen sardines sluiced down with a small glass of white wine will set you back €3.50. It's beside The Lounge cafe.

Still strictly from the sea and an easy walk away is: *Bar Pilar* (☎ *96 391 04 97, Calle Moro Zeit 13)*. Just off Plaza del Tossal, Bar Pilar does the finest, freshest mussels in town. Ask for an *entero* (€3), a portion of mussels in a spicy soup, which you scoop up with a spare shell. If you're eating at the bar, etiquette demands that you dump your empty shells in the plastic trough at your feet. Although cramped, it's also an excellent place for tapas.

Sandwiches & Snacks
Ñam Ñam (☎ *96 351 48 37, Calle San Andrés 4)* Sandwiches €2.30-4, salads €3.50-6.25. Open Mon-Fri & Sat lunch. Ñam Ñam

(Yum Yum in English – call by and you'll know why) is several cuts above your average sandwich place. Be sure to finish off with one of their homemade desserts.

S'Horabaixa (☎ *96 391 21 77, Calle Conde Almodóvar 2)* Open Tues-Sun, eve only. With its cosy decor, S'Horabaixa is popular for its crisp salads and imaginative selection of tasty, open sandwiches, many based upon Mallorcan recipes.

Bocatame (☎ *96 391 08 70, Calle Turia 61) Bocadillos* €6-10. Open from 8pm Tues-Sun. Bocatame (Eat Me) is the place to go for scrummy bocadillos (French-bread sandwiches) in a pleasant setting, especially when its summer *terraza* (terrace) is open.

Eating Ethnic
New trattorias, pizza and pasta joints seem to spring up weekly.

Pizzeria La Vita é Bella (☎ *96 352 21 31, Calle d'En Llop 4)* Mains €4.50-7.50. Just off Plaza del Ayuntamiento, this cosy cafe-bar occupies a tastefully restored draper's shop. In addition to good pizzas and pastas, it also does mouth-watering ice creams.

In the heart of town, there's a trio of good, stylish Italian restaurants, all under the same ownership and all are open daily.

La Pappardella (☎ *96 391 89 15, Calle Bordadores 5)* Meals around €10. Built around a central patio, La Pappardella has an ultrafriendly young staff.

Al Pomodoro (☎ *96 391 48 00, Calle del Mar 22)* Pizzas €5-7.50, salads €5-6.50. The food is great and the clientele primarily young at this attractive split-level place, all bare brickwork and beams.

Maramao (☎ *96 392 31 74, Calle Correjería 37)* Meals about €20. Open eve only. Youngest of its three cousins, it plays the kind of background music you actually want to listen to – great, raw, growling sax jazz when we last visited; the food, by contrast, was altogether subtler. They have live music most Wednesdays from 10pm onwards.

La Bottega dell'Ozio (☎ *96 391 10 70, Calle Salvador Giner 1)* Meals around €8. From this tiny Cinderella of a place, the three sisters mentioned above grew. Now a mite upstaged, it remains a favourite with locals who have longer memories.

Alghero (☎ 96 333 35 79, Calle de Burriana 52) Meals €20-30. Menú Alghero (4 dishes & dessert) €30, midday menú (2 dishes & dessert) €17. Alghero, where everything is attractively presented and mouthwatering, couldn't be further from your average trattoria. Try in particular their rice dishes (for a minimum of two) and fish.

Chinese Valencia, like any other European city, large or small, has its share of Great Wall of China and Jasmine Blossom places serving up economical, edible but unexceptional Chinese fare.

Mey Mey (☎ 96 384 07 47, Calle Historiador Diago 19) Meals €15-20. Open Sept-July. Mey Mey is way above your average Chinese joint in both price and quality, and maintains an excellent ratio between the two. Share a basket of their delicate *dim sum* (€11), followed by *fantasía Mandarin* – shrimps, chicken, maybe a strip or two of duck, veal and vegetables in an edible basket of crispy noodles (€8.50). Its low ceiling exudes positive feng shui, though the large pair of kitsch herons, spouting water into a central pool may not be entirely to your liking.

Indian *Taj Mahal (☎ 96 330 62 64, Calle Doctor Manuel Candela 20)* Mains €5-8. If you're craving a curry, this is the best of the very limited Indian options in town.

Latin American *Aire Latino (☎/fax 96 333 11 29, Calle Martí 20)* Meals €15-20. Open Tues-Sun. Aire Latino, with its self-consciously folk decor and staff bedecked likewise, serves up Colombian cuisine and, on weekend evenings, live music. For maximum variety, go for their Picada Aire Latino (empanadas, arepas, yuca and fried plantain; €4) as a starter, chased by the Bandeja Paisa (rice, fried beans, fried egg, minced beef, cubes of pork, avocado, chorizo and fried plantain; €11) and wash them down with one of Aire Latino's fresh fruit juices. Both dishes offer a selection of Colombian specialities.

Rincón el Gaucho (☎ 96 395 20 17, Calle Conde de Altea 51) Meat mains €10-15.

Open daily, eve only. Rincón Gaucho serves the juiciest beef in town, cooked the way only Argentinians can. The weight of the meat is indicated so you know exactly what you're getting.

Arabian *Beirut (☎ 96 374 59 05, Calle Conde de Altea 39)* and *Beirut King (☎ 96 337 21 64, Calle Felipe Garín 4)* Open Mon-Sat. These twin institutions on either side of the river, the former more restaurant, the latter informal cafeteria, share the same owner. Menus are much the same and both offer very reasonably priced Lebanese cuisine. Their *menú degustación*, with its eight different dishes, is especially good value at €6.

Turkish *Istanbul (☎ 96 395 00 75, Calle Salamanca 15)* Open Tues-Sat & Sun eve. Menú €6, menú degustación €12 for 2 people, mezze €2-3. At 10pm, Thursday to Saturday, a belly dancer wiggles her hips. They also do takeaway.

Japanese *Suchi Cru (☎ 96 448 31 93, Calle Pintor Zariñena 3)* Open Tues-Sun. Enough to fill you €12-15. It's sushi and only sushi at this intimate place, one of Valencia's few Japanese options. Eat at the bar and you can watch the deft way the staff prepare the subtle morsels. Since almost everything is prepared fresh and on the spot, don't expect quick service. Curiously, this tiny touch of the Orient is run by Heike, a friendly German.

Vegetarian Cuisine

La Lluna (☎ 96 392 21 46, Calle San Ramón 23) Menú €6. Open Mon-Sat. Tiny La Lluna in the Barrio del Carmen does simple, good-value vegetarian food.

Ana Eva (☎ 96 391 53 69, Calle Turia 49) Meals €12-15. Open Tues-Sat & Sun lunch. Altogether more sophisticated – and more pricey – than La Lluna, Ana Eva has tasteful decor and a delightful patio.

La Llavoreta (☎ 659 457170, Calle Pepita – also called Carrer Pepica – 11) Set 3-course lunch €9. Open only Tues-Thur lunch. Just north of the old riverbed, La Llavoreta is run by a food cooperative and serves only organic produce.

Cafes

La Tienda del Astoria (☎ 96 351 88 04, Calle del Poeta Querol 10) This cafe, an offshoot of the top-end Hotel Astoria Palace (see Places to Stay – Top End earlier in this chapter), does great cakes and coffee, functions as a tea room in the afternoons – and does a good midday menú at €10.

For quite the finest, gooiest ice cream in town, indulge in a couple of authentic, melt-in-the-mouth scoops from *Stortini (☎ 96 391 91 21, Calle Muro Santa Ana 3)*, opposite the Cortes.

While in town, you ought to try a glass of *horchata,* an opaque, local drink made from pressed *chufas* (tiger nuts) into which you dip large finger-shaped buns called *fartons*. Two traditional horchata houses are *Horchatería de Santa Catalina* and *Horchatería el Siglo*, both on Plaza de Santa Catalina. For the real horchata experience, however, you need to head out of town to *Horchatería Daniel (☎ 96 185 88 66, Avenida de la Horchata 41, Alboraya)*. Take metro Line 3 to the Palmaret stop.

Self-Catering

A visit to the magnificent covered market, *Mercado Central*, on Plaza Mercado, is a must, even if you only browse. It's open until 2pm daily Monday to Saturday.

No Solo Pasta (☎ 96 391 88 60, Calle Mantas 5) Open Tues-Sun. This modest place near the Mercado Central does both Italian and Spanish dishes to take away.

Villanueva (☎ 96 351 03 41, Calle Juan de Austria 28) Renowned for its cakes and pastries, this is also a popular drop-in place if you want to grab a mid-morning cake or bocadillo.

For the best in local cheeses and meats – at a price – visit *Las Añadas de España (Calle Xàtiva 3)*.

Castillo (Gran Vía Marques de Turia 1), another wonderful delicatessen for cheeses, sausages and so on, has been run by the same family for more than 80 years and its long pedigree shows.

If you're vegetarian and self catering, you'll find the largest selection of produce, including organic vegetables, at *Navarro*

(Calle Arzobispo Mayoral 20) just behind the Ayuntamiento. In the old quarter, the friendly *Herboristería del Carmen (Calle Roteros 13)* carries a smaller but still respectable range. For fresh daily organic produce at normal market prices, call by *Eduardo*, stall No 508 near the rear of the Mercado Central. Look for the small crowd of shoppers around his stall – and get there early since he's popular among those in the know.

ENTERTAINMENT

Fuelled by a large student population and a keen sense of competitiveness with Madrid and Barcelona, Valencia has a reputation as one of Spain's best nightlife scenes. For many visitors, Valencia's 'party long and hard' attitude is the motivation for coming.

By decree of the town hall, bars must close in winter by 2.30am, Monday to Thursday, and by 3.30am, Friday to Sunday. Equivalent summer closing hours are 3am and 4am. This said, there's quite a lot of winking at the law. Most pubs will be pulling pints by 10pm. The majority of discos, by contrast, don't deign to open their doors until midnight – or even later.

The **Barrio del Carmen** has both the grungiest and grooviest collection of bars. The other major area is around the **university**; along Avenidas Aragón and Blasco Ibáñez and around Plaza de Xuquer there are enough bars and discos to keep you busy beyond sunrise. Two other areas worth checking out are around the **Mercado de Abastos**, near the port, and **Plaza de Cánovas del Castillo**. In summer, the *movida* (night-time action) moves to Malvarrosa and the beach area north of the port while El Perellonet, some 20km south, comes alive with disco fever.

Grab Your Bag

At night, the Barrio del Carmen is generally as safe as anywhere else in town. However, give a wide berth to the hash dealers in the Plaza del Carmen, who aren't averse to supplementing their income by a little bag-snatching.

Bars & Pubs

Barrio del Carmen & Around 'El Carmé', as Barrio del Carmen is also known, has everything from upmarket designer bars and yuppie pubs to grungy thrash-metal haunts and squat punk bars. At weekends, Calle Caballeros, the main street, seethes with people seeking out *la marcha* (the action).

Calle Roteros, just a well hurled stone away from the Serranos towers, has a couple of stylish bars.

Records de l'Avenir *(☎ 96 392 01 37, Calle Roteros 14)* Recently revamped, 'Memories of the Future' has occasional art and photographic displays and recitals. It draws a mainly intellectual and wannabe intellectual clientele. The background music of old film scores will appeal to cinema buffs.

Santa Companya *(☎ 96 392 22 59, Calle Roteros 21)* Almost opposite Records de l'Avenir, Santa Companya carries a good selection of mainly Spanish wines that you can quaff by the glass or bottle.

Plaza del Tossal has some of the most sophisticated bars this side of Barcelona.

Café Bolsería is a stylish place that attracts a smart crowd of 30-somethings. Opposite, ***Café Infanta*** is a swanky, stylish bar. Also in the square, the first floor of ***San Jaume***, a converted pharmacy, is all quiet crannies and poky passageways.

Hanax *(Calle Caballeros 36)* Admission €7.25, free Thursday. Built around a huge chunk of Valencia's Arabian wall, multilevel Hanax, good for a drink or a dance, plays bacalao and house and attracts a classy clientele. Drinks are expensive and there's a dress code.

From Hanax, head eastwards along Calle Caballeros to ***Johnny Maracas*** at No 39, a suave salsa place with fish tanks on the bar. The music, like the clientele, is energetic and loud. At No 35, ***Fox Congo*** has a cool marble bar, patchwork suede benches, scrap-metal montage ceilings – and glass-walled toilets.

At ***Cafe-Bar Negrito***, a block south on Plaza del Negrito, the crowd and music spill out onto the square. Traditionally, it attracts an intellectual, left-wing crowd. On the same square, ***Cava del Negret*** is more intimate, pipes great jazz and blues and does a mean Agua de Valencia.

Bars north of Plaza del Tossal along Calle Alta are cheaper, with tables flanking the street. At No 8 is ***John Silver***, low, dark and named after the monopod old pirate himself (his wooden leg hangs behind the bar).

Just north of Plaza de la Virgen is ***Café de las Horas*** *(Calle Conde de Almodóvar 1)*, a wonderfully baroque place with tapestries, classical music and candelabras dripping wax. Sample their exotic cocktails.

On Plaza de la Reina, ***Finnegan's***, one of Valencia's several Irish bars, is a popular meeting place for speakers of English.

For a true Irish bar without a false fiddle or unread copy of James Joyce in sight, visit ***The Lounge*** *(☎ 96 391 80 94, Calle Estameñaría Vieja 2)*. Run by Lisa from the North and Fiona from the Republic, this popular haunt of foreign students is a friendly, tranquil place with deep sofas, a selection of local and English language newspapers and an Internet terminal.

Mercado de Abastos Near the Mercado de Abastos just west of the town centre, the intersection of Calle Juan Lloréns and Calle de Calixto III is very much the 'in' area.

Akuarela *(☎ 96 382 29 58, Calle Juan Llorens 49)* Open nightly from 6pm. Akuarela is packed at weekends with punters of all ages, there for the pop and rock. Call by between Monday and Thursday and La Bruja (The Witch), their resident fortune teller, will tell you your fate. On Monday and Tuesday, there are free salsa classes and Thursday is Casino Night. On Friday and Saturday, a free bus takes you to their second disco on the outskirts of town, Akuarela Auditorium. If you've already bought a drink back at Akuarela, admission to Akuarela Auditorium is free.

Maruja Limón *(☎ 96 354 01 26, Calle Juan Lloréns 54)* Open Wed-Sat. If you want to get a grip on the latest in Spanish pop, there's no better place than popular Maruja Limón, where the dance floor's usually heaving.

Café Carioca *(☎ 96 384 67 92, Calle Juan Lloréns 52)* Open nightly. This well established place was packing in dancers long before the area became fashionable for nightlife and it continues to pull them in.

Havana Club *(Calle Juan Llorens 43)* Admission including first drink €9-12. Open Wed-Sat Sept-July. The product's well worth paying for.

Peatonal *(☎ 96 385 65 85, Calle Juan Lloréns 39)* Open nightly from 7pm. Next door to Havana Club and specialising in Spanish and Latino, Peatonal offers free salsa classes on Monday and Tuesday.

Around Plaza de Cánovas del Castillo

Just east of the centre, Plaza de Cánovas del Castillo, tamer and more upmarket, attracts a younger crowd. ***Plaza*** *(☎ 96 374 41 40)* is a stylish corner bar on the square itself. Around the corner there are a string of places along Calle Serrano Morales.

Década Loca *(☎ 96 333 0069)* at No 7 has karaoke Sunday to Thursday and go-go dancer on Friday and Saturday. Next door at No 9, ***Sambando Salsa*** is strictly Latino. Among the bars on Calle Salamanca, ***Andromeda Cyber-Pub*** at No 37 (see also Email & Internet Access, earlier in this chapter) is a particularly welcoming place.

Avenida de Aragón & Plaza de Xuquer

Plaza de Xuquer, where students pack the bars, is the place to go early to. Wednesday night tends to be student night.

Rocafull Cafe *(☎ 96 332 09 54, Plaza de Xuquer 14)* Open daily from 3.30pm. Rocafull hosts events, sometimes with live music. Wednesday night is normally Erasmus (European Community exchange scheme) student night.

Max Max *(Calle Vinalopó 11)* Just north of the square, Max Max is run by Toni, the owner, who himself is from Galicia and Spain's Celtic fringe. His pub embraces all Celtic cultures and is much more than just another Irish bar. Warmly recommended for its live music, house cider and sheer friendliness. Student night is Wednesday.

Samet Ville *(Plaza de Xuquer 10)* Open Wed-Sun. This place may be small, but it's the place to head for hip hop and has great weekend DJs.

On the corner, ***Carajillo*** attracts a young crowd, spilling out onto the pavement. ***Farandula*** and, right opposite, ***La Salamandra***, are normally altogether quieter places where you can catch your breath before plunging again into la marcha.

Don't discount heading for Avenida de Aragón, where new bars are opening by the month.

Cachao *(☎ 616 941162, Calle Periodista Ros Belda 5)*, just off Avenida de Aragón, is a salsa bar, open daily, that was one of the first to offer free lessons before every hybrid place with pretensions started to do the same.

At night, ***New York***, or just ***NY*** *(☎ 96 362 99 80, Avenida de Aragón 28)* is open daily and plays funky music. Before the night owls start to flit and on match days (even if you aren't football crazy, you will be by the time you leave) as many as three games may be playing live and simultaneously on three different monitors.

Set back from Avenida de Aragón with its entrance at Calle Bélgica 5, ***Caribbean's***, open Tuesday to Saturday, plays a mix of salsa and merengue at eardrum-shattering levels, and pulls in a mainly young crowd. Don't go expecting polite conversation. Or, indeed, any conversation...

Malvarrosa As the summer nights get warmer, the action moves eastwards, to Malvarrosa and the coast. Most of the places that follow are open only from mid-July to mid-September.

Vivir sin Dormir *(Paseo de Neptuno 42)*, literally 'live without sleep', is a popular last-stop late-night/early morning bar overlooking the sea. For somewhere a little classier, relax in ***La Champaneria***, Calle Eugenia Viñes 118.

In summer, you can see stars while you dance at open-air ***Caballito del Mar*** *(☎ 96 371 07 63, Calle Eugenia Viñes 22)*, where the music goes from funky to Latino to house. Admission costs €10 and includes the first drink.

The ever-inventive ***Akuarela*** *(Calle Eugenia Viñes 152, Edificio Termes Victoria)* has a summer offshoot (see the Mercado de Abastos, earlier).

Live Music & Jazz

Black Note *(☎ 96 393 36 63, Calle Polo y Peyrolón 15)* Admission, including first drink, €6-15 depending on who's playing. Valencia's best jazz venue has live music Monday to Thursday and good canned blues, soul and jazz Friday and Saturday.

Jimmy Glass *(Calle Baja 28)* is just what you want from a jazz bar – dim, smoky, serving jumbo measures and with the coolest of jazz from the owner's vast CD collection. It's a regular venue for live performers.

Cervecería Madrid *(Calle de la Abadía de San Martín 10)*. Upstairs at this long-established cafe, there's jazz (usually weekends only), courtesy of the owner on piano accompanied by his friends.

The Italian restaurant **Maramao** (see Places to Eat earlier in this chapter) has regular live jazz on Wednesday evenings.

La Linterna Jazz Café *(Calle de la Linterna 11)*, a place where the beautiful people come to be seen, plays good background jazz and hosts live musicians.

Café del Duende *(☎ 630 455289, Calle Turia 62)*, a little corner of southern Spain, has live flamenco on Thursdays and folk on Wednesdays.

Roxy Club *(☎ 96 380 38 52, Calle San Vicente Mártir 200)*, south of the train station, has live pop and rock and brings in the big names.

Discos

Discos, even more than bars, tend to come, go and change their names almost as often as the DJ changes the CDs. The ones we highlight are as stable as any in this volatile sector. Expect an admission or first drink fee, which rarely exceeds €9. Discounted passes are often available from local bars.

A handful of discos are scattered around the centre, but if you really want to experience life after 3am in Valencia, head for the zone along and around Avenida Blasco Ibáñez, towards the university (€3 to €5 by taxi from the centre).

Around 3am the stayers with cash to splash move on to the big discos along Blasco Ibáñez.

Rumbo 144 *(☎ 96 371 00 25, Avenida Blasco Ibáñez 144)* Open 1am-7am Thur-Sat Sept-July. Rumbo 144 is a funky, three-barred, large-floored place with light show. Salsa is a speciality. Don't be deterred by the gorillas with FBI-type earpieces at the door. They're quite cuddly really.

Warhol *(☎ 96 371 65 96, Blasco Ibáñez 111)* Admission including the first drink €6. Open 12.30am-6am Wed-Sat. Across the road from Rumbo 144, this smallish venue plays eclectic music and attracts a predominantly student crowd. They do a special Wednesday night for Erasmus students.

Woody *(☎ 96 361 85 51, Calle Menéndez Pelayo 25)* In the heart of the faculty area, Woody attracts a younger student set and plays bacalao and house.

Jam *(Calle Cuba 8)* Open 2am-5.30am Thur, 2am-6.30am Fri-Sat. South of Estación del Norte, Jam has great music, lights, atmosphere – and Valencia's hottest go-go dancers, both boys and girls.

Akuarela Auditorium *(Calle San Vicente Mártir 305)* Open midnight-6.30am Fri-Sat. For a free bus and free admission to this popular disco (see Akuarela, its sister pub earlier under Mercado de Abastos). If you're taking a taxi, ask for the Cruz Cubierta, a large cross with canopy and well known landmark that's right in front of the disco. Alternatively, take night bus No N6.

Bananas *(☎ 96 178 17 06, Carretera Valencia-Alicante, El Romaní)* Midnight onwards Fri-Sat. Truly the 'maxi-disco' it proclaims itself to be, this complex is the haunt of thousands at weekends. Leave the car at home, forget waiting hours for the next free taxi and take the train. A disco special service leaves Estación del Norte every Saturday at 1.15am for El Romaní and returns at 6.15am.

Two other megadiscos outside of town, each deep into *bacalao* (see Music in the Facts about Valencia chapter for details), are **Sound Factory** *(☎ 96 324 80 25, Carretera del Río 399)* and, close by, **The Face** *(☎ 96 324 87 40, Calle Montañares 141)*, both in Pinedo, between Valencia and El Saler.

Gay & Lesbian Venues

There's a small gay rectangle at the west end of the Barrio del Carmen.

La Goulue (Calle Quart 32) Open Wed-Sat. Weekends are packed at this disco-pub, a particular favourite of the young set.

Venial (☎ 96 391 73 56, Calle Quart 26) Admission €7.50, drinks €6. Venial, with its house and techno music is far and away the city's most popular gay dance venue.

Café Sant Miguel (☎ 96 392 31 29, Plaza Sant Miguel 13) Open from 7pm Wed-Sun in winter, daily in summer. With its soft background music and summer terraza, this is *the* place to meet, converse and communicate. It's worth a visit for the food alone.

Dona Dona (☎ 96 391 18 38, Calle Portal de Valldigna 2) Open Wed-Sat. Strictly for the girls, the music's good and the bar billiards always busy.

Turangalila (☎ 96 391 02 55, Calle del Mar 34) With its restaurant, cabaret and drag shows, Turangalila is a popular mixed gay and straight venue.

Theatre & Opera

The *Teatro Principal (☎ 96 351 00 51, Calle Barcas 15)* is Valencia's main venue for opera and the performing arts. The *Palau de la Música (☎ 96 337 50 20, Paseo de la Alameda 30)*, a huge, glass-domed concert hall above the Jardines del Turia, hosts mainly classical music recitals. Its current programme can be viewed on the Web site at W www.palauvalencia.com.

Teatro Rialto (☎ 96 351 23 36, Plaza del Ayuntamiento 17) also frequently puts on plays.

Cinemas

On the 4th floor of the Teatro Rialto building, the *Filmoteca* screens undubbed classic, art-house and experimental films. Admission costs €1.20 – one of Valencia's best bargains.

During August and the first week of September, the Filmoteca shows undubbed films on a giant screen in the Turia riverbed, below the Palau de la Música.

Two multiscreen cinemas show undubbed films: *Albatros (☎ 96 393 26 77, Plaza Fray Luis Colomer)* and *Babel (☎ 96 362 67 95, Calle Vicente Sancho Tello 10)*. Movies, normally €5.50, are cheaper on Monday. Both cinemas share a Web site, W www .cinesalbatrosbabel.com (Spanish only).

SPECTATOR SPORTS
Football

Valencia Club de Fútbol were European Championship runners-up in both 2000 and 2001. Their steeply raked stadium, known as La Mestalla or Estadio Luis Casanova (☎ 96 337 26 26), is at the junction of Avenidas Aragón and Blasco Ibañez. Tickets start at €15 for a bird's-eye view. The seriously football-crazy might want to pick up a scarf, woolly hat or shirt from the club's official shop at Calle Pintor Sorolla 25, where you can also buy tickets for the game.

The other professional club in town, Levante (☎ 96 365 08 00), are to Valencia as Leyton Orient are to Arsenal, Essendon Bombers to St Kilda Saints or the Mets to the Yankees; worthy but not in the same league – literally; so as they put up a plucky fight in the second division. Undoubtedly more in need of your support and with a cheaper admission fee of around €6, they

JANE SMITH

**Catch a bit of Spanish passion
at a Valencia game.**

play in the Levante stadium on the north side of town.

For both teams, home games normally (but not always) take place on Sundays between September and May.

Bullfights ✓

Bullfights, which are usually staged to coincide with local fiestas, take place in the Plaza de Toros (☎ 96 351 93 15, Calle Xàtiva), which can accommodate over 20,000 spectators.

SHOPPING

Calle de Colón is Valencia's main shopping street. On it, you'll find a couple of branches of the Corte Inglés department store and a multitude of good clothing shops. You might also like to window shop along Calles Ribera and Ruzafa, which branch off it. Within easy walking distance, too, and rich in clothes outlets are Calles del Poeta Querol and Juan de Austria. For antiques, whether you're seriously buying or just browsing, drift in and out of the specialist shops on Calle Avellanas. For US-style shopping malls, called *centros comerciales*, lose yourself around the Nuevo Centro or Centro El Saler.

Clothes ✓

Zara, the stylish yet inexpensive Spanish clothing chain, has shops at Calle de Colón 11 and, right opposite, at No 18. Prices in Spain can be up to one third cheaper than at its branches elsewhere in Europe. *Mango*, at No 31, is another Spanish chain with fresh, exciting designs. It also has an outlet at Calle Juan de Austria 7.

Spaghetti & Co. (Calle Pascual y Genís 11) a chain with its headquarters in Catalunya, despite the name, goes for the light and frivolous. *Massimo Dutti*, with one of its several branches at Calle Juan de Austria 4, opposite Mango, and another at Calle de Colón 9, goes more for the comfy and practical – yet with considerable flair. For no-nonsense, easy-to-wear women's fashions, try on a garment or two at *Cortefiel (Calle de Colón 66)*, which consistently maintains a good price-quality ratio.

Designer Shops

For that label that few others can flash, Valencia has plenty of choice, including a number of its own designers who are making their mark internationally. A couple of designers from Galicia in the north-west of Spain merit a visit; *Purificación García (Calle de Colón 17)* combines both classic design and more avant-garde creations while *Adolfo Domínguez* at No 52 also creates for both men and women. The range of garments at *Max Mara (Calle Pascual y Genís 18)*, strictly for the ladies, runs from sportswear to the most formal occasion. You might also want to press your nose against the window of *Loewe (Calle del Poeta Querol 7)*. Its clothing and accessories are, well, exquisite – and accordingly priced.

Things Valencian

If you want to take home a traditional *fallera* dress and accessories, visit *Casa de los Falleros (Calle Quevedo 3)* or, opposite at No 6, *Artesanía Fidela*. However, they don't come cheap – a typical ensemble will set you back at least €300.

Fans may be the most hackneyed of Spanish stereotypes but they're really practical when heat and humidity are high. They can cost anywhere from €1 to €175 for a really fancy, hand-painted one. For a wide choice, visit *Nela (Calle San Vicente Mártir 2)* who also do a nice line in umbrellas and walking sticks, *Rosalén* at No 19 or *Abanicos Carbonell (Calle Castellón 21)*.

Manilla shawls too vary enormously in price – from €35 for a simple, machine-spun version, to as much as €300 for a special silk number.

Accessories

Valencia has enough footwear shops to shoe an army. Many of the pairs you might squeeze into will have been manufactured within the Comunidad, in and around towns such as Elda and Novelda in Alicante province. For style, peek into *Calzados Beguer (Calle Colón 58)* who manufacture in Torrente, a dormitory town south-west of the city. Or visit *Camper (Calle Colón 13)*.

Camper, with branches in larger towns, is something of a Spanish institution. But just because it's popular does not mean that its output is run-of-the-mill. Choose wisely and you can dance out, toes tapping with satisfaction.

A pair of *alpargatas*, the traditional Valenciano footwear – canvas on top with a sole of dried, woven grasses and bound to the ankle by cross-gartered tape – makes an original present for the folks back home and a practical alternative to sandals, especially where it's sandy or dusty.

One of the pleasant things about Spain, in general, and Valencia, in particular, is that small, specialist, single-product shops still manage to cling on despite heavyweight competition from all-purpose department stores. If you rather fancy yourself strutting in a stylish hat, *Albero (Calle Xàtiva 21)* established in 1820, can set you up with dapper panamas, trilbies and berets, as well as striking headwear for those who want to be noticed.

Even if you don't buy a thing, at least have a look at the window of **Guantes Camps** *(Calle San Vicente Mártir 3)*. In a city where the temperature rarely tumbles below 0°C, they specialise in gloves for all occasions, from cycling and skiing to weddings and horse riding.

Lladró

The Lladró brothers, Valencia born and bred, set up the factory that nowadays turns out hand-painted ceramic statuettes by the thousand. Their winsome creations appeal to collectors around the world. At their factory in the suburb of Tavernes Blancas (take bus No 16 from Plaza del Ayuntamiento), their seconds shop is a particular bargain. Pick up a piece or two, marginally flawed but you'll scarcely notice, present it with a flourish back home and you'll be in your Great Aunt's good books for ever.

IVAM

If you're looking for a coffee-table art book or some stylish bauble to take home, the Instituto Valenciano de Arte Moderno (IVAM; see the section earlier in this chapter) on

---

El Palleter

It's the year 1808. Spain's gullible leaders have granted French troops under Napoleon safe passage in preparation for a joint attack on Portugal. But the French stop, fan out and occupy much of the north. On 2 May, Madrid rises against the court and in favour of Fernando, the weak monarch and son of Carlos IV.

Three weeks later, many towns have risen against the distant, ineffectual court and the foreign invader but, although tension is high, Valencia still wavers.

In the former Placeta del les Panses, just behind the Lonja, Vicente Doménech, a *palleter*, or seller of straw firelighters, takes off his broad woollen belt, hoists it to a handy stick and leaps onto the nearby steps. Waving his impromptu standard, he shouts to the crowd, *'Un pobre palleter li declara guerra a Napoleón. Visca Fernando Sèptim y muiguen els träidors!'* ('A humble palleter declares war upon Napoleon. Long live Fernando VII and death to the traitors!') And the townspeople, their resolve stiffened, rise in revolt.

No doubt embellished after the event, the story of the palleter, a symbol of individualism and justified revolt, painted by Joaquin Sorolla, sculpted by Mariano Benlliure and commemorated by a plaque on Calle Lonja, is an essential part of the Valencian sense of identity.

Calle Guillem de Castro has a great bookshop and store that are both well worth a browse in their own right.

Flea Markets

Valencia's largest flea mar-ket occurs every Sunday morning in **Plaza Luis Casanova**, sandwiched between Estadio Luis Casanova (Valencia's major football stadium) and Avenida Blasco Ibañez. Much of the stuff looks as though it's been hauled out of someone's rubbish bin but the occasional gem twinkles up at you. Take the new Metro No 5 to Aragón.

There's a smaller Sunday market, dealing particularly in caged birds and sad, wide-eyed pets, in the **Plaza Redonda** (see Iglesia de Santa Catalina & Plaza Redonda, earlier in the chapter).

Every Thursday, there is a large market on the east side of town in the district of **Cabanyal**, heading towards the beach. If you are prepared to ferret around you can find some good clothing bargains. To get there just hop on bus No 81 from the Plaza del Ayuntamiento.

Collectors

Numismatists, philatelists and the just plain curious can have fun and do a spot of useful business at the Sunday morning exchange and mart in the main hall of La Lonja (see earlier in this chapter).

GETTING THERE & AWAY
Air

Valencia's Aeropuerto de Manises (☎ 96 159 85 00) is 10km west of the city centre on the Madrid highway. For details of airlines and flights, see the Getting There & Away chapter.

Bus

The main bus station (☎ 96 349 72 22) is on the north side of the riverbed on Avenida Menéndez Pidal. Recently refurbished, it's a pleasant enough place but would be even more agreeable if they swept away more regularly the refuse that swirls through its platforms. It has a bank of luggage lockers (€3 for up to 24 hours) that can take the bulkiest backpack. Bus No 8 connects it to Plaza del Ayuntamiento.

For transport companies operating from the bus station and the routes they serve, see the Getting There & Away chapter.

Autocares Herca buses for El Saler beach and the Albufera, some of which continue to El Palmar and/or El Perelló (see Around Valencia City for details) leave from the junction of Gran Vía de las Germanías and Calle Sueca.

Train

From Estación del Norte (☎ 96 352 02 02 or 902 24 02 02) there are 10 *Alaris* express trains daily to and from Madrid (€34.85, 3½ hours) via Albacete as well as three

regional services via Cuenca (€18.10, 5½ hours).

A dozen trains daily make the three- to five-hour haul northwards to Barcelona via Tarragona, including the high-speed *Euromed* (€31.25, six daily) and the slightly slower *Arco* (€28.25, three daily). Up to eight trains head daily to Alicante (€8.60 to €18.65, 1½ to two hours).

Most of the frequent northbound trains stop at Sagunto (€2.05, 30 minutes) and Castellón (€3.15, up to one hour).

For other popular train destinations within the Comunidad Valenciana, see the Getting There & Away chapter.

Boat

In summer, Trasmediterránea (reservations ☎ 902 45 46 45) operates daily car and passenger ferries to/from Mallorca and Ibiza and has a weekly connection with Menorca. During the rest of the year, sailings are less frequent. Buy your ticket at the Estación Marítima (☎ 96 367 39 72) or any travel agency.

GETTING AROUND
To/From the Airport

A regular round-the-houses MetroBus service (€0.85, 45 minutes) connects the Aeropuerto de Manises with the bus station. The local train line C-4 passes nearby and runs at least every 20 minutes (less frequently at weekends). It isn't practical if you're laden with luggage since the station is a good 300m walk from the terminal. A taxi into town costs about €10 – less on the trip from town as there's a mandatory €2.25 supplement for journeys from the airport. There are plans to extend the metro to the airport but they are unlikely to be realised during the lifetime of this book.

Bus, Metro & Tram

Valencia has an impressive integrated transport system embracing bus, metro and high-speed tram routes.

Buses of the Empresa Municipal de Transportes (EMT; ☎ 96 352 83 99, ⓦ www .emtvalencia.es) service routes within the city and run until about 10pm. A single journey

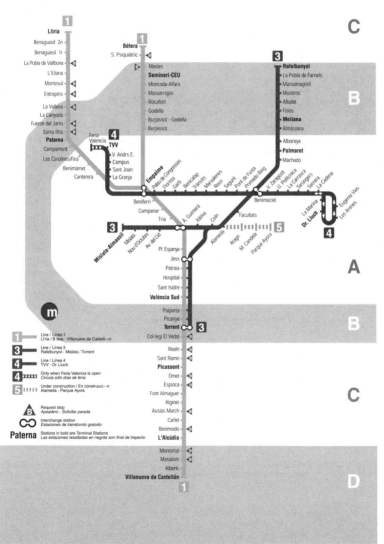

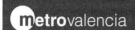

metrovalencia — **Zonal map**

C

Llíria
Benaguasil 2n
Benaguasil 1r
La Pobla de Vallbona
L'Eliana
Montesol
Entrepins
La Vallesa
La Canyada
Fuente del Jarro
Santa Rita
Paterna
Campament
Les Carolines/Fira
Benimàmet
Canterera

Bétera
S. Psiquiàtric

Masies
Seminari-CEU
Moncada-Alfara
Massarrojos
Rocafort
Godella
Burjassot - Godella
Burjassot

Rafelbunyol
La Pobla de Farnals
Massamagrell
Museros
Albalat
Foios
Meliana
Almàssera

Alboraya
Palmaret
Machado

B

Feria Valencia
4 TVV
V. Andrs E.
Campus
Sant Joan
La Granja

Empalme
Palau de Congressos
Florista
Garb
Benicalap
Transits
Maravelenes
Reus
Sargent
Pont de Fusta
Primado Reig
V. Zaragoza
U. Politècnica
La Carrasca
Tarongers
Serreria
La Cadena

Beniferri
Campanar
Tria
A. Guimera
Xàtiva
Coln

Benimaclet

La Marina
Eugenia Vies
Les Arenes
Dr. Lluch

3 Mislata-Almassil
Mislata
Nou d'Octubre
Av. del Cid

Facultats
Alameda
Aragn
M. Candela
Parque Ayora
5

4

Pl. Espanya
Jess
Patraix
Hospital
Sant Isidre
València Sud

A

Paiporta
Picanya
Torrent ∞ **3**
Col·legi El Vedat

B

Line / Línea 1
L'ria / B tera - Villanueva de Castell—n

1

3
Line / Línea 3
Rafelbunyol - Mislata / Torrent

4
Line / Línea 4
TVV - Dr. Lluch

4 ····
Only when Feria Valencia is open
Circula solo días de feria

5 ||||||
Under construction / *En construcci—n*
Alameda - Parque Ayora

Ⓐ **B**
Request stop
Apeadero - Solicitar parada

∞ Interchange station
Estaciones de transbordo gratuito

Paterna Stations in bold are Terminal Stations
Las estaciones resaltadas en negrita son final de trayecto.

Realn
Sant Ramn
Picassent
Omet
Espioca
Font Almaguer
Alginet
Ausiàs March
Carlet
Benimodo
L'Alcúdia

C

Montortal
Masalavs
Alberic
Villanueva de Castellón
1

D

Ⓜ

ticket, purchased on board on buses and from machines for tram and metro, costs €0.80. If you're a group or in town for even just a couple of days, consider a BonoBus (€4.50), which allows 10 journeys. With the Bono10 (€5.35), you can catch a connection within 50 minutes of having started your journey. The T1 card (€3) gives you a day of unlimited travel by bus and within the central metro zone A. All three multiple-journey cards are available from just about any newsagency.

Yellow Metrobus services, most of which terminate at the bus station, connect outlying towns and villages with Valencia.

From 11pm to 2.45am on Thursday, Friday and Saturday nights, night buses radiate out from Plaza del Ayuntamiento every 45 minutes (less frequently in winter). They follow seven routes, one of which will get you to within a reasonable walk of where you're staying, even if you're in the outer suburbs.

The smart high-speed tram is a pleasant way to get to the beach, paella restaurants of Las Arenas and the port. Pick it up at Pont de Fusta or where it intersects with the Metro at Benimaclet.

Metro lines serve the outer suburbs. The closest stations to the centre are Ángel Guimerá, Xàtiva (for the train station), Colón and Pont de Fusta.

Tourist offices stock maps for both EMT and Metro services.

Car

Major car-hire companies include Europcar (☎ 96 152 18 72 airport, ☎ 96 351 90 55 train station/town) and Avis (☎ 96 152 21 62 airport, ☎ 96 352 24 78 train station/town).

Reliable local – and normally quite substantially cheaper – companies operating from Valencia airport include Javea Cars (☎ 96 579 3312, fax 96 579 60 52, W www .javeacars.com), Solmar (☎ 96 646 10 00, fax 96 646 01 09, W www.solmar.es) and Victoria Cars (☎ 96 579 27 61, fax 96 583 20 00, W www.victoriacars.com).

Street parking can be a real pain. There are large subterranean car parks beneath Plazas de la Reina and Alfonso el Magnánimo and on Calle Roger de Lauria, off Calle Colón.

Taxi

Call Radio-Taxi (☎ 96 370 33 33) or Valencia Taxi (☎ 96 357 13 13). The flag fall is €1 and there's a minimum charge of €2.50. Journeys within town cost 0.60 per km, plus waiting time at €11.15 per hour.

Bicycle

Ergobike (☎ 96 392 32 39), on Calle Museo, rents out town bikes and recumbents (see also Organised Tours, earlier).

Around Valencia City

SAGUNTO (SAGUNT)
postcode 46500 • pop 56,750

Sagunto, 25km north of Valencia, was a thriving Iberian community as early as the 5th century BC. Named – infelicitously, with hindsight – Arse, it minted its own silver and bronze coins and traded with both Greeks and Phoenicians.

In 219 BC Hannibal, the Carthaginian, wiped out the inhabitants and destroyed their town after an eight-month siege, an event that led to the Second Punic War between Carthage and Rome. Rome won, renamed the town Saguntum and set about rebuilding it.

Do you remember *Rodrigo's Guitar Concerto* (known in Spain as the *Concierto de Aranjuez*), available in every version under the sun, from throbbing classical guitar to bland musical wallpaper? Joaquin Rodrigo, responsible only for the former, was born in Sagunto in 1901.

Most people visit Sagunto as a day or half-day excursion from Valencia.

Orientation & Information

The Roman ruins are atop an inland hill behind the new town, which itself is of little interest. From the train station beside the N-340 highway, which cuts a noisy swath through town, it's a 10-minute walk to the tourist office (☎ 96 266 22 13) on Plaza Cronista Chabret. It usually opens 8am to 3pm and 4.30pm to 6.30pm Monday to Friday,

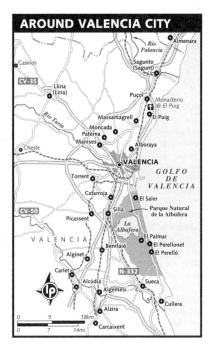

AROUND VALENCIA CITY

gunto's three-week open-air arts festival in August (mainly theatre).

Higher up, the old, stone defensive walls of the rambling complex, mostly in ruins, wind around the hillside for almost a kilometre. Most interesting, because it is the best preserved, is the **Plaza de Armas**, just to the left (east) of the main entrance, and, beyond it, the massive Muslim gateway of the **Plaza de Almenara**. There's also a small **Antiquarium Epigráfico** *(open 10am-2pm & 5pm-dusk Tues-Sat, 10am-2pm Sun)*, a collection of stones bearing inscriptions, mainly from the Roman era. However, perhaps the main charm of a ramble through the overgrown cactuses and chaos of shaped stones is the great views afforded of the town, coast and hectare upon hectare of orange groves.

Down in the town, other monuments include the remaining wall of the ruins of the 4th-century BC **Templo de Diana** on Calle Sagrario, just off the Plaza Mayor; the adjacent **Iglesia de Santa María**, in the south-west corner of the square, with its Gothic and baroque doorways; and the 17th-century **Ermita de la Sangre**.

Getting There & Away
There are frequent trains between Valencia and Sagunto (one way/return €2.10/3.45), and AVSA runs a half-hourly service (€2) from Valencia's bus station.

LA ALBUFERA & EL SALER
La Albufera
About 15km south of Valencia, La Albufera is a huge, freshwater lagoon that's separated from the sea by a narrow strip of sand dunes and pine forests known as La Devesa. The unspoiled sections of La Albufera have a serene beauty and the area is noted for its spectacular sunsets. The lake's current area, which expands and contracts according to season, averages a little over 2800 hectares. In most places it's scarcely 1m deep; hence the distinctive flat-bottomed boats that the local fisherfolk use to harvest fish and eels from the shallow waters.

The lake and surrounding areas, a breeding ground and sanctuary for migrating and indigenous birds, nowadays are afforded

plus 8.45am to 1.45pm on Saturday and 9.30am to 2.30pm on Sunday.

From the tourist office, a further 15-minute uphill walk through narrow streets – passing beside the *Judería*, the former Jewish quarter – brings you to the Roman theatre and castle. Alternatively, take a taxi ride from the station.

Things to See
You can happily spend a couple of hours meandering around the **castle complex** *(☎ 96 266 55 81; admission free; open 10am-dusk Tues-Sat, 10am-2pm Sun)*, more accurately called the acropolis, a group of hilltop defences rather than a single, unified creation.

The first monument you reach is the **Roman theatre**, built into the hillside during the 1st century AD. Centuries of use and disuse had left it in poor shape, but its controversial modern 'restoration' is in questionable taste. Still, the acoustics remain outstanding, and it's the main venue for Sa-

protected status as a nature park. Keen bird-watchers flock to the **Parque Natural de la Albufera** to spot kingfishers, mallards, white herons, coots and red-crested pochards, among others. Around 90 species regularly nest in the area, while more than 250 use it as a staging post during their migrations.

Build in a visit to the **Racó de l'Olla visitors centre** (*☎ 96 162 73 45, Carretera El Palmar s/n; admission free; open 9am-2pm & 4.30pm-6.30pm Mon-Fri in summer, 9am-2pm & 5.30pm-6.30pm Mon-Fri in winter, 9am-2pm Sat & Sun year round).* At the centre, there's an informative pamphlet in English, a guided walk, a hide for watching the birds that flock to the pools in this small protected area –and closed-circuit TV cameras that you can operate in order to eavesdrop on unsuspecting species.

El Saler

The long strand of El Saler, backed by shady pine woods, is scarcely 10km and a half-hour bus ride from the heart of Valencia. The northern end of the beach and parallel dunes, reached from the *playa* (beach) bus stop, are a permitted nudist area, popular with the gay community. For the main, mainstream beach area, continue to El Saler village. The southern limit of the beach, in the region of the Parador de El Saler hotel, is also a permitted nudist zone.

El Palmar

El Palmar has a long, fishy history. It was King Jaime I who granted the original inhabitants the right to fish the lake back in 1250.

The journey to El Palmar is almost as good as getting there. As you head from the coast towards El Palmar, crossing locks and reed-fringed side canals, look out for *barracas*, the typical Albufera houses with their steeply pitched, thatched roofs.

At weekends, you won't be alone. Carloads and coach parties descend upon this fishing village that, at first sight, seems to be all restaurants – and indeed catering has overtaken fishing as the main source of income for El Palmar. They come for paella and for *all i pebre*, eels, hauled wriggling from the lake and simmered in a garlic-rich

peppery stew. The restaurants all serve much the same fare but, for added pleasure, choose one that has a picture window overlooking the lake or the paddy fields.

Restaurante l'Establiment (*☎ 96 162 01 00, Camino Estell)* Meals around €20. Open Wed-Mon. A cut or two above your average paella place, L'Establiment, at the southern limit of the village, is famous for its rice dishes (€8.50 to €11) – so famous that you'd be well advised to reserve a table in advance.

You'll probably want to linger over lunch but build in time for a boat trip on the Albufera, the only way to get a sense of this unique watery expanse. Expect to pay about €3, with a minimum of €12 per boat.

Getting There & Away

Autocares Herca (*☎ 96 349 12 50)* buses run hourly (every half-hour in summer) from the junction of Gran Vía de las Germanias and Calle Sueca (30 minutes, €1.25) from Valencia to El Saler. Some head inland to El Palmar, while the majority continue down the coast to the small and very Spanish resorts of El Perelló and Perellonet. Either will bring you closer to La Albufera, which, even if the bus terminates in El Saler, is a comfortable and attractive walk away if you hug the coast.

If your goal is El Palmar, another option is to take one of the Valencia Bus Turístico (*☎ 96 342 02 85)*. At other than peak times, you can hop off, have a paella lunch in El Palmar, then catch a later bus back into town. Be sure to alert the driver at the outset of the journey; El Palmar's no fun as an impromptu overnight destination.

MANISES & PATERNA

Manises, out near the airport and under 10km from the centre of Valencia, has been a centre for the ceramics-making ever since the 11th century and Moorish times.

To get a sense of the huge range of items and styles over the centuries, visit its **Museo Municipal de Cerámica** (*☎ 96 152 10 44, Calle Sagrari 22; admission free; open 10am-1pm & 4pm-7pm Mon-Sat, 11am-2pm Sun).* This museum also displays some original contemporary designs and you can watch a demonstration of traditional ceramics-making. Flaunting the town's wares, the market and quite a few of the houses are elaborately decorated with ceramic tiling. If you have room in your luggage, Manises is the ideal place to pick up a little – or larger – something for back home at factory prices.

Take local train C-4 from the Estación del Norte or a bus from the bus station. Both services are frequent.

Paterna, at one time an arch rival to Manises, is still a major producer, if nowadays not in the same league. It has a tower, of Arab origin, from whose top you get a fine view of the surrounding huerta. And it, too, has its ceramics museum, the **Museo de Cerámica** (☎ 96 137 96 00, Plaza del Pueblo 1; admission free; open 10am-2pm & 6pm-8pm Tues-Sat) in the old town hall. Less strong on contemporary design, it has some interesting pieces from the 11th to 18th centuries.

To get there, take Metro Line No 1.

MONASTERIO DE EL PUIG

This monastery (☎ 96 147 02 00; admission €2.40; open daily 10am-1pm & 4pm-5.30pm in winter, 10am-1pm & 4pm-7.30pm in summer), prominent on a low hillock (puig in Valenciano) to the west of the motorway, lies 18km from the centre of Valencia. The Real Monasterio de el Puig de Santa Maria, to give it its full and flowing title, is not the first to bring fame to this small rise amid the wide plain of orange orchards. Here, the Christians enjoyed a decisive victory over the Arabs, motivating King Jaime I to begin his assault on the occupied city of Valencia. The small commemorative chapel was overshadowed in the 17th century by the present solid, four-towered construction with its central cloister. The monastery is home to a fine image, in the Byzantine style, of La Virgen del Puig, patroness of the former Reino de Valencia (kingdom of Valencia). Within it, as well, is the **Museo de Artes Gráficas y la Imprenta** (Museum of Graphics and Printing), which, among many fascinating articles, has what is claimed to be the smallest book in the world.

Frequent trains of the local line C-6 serve El Puig from the Estación del Norte.

Northern Valencia

Costa del Azahar

Stretching north from Valencia is the Costa del Azahar – the orange-blossom coast. Backed by a mountainous hinterland, its coastal plain is a green sea of orange groves, from whose heady-scented flowers *(azahar)* the region takes its name.

Getting There & Away

The Valencia-Barcelona railway follows the coast and regional trains stop at all main towns. From Valencia, trains run every half hour to Castellón (€3.15). Seven trains daily call at Benicàssim (€4.10), three at Oropesa del Mar (€5) and eight at Benicarló, Peñíscola and Vinaròs (all €6.90).

The above fares are the cheapest. Rates differ considerably from stop-at-every-station *cercanías* and *regionales* to the swifter *Euromed* and *Arco* services that only stop at main stations.

CASTELLÓN (CASTELLÓ) DE LA PLANA
postcode 12005 • pop 142,300

The outskirts of Castellón are drab, industrial and rambling so the centre comes as quite a pleasant surprise to the few tourists who penetrate to its heart. Like its immediate neighbours, Benicàssim and Oropesa to the north, the old part lies well inland. Like smaller Vinaròs further north, El Grau retains an active fishing fleet. It also bustles with commercial traffic and has an attractive marina for pleasure boats.

Castellón itself is a prosperous commercial centre and university town. It boasts an impressive, recently renovated fine arts museum, some interesting monuments and a few examples of *modernista* architecture.

Orientation

The Plaza Mayor and, just to its south, Plaza Santa Clara, lie at the heart of the interesting part of Castellón. The spanking

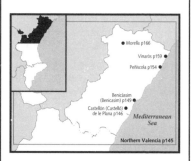

new subterranean train station, with the intercity bus station above it, is around 1km north-west beyond leafy Parque Ribalta. El Grau, the port area, is 4km east of downtown and is best reached by Avenida del Mar or Avenida Hermanos Bou.

Information

Tourist Offices The tourist office (☎ 96 435 86 88), Plaza María Agustina 5, opens 9am to 2pm and 4pm to 7pm Monday to Friday (through lunch in July and August) plus 10am to 2pm Saturday.

Post The main post office occupies a fine neo-Mudéjar building, all mellow brickwork

NORTHERN VALENCIA

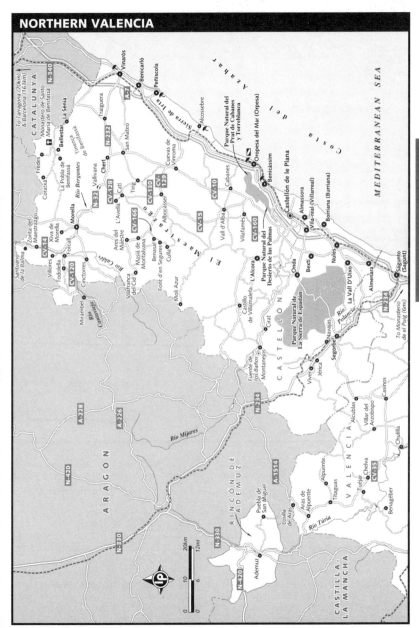

CASTELLÓN (CASTELLÓ) DE LA PLANA

NORTHERN VALENCIA

PLACES TO STAY
16　El Maestrat
21　Hotel Real
22　Hostal La Esperanza
23　Hotel Intur Castellón
25　Mare de Déu del Lledó

PLACES TO EAT
3　Lizarran
4　Julivert
7　Mesón Navarro I
8　Mesón Navarro II
10　Mercado Central
　　(Covered Market)
14　Mesón Navarro III
20　Restaurante Casino
　　Antiguo

OTHERS
1　Tourist Office
2　Convento de las
　　Capuchinas
5　Nómada
6　Post Office
9　Town Hall
11　El Fadrí
12　Concatedral de Santa
　　María
13　Museo Etnológico de la
　　Diputación
15　Bus Stop
17　Museo de Bellas Artes
18　Bus Stop
19　Ciberkantina
24　Bus Stop

punctuated by intricate tile work, that graces
Plaza Tetuan. It's well worth passing by even
if you have no letters to post.

Email & Internet Access Ciberkantina
(☎ 96 422 30 88), Calle Asensi 20, has nine
machines. Open 9am to 11pm daily, it charges €2.40 per hour and serves a mean cup
of coffee.

Bookshops For a town of its size, Castellón
has quite a splendid travel and outdoor activities bookshop. Recently established, intimate and well stocked, Nómada (☎ 96 472

28 61), Calle Cervantes 20, carries a wealth
of unputdownable titles in Spanish as well as
a good selection of Lonely Planet titles in
English.

Things to See & Do

It's almost worth diverting to Castellón just
to take in the town's **Museo de Bellas Artes**
(☎ 96 472 75 00, Avenida Hermanos Bou 28;
admission €2.10; open 10am-8pm Mon-Sat,
10am-2pm Sun). Housed in spanking new,
award-winning premises, its artefacts, many
of them on public display for the first time,
aren't overawed by the impressive setting.

There are displays devoted to archaeological finds from the area, folk costumes and artefacts and, as you'd expect, a large and impressive ceramics section, focusing on the region's major industry.

If you're interested in folk art and history, you might also want to poke your nose into the **Museo Etnológico de la Diputación** (☎ *964 35 97 03, Calle Sanchis Abella 1; admission free; open 10am-2pm & 4pm-6pm Mon-Fri, 10am-12.30pm Sat in winter, 9am-2pm Mon-Fri, 10am-12.30pm Sat in summer).* It's possible that, during the lifetime of this book, the collection will be transferred to the Museo de Bellas Artes, so check first.

Art lovers will enjoy a visit to the chapel of the **Convento de las Capuchinas** (☎ *96 422 06 41, Calle Núñez de Arce 11; admission free; open 2pm-6pm daily),* which houses 10 fine paintings by Zurbarán.

From Plaza Mayor, bordered by the early-18th-century **town hall** and bustling covered market (see Places to Eat later in this chapter), thrusts the long finger of **El Fadrí**, an octagonal bell tower erected in 1604 and a symbol of the city. Beside the tower is the reconstructed **Concatedral de Santa María** (☎ *96 422 34 63, Plaza Mayor s/n; open 8am-1pm & 5pm-8pm Mon-Sat, 9.30am-11am & 6pm-8pm Sun).* Virtually demolished during the civil war, it has been carefully restored to its original state.

In the centre of the adjacent **Plaza Santa Clara** is a monumental sculpture by Llorens Poy depicting Castellón's history.

Four kilometres east of the centre is **El Grau de Castellón**, a harbour that handles this industrial region's exports, as well as the local fishing fleet and a shoal or two of pleasure craft. Castellón's beaches start north of here.

At the northern edge of El Grau, Castellón's **planetarium** (☎ *96 428 29 68, Paseo Marítimo s/n; adult/child €2.10/1.50; open 4.30pm-8pm Tues-Sat, 11am-2pm Sun)* looks to the stars. It offers a version in English during summer months. Here, too, is an informative display about the Islas Columbretes (see later in this chapter for more details).

In summer, **Golondrina Clavel** (☎ *96 448 08 06, 608 123129)* offers 45-minute boat trips (€6) around the harbour. They also sail to the Islas Columbretes, some 60km offshore from Castellón. This full-day outing costs €42.10/24 per adult/child.

Special Events
The big folk-cultural event of Castellón's year is La Magdalena, a week-long fiesta in the first half of March (see the special section 'Fiestas' for details). Of much more recent origin is the Harley, a long weekend in early September when Harley-Davidson aficionados bike in from all over Europe. Bring your bandanna – and a pair of particularly thick earplugs. To check the arrangements, visit W www.bigtwin-club-spain.com. Even if you don't read Spanish, you can enjoy the startup and soft purr of an idling Harley.

Places to Stay
Hostels Castellón has a couple of Hostelling International (HI) affiliated youth hostels, open to everyone in July and August, and functioning as student residences during the academic year. Both charge €8.50/5.50 for over/under 25s.

El Maestrat (☎ *96 422 04 57, fax 96 423 76 00, Avenida Hermanos Bou 26)* The rooms, seven of them with bathroom, each accommodate four guests.

Mare de Déu del Lledó (☎ *96 425 40 96, fax 96 421 66 77, Calle Orfebre Santalínea 2)* This hostel was being comprehensively gutted at the time of writing but should have been reassembled by now. All rooms are doubles.

Hotels *Hostal La Esperanza* (☎ *96 422 20 31, Calle Trinidad 37)* Singles/doubles/triples €14.40/24/36. The spotless rooms above the small bar-restaurant all have external bathrooms at this cosy family-run place.

Hotel Real (☎ *96 421 19 44, fax 96 421 19 66, Plaza Real 2)* Singles/doubles/triples €34.85/46.45/61.45. Don't be deterred by the rather gloomy reception area. Rooms are pleasant with '70s decor and mod-cons.

Hotel Intur Castellón (☎ *96 422 50 00, fax 96 423 26 06, Calle Herrero 20)* Singles/doubles €98.50/123 Mon-Thur, €52/62 Fri-Sun. Weekend rates are a particular bargain at this award-winning top-end hotel.

NORTHERN VALENCIA

Places to Eat

Julivert *(☎ 96 422 37 26, Calle Caballeros 41)* Open lunchtime only Mon-Fri. Julivert has a good three-course *menú* with vegetarian option for €7.60 and an imaginative choice of *bocadillos* (French-bread sandwiches) and tapas.

Lizarran *(☎ 96 422 69 70, Calle Caballeros 18)* This restaurant, member of a thriving national chain, offers primarily Basque cuisine with a wide range of soups, salads and tapas.

There are three ***Mesón Navarro*** restaurants around town, all bustling and all offering excellent value for meat dishes. The one at Calle Amadeo I 8 *(☎ 96 425 09 66)* also specialises in fresh fish. At their Calle Sanchis Abella branch *(☎ 96 426 11 33)*, the *plato de embutidos* (€7.25), billed as a starter though copious enough to be a meal in itself, is a selection of the finest ham, salami and chorizo, all cut wafer-thin. The third *(☎ 964 21 31 15)*, equally agreeable, is at Plaza Tetuán 26.

Restaurante Casino Antiguo *(☎ 96 422 58 00, Plaza Puerta del Sol 1)* Castellon's casino, with its rich neoclassical facade, is strictly members only, but anyone can eat in style at its restaurant, which is popular with local dignitaries. The patio beyond the restaurant's separate garden entrance is a pleasant spot for summertime dining or simply a drink.

For self-caterers, the ***Mercado Central***, sandwiched between Plazas Mayor and Santa Clara, offers all you might need. Smallish for a town the size of Castellón, it compensates for its lack of size in the richness of its produce. The fish section, the market's largest, teems with seafood, both scaly and in shells.

Entertainment

You'll find a profusion of small bars and simple eateries, most of which come alive only after dark, in the narrow streets just south of Plaza Santa Clara. In summer, the scene moves to El Grau to catch the sea breezes. Paseo Buenavista is lined with bars and cafes, which also encircle the recently designed Plaza del Mar, at the dividing line between leisure and fishing ports.

Getting There & Around

Castellón has a smart new combined bus and train station that may not feature on older town maps.

Most intercity services leave from the new bus station (☎ 96 424 07 78). Buses for El Grau and the beaches to its north leave from Plaza Borrull. Frequent buses for Benicàssim set out from Plaza Fadrell while those to and from Valencia operate from Plaza del País Valenciano.

For both Valencia and the resorts to the north, except for Benicàssim, trains are both swifter and more frequent than buses.

To hire a taxi, either call ☎ 96 422 74 74 or ☎ 96 425 46 46.

ISLAS COLUMBRETES

The Islas Columbretes, a cluster of tiny volcanic islands, lie some 60km (33 nautical miles) offshore from Castellón. Once the haunt of smugglers, pirates and the occasional shipwrecked fisherman, they're now a nature reserve and vital stopover for migratory birds.

Visitors are only allowed on the largest horseshoe-shaped island, Isla Grossa, a mere 60m wide at its broadest point, which has a lighthouse and small cemetery. Its clear waters seethe with marine life and make for excellent diving.

In high season, boats from Vinaròs, Peñíscola, Alcossebre, Oropesa (divers only) and – the nearest departure point – Castellón visit the islands. For more information on each destination, see the section on each town later. A maximum of 250 visitors per day are allowed to disembark so it's wise to reserve a day or two in advance. Divers need special permission, which the boat operator normally obtains.

BENICÀSSIM (BENICASIM)

postcode 12560 • pop 11,900

Benicàssim (People or Family of Kassim in Arabic) was founded by the Muslims. Some 13km north of Castellón, it has been a popular seaside resort since the 19th century. The impetus was the railway pushing northwards in 1872, making the coast more accessible and attracting from both Castellón

BENICÀSSIM (BENICASIM)

NORTHERN VALENCIA

PLACES TO STAY
1 Camping Azahar
8 Hotel Avenida
9 Hostal el Forcat
17 Albergue Argentina
19 Camping Florida

PLACES TO EAT
5 Fibercafe
10 Ribalta
12 Restaurante Plaza

OTHER
2 Post Office
3 Main Tourist Office
4 Iglesia de Santo Tomás
  de Villanueva
6 Train Station
7 Deportes Marqués
11 Locutorio (phone centre)
13 Bodegas Carmelitano
14 Bus Stop
15 Torre San Vicente
16 Tourist Kiosk
18 Aquarama
20 Tourist Kiosk

and Valencia wealthy families who chose this stretch of coast to build their summer residences.

Although Benicàssim's more recent architectural legacy can't rival the charm of Peñíscola's old quarter, the town certainly vies with its northern neighbour for the title of the Costa del Azahar's best coastal playground. And, unlike both Peñíscola and the Costa Blanca, it isn't overrun by foreigners. A high 80% of the town's visitors are Spanish and many residents of Madrid, Valencia and Castellón own holiday apartments here.

Orientation & Information
Benicàssim, like other resorts along the coast of the Comunidad Valenciana, such as Oro-pesa and Benicarló, is really two places with two quite different personalities. The old town, originally established inland to provide protection from the raids of Turkish and Barbary pirates, has been emphatically upstaged by the strip of development, in many parts barely a couple of blocks deep, which stretches for 6km along the coast. Above all five of its sandy beaches flutters the European Union (EU) blue flag, which is awarded only to those parts of the coast that meet strict standards of cleanliness and facilities.

Tourist Offices At the time of writing, the tourist office (☎ 96 430 01 02) was within the Ayuntamiento (Town Hall). Within the lifespan of this book, it will transfer to new premises beside Iglesia de Santo Tomás de Villanueva, a mere 150m away on Calle de Santo Tomás. It opens 9am to 3pm and 5pm to 7.15pm (to 8.30pm in summer) Monday to Saturday, plus 10am to 1pm and 5pm to 7.15pm on Sunday.

From June to mid-October, two other offices function along the beachfront.

Post The post office is on Calle Correus.

Email & Internet Access The Locutorio (phone centre), at Calle Castellón 17, has nine computers and charges €3.60 per hour. It opens 10am to 2.30pm and 4.30pm to midnight daily.

Things to See & Do
Benicàssim's 6km of broad beach and shallow waters are the town's main attraction. If you're feeling active aquatic-wise, head inland to **Aquarama water park** (☎ 96 430 33 21, N-340 km 987; adult/child €13/9 from 11am, €10.25/7.75 from 4pm; open 11am-7pm mid-June–mid-Sept). Back at sea level, there's a **sailing school** (☎ 96 430 32 51) on Playa els Terrers. The same people also offer windsurfing lessons and equipment hire, operating from Playa Heliopolis.

At the north-eastern end of the beach are **Las Villas**, summer bourgeois residences whose construction in the late 19th and early 20th centuries launched Benicàssim as a holiday resort. Mercifully, many have been saved from destruction before they could be supplanted by yet another looming high-rise. Information plaques are in Spanish. Ask at the tourist office for the English version of the free pamphlet *Ruta de las Villas* and stroll pedestrianised Paseos Marítimo Pilar Coloma and Bernat Artola to view the residences from the exterior. As befits seaside architecture, breaking free from the usual constraints of urban design, the style of many is eclectic, even frivolous.

At the southern end of the Bernat Artola sits the 16th-century **Torre San Vicente**, one of 18 watchtowers constructed along the length of this coastline to give advance warning and a place of last retreat if pirates appeared offshore.

Backing Benicàssim and approximately 6km inland is the **Desierto de las Palmas**, a mountain range with a still-functioning Carmelite monastery at its heart. Far from being a desert (for the monks it meant a place for meditation and spiritual withdrawal), it's now a nature park and a popular outdoor activities area for walkers, climbers and mountain bikers. The greenness of the area contrasts with the more desiccated countryside all around it. For trail information, call by the La Bartola information centre (☎ 96 476 07 27), Benicàssim–Ermita de la Magdalena road km 7.8, which opens 9am to 2pm and 3pm to 5pm Monday to Friday, and 9.30am to 3pm Saturday and Sunday. High spots are the ruins of the Arab fortification, **Castillo de Montarnés**, a short clamber from the road, and **Monte Bartolo**, the highest point at 728m, from where there are staggering, wrap-around views.

Bodegas Carmelitano (*☎ 96 430 08 49, Calle Bodolz s/n; admission free; open 9.30am-1.30pm & 3pm-7.30pm daily*) continue to distil – among other firewater products – the Licor Carmelitano that was originally crafted by the monks of the Carmelite monastery. They offer free tours and sampling and there's an information sheet in English.

There are three golf courses within easy driving distance from Benicàssim: the nine-hole Club de Golf Costa Azahar (*☎ 96 428 09 79*), the 18-hole Club de Campo del Mediterráneo La Coma (*☎ 96 432 12 27*) and Club de Golf Panorámica (*☎ 96 449 90 02*), also full size.

Special Events

Whatever your taste in music, Benicàssim offers something that will set your fingers snapping.

If you're a Latino lover, try to coincide with Mulabe, held at the end of June and in the first week of July. Between 6pm and 5am, Benicàssim sways to a salsa and samba beat at this festival of Latin American music, dance, handicrafts and culture. Season tickets allowing admission to all concerts are a very reasonable €30. For details, check out W www.mulabe.com.

In early August young people converge by the thousand for the town's annual Festival Internacional de Benicàssim (FIB), now one of Spain's – Europe's even – top outdoor music fests, which also embraces short films, dance and alternative theatre. Over three days, it brings in the big international names across a variety of music genres. Recently, for example, the city throbbed to the sounds of Fat Boy Slim, the Manic Street Preachers, Pulp, The Avalanches, and many other groups, both famous and carefully selected up-and-coming acts. Two special areas are set up with space for up to 22,000 campers.

To close the season, Benicàssim stages its annual Certamen Internacional de Guitarra in late August/early September. One of the

world's major moots of its kind, it will strike a chord with all lovers of classical guitar.

Places to Stay

Camping Benicàssim's seven camp sites are all within reasonable walking distance of the beaches. Take your pick and plant your poles. The following two remain open year-round:

Camping Florida (*☎ 96 439 23 85, fax 96 439 23 85, Calle Sigalero 34*) 2 people, tent & car €17. This is a shady spot in the heart of the resort.

Camping Azahar (*☎ 96 430 31 96, fax 96 430 25 12, Partida Villaroig s/n*) €3/6/3 per person/tent/car Jan-June & Sept-Dec, €3.15/7.75/3.15 July, €3.55/9/3.55 Aug. Camping Azahar is a first-class camp site, particularly popular in winter with northern Europeans. Its only downside is intermittent noise from the railway that passes close by.

Hostels *Albergue Argentina* (*☎ 96 430 27 09, fax 96 430 04 73, Avenida Ferrandis Salvador 40*) €4.85/6.60 juniors/seniors in rooms for 2-4. Open Feb–20 Dec. This HI hostel, right on the seafront, is a whopping, whitewashed complex with two pools and 140 bunks. Forget it in July and August, when it's always booked solid.

Hotels *Hostal el Forcat* (*☎ 96 430 50 84, fax 96 430 06 98, Avenida Castellón 20*) Singles/doubles with bathroom €18/30. Up in the old town, rooms at Benicàssim's cheapest option are perfectly adequate, although the affiliated bar below attracts a sometimes seedy clientele.

Hotel Avenida (*☎ 96 430 00 47, fax 96 430 00 79, Avenida Castellón 2*) Rooms €29.75 Mar-June & Oct, compulsory B&B €43.90 July & Sept, from €54.10 Aug. Open Mar-Oct. Hotel Avenida is a friendly, appealing mid-range hotel with a pool and shady courtyard. It's particularly good value outside the summer season.

Places to Eat

Plenty of economical *eateries* line Calle de Santo Tomás and Calle Castellón, the old town's main street.

NORTHERN VALENCIA

Fibercafe (☎ 96 430 12 00, *Calle Santo Tomás 62)* Open daily July-Sept, Wed-Sun Oct-June. This hip place serves vegetarian food to a background of indie, radical music.

Ribalta (☎ 96 430 23 99, *Calle Castellón 7)* Pizzas €6.60, mains €10.85-13.85. Closed Mon & Jan. Ribalta, light, airy and tastefully designed, is an intimate, friendly place that functions as a restaurant, pizzeria and sandwich joint.

Restaurante Plaza (☎ 96 430 00 72, *Calle Cristóbal Colón 3)* Meat mains €7-10, fish mains €12.50-15. Although this restaurant has recently changed hands, it remains stylish, reasonably priced and a favourite with locals.

Entertainment

During summer and at weekends, Benicàssim has a vibrant nightlife. Once a large new leisure area, the Ciudad de Ocio (under construction at the time of writing), comes alive, it will probably spell the death of most of the old town's characterful bars, which will either be compelled to close or convert to something more restrained.

Get yourself to Calle de los Dolores (Els Dolors) in the old town while there's time. Here you'll find a great collection of lively bars including *Pay Pay*, *Bumerang*, *Pedal*, *Campus* and *Resaca* (the perhaps appropriately named Hangover).

Getting There & Around

Autos Mediterraneo (☎ 96 422 00 54) buses run to and from Castellón every 30 minutes (every 15 minutes in summer).

There are seven trains daily to and from Valencia (€4.10, one hour). For a wider choice of transport both north and south, take the bus to Castellón, from where trains are more frequent.

You can hire mountain bikes from Deportes Marqués (☎ 964 30 05 89), Calle Secretario Chornet 18, for €14.50/26.50/57.70 per day/three days/week.

OROPESA (ORPESA) DEL MAR

It's a fine scenic drive from Benicàssim to Oropesa along a narrow road that winds around the rocky coastline. This small but expanding resort is a relatively tranquil alternative in the high season to seething Peñíscola and Benicàssim, to the north and south. What remains of the old quarter of Oropesa, like that of its larger sister Benicàssim, is set a little inland and back from the strip of development that hugs the shore.

The beaches of **Morro de Gos** and **Les Amplaries** on the north side are great for swimming and water sports. To the south, the protected beach spot of **La Concha** shelves gradually and is ideal for families.

The main tourist office (☎ 96 431 22 41) is at Avenida de la Plana 1 in the old town. A second one (☎ 96 476 66 12) operates in summer from Plaza París beside Playa de la Concha.

Azahar Submarinismo (☎/fax 96 431 23 13) at Puerto Deportivo, Local 6, offers diving courses in English from March to December and also arranges diving visits to the Islas Columbretes.

ALCOSSEBRE (ALCOCEBRE)

Alcossebre has resisted high-rise development. Although the town is starting to spread, construction is restrained and mainly tasteful. It's a good place for a quiet break and an excellent spot for a family holiday.

The Sierra de Irta runs northwards from town towards Peñíscola, its flanks incised by rocky coves accessible only by dirt road. This brief stretch is one of the very few parts of the Valencian coastline that, thanks to its very ruggedness, has not been exploited for tourism or agriculture. Southwards lies a flatter land of shade-giving pine, olive groves, salt flats and good, uncrowded beaches.

The tourist office (☎ 964 41 22 05), Calle San José 59, opens 10am to 1.30pm and 5pm to 7.30pm Monday to Saturday, plus 10am to 1pm Sunday morning from June to October (9.30am to 1.30pm, Monday to Saturday from November to May).

Barracuda (☎ 964 41 26 23) offers diving courses in English and rents equipment. They organise visits to the Islas Columbretes (€93 for two dives including equipment hire or €60 if you're just along for the cruise). You'll find their office beside the small leisure craft port of Las Fuentes.

Also beside the port is **Cheers Bar**, known locally as the 'British Embassy'. Drop in for a drink and for the lowdown on Alcossebre in your own lingo.

Masía del Rull (☎ 630 77 94 96; €15 per hour; open daily June-Aug, Sat & Sun only Sept-May) offers gentle horse riding along the coastal plain. Follow the signs southwards along the coast from Alcossebre.

Camping Playa Tropicana (☎ 964 41 24 48, fax 964 41 28 05) 2 people, tent & car €24.75. Open mid-Mar–Oct. 'Tropical Beach Camping' is an apposite name for this green, well managed Class 1 camp site fronting a sandy beach. Not without its pretensions (reproduction classical statues flank the alleys and even greet you in the washrooms), it's probably the most luxurious, not to say expensive, camp site you'll ever pitch your tent at. Prices go up by 30% in July and August.

Discoteca Túnel (☎ 964 76 10 62) Admission including first drink €9. Open daily July & Aug, Sat & Sun only Easter-June & Sept–mid-Oct. If the tranquillity of Alcossebre becomes a mite oppressive, step up the pace at this disco, a mock castle on the shoreline beside Playa Capicorb at the southern limit of the development.

To get there, take the train to Alcalá de Chivert, on the main coastal line, then bus (six daily) onto Alcossebre. For a taxi, call ☎ 964 41 01 52 or ☎ 629 63 40 03.

PEÑÍSCOLA
postcode 12598 • pop 4550
Peñíscola's old town, all narrow cobbled streets and whitewashed houses, perches on a rocky fortified promontory jutting into the sea. It's pretty as a postcard – and just as commercial, with dozens of souvenir and ceramics shops and clothes boutiques catering to the ascending hordes of tourists. It's pleasantly higgledy piggledy, though at high noon in high summer it's difficult to prise your way through the throngs of visitors. As you meander through its streets and around the castle, you're following in the footsteps of Sophia Loren and Charlton Heston; it was

in Peñíscola that large sequences of the Hollywood blockbuster epic El Cid were shot.

By stark contrast, the modern high-rises sprouting northwards along the coast are mostly leaden and charmless. But the **Paseo Marítimo** (seafront promenade) makes pleasant walking and the Playa Norte, a 2km strand, is one of the best beaches on the Valencian shoreline. Playa Norte is being extended a further 3km northwards, an enterprise requiring, say the authorities, the importing of – such precision may raise an eyebrow – 1,703,806 cu metres of sand.

August is the cruellest month. Facilities are swamped, the old town heaves with humanity and accommodation prices can be as much as double their low-season ·equivalent. By contrast, October to June – especially the winter, under cobalt blue skies – is delightful as the town breathes again and recovers from its annual summer invasion.

History
The rocky promontory on which the old town sits was first settled by the Phoenicians as a coastal trading post. In succeeding centuries, Carthaginians, Romans, Byzantines, Arabs and Knights Templar (a medieval military religious order), all recognising Peñíscola's defensive potential, cast covetous eyes from the sea and occupied the outcrop, each in turn.

Its mainly 14th-century castle was also briefly the very centre of Christendom. Between 1421 and 1429, at a time of schism within the Catholic church, Pope Benedict XIII, known as Papa Luna (the Moon Pope; you'll see his crescent symbol all over the old town), and his successor, Clement VIII, established themselves and their entourage in the castle.

The present city walls, commissioned by Philip II and designed by the Italian civil engineer Juan Bautista Antonelli, date from 1578 and are still largely intact.

Information
Tourist Offices The main tourist office (☎ 964 48 02 08, Ⓦ www.peninscola.org) is at the south end of the Paseo Marítimo. It opens 9.30am to 8pm Monday to Friday, 10am to 1pm on Saturday and Sunday, and

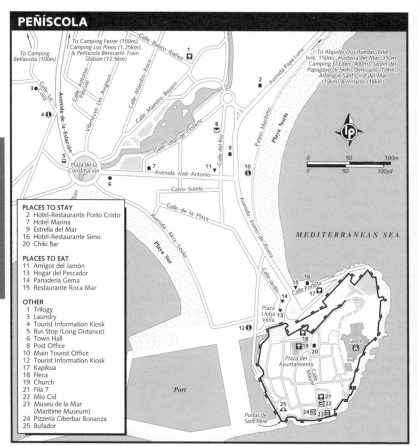

PEÑÍSCOLA

To Camping Bellavista (100m)

To Camping Ferrer (150m), Camping Los Pinos (1.25km), & Peñíscola Benicarló Train Station (12.5km)

To Alquiler Dos Ruedas (bike hire; 150m), Hostería del Mar (350m), Camping El Edén (400m), Jardin del Papagayo (6.5km), Benicarló (10km), Albergue Sant Crist del Mar (10km) & Vinaròs (18km)

Calle-Blasco-Ibañez
Calle-Maestro-Roca
Calle-Maestro-Bayarri
Calle-Antonio-Pascual
Avenida-de-la-Estación
Avenida-de-la-Estación
Villeneuve-Les-Avignon
Calle-La-Cova
Calle-Ullal-de-l'Estany
Calle-del-Río
Avenida-José-Antonio
Plaza-de-la-Constitución
Calvo-Sotelo
Calle-de-la-Playa
Avenida-Akra-Leuke
Playa Sur
Port
Avenida-Primo-de-Rivera
Avenida-Papa-Luna
Paseo-Marítimo
Playa Norte
MEDITERRANEAN SEA
Calle-Jardín
Plaza Llotja Vella
Calle-Porteta
Plaza del Ayuntamiento
Calle Mayor
Castle
Portal de Sant Pere

0   50   100m
0   50   100yd

MEDITERRANEAN SEA

PLACES TO STAY
2 Hotel-Restaurante Porto Cristo
7 Hotel Marina
9 Estrella del Mar
16 Hotel-Restaurante Simo
20 Chiki Bar

PLACES TO EAT
11 Amigos del Jamón
13 Hogar del Pescador
14 Panadería Gema
15 Restaurante Roca Mar

OTHER
1 Trilogy
3 Laundry
4 Tourist Information Kiosk
5 Bus Stop (Long Distance)
6 Town Hall
8 Post Office
10 Main Tourist Office
12 Tourist Information Kiosk
17 Kapikua
18 Fleca
19 Church
21 Fila 7
22 Mío Cid
23 Museu de la Mar (Maritime Museum)
24 Pizzería Ciberbar Bonanza
25 Bufador

4pm to 8pm on Saturday from July to mid-September. Hours during the rest of the year are 10am to 1.30pm and 4pm to 7pm Monday to Saturday and 10am to 1pm on Sunday. There are three other tourist information booths around town, staffed in summer only.

Post The post office is at Calle del Río 13.

Email & Internet Access There are two places in the old town where you can log on. The place you choose depends whether you fancy skimming your emails over a pizza or a pint. Pizzería Ciberbar Bonanza, ☎ 964 48 00 82, Calle Mayor 44, has six machines and opens from 6pm to at least 1am daily, as well as 1pm to 3.30pm in July and August.

Mío Cid, almost opposite at No 43, has a couple of computers and opens 8pm to 4am daily.

Laundry Lavandería Rosa Mari, Calle La Cova s/n, will spin you a load of washing for €5.50 (€11 for it to be returned dried).

Things to See

The 14th-century **castle** (☎ 964 48 00 21; admission €1.20; open at least 9.30am-2.30pm

& 4.30pm-8.30pm daily Easter–mid-Oct, 9.30am-1pm & 3.15pm-6pm daily mid-Oct–Easter) was built by the Knights Templar on Moorish foundations. It's fun to ramble around its courtyards and upper walls, which offer great views of the old town and fishing port, the mountains of Sierra de Irta snaking southwards and bounded by tight rocky bays, and the broad sandy sweep of the Playa Norte extending as far as Benicarló. Poke your nose into the barrel-vaulted Gothic hall, a regular venue for summertime concerts that exploit its superb acoustics. The Pontifical Chamber is a grand term for Papa Luna's small study and library, its seaward windows facing distant, longed-for Rome. Signing is multilingual throughout.

The small, well designed **Museu de la Mar** (Maritime Museum; ☎ 964 48 16 03, Calle Príncipe s/n; admission free; open 10am-2pm & 4pm-dusk daily Apr-Sept, Tues-Sun only Oct-Mar) brings together a range of artefacts illustrating the town's former preoccupation with things maritime. Three aquariums seethe with specimens of offshore life.

A rainbow of exotic tropical birds squawk, trill and look admonishingly at you in the **Jardín del Papagayo** (Parrot Garden; ☎ 964 46 12 24, Camino del Término; adult/child €5.50/4; open 11am-2.30pm & 4.30pm-dusk Oct-June, 11am-dusk July-Sept), 6.5km from Peñíscola. Every so often the stars are put through a series of tricks and hoops. Even if such manipulation leaves you cold, the birds can't fail to impress by just being themselves.

As you walk up to the old town, enjoy a moment of fun for free. On your left at the first bend beyond Portal de Sant Pere is the **Bufador**, a sink hole in the cliff from where, if there's any swell at all, you can hear the sea slurp and gurgle. If the waves are a little stronger, it will even behave like a whale's blowhole and soak the unwary passer-by.

Activities

From Easter to October, boats (€4.25 per person) depart hourly from the port for a 30-minute trip around the peninsula. Between May and mid-October, you can also undertake a full-day outing (€30) to the Islas Columbretes (see earlier in this chapter). It can be a choppy ride but the destination, a cluster of tiny volcanic stubs sticking out of the Mediterranean, make a little queasiness almost worthwhile. For information and reservations, you can ring ☎ 964 48 02 00 or ☎ 964 48 08 65.

A day or half-day's hiking in the Sierra de Irta makes an effective antidote to too much intensive flat-on-your-back beach work. A 26km trail, the PRV-194, winds through this long flank of mountain running parallel to the coast south of Peñíscola. It embraces, among other features, a deserted chapel, a ruined castle and a beach which only the most energetic ever reach. Less strenuous variants allow you to pick and mix your route. Ask for the English version of the pamphlet Senderos de Irta at the main tourist office.

Special Events

The main fiesta among Peñíscola's several annual celebrations takes place on 8 and 9 September. Les Danses, in addition to all the usual elements of fiesta fun, includes some unique folk dancing and, like many pueblos further south in the Comunidad, a Moros y Cristianos parade. For details, see the special section 'Fiestas'.

Places to Stay

Most hotels close for at least part of the winter period; quite a few are shuttered from early October until the following Easter. Prices rise very substantially during August and, for many places, in July, too. You may need to call upon your calculator or an abacus to work out the complex tariff system of some hotels.

Camping Peñíscola boasts as many as 12 camp sites in and around the resort. The ones listed below all have at least one swimming pool.

Camping El Eden (☎ 964 48 05 62, fax 964 48 98 28, Ⓦ www.camping-eden .com, Avenida Papa Luna s/n) 2 people, tent & car €21.65 July & Aug, €13.65 June & Sept, €12.65 Oct-May. Handiest for both beach and old city, this camp site is geared very much to caravans rather than tents.

NORTHERN VALENCIA

Camping Bellavista *(☎ 964 48 01 35, fax 964 48 16 49, Partida la Cova s/n)* €4.10 each person/tent/car. Open year round. This place, convenient for the Playa Sur (South Beach) and old city, also caters mainly for the caravan visitor.

Camping Ferrer *(☎/fax 964 48 92 23, Avenida Estación 27)* €4.20 each person/tent/car. Open Easter-Sept. If you're packing a tent, this well shaded place offers a much better chance of finding a pitch. The adjacent ***hostal*** has rooms with bathroom for €36 from September to June (€48.10 July to August).

Camping Los Pinos *(☎/fax 964 48 03 79, Calle Abellers s/n)* €3.35/3.50/3.35 per person/tent/car. Just off Avenida Estación and well signed, this is a pleasant, deeply shaded option, a mere 2km from town yet remote enough to be away from its bustle. It has a small shop and bar/restaurant.

Hostels There's a HI hostel, ***Albergue San Crist del Mar*** (open summer only) at Benicarló, 8km northwards up the coast.

Hostales & Hotels *Chiki Bar (☎ 964 48 02 84, Calle Mayor 3)* Rooms with bathroom €24-36 according to season. Up in the old town, welcoming Chiki Bar, in addition to its engaging name, offers great value. Rooms are modern, clean as a new pin and offer great views. Its restaurant, open Easter to October, does reasonable set-price meals. Its sole disadvantage: the church bells, but a hurled stone away, chime tinnily on the hour, every hour.

Hotel Marina *(☎/fax 964 48 08 90, Avenida José Antonio 42)* Singles/doubles €15/27 Apr-May & Oct, €16.25/33 June–mid-July & Sept, €18/42.10 mid-July–Aug. Open Easter-Oct. Hotel Marina's 19 rooms, all with bathroom, are nothing fancy but they are reasonably priced, particularly given their position at the base of the old town.

Hotel-Restaurante Simo *(☎ 964 48 06 20, Calle Porteta 5, ⓦ www.restaurantesimo .com)* Singles/doubles with bathroom from €31.50/37, €45/57 Aug. Open Mar-Sept. Along a lane at the base of the old town, the majority of the 10 rooms at the friendly Simo offer great sea views.

Estrella del Mar *(☎/fax 964 48 07 45, Avenida Primo de Rivera 31)* Rooms with bathroom €33. Open Apr–mid-Oct. Down at shore level, most of Estrella del Mar's rooms look out over the beach.

Hotel-Restaurante Porto Cristo *(☎ 964 48 07 18, fax 964 48 90 49, Avenida Papa Luna 2)* Singles €30-42, doubles €40-50.50 according to season, €81.25 Aug. Open Apr-Nov. The rooms here are a trifle gloomy but all have a balcony, air-con, heating and TV.

Hostería del Mar *(☎ 964 48 06 00, fax 964 48 13 63, Avenida Papa Luna 18)* Singles/doubles €41.50/55.30 Jan-June & mid-Sept–Dec, €59/83.55 July & 1-15 Sept, €83/110 Aug. Open year round. This hotel has considerably more character than most of its undistinguished beachside multistorey neighbours on the north side of town. Its restaurant does a very respectable menú for €15.75. It does a Saturday night medieval banquet that may set you searching for an alternative round table that evening...

Places to Eat

The Paseo Marítimo, the main waterfront promenade, is lined with ***restaurants*** specialising in local seafood (and high prices).

Amigos del Jamón *(☎ 964 46 75 18, Avenida José Antonio 4)* Platters €7.50-12. 'Ham Lovers' is for the seriously carnivore. Order a wooden platter packed with *butifarras*, *salchichones* or *chorizo*, all local variants of the humble sausage, or go for something less processed in the ham line. Dishes are accompanied by *pan y tomate*, bread smeared with grated tomato, a speciality of Catalunya, only a few kilometres up the coast.

Hogar del Pescador *(☎ 964 48 95 88, Plaza Llotja Vella s/n)* Fish mains €8.50-15. In a town where, even though fresh fish is caught daily, many restaurants serve up defrosted fare, you can be sure that this place offers only the freshest fish, bought daily from Peñíscola's market. It doesn't come cheap but you won't find a better *mariscada* (seafood selection) in town – or get better value for your euro – than Hogar del Pescador's at €30.

***Restaurante Roca Mar** (☎ 964 48 06 21, Calle Porteta 3)* Meals €13-24. The food isn't significantly better than that of many other places but the ambience of the terrace, where the sea laps at your feet and the lights shimmer across the water, makes the meal. If you aren't in the mood for a full meal, go for one of their rice dishes (€8 to €13; minimum two people).

***Panadería Gema** (☎ 964 48 18 71, Calle Jardín 4)* Open to 9pm Mon-Sat, Sun morning. Tucked away from the main tourist trails, Gema's is an uplifting way to start the day. There's a great selection of freshly baked breads and local cakes, lipsmacking fruit juices and the coffee is several degrees tastier than the usual hotel slop. You can also have a tasty sandwich at any time of the day.

Entertainment

Three of Peñíscola's four discos are up in the old town – and the fourth's an easy walk from it. They mostly pound and heave nightly from July to mid-September, open on Friday and Saturday nights at other times between Easter and mid-October, and close for winter.

***Fleca** (Plaza del Ayuntamiento s/n)* is no more than 150m from ***Fila 7** (Calle Mayor 35)*, which has taken over an old cinema. A little lower down is ***Kapikua** (Calle Porteta 14)*, while ***Trilogy** (Calle Blasco Ibañez s/n)* is set back on its own, across the small artificial lake at the neck of the peninsula. Trilogy and Fleca have an admission fee of about €6, while at the other two, which function more as disco pubs, you pay only for what you drink.

Getting There & Away

Auto Res (☎ 902 020999) has at least one bus daily to and from Madrid. Autocares Hife (☎ 902 119814) runs at least two services a day to and from Barcelona, and one/two daily to and from Zaragoza. The Peñíscola intercity bus stop is on Plaza de la Constitución and most services also pass by Benicarló and Vinaròs.

Local buses also run roughly every 30 minutes between Peñíscola, Benicarló and Vinaròs.

The nearest train station is in Benicarló, about 10km away. Between July and mid-September, a bus runs between Peñíscola and the station every half hour. For train services along this stretch of the coast, see the Getting There & Around under Vinaròs.

Getting Around

Only residents and the seriously antisocial take their cars into the old town, where distances are so short and gradients so steep that two legs are the best form of propulsion anyway. Unless you're marooned in one of Peñíscola's northernmost hotels, you'll find the walk into town along the Paseo Marítimo an agreeable experience in itself.

Another safe and pleasant way to get around at shore level is to hire a bike from Alquiler Dos Ruedas (☎ 964 48 14 78), Avenida Papa Luna 27, 150m south of the Peñíscola Palace hotel. Prices per day start at €8.40.

To hire a taxi, call Union Radio-Taxi 964 46 05 06. For car hire, contact Rent a Car Peñíscola, ☎ 964 48 92 26, in the Forner building, Plaza de la Constitución. Perhaps because they have a monopoly in town, they don't come cheap.

BENICARLÓ
postcode 12580 • pop 19,900

The most exciting thing about Benicarló is its artichokes. Faint praise, you may well say, and indeed there's not much to make you linger in town. Like Vinaròs to the north, Benicarló is a commercial and industrial centre – only not so much and not so successfully. And like its northern neighbour, Benicarló has tourism aspirations, however, the place is all but eclipsed by Peñíscola just to its south. So perhaps God relented and gave the town what must rank as Europe's finest artichoke (see the boxed text 'Putting the Art in Artichoke' later in this chapter).

All but destroyed by Turkish pirates in 1556, then besieged by the French in the early-19th-century War of Independence

Putting the Art in Artichoke

The bottle of Spanish wine on your table may well bear a *denominación de origen* label, which indicates that it's from a specific area and, if that area's a good one for grapes, guaranteeing a certain level of quality. Nowadays, a few privileged regional cheeses also carry a similar endorsement.

But not until 18 September 1998 did the humble artichoke achieve such status and was given a *denominación de origen* label of its own, indicating that it grew and was lovingly cared for around Benicarló.

Inland from town stretches a silvery-green triangle formed by field upon field of spiky artichoke plants. However, these are not just any old artichokes. A combination of soil and a gentle Mediterranean climate, plus careful tending, produces a firm, round, compact head, ripe for plucking in a season which begins in October and lasts right through until June.

Should you happen to hit Benicarló at the right time in January (the exact date varies from year to year), you can join in the town's annual artichoke festival Fiesta del la Alcachofa de Benicarló.

(Peninsula War) then attacked and put to fire during the Carlist wars later in the same century (see History in the Facts about Valencia chapter), Benicarló has taken a battering from history. Nowadays, too, squeezed between its two more attractive neighbours and with little in the way of beaches to pull in visitors, it sees tourism euros being spent enticingly near but not near enough.

Benicarló's tourist office (☎ 964 47 31 80), on Plaza de la Constitución, opens 10am to 1.45pm and 5pm to 8pm, Monday to Friday.

You can surf the Web (€0.90/15 minutes) at Power Internet, Calle Hernán Cortés 28.

The early 18th-century **Iglesia de San Bartolomé**, in the square of the same name, has an elaborate baroque door surrounded by four bulky, twisted columns and a larger-than-life statue of St Bartholomew lodged in the niche above. The church's other glory is its tall, free-standing octagonal tower.

Less than 100m along Calle Mayor is the **Museo Histórico Arqueológico Municipal** *(☎ 964 47 00 50, Calle Mayor 7; admission free; open 6.30pm-9.30pm daily)*. Occupying the former town jail, it has some interesting finds from nearby Iberian settlements.

Albergue Sant Crist del Mar (☎ 964 47 08 36, fax 964 46 02 25, Avenida Yecla 29) Dorm beds under/over-25s €5.40/8.40 including breakfast. Open daily July–mid-Aug, Mon-Fri mid-Sept–June. This 76-bed, HI hostel, serving the three towns of Peñíscola, Vinaròs and Benicarló, is a convenient 150m from both beach and port.

For buses see Getting There & Away under Peñíscola earlier in this chapter.

A taxi (☎ 964 46 05 06) to or from the station, 2km from town, costs about €4.25. For Renfe trains, see Getting There & Around under Vinaròs, later. There's a Renfe booking office (☎ 964 47 01 99) at Calle Alcalá de Xivert 20 in Benicarló.

VINAROS
postcode 12500 • pop 22,500

Unlike its sybaritic neighbours, Vinaròs is a working town whose port is still used commercially and by in-shore fishing boats. Consequently, it's about the best place along the coast to enjoy fresh sea produce, especially shellfish – and most especially its succulent scampi. A fairly grim, dreary place away from the seafront, its redeeming feature is its fairly small but sandy beaches, and the Paseos of Blasco Ibañez, Colón and San Pedro, three waterfront promenades lined with restaurants and cafes. It's a very Spanish resort, perhaps more than any other on the Valencian coastline.

Information

Tourist Offices The tourist office (☎ 964 45 33 34) is at Paseo Colón s/n. It opens 10.30am to 2pm and 5pm to 8pm daily, June to October, and 8am to 3pm Monday to Friday, November to May.

Post The post office is in Plaza Jovellar.

Email & Internet Access K'em@scentro, Calle San Francisco 13, opens 10.30am to 2pm and 5.30pm to 10pm daily. It charges €0.05 per minute, €2.40 per hour. Powernet, Calle Remedios 1, has nine computers and charges €3.60 per hour.

Laundry There's a laundry, open 9am to 1pm, at Calle San Francisco 34.

Things to See & Do

The **Iglesia Arciprestal** is a fine baroque church with a tall bell tower and elaborate main doorway decorated with candy-twist columns. From here, pedestrianised Calle Mayor leads to the **covered market**, which makes for an enjoyable browse – savouring the fresh fish, fruit and vegetables, and the attractive lines of its modernista architecture.

Of the town's two beaches, **Playa Fortí** is the larger. **Playa Fora Forat**, more attractively landscaped, offers some shade.

Aqua Sub (☎ 964 45 66 61, fax 964 49 61 62, Calle Doctor Fleming L-6), runs PADI diving courses year round in five languages, including English, and also hires out equipment. *Buenaventura del Mar* (☎ 608 048 948, fax 964 45 67 03, W www.columbretes .com, Calle San Francisco 27, 3rd floor) organises deep-sea fishing expeditions and day trips to the Islas Columbretes (see the section earlier in this chapter) and the Ebro delta, just into Catalunya.

Special Events

The good folk of Vinaròs conveniently space their celebrations throughout the year. The

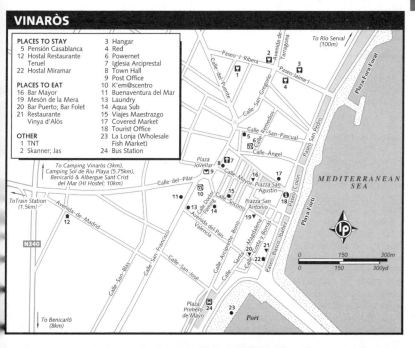

VINARÒS

PLACES TO STAY
5 Pensión Casablanca
12 Hostal Restaurante Teruel
22 Hostal Miramar

PLACES TO EAT
16 Bar Mayor
19 Mesón de la Mera
20 Bar Puerto; Bar Folet
21 Restaurante Vinya d'Alòs

OTHER
1 TNT
2 Skanner; Jas
3 Hangar
4 Red
6 Powernet
7 Iglesia Arciprestal
8 Town Hall
9 Post Office
10 K'em@scentro
11 Buenaventura del Mar
13 Laundry
14 Aqua Sub
15 Viajes Maestrazgo
17 Covered Market
18 Tourist Office
23 La Lonja (Wholesale Fish Market)
24 Bus Station

To Río Serval (100m)

Playa Fora Forat

Paseo J-Ribera

Avenida de Tarragona

Paseo Jaime-I

Calle-del-Puente

Calle-San-Gregorio

Calle Remedios

San-Pascual

Paseo San Pedro

Calle San-Pascual

Calle-Ángel

Plaza Jovellar

Calle Mayor

Piazza San Agustín

MEDITERRANEAN SEA

To Camping Vinaròs (3km),
Camping Sol de Riu Playa (5.75km),
Benicarló & Albergue Sant Crist
del Mar (HI Hostel; 10km)

Calle-del-Pilar

To Train Station (1.5km)

Avenida-de-Madrid

N340

Calle-San-Blas

Calle San Francisco

Calle-San-José

Calle Doctor Fleming

Calle-Socorro

Avenida del País Valencià

Santa Magdalena

Calle-Arcipreste-Bono

Costa-y-Borrás

Paseo Blasco Ibáñez

Piazza San Antonio

Playa Fortí

0   150   300m
0   150   300yd

To Benicarló (8km)

Plaza Primero de Mayo

Port

town's *carnaval* celebrations occupy a full week of festivities just before the onset of Lent. Its processions, featuring over 3000 extravagantly dressed participants, are famous throughout the Comunidad. Then follows a whole week of action at the end of June in honour of San Juan and San Pedro. On 15 August, coinciding with the Feast of the Assumption, the decidedly pagan Fiesta del Langostino (Prawn Festival) takes place in honour of the juicy, prized Vinaròs scampi.

Places to Stay

See Benicarló, earlier in this chapter, for the nearest HI hostel.

Camping Vinaròs has a couple of excellent camp sites, both open year round and just off the N-340, north-east of town.

Camping Vinaròs (☎/fax 964 40 24 24, Carretera N-340 km 1054) 2 people, tent & car €13.85. This quality camping ground with a pool and a bar/restaurant has many long-term stayers, especially during the winter, but there's usually room for all. Choose a pitch on the more mature, better-shaded southern part.

Camping Sol de Riu Playa (☎ 964 49 63 56, Partida Deveses s/n) 2 people, tent & car €16.15, €10.25 mid-Sept–June. This camp site, like Camping Vinaròs, has a pool, restaurant and supermarket. A bus (€0.60) runs to town and back six times daily.

Hotels & Pensiones *Pensión Casablanca* (☎ 964 45 04 25, Calle San Pascual 8) Singles/doubles €11/19.50. Open Mar-Sept, Pensión Casablanca has presentable budget rooms with external bathroom. Ring first to check since the owners are elderly and are likely to retire soon.

Hostal Miramar (☎/fax 964 45 14 00, Paseo Blasco Ibañez 12) Singles/doubles/triples with bathroom €25.85/41/54. This 17-room family hotel has a pleasantly old-fashioned air about it. Fronting onto the promenade, it couldn't be handier for the beach.

Hostal Teruel (☎/fax 964 40 04 24, Avenida de Madrid 34) Singles/doubles with bathroom €27/39, €33/47 mid-July–mid-Oct.

Set back in town yet within an easy walk of the beach, this is a businesslike, pleasant enough option; prices include breakfast.

Places to Eat

You've plenty of eating choices on the waterfront, most of them specialising in seafood.

For a bocadillo or snack, made with bread baked fresh on the premises, call by *Bar Mayor* (Calle Mayor 39).

Bar Puerto (☎ 964 45 00 04, Calle Costa y Borrás) and its neighbour, *Bar Folet*, are a couple of modest, delightfully unassuming places, each within a well lobbed sardine's throw of *la lonja*, Vinaròs's fish market. Rich in tapas, the service is friendly and their fish dishes couldn't be fresher. Bar Puerto retains one of the Comunidad's last remaining giant's footsteps squat toilets. Rush before they're ripped out in the name of progress.

Mesón de la Mera (☎ 964 40 16 17, Plaza San Antonio 27) Meals €10-17. This cosy place is a great choice in the heart of town. It does a great value midday menú for €7.25.

The *restaurant* of Hostal Teruel (see Places to Stay) has a house menu at €8.75 and generous meat mains for €5.75-9.75.

Restaurante Vinya d'Alòs (☎ 964 45 49 62, Paseo Blasco Ibañez 6) Meals €22-30. As befits a restaurant right on the seafront, this place offers the freshest of fish and seafood, imaginatively prepared. Try, for example, their *chipirones salteados en habitas tiernas* (sautéed baby squid and tender broad beans; €12.60) or go for one of their rice dishes (€8 to €15.50).

Entertainment

You'll find all the action at the east end of town, where five discos all vie for your custom. *Hangar* (Paseo Jaime I), plays funky and underground house, and admission including the first drink costs €6. Just opposite is *Red* while a short stagger to the junction with Avenida de Tarragona brings you to *Skanner* (Paseo J. Ribera) and *Jas*, side by side. *TNT* (W www.tntdisco.com) most prestigious of the pack, is just up the road. Check out their Web site for upcoming programmes. Most discos groove on Friday and Saturday only, except during August when they fire up nightly. Turn up before midnight and you'll be dancing alone.

Getting There & Around

Buses, leaving from Plaza Primero de Mayo, run to Castellón via the autopista (€4.55) and Morella (two daily, €4.80). For long-distance routes, see Getting There & Away under Peñíscola.

Eight trains daily run southwards to Valencia (€6.90, 1¾ hours) via Castellón (one hour) and northwards to Barcelona (two hours) via Tarragona (one hour). All stop at Benicarló/Peñíscola, the next station up the line. To save yourself an extra journey to the station, you can reserve long-distance train and bus tickets at Viajes Maestrazgo (☎ 964 45 53 00), Calle Socorro 29, in Vinaròs.

At taxi between town and the train station costs €4.20; call ☎ 964 45 51 51.

Maestrazgo & Around

Straddling north-western Valencia and south-eastern Aragón, El Maestrazgo (El Maestrat in Valenciano) is a mountainous land, sparsely dotted by ancient pueblos huddled on rocky outcrops, cones and ridges, as if seeking protection from warrior enemies and insulation from the area's harsh winters.

One such pueblo, San Mateo, was chosen in the 14th century by the *maestro* (hence the name El Maestrazgo) of the Montesa order of knights as his seat of power.

The area is a world away from the coastal resorts and is not much visited by non-Spaniards. Ask at local tourist offices for the *Guía de Alojamientos del Maestrazgo*, a comprehensive guide to accommodation from four-star hotels to *casas rurales* (village or country houses) to camping grounds in both the Valencian and Aragonese sectors of the Maestrazgo.

The easiest way into this hinterland is to strike westwards for Morella along the N-232 from Vinaròs on the Costa del Azahar. A slower but more varied route to Morella runs north-west from Castellón along good quality but more minor roads, that take in a number of typical inland villages and towns along the way. Best of all, if you can spare the time, is to complete the whole large triangle, Vinaròs, Morella and Castellón at its angles, and its hypotenuse the fast A-7 running parallel to the coast.

A limited bus service runs to San Mateo and Morella from Castellón and Vinaròs.

CASTELLÓN TO MORELLA

If you have wheels, the optimum way to approach the Maestrazgo and Morella is to head inland from Castellón. This way, you gradually leave behind the coastal plain to immerse yourself in the increasingly rugged beauty of this inland and relatively untrodden – by non-Valencianos at least – corner of the Comunidad. This option also makes for an ideal cycle tour, except in high summer when the heat can be a bit wearing. This said, it becomes drier and less intense as you climb – and climb you will, though not lung-searingly. If you're exercising pedal power, you might want to turn what makes for a fulfilling one day's drive into a two-day ride. Leave Castellón by the CV-10, which strikes inland from the N-340. To reach it, take the Castellón north exit from the A-7 and head briefly southwards along the N-340 until you meet the junction.

Vilafamés

A strongly recommended 4km detour up the CV-15 and along the CV-160 brings you to the tiny village of Vilafamés. What draws visitors to this hillside town, 26km north of Castellón, is its excellent **Museo Popular de Arte Contemporáneo** (☎ 96 432 91 52, Calle Diputació 20; admission €1.80; open 10am-1.30pm & 4pm-7pm, to 8pm in summer, Tues-Sun). Within the 15th-century Palacio del Batlle – which is worth a visit in its own right – is an excellent, highly eclectic collection of contemporary paintings and sculpture.

The small old town is an agreeable clutter of whitewashed houses and civic buildings in rust-red stone. The 18th-century **Iglesia de la Asunción** features some unique ceramic artworks. From Plaza de la Sangre, stone steps take you up to the **castle**, with its

Arabian foundations, rebuilt circular turret and sensational panoramas.

Hotel El Rullo (☎ *964 32 93 84, Calle de la Fuente 2)* €16 per person. Scarcely 200m below the museum, Hotel El Rullo has eight rooms with bathroom offering great views. Down the road, you can get a menú for €7.50 at *Meson El Rullo*.

Retrace your tracks to the CV-10.

Albocàsser (Albocácer)

Albocàsser, best reached by taking the CV-129 westwards, merits a short stop. Its mere 1500 inhabitants make it one of the more heavily populated pueblos of the Maestrazgo. Amid much contemporary brick construction, many of the thick-walled old town houses are being restored, not always with great sensitivity (the shocking-pink tile work plastered over the facade of one such building behind the church, will set your teeth on edge). Sadly, it's not the only village around to fall victim to such architectural vandalism.

In the main square at the end of Calle Mayor, the classical facade of the 17th-century parish church of **La Asunción** outstares Albocàsser's trim, arcaded and altogether more modest town hall. Round the corner is the even more modest 13th-century **Ermita de los Santos Juanes**. Although constructed in medieval times, the sculpted blocks on each side of the door have clearly been recycled from some much earlier structure. Back on the main street, spare a glance for the town wash house, a stylish early-20th-century construction, still sudsy and used by some of the older women in the village.

Before moving on, you might want to pick up a jar of honey, culled from hives in the surrounding countryside, or some local olive oil, equally prized hereabouts.

From Albocàsser, you could then make a 10km detour along the CV-130 northeastwards to Tirig and the **Museu de la Valltorta**, devoted to prehistoric rock paintings (see Around San Mateo, later). Otherwise, strike west to rejoin the CV-15.

Benasal (Benassal)

Benasal, too, deserves the brief 3.5km detour off the main CV-15. In the main Plaza del Ayuntamiento, a giant three-dimensional metal mural grafted onto the south wall of the church commemorates the 750th anniversary of the recapture of the town from the Arabs. A cobbled street to the west of the church, bordered by a couple of elegantly restored *señorial* (noble) mansions leads to the small **Museo Arqueológico de l'Alt Maestrat** (☎ *96 443 10 02, Calle La Mola 10; admission €0.60; open 11am-2pm July-Aug)* housed in a pleasant, deeply vaulted sandstone building. Beside it and set into one of the last remaining hunks of the old town wall is the **Porta de la Mola**, its horseshoe shape indicating its Islamic origin. Two blocks southwards of the Plaza del Ayuntamiento, there's a slender, well preserved stone defensive tower typical of the region (you'll pass beneath another in Mirambel further along the route).

Continuing southwards for another couple of kilometres on the road leading to Culla brings you to **Font d'en Segures**, the natural spring from which water is tapped and sold under the Benassal brand name throughout the Comunidad. Once a modest health spa, it's now rather run down. After filling your containers with the reputedly health-enhancing waters at the higher of two terraces above the bottling plant, drop to the lower one for a fine view of the valley and steep, surrounding cliffs.

If it's around mealtime, you might want to push on for a further 7km to Culla itself and *La Carrasca* (☎ *96 476 21 76, Calle Torre Embesora, Culla km 12; open daily Aug & Sept, Sat & Sun only Oct-July)*. Renowned for its rabbit dishes, this restaurant takes its name from the giant *carrasca* (kermes oak) nearby, which is reputedly the oldest in Spain.

Ares del Maestre

postcode 12165 • pop 250
• elevation 1194m

Back on the CV-15, stop after about 4km at the **Masía de Montalvana** if you've an interest in prehistoric rock paintings and fancy a short stroll. The farmer here is the official guide who will escort you down the Barranco de la Gasulla to the **Cueva Remigia**

NORTHERN VALENCIA

(Remigia Cave; ☎ 964 76 21 86; admission free; open 9.30am-12.30pm & 4pm-5.30pm Tues, Wed & Fri-Sun). Here, with the right light and just a touch of imagination, you can make out hunting scenes and stick figures harassing bulls, wild boar and goats.

Beyond the Masía the terrain becomes increasingly rugged as you approach the village of Ares, at first no more than a broad white smudge on the cliff high above. Fronting the small Plaza Mayor is *Hotel d'Ares* *(☎ 964 44 30 07, Plaza Mayor 4, open Dec-Oct).* Singles/doubles with bathroom & TV €24/36. At the *bar/restaurant* below this cosy, recommended hotel, you can get a full meal, including coffee and wine, for around €25.

The tiny village is quickly explored. Note the twisted columns of the main entrance to the 18th-century church and, beside it, the town hall, in its time the meeting hall of the Knights Templar, who controlled the village in the Middle Ages. But Ares' trump card is its views, already impressive from the village itself and even more breathtaking if you're prepared to make the 15-minute ascent to the summit of the **Mola d'Ares** (1318m), the wedge of mountain that broods over the village. On the way, note the 16th-century *nevera*, or ice house, where snow was packed down and stored for use in warmer months.

Vilafranca del Cid (Villafranca del Cid)
postcode 12150 • pop 2800
• elevation 1125m

Vilafranca, 12km of attractive mountain road beyond Ares, is a small textile town, specialising in socks and tights (hose), where you can pick up a pair or two of designer specials at factory prices. As you approach, notice the line upon line of walls, piles of rocks, tool sheds and emergency shelters, all in stone and constructed as much to clear this bitter, unfruitful land as for any secondary purpose.

The tourist office (☎ 964 44 10 44), is open July and August only, and occupies a part of the Gothic town hall at Plaza de la Iglesia 3. Beside it, a pair of worldly, winged cherubs sit astride dolphins above the otherwise sober main entrance to the 16th-century parish church, the Iglesia de la Asunción.

Both give onto Calle Mayor, the main street, which, heading south, changes its name to Calle San Roc in honour of the town's patron saint. Portal San Roc is the only remaining gate of four that once punctuated the defensive walls. Unless you happen to pass by in Vilafranca's week of festivities in honour of San Roc following 15 August, you'll find its stolid, wooden 1st-floor doors firmly shut.

Camping Llosar (☎ 964 44 14 09, Partida Vegas Tejería) €9 for two adults, tent & car. Open June-Sept. This municipal camp site, just west of Vilafranca on the CV-15, is one of the Maestrazgo's few camping grounds.

Mirambel
We're cheating just slightly here, albeit for the best of motives. Mirambel is just over the regional border, in the neighbouring region of Aragón. Disregarding the ancient frontiers artificially imposed by humankind, Mirambel is as much Maestrazgo in spirit as any village you'll visit. There is, however, one significant difference; even though you penetrate only 2.5km into Aragón, you'll notice the switch in the preferred local language from Valenciano to Spanish.

The route, as you approach it from Vilafranca, takes in some soul-stirring, rugged scenery as you descend to the Cantavieja valley. More adventurously, you can approach Mirambel on foot from Forcall (see the following section) along the PRV-112 walking trail, which is of medium difficulty. Allow five hours one way.

Mirambel gives a good sense of what a small, walled medieval town looks like without the usual modern-day add-ons. Enter by the main gate, the Portal de las Monjas (Nuns' Gate) in the north-west corner of the town walls. The fine plaster geometrical window screens of the gate's upper storey were originally part of a convent, built in 1564. They were designed, as with similar window features in the Islamic world, to allow the breeze to flow and the women to look out without themselves being observed.

Created by order of the Knights Templar in 1243, Mirambel boasts several magnificent, robust, thick-walled señorial mansions, most with finely turned wooden balconies and overhanging eaves. The town served as the headquarters of the Carlist forces of Valencia, Aragón and Murcia in the 19th century, when its population reached the dizzy heights of 950. Today less than 150 people remain, many of whom appeared as extras in Ken Loach's film about the Spanish Civil War, *Land and Freedom* (1995), which used Mirambel as its main location.

Fonda Guimera (☎ 964 17 82 69, fax 964 17 82 93, Calle Agustín Pastor 28) Singles/doubles with bathroom €12/21. On the main street, the cafe/restaurant below this modest but quite adequate place can serve you up a menú for a bargain €7.20. It's a question of pot luck; there's no a la carte and you enjoy what's cooking that day.

Forcall

Following the valley of the Río Cantavieja along the CV-120 for about 20km brings you to Forcall. This quiet village, perched at the confluence of the Ríos Caldés and Cantavieja, makes a decent alternative to Morella for an overnight stop.

Each weekend closest to 17 January, the Santantonà (also known as Fiesta de San Antón), a winter festival celebrating fire, briefly dispels the prevailing calm as local youths sprint through a blazing tunnel. At the end of Calle San Vicente, at the western limit of the village, is a fine nevera, sunk in 1638.

On opposite sides of the Plaza Mayor stand two fine, renovated, 16th-century Aragonese palaces. One has been converted into an up-market hotel, *Hotel-Restaurante Palau dels Osset-Miró (☎ 964 17 75 24, fax 964 17 75 56)*. Rooms with air-con & heating €72-90. Half-board (an extra €25 per person) compulsory Sat & Sun. Its *restaurant* (meals €24 to €30), the most elegant of Forcall's limited choices (no blaring TV here), has more than a hint of *Fawlty Towers*. Take a paperback or a scintillating dining companion since the service is excruciatingly slow (a Spanish family walked out and a party of Germans were reduced to helpless laughter, maybe

tears, when we last ate there). On that occasion, you had to take your table candle (it's that sort of place) to the toilet since lighting didn't extend as far as the loos.

Beyond your budget? Then check in at friendly, earthy *Hostal Aguilar (☎ 964 17 11 06, Avenina 3° Centenario 1)*, Forcall's most easterly building, where rooms with bathroom, central heating and TV offer unbeatable value at €12/21 (€18/30 in Aug).

Mesón de la Vila (☎ 964 17 11 25, Plaza Mayor s/n; open Tues-Sun lunch), with its attractive terracotta floors, stone arches and whitewashed walls, does a copious, excellent-value menú for €7.80, even if the service is short on smiles.

Around Forcall

Morella is 13.5km south-east of Forcall along the freshly upgraded CV-14. If you have time, or if you choose to stay overnight in the latter, you might want to sample another Maestrazgo village that's well and truly off the tourist path or visit a remarkable, equally off-the-beaten-track mountain shrine.

The **Santuario de la Balma** lies less than 15km north of Forcall along the CV-14, a little beyond the village of Zorita del Maestrazgo. Dedicated to Nuestra Señora de la Balma, this extraordinary chapel is set inside the rock face. Behind the main altar is a forest of items donated to Our Lady – wax limbs, baby clothes, bridal dresses, military berets and so on, each accompanied by a note of thanks to the Virgin for her protection or intercession. While most of these votive offerings are relatively recent, the sanctuary, first mentioned in the 14th century, has a long history of special powers. In its antechamber is a *bar/restaurant*, where a scrummy plate of frogs' legs costs €4.

Just 3km north of Forcall, a minor road crosses a medieval bridge to snake up another couple of kilometres to the trim, whitewashed working hamlet of **Villores**, its balconies bright with flowers. There are no monuments, hostal, cafe or concessions to tourism, here. But it's pleasant just to ramble the sparse streets, then enjoy the view of the wide Río Bergantes valley as you descend, retracing your tracks.

Todolella, 6km west of Forcall, is larger and manifestly more prosperous. Leave your car down on the CV-122 and walk up through the village's narrow alleys as far as the massive square presence of its castle. Privately owned, it's been sensitively preserved and restored. Even though you can't visit the castle, both it and the valley below make for a good photo opportunity.

MORELLA
postcode 12300 • pop 2700
• elevation 1000m
The fairy-tale town of Morella commands the northern part of Valencia's share of El Maestrazgo, which the Comunidad shares with Aragón. It's also the ancient capital of Els Ports, the 'mountain passes', an area offering some outstanding scenic drives and strenuous cycling excursions, as well as potential for hikers and mountain climbers. The town is an outstanding example of a medieval fortress. Perched on a hill top and crowned by a castle, it looks from a distance like a giant layered cake. Enclosed by a wall over 2km long, it's one of Spain's oldest continuously inhabited towns.

Orientation & Information
The town walls of Morella are broken only by seven entrance gates. Calle de la Muralla runs around the inner perimeter while the rest of town is a confusing, compact jumble of narrow streets, alleys and stairs. The main street, which runs from east to west, from the Puerta de San Miguel to the Puerta de los Estudios, compounds the confusion by assuming five different names along its length of less than a kilometre.

The tourist office (☎/fax 964 17 30 32), Plaza de San Miguel 3, is open 10am to 2pm and 4pm to 6pm (to 7pm in summer), Tuesday to Saturday and Sunday morning. It's just inside the Puerta de San Miguel, Morella's main entrance. In principle, it only covers the town but it also carries useful information on Els Ports and the Maestrazgo as a whole.

Things to See
Morella's **castle** *(open 10.30am-6.30pm Sept-Apr, to 7.30pm May-Aug; admission*

€1.80; combined ticket to castle & town's museums €6)*, although in ruins, remains imposing. You can almost hear the clashing of swords and clip-clop of horses that were a part of fortress life. A strenuous climb is rewarded by breathtaking views of the town and surrounding countryside.

The old town is best explored on foot. A good starting point is Puerta de San Miguel, most impressive of the town's seven entrances and flanked by twin 14th-century towers. In one of them, the **Museo Tiempo de Dinosaurios** presents a handful of dinosaur bones – the Maestrazgo's remote hills are a treasure trove for palaeontologists – and a video (in Spanish). Two other towers set into the town walls house small museums. The **Museo Tiempo de Imagen** *(Torre Bebeito)* has a collection of old black-and-white photos of Morella, while the **Museo Tiempo de Historia** *(Portal de la Nevera)* charts the history of the town. Morella's other museum, the **Museo del Sexenni** *(Iglesia de Sant Nicolau)*, evokes the atmosphere of this major fiesta (see Special Events, later). Admission to each costs €1.80 or you can buy a combined ticket, which also includes admission to the castle, for €6.

The Gothic **Basílica de Santa María la Mayor** *(Plaza Arciprestal; open 11am-2pm & 4pm-8pm daily)* is the Maestrazgo's finest church. The two elaborately sculpted doorways on its south facade only partially prepare you for the extraordinarily elaborate gilded altarpiece within. Equally impressive and considerably more sober is the spiral staircase at the west end. Finely carved with figures in bas relief, it leads to the first-floor choir. At the base of the choir's stonework screen, delicately carved in geometrical shapes, stand guard a phalanx of charmingly disproportionate, stunted human figures. Beside the main altar is the **Museo Arciprestal** *(admission €1.20)*.

Also worth seeing are the 14th-century **Ayuntamiento** (Town Hall), the **Convento de San Francisco** *(Plaza San Francisco)* – through whose tranquil cloister you pass to reach the castle – together with its adjacent church, and several impressive manorial houses, such as the **Casa de la Cofradía de**

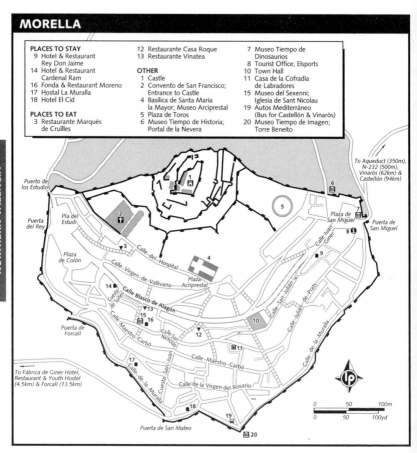

MORELLA

PLACES TO STAY
9 Hotel & Restaurant
   Rey Don Jaime
14 Hotel & Restaurant
   Cardenal Ram
16 Fonda & Restaurant Moreno
17 Hostal La Muralla
18 Hotel El Cid

PLACES TO EAT
3 Restaurante Marqués
   de Cruïlles

12 Restaurante Casa Roque
13 Restaurante Vinatea

OTHER
1 Castle
2 Convento de San Francisco;
   Entrance to Castle
4 Basílica de Santa María
   la Mayor; Museo Arciprestal
5 Plaza de Toros
6 Museo Tiempo de Historia;
   Portal de la Nevera

7 Museo Tiempo de
   Dinosaurios
8 Tourist Office; Elsports
10 Town Hall
11 Casa de la Cofradía
   de Labradores
15 Museo del Sexenni;
   Iglesia de Sant Nicolau
19 Autos Mediterráneo
   (Bus for Castellón & Vinaròs)
20 Museo Tiempo de Imagen;
   Torre Beneito

Labradores (House of the Guild of Farmers), constructed in 1640 and today headquarters of an agricultural cooperative.

If you look north-east from the Puerta San Miguel, you'll see, beyond the town, the arches of a 13th-century double-storey **aqueduct** that used to supply the city with water.

Activities

Morella makes an excellent base for a few days' wild walking. The PRV-116, a 15km trail, runs between Morella and Forcall, overlooking the Bergantes valley. Another route, the PRV-119, also about 15km long, joins Morella and Cinctorres. Alternatively, the 8km PRV-216 between Morella and Xiva makes for a pleasant shorter stroll. For something altogether more stretching, the Els Ports loop, described in Lonely Planet's *Walking in Spain*, offers four to five days of magnificent trekking. If you prefer a unidirectional trek of several days, the long-distance GR-7 walking trail crosses the Els Ports and Tinença de Benifassá districts.

Elsports (☎ *964 17 31 17, fax 964 17 31 31, Plaza de San Miguel 3*) offers a range of weekend outdoor activities including walking, climbing, caving and mountain-biking.

Special Events

Morella's major festival is the Sexenni, held in August every six years (the next is in 2006) in honour of the Virgen de Vallivana. Visit the Museo del Sexenni (see Things to See earlier) to get the flavour of this major celebration. Annually in August, there's a baroque music festival, starring the huge organ in the Basílica de Santa María la Mayor.

Places to Stay

Cases de Morella (☎ 964 17 31 17, Ⓦ www .morella.net) is an agency that has a range of rural accommodation and farmhouses on its books.

For details of Morella's HI youth hostel, see Hotel Fábrica de Giner at the end of this section.

Fonda Moreno (☎ 964 16 01 05, Calle San Nicolás 12) Rooms €15. The cheapest option in town, this friendly, recommended *fonda* (inn), a neighbour to the Museo del Sexenni, has six quaint, basic doubles. Their price, despite the introduction of the euro, has scarcely changed in the last five years.

Hotel El Cid (☎ 964 16 01 25, fax 964 16 01 51, Puerta de San Mateo 3) Singles/ doubles with bathroom €23.80/38.30. Rooms are spruce at this recently renovated and upgraded place. The ones at the front have magnificent views over the valley.

Hostal La Muralla (☎/fax 964 16 02 43, Calle de la Muralla 12) Singles/doubles with bathroom €21/33. Around the corner from Hotel El Cid and just as trim and more economical, Hostal La Muralla raises its prices by a modest €3 between July and September. It does a particularly good breakfast of croissants, rolls and espresso coffee. Rooms have TV and central heating.

Hotel Rey Don Jaime (☎ 964 16 09 11, fax 964 16 09 88, Ⓦ www.reydonjaimemorella .com, Calle Juan Giner 6) Singles/doubles €28.55/47.50. Rooms all have satellite TV and central heating at this pleasant mid-range hotel.

Hotel Cardenal Ram (☎ 964 17 30 85, fax 964 17 32 18, Ⓔ hotelcardenalram@ ctu.es, Cuesta de Suñer 1) Singles/doubles €33/51.25. With its ancient stone floors, high ceilings and antique furniture, this hotel

occupies a wonderfully transformed 16th-century cardinal's palace.

On the Forcall road, 4.5km west of town, is the Fábrica de Giner complex, a former textile factory.

Hotel Fábrica de Giner (☎ 964 17 31 42, fax 964 17 31 97, Carretera Morella-Forcall km 4.5) Singles/doubles €48.10/56.50, €59.50/65.50 Fri, Sat & July-Sept. This up-market hotel occupies the former factory-owner's sumptuous dwelling.

In the former workers' housing of this same 19th-century industrial complex is Morella's *Youth Hostel (☎ 964 16 01 00, fax 964 16 09 77)*, which has dorm beds for €6.60 and half-board for €11.45.

Places to Eat

The upstairs restaurant at *Fonda Moreno* (see Places to Stay, earlier) does a hearty menú for €7.20 and has an ample a la carte selection.

Restaurante Casa Roque (☎ 964 16 03 36, Cuesta San Juan 1) This locally famous restaurant, having gone through something of a bad patch, seems to be righting itself after a move to new premises in an attractive 17th-century mansion. Popular with groups, it does a good value weekday menú at €8.25. For a selection of typical Els Ports dishes, go for their *menú degustación* at €15 or, if you've the time and the appetite, their blow-out *menú gastronómico* at €21.

The *restaurant* of Hotel Cardenal Ram (see Places to Stay, earlier) also does a first-class menú degustación for €15. Value for money, too, is their *menú del día* at €10.75.

The *restaurant* of Hotel Fábrica de Giner (see Places to Stay) is decent, too. Meals cost from €15 to €21.

Restaurante Vinatea (☎ 964 16 07 44, Calle Blasco de Alagón 17) Open Tues-Sun. Meals around €12. On the main street, the Vinatea is another place that does a bargain menú, rich in local dishes, for €9.

Restaurante Marqués de Cruïlles (☎ 964 16 09 90, Carrer de l'Hospital) Open Thur-Tues lunch. This restaurant's peaceful garden, just opposite the castle entrance, makes a restful drinks stop. It also offers mainly regional cuisine and has a fine menú at €12.

NORTHERN VALENCIA

Shopping

Morella's main street is lined with shops selling produce of El Maestrazgo – cheese, hanks of sausage, cold cuts, pâtés, nuts and honey. For such a small place, it has a wide range of cakes and desserts, some of which you really ought to sample. There are *coca de frutos secos*, also called *coca de miel*, a crispy open tart garnished with walnuts, almonds, hazelnuts and honey; *flaon*, a covered *empanada* (pie) or pasty, filled with *requesón*, a soft white cheese; and *pastiset de calabaza*, made with soft yellow pumpkin glazed with honey. Just as delightfully fattening are the large, puffy *almendrados*, meringues of egg-white, sugar and – like so many dishes around here – almonds. Try also *pinyonades*, bite-size balls made from pine nuts and, sold especially around the feast of San Antonio, and *sequillet de panoli*, with a base of sugar, moscatel sweet wine and *aquavita* (brandy).

Getting There & Around

On weekdays, Autos Mediterráneo (☎ 964 22 05 36) runs two daily buses to and from both Castellón and Vinaròs. There's also one Saturday bus to and from Castellón. The once-daily, Monday-to-Friday bus between Morella and Forcall, designed primarily for those who travel to work, could scarcely be more inconvenient for travellers. It leaves Forcall at 6am and returns from Morella at 6pm.

Drivers can leave their vehicles in the large car park (€1.80) just north of the main San Miguel gate.

For a taxi, call ☎ 659 48 78 61. This local company also offers fixed-rate tours to nearby places of interest. Typical prices per vehicle are:

destination	cost (€)	km	hrs
La Balma	27	50	2
Mirambel	33	70	2½
Tinença de Benifassá	60	115	5

TINENÇA DE BENIFASSÁ

Tinença de Benifassá is the collective name of seven isolated hamlets in the northernmost reaches of Valencia. Often snowbound in winter, they belonged in feudal times to the vast **Monasterio de Santa María de Benifassá**. The convent is still in use but you'll be lucky to find it open; the nuns open their church to visitors only between 1pm and 3pm on Thursdays.

Around 7km south-west is **La Pobla de Benifassá** with its distinctive local stone houses fronted by timber balconies. **Hotel Tinença de Benifassá** (☎ 977 72 90 44, Calle Mayor 50), set in a restored villa, has 10 attractive singles/doubles with heating and TV at €46.30/57.75.

Most other villages in the area, including **Bellestar**, **Fredes** and **Coratxá** are uninhabited in winter.

MORELLA TO PEÑÍSCOLA
Catí

An 8km diversion south from the N-232, following the CV-128, leads to the village of Catí. It still retains one or two well preserved Renaissance noble houses on the main Calle Mayor, a reminder of the days when this small town enjoyed the wealth generated by the wool trade. The ground floor of the Casa de la Vila, with its four sweeping 15th-century ogival arches, has served variously over the centuries as a commodity exchange, prison, butcher's and the village wheat store.

An obligatory stop for those with a sweet tooth is the **Fábrica de Turrones y Mazapanes J Blasco** at the northern entrance to town. Processing the almonds that constitute the valley's main crop, this small factory transforms them into marzipan and *turrón*, a popular Valencian variant of nougat, both of which you can sample and buy.

Pensión el Prigó (☎ 964 40 90 33, Calle Santa Ana s/n) Rooms with bathroom, heating & TV €12 per person, full board €27. Pensión el Prigó ranks as one of the Comunidad's best bargains. You can stay either in the main building with its *restaurant*, serving rich and reasonable local fare, or in one of their five renovated houses in and around the village.

Up in the mountains 5km north-west, the tiny spa village of **L'Avellá** is no more than a dozen buildings, a 16th-century chapel and a plant for bottling its spring water. **Fonda Miralles** (☎ 964 76 50 51) is a simple hostal, open July to September.

San Mateo (Sant Mateu)
postcode 12170 • pop 1800
• elevation 325m

A 5km detour south from the N-232 along the CV-132 brings you to San Mateo del Maestrat (to give it its full, if rarely used, title), the ancient capital of El Maestrazgo. Although long since overtaken and outgrown by Morella, the town's impressive mansions and elaborate facades are reminders of a more illustrious past and former wealth, based upon the wool trade. But don't go expecting a miniature Toledo or Seville; San Mateo is a pleasant little town with a number of buildings that are impressive – within the context of the traditionally poor, rural Maestrazgo.

It's easy to find your way around since all major sights are well signed. The heart of this small community is, as so often in Spanish towns, the Plaza Mayor, colonnaded, deeply shaded and fringed by bars and cafes. From here radiate all San Mateo's major streets. The tourist office (☎ 964 41 66 58) is just off the Plaza Mayor at Calle Historiador Betí 6. It opens 10am to 2pm, Tuesday to Sunday plus 5pm to 7pm Saturday. The better of the noble mansions and minor palaces are along Calles La Cort and Morella, both of which take off from the square's north-west corner, and Calle Zaragoza, which leads westwards from Plaza de la Mare de Déu de la Font. Richest of all is the 16th-century **Palacio del Marqués de Villores** on Calle Valencia, its windows and main portal framed by ornate, purely decorative pilasters.

From the Plaza Mayor, signs point to San Mateo's four municipal museums, all small and on the local scale. Hours are often not officially published so you'd do well to ring or call by the tourist office for the current, often shifting situation.

Just off the Plaza Mayor on Calle San Bernardo, the Romanesque main door of the parish church leads into the **Museo Arciprestal**

(admission €0.90; open 10am-2pm & 4pm-7pm daily mid-June–mid-Sept, 10am-2pm & 4pm-6pm Sat, 10am-2pm Sun mid-Sept–mid-June), which has a small collection of religious art and adornments, vessels and ornamentation used in the sacraments. The **Museo Histórico-Etnológico** office, sharing a fine 15th-century building with the town hall and tourist office, observes the same hours as the latter. The **Museo Paleontológico** (Calle Barcelona 21; admission €1; hours as per Museo Arciprestal) contains a few local prehistoric finds. If it's closed during the hours it purports to be open, ring the bell at No 25, two doors down. The **Museo les Presons** is in the former jail. Closed at the time of writing because of work on adjacent buildings, it should be up and functioning again by the time you read this.

If you pass by in the morning, when they're still baking, you can peer into the **Horno Medieval** (Calle Historiador Betí 13), a bakery that's been turning out bread since the 14th century.

Places to Stay & Eat San Mateo has a number of worthwhile options.

Hotel-Restaurante La Perdi (☎ 964 41 60 82, Calle Historiador Betí 9) Singles/doubles with bathroom €18/30, €24/36 mid-July–mid-Sept. Rooms are modern and comfortable with TV and heating and its restaurant has a good menú costing only €7.25.

Hostal el Cubano (☎ 964 41 63 95, Calle Historiador Betí 26) Singles/doubles with bathroom €18/30. Cheaper in summer but less welcoming, Hostal el Cubano is another budget option; rooms have TV.

Hotel Restaurante Montesa (☎ 964 41 60 00, fax 964 41 66 48, Avenida Constitución 21). Singles/doubles €18/36 Oct-June, €21/42 July-Sept. In the newer part of town – yet no more than a 400m walk from the Plaza Mayor – this hotel, inaugurated in 1997, is San Mateo's most modern and the best that the town has to offer.

Restaurante Mare de Déu (☎ 964 41 60 07) Menú €15. Open Wed-Mon July-Sept, Fri & Sat only Oct-Apr. On a rocky hillside and a 20-minute walk east of San Mateo, this restaurant was a monastery until the Spanish Civil War (take a peep at its over-the-top baroque chapel). It's now a warren of barrel-vaulted, whitewashed dining areas. Sadly, neither the food – albeit reasonably priced – nor the service is what such a magnificent site merits. To get there, follow the signs from San Mateo's Plaza Mayor.

Getting There & Away Weekday Autos Mediterráneo buses link San Mateo with Vinaròs (€2.25, one hour, four daily), Castellón (€4, up to two hours, three daily) and Morella (1¼ hours, two daily). On Saturday, one bus runs from Castellón to Morella via San Mateo. The bus stop is 100m east of Hotel Restaurante Montesa.

Tirig

If you're interested in prehistoric rock paintings, or just fancy a walk with great views of the sweeping cliffs and river valley of the Barranco de Valltorta, push on a further 10km south-west of San Mateo to Tirig. Signposted from the village is the **Museu de la Valltorta** (☎ 964 76 10 25; admission free; open 10am-2pm & 5pm-8pm Wed-Sun May-Sept, 10am-2pm & 4pm-7pm Wed-Sun Oct-Apr). The museum's illustrative panels document the rich history of cave paintings in the area and staff lead guided walks to the Barranco and the most significant cave site.

Traiguera

At the village of Traiguera, on the N-232 42km from Morella and 17km short of Vinaròs, look for the sign Reial Santuari Verge Font de Salut. A 3.5km detour, winding through olive groves, brings you to this sanctuary and popular local pilgrimage destination in honour of the Virgin of the Spring of Health. Dating from the 15th century, it's an agreeably motley jumble of buildings, including a noble house, pilgrims' hostel, contemporary cafe and outbuildings. The fine exterior of the central chapel was constructed in 1588. The interior, by contrast, is disappointing, the Virgin herself perched atop a disproportionately chunky pillar like a richly caparisoned Barbie doll.

In that agreeably Spanish way, the sanc-tuary happily functions both as a place of worship and a convivial meeting place and picnic spot with ranks of barbecue pits set into its surrounding wall.

Vallivana

Vallivana, 24km from Morella and nowadays a cluster of houses, bypassed by the highway and largely ignored by passing traffic, once knew fame. Once a year, on the first weekend in May, its Virgin, patron of Morella, still enjoys the attentions of pilgrims, who descend from the town (many of them on foot) to pay tribute to her. She's a beauty – tiny and encrusted with jewels, peeking from the heart of a richly gilded altarpiece.

The rough-and-ready bar next door was once the heart of the pilgrims' quarters. With its vast wooden counter, it makes a handy drinks or snack stop.

Vall del Palencia & Around

The N-234, linking Sagunto with Teruel, over the border in Aragón, climbs gradually and consistently for over 50km. It follows the upper reaches of the Río Palancia, in whose valley there are a couple of worthwhile destinations.

SEGORBE
postcode 12400 • pop 7850
• elevation 395m
Segorbe, 33km north-west of Sagunto and 56km from Valencia, is the main town of the Alto Palancia (Upper Palancia) region.

Information
The tourist office (☎/fax 96 471 32 54), Calle Marcelino Blasco 3, is beside the municipal car park. It's open 10am to 2pm and 4pm to 7pm Tuesday to Sunday.

Things to See & Do
Segorbe has been a bishopric ever since the 3rd Council of Toledo in AD 589. Its **cathedral**, of Gothic origin, has been much amended over the centuries. What remains

from the original construction is a tranquil cloister, its most delicate feature. Inside one of the alcoves is a small museum, closed at the time of writing and its future uncertain, which displays canvases by, among others, Ribalta and Jacomart.

Segorbe's other buildings of interest sit in a cluster at the western corner of the old town. A pair of cylindrical towers were originally embedded within its protective walls. The **Torre de la Carcel** for a time served as the town's lock-up while the town executioner, for those prisoners whose fate was even worse, lived nearby in the **Torre del Botxí**. The medieval aqueduct, of which a healthy hunk remains, brought water from the fountain of La Esperanza (Hope), from where it still springs eternal.

Here, too, is Segorbe's **Museo Municipal** (*☎ 96 471 21 54, Calle de la Esperanza s/n; admission free; open 10am-2pm & 6pm-8pm Tues-Sun June-Aug, 10am-2pm Sat & Sun, 6-8pm Sun Sept-May)*. This small museum displays local finds dating from Palaeolithic times to the Middle Ages.

The **castle** – or rather what's left of it – is on a hillock overlooking Segorbe. It's well worth the short, steep walk up, not so much for the sake of the largely restored tower and a trace or two of battlement but for the glorious view of the town below, the Sierra de Espadán to the north and the Sierra Calderona stretching across the southern skyline.

Segobriga Park, also overlooking the town, is a water park, run by the municipality, that squirts and flows in summer.

Places to Stay & Eat

Camping San Blas (☎/fax 96 471 11 81, **e** *sanblas2001@terra.es, Cerro de San Blas s/n)* €2.65/3.20/2.65 per person/tent/car. Right beside Segobriga Park (see Things to See & Do), this municipal camp site also boasts its own pool.

Tasca el Pelen (☎ 96 471 07 40, fax 96 471 24 10, **e** *elpalen@infobit.es, Calle Franco Ricart 9)* Singles €24.05-36.05, doubles €45.10-54.10 according to season. Occupying a one-time bakery and oil press constructed in 1799, this hotel has been tastefully restored and converted. Each of the eight

> ## Horse Play
>
> Blink and you've missed the Entrada de Toros y Caballos (Entry of the Bulls and Horses), Segorbe's unique variant upon running the bulls. Bang on the dot of 2pm, a cannon sounds (only where bulls and fireworks are concerned are events guaranteed to start on time in Spain) and the bulls begin their 500m, scarcely-a-minute-long canter.
>
> A dozen or so men on horseback skilfully guide and prod the bulls down Calle Colón, between two human walls of spectators, unprotected by any barrier, and into the Plaza de la Santa Cueva.
>
> As part of Segorbe's annual fiesta in honour of its patron saints, bulls and horses run daily during the second week of September in an event that has its roots in the 16th century, and perhaps even earlier.
>
> At other times of the year – and outside that brief minute of spectacular action – ask the tourist office to put on its short video of the Entrada.

rooms has its own decor and the barrel-vaulted restaurant beneath serves hearty mountain food. Highly recommended.

Hotel María de Luna (☎ 96 471 13 13, fax 96 471 12 13, Avenida Comunidad Valenciana 2) Doubles €60-66 according to season. This hotel, also recently established, runs a highly regarded restaurant.

Getting There & Away

Autocares Herca (☎ 96 349 12 50) runs eight buses daily between Segorbe and Valencia (1¼ hours) via Sagunto (40 minutes). Five buses of Autocares Samar (☎ 96 349 56 09) do the journey directly (45 minutes). Autobuses AVSA (☎ 96 469 97 900) have two buses daily to and from Castellón. There are six direct trains a day to Valencia plus others requiring a change in Sagunto.

NAVAJAS

Navajas, shaded by cypress and palm trees, sits amid orchards, almond and olive groves. To nourish them, there are springs and fountains spurting everywhere. Once a small spa town (there's talk of reviving the facility) and still an escape from the summer heat of Valencia, it's been a popular holiday spot ever since the late 18th century. Note the charming tiled and pastel-painted summer villas, built during the 19th century by rich Valencians.

The tourist office (☎ 96 471 39 13) is at No 3 on tranquil Plaza del Olmo. It opens 11am to 2pm and 6pm to 9pm Tuesday to Sunday between July and September. During the rest of the year, it functions from 11am to 2pm and 5pm to 8pm on Saturday and from 11am to 2pm on Sunday. Check out their Web site at W www.navajasturismo.com (Spanish only) to get an idea of what the town has to offer, such as the Saturday night musical concerts held throughout July and August in the magnificent setting of the **Salto del Novio** (Lover's Leap), against a backdrop of the Cascada el Brezal, a waterfall that tumbles over 50m.

Anglers can fish in El Regajo, a reservoir that supplies the town with its water. Walkers can follow four trails, each signed and about 12km long, that start and finish in Plaza del Olmo. In a recent initiative, Navajas has developed the first stretch of an inland cycle trail. Eventually, this will lead from Puerto de Sagunto on the coast to Ojos Negros in Teruel province, following an old railway track that once supplied coal from the interior to Puerto de Sagunto's long defunct iron smelter. You can hire a bike (€6 per day) from Camping Altomira.

Camping Altomira (☎ 96 471 32 11, fax 96 471 35 12, W www.campingaltomira.com, Carretera Navajas-Pantano del Regajo km 1) €3.80/3.20/3.20 per person/tent/car. Open year round. They also have chalets accommodating up to six people (from €55 per night). You're assured of a friendly welcome at Camping Altomira. It has both pool and bar/restaurant and makes an ideal base for an active few days.

Hostal el Jardín de Estornell (☎/fax 96 471 11 98, Calle Valencia 1) Doubles with bathroom from €38. Open year round. For a roof over your head, this place offers rooms with full facilities.

MONTANEJOS
postcode 12448 • pop 415
• elevation 460m

Two attractive mountain drives bring you to the popular resort and spa village of Montanejos. The CV-20 from Castellón via Onda snakes its way up the spectacular Río Mijares gorges. The CV-195 heads northwards from the main N-234 Sagunto-Teruel road and Jérica (in passing, note the village's fine Mudéjar church tower). It runs through more open but scarcely less scenic terrain, crossing the watershed at the Collado de Arenillas (1009m).

Surrounded by craggy, pine-clad mountains, Montanejos lies at the heart of the Sierra de Espadán. The warm springs of the nearby **Fuente de Los Baños**, dispense 5000L per minute at a constant 25°C into a series of natural swimming pools. The cool, fresh mountain air attracts hordes of mainly Spanish visitors in summer.

The tourist office (☎ 96 413 11 53) is within the Balneario (spa) on Carretera Tales.

The village, uninteresting in itself, is a popular base for mountain sports. Climbers can pick up all the information they need at Refugio de Escaladores (see Places to Stay & Eat below). Walkers will be well served with routes by the tourist office. If you fancy seeing the countryside the cosy way, *Centro Equestro la Garrocha (☎ 600 535180)* does 45-minute pony and trap rides from €6 per person and also hires out horses.

Places to Stay & Eat
Refugio de Escaladores (☎ 96 413 13 17, e erlopsas@teleline.es) Dorm beds €7.50 including breakfast. There's also limited camping space (€3.50 per person). This is the place to meet friendly outdoor folk. The dynamic duo who run it have also constructed some simple wooden cabins (€15 per person) and run a restaurant, open to all and serving home-made pizzas (€5-5.75) and *platos combinados* (€6-7.25).

Casa Ovidio (☎ 96 413 13 09, Avenida Elvira Peiró 41) Menú €12, mains €6-10.50. This immensely popular restaurant also has a few rather overpriced rooms with bathroom (€60 to €66 according to season).

Hotel Rosaleda del Mijares (☎ 96 413 10 79, fax 96 413 11 36, W www.hotelesrosaleda .com, Carretera Tales 28) Singles/doubles from €27.05/41.75 in winter, from €37.85/ 51.40 in summer. Most Montanejos hotels opens only in summer and at the weekend. This upmarket option, open year round, is barely 100m from the Balneario.

VALL D'UIXÓ

The valley is famed for its **Grutas de San José** *(☎ 96 469 67 61, W www.riosubterraneo .com; adult/child €5.70/4.20; open 10.30am- 1.30pm & 3.30pm-dusk May-Sept, 11am- 1.15pm & 3.30pm-dusk Oct-Apr)*, a series of limestone caves through which flows Europe's longest navigable underground river.

NORTHERN VALENCIA

Central Valencia

Vall del Turia & Around

Beyond the bustling provincial town of Llíria, people and cars recede by the kilometre as you climb gradually and higher up the Turia valley. Here are communities where the bars are still very much a male preserve, where whole families sit out in the street to enjoy the cool of evening and where your passage will probably not go unnoticed.

This is El Secano, a region of nonirrigated agriculture, relying upon rainfall to swell its watermelons, peaches, apricots, vines, olives and carob.

You don't come to the Alto Turia (High Turia) for architectural gems, fine food or hectic nightlife. And it might take a measure of sensitivity on your part to appreciate the tranquillity of its villages, where you're as likely to find a tractor as you are a truck blocking your way along the narrow streets. Most people still live primarily from the land, cultivating cereals, fruit trees, vegetables and vines. And the Alto Turia wines, primarily white and dry, are good if not great.

You come here for the countryside and to enjoy the small, one-mule, single hotel villages, depopulated but still alive, kicking and turning towards rural tourism to supplement the hazardous income from agriculture.

There's nothing subtle about the cuisine up the valley, which owes more to the hearty, meat-rich dishes of neighbouring Aragón and Castilla la Mancha than to the Mediterranean. But you won't eat badly and you won't leave hungry since portions are usually more than generous.

Activities

Most villages have at least one walking route in the vicinity. To stretch the legs further, both the GR7 and GR10 long-distance trails thread through the valley's upper reaches. To really get the feel of the area, set aside three or four

Highlights

- Wandering the streets of Guadalest, almost alone once the last tourist bus has pulled out
- Watching Alcoy's Moros y Cristianos (Moors and Christians) parade
- Walking the Sierra de Mariola
- Savouring Novelda's *modernista* architecture
- Hurling tomatoes during La Tomatina, Buñol's annual hour of sticky mayhem
- Gradually losing contact with reality at Requena's Fiesta de la Vendimia, which celebrates the wine harvest

Xàtiva (Játiva) p184

Mediterranean Sea

Central Valencia p175

days to walk the recently established GR37. Circular and 62km long, it follows ancient *vías pecuarias* (drovers roads), established in medieval times, and takes in Aras de Alpuente, Titaguas and Alpuente. Throughout the walk, note the tiny chapels, called *verónicas* in the local dialect, usually marking crossroads and built to invite divine protection for both shepherds and their flocks.

Getting There & Away

Trains run every half hour between Valencia and Llíria.

Hispano Chelvana (☎ 96 198 50 09) runs buses to and from Valencia, serving towns

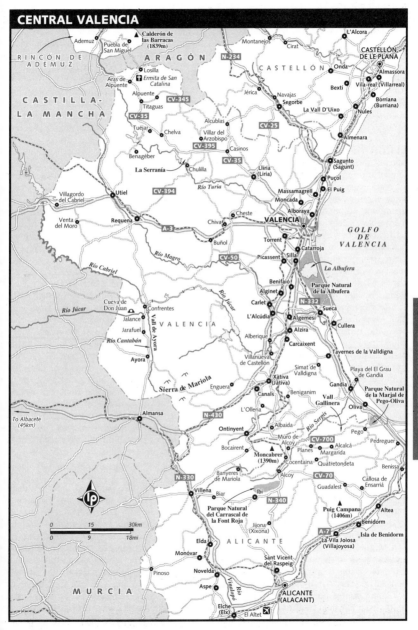

CENTRAL VALENCIA

and villages along the CV-35 (previously called the CV-234 and still featuring as such on many maps). Two services daily, departing from Valencia at 9am and 7.30pm, run as far as Ademuz (€8.60, 3¼ hours) while two more terminate in Tuéjar (€5.10, two hours). All buses pass through Villar del Arzobispo (€3.30, one hour). Alpuente (€5.25, 1½ hours) has one service daily from Monday to Saturday.

LLÍRIA (LIRIA)
Llíria is the first and only town of any consequence up the Turia valley. Nowadays an agreeably sleepy place, it was a settlement of some significance during Iberian times. On the mound of San Miguel, the Iberians built themselves Edeta, an important provincial settlement round about the 4th century BC.

Excavations on the hillock have yielded the most important finds so far of coloured Iberian pottery, now lodged in Valencia City's Museo de la Prehistoria within La Beneficencia.

Edeta, comprehensively sacked by the Romans, was abandoned and those of its populace who were spared moved down to the plain below to swell the numbers of the imperial town of Lauro. A magnificent mosaic from this era of the 12 Labours of Hercules is now displayed in the Museo Arqueológico Nacional in Madrid.

Contemporary buildings of interest are mostly around or near Llíria's Plaza Mayor. Dominating it is the magnificent Renaissance bulk of what is nowadays the **town hall**. Here too, you'll find the 18th-century **Iglesia Arciprestal de Nuestra Señora de la Asunción**, with a fine baroque facade divided into three sections and a baroque cupola up above. Nearby, the **Iglesia de la Sangre**, constructed in the 13th century as the Romanesque was ceding to the Gothic, betrays elements of each. The **Monasterio de San Miguel** may not have too much architectural merit in its own right, but local tradition has it that it houses a feather from the wings of no less than the Archangel Gabriel.

Llíria's contemporary claim to fame lies in its strong musical tradition. Nearly every pueblo in the Comunidad Valenciana has its own *banda* and, in La Primitiva and La Unión Musical, the town boasts two of the region's best bands. Rivalry is keen and has been known to split families asunder...

Getting There & Away
Llíria is served by infrequent buses heading up the Turia valley. A better bet is Metro line No 1 from Valencia, which terminates in Llíria. Trains (€1.85, 45 minutes) run about every half hour.

CASINOS
From Llíria take the CV-35. If you've a sweet tooth, stop off briefly in Casinos, 13km westwards, to pick up a packet or two of *peladillas* (sugared almonds), *garrapiñadas*, a type of praline, or a slab of *turrón*, a kind of soft nougat. All are gloriously sweet confections, made mainly from almonds, which grow in profusion hereabouts.

VILLAR DEL ARZOBISPO
It's worth taking a brief detour off the CV-35 to Villar del Arzobispo. Almond trees give way to olive groves and then, once you've crossed the dry riverbed of Río Acaña, vineyards. Villar's main produce is its wines – the dry, white Villar del Arzobispop itself; Cerro Gordo, named after the squat hillside in the middle ground; and Viña Villa, a red, aged in oak barrels. To sample each, call by the **Cooperativa Agricola el Villar** *(Avenida Ingeniero Tamarit 8-12; open 9am-1pm & 4pm-7.30pm Mon-Sat, 9am-1pm Sun).* Next door is the private **Bodegas Comache**, which also welcomes visitors.

Just opposite the Cooperativa Agricola el Villar, *Hostal Restaurante La Posá (☎ 96 272 07 19, Avenida Ingeniero Tamarit 9)* does a *menú* for €5.70 and has singles/doubles with bathroom for €15/28.85.

Granja-Escuela La Serranía (☎ 96 272 01 67, off Avenida Jorge de Austria) €12-15 per person according to season. These rooms are in a working farm, tucked away down a lane beside the Convento Carmelita (Carmelite Convent). Here, you can feed the livestock, go horse riding (€9 per hour) or hire a mountain bike (€2.40 per hour). It's popular with school groups during term time.

CHULILLA

Another detour southwards off the CV-35 along the CV-394 leads, after 6km, to the higgledy-piggledy, split-level village of Chulilla whose narrow, traffic-free streets, silent as the grave outside holiday periods, merit a meander. The more energetic will relish the fairly strenuous 20-minute round trip ascent to the ruins of the **Arabian castle** that frowns over the village. From its breezy battlements, there are fine views of the village and the wide, cultivated plain, hemmed in by precipitous cliffs, which are an internationally popular challenge for rock climbers in the know.

Hotel Balneario de Chulilla (☎/fax 96 165 70 13, e termas@infase.es) Singles €33.60-39.60, doubles €53.50-63.10 according to season. Open Mar–mid-Dec. A further 4.5km from the ruins will bring you to Hotel Balneario de Chulilla. Down at river level, this place is both a hotel and health spa. The heated spring, from which every hour gush over 180,000 litres of water rich in lime, magnesium and sulphates, has been recognised for its medicinal properties for over 200 years. You can dunk yourself in the large naturally heated swimming pool for €6 or, for €27, select a couple of activities from its range of showers, whirlpools and other things that squirt.

For somewhere similarly healthy and decidedly more cheap and cheerful, rest your head at *Refugio de Montaña El Altico (☎ 96 165 70 10)*, just before Chulilla on its north side. A popular climbers venue (there are even a couple of practice walls within the grounds), it enjoys a stupendous view of the valley below and sheer rock wall beyond.

CHELVA

Upstream from Chulilla, the Río Turia, often reed-choked or presided over by tall poplars, cuts a narrow swath through the main, thin pine forest, at risk annually from forest fires. Where the land is flat, whether naturally or carved by human labour into hard-won terraces, fruit trees and, in particular, almond trees stand in military order.

Chelva, first of the Alto Turia towns and villages, is also among its most typical. Parish

church and town hall, spiritual and temporal power, face each other across the Plaza Mayor. The church of Nuestra Señora de los Angeles has a fine, confident facade; its conche-shaped niches sadly stripped long ago of their statues. More interesting than the modern town hall – referred to as the Casa Consistorial – is its Renaissance predecessor, a short walk away along Calle Caballeros.

La Posada (☎ 96 210 01 24, Avenida Mancomunidad Alto Turia 20) Singles/doubles €18/30. This fairly functional place makes a good base for exploring the upper valley. While it can be noisy (ask for a room facing away from the main road), rooms, all with bathroom, heating, air-con and TV, are good value. Next door, *Rincón de los Pasos* does a la carte and a menú for €6.

Each Saturday, three tourist buses, called La Juanita in memory of a long-defunct intervillage service, leave at 10am and follow three different routes around the Alto Turia, all returning at around 6pm. They're an excellent way to experience the area if you haven't got your own wheels.

TUÉJAR

The tourist office on the outskirts of Tuéjar serves the five pueblos of the Alto Turia region. It opens 10am to 2pm and 4pm to 8pm, Monday to Saturday, plus Sunday morning in July to September. For the rest of the year, it observes the same weekend hours but opens only from 10am to 1pm, Monday to Friday.

From Avenida Ramón Villanueva, the main traffic route through the town which skirts the older town above, follow Calle Larga uphill to the Plaza Mayor. Here is Tuéjar's Casa Consistorial, or town hall, faced by the decidedly gaudy parish church, overpopulated with fleshy, winged cherubs, all of whom clearly need to go on a diet.

A pleasant walk up a side valley 1km north of town (take the turning for Hecu Camping) brings you to **El Azud de Tuéjar**, a shaded riverside picnic spot, where there's also a *restaurant (☎ 96 163 51 30)*, terrace cafe and **swimming pool** *(adult/child €2.10/1.50)*. From here, you can do a range of outdoor activities, as well as hire bikes. The area can become quite crowded in July and August, but if you continue walking up the wide valley, you can shake off the crowds and follow a signposted trail to Corrales de Silla and some scarcely distinguishable rock paintings.

Tuéjar also has the area's only camp site. *Hecu Camping (☎ 96 213 00 12)*, a couple of kilometres north of the village, charges €2.40/2.25/2.25 per person/tent/car. Hacked from the hillside, it offers shade, a stirring view over the valley towards Tuéjar and a welcome swimming pool (€1.80) at the end of a day's walking.

Hotel Restaurante Álvarez (☎ 96 163 52 82, fax 96 163 52 24, Avenida Ramón Villanueva 69) Singles/doubles €24/32.40. For a roof over your head, this place, on the main road that passes through the village, offers comfortable rooms, all with bathroom. You can eat simply and well here for under €12, including wine.

If you're self-catering or thinking of next-day's picnic, follow your nose to butchers *Hermanos Lance Llovera (Avenida Ramón Villanueva 3)* where the aroma of freshly despatched flesh fills the air. Sausages hang in swags, whole legs of ham drip into bowls, rich pâtés sit deep in basins and meat of every hue and texture hangs around.

For a nightcap, cross the road to *Pub Pérez (Avenida Ramón Villanueva 44)*. Then, if you've energy still to spare and it happens to be the weekend or high summer, dive into *Discoteca Tío Pepe* next door, where you can dance until the sun peeks over the horizon.

BENAGÉBER
The Benagéber dam, 17km south-west of Tuéjar, temporarily holds back the Río Turia. If it hasn't been raining for ages in the hills upstream, you can still see the remains of the original village peeking above the waters. When the dam was constructed in the 1950s to hold back the river, villagers were given a choice: to follow the migratory pattern to the towns and be relocated on the outskirts of Valencia City or to up sticks and shift up the mountainside to what is now present-day Benagéber. The latter is a place which, half a century later, still seems to be searching for an identity. What's likely to draw you here are the opportunities for water sports and for

walking. *Aventuria (☎/fax 96 213 90 81, ℮ aventuria@hotmail.com)*, down at river level about 4km north of the dam, is the place for activities of an aquatic kind. It's open from Easter to mid-October. José, head honcho of this small, friendly operation, speaks good English. Here, you can windsurf, sail, water ski, wake-board, canoe or just potter around on a pedalo. It has a small cafe/bar with a free camping zone just above it.

The *Centro de Vacaciones (Holiday Centre; ☎ 96 342 04 26, fax 96 320 29 84, � www.alberguebenageber.com – Spanish only)* is a mini-village that occupies quarters once used by the dam construction team. It offers mountain biking, horse riding and rock climbing. Full board, which is obligatory, costs a very reasonable €18 for a bed in a dorm or €30 in rooms with bathroom. Since the Centro is so popular with school groups, it's advisable to reserve in advance.

TITAGUAS
Titaguas, 14km north of Tuéjar, merits a brief stop to sample the village's dry white wines at one of its two wineries: **Bodegas Polo Monleon** (come away with a bottle or two of their excellent-value Hoya del Castillo at €1.50) at the junction of the main CV-35 and the CV-345 leading to Alpuente; and **Cooperativa Santa Barbara**, 200m down the CV-345.

Barely 500m west of the village, the *Zona de Acampada Rincón de la Olivera* offers free camping. Beside it is an open-air swimming pool.

Habitaciones Fuente Vieja (☎ 961 63 52 44, Avenida Don Ramón Villanueva 55) €9 per person, €12 with bathroom. This simple place on the main street is Titaguas' only option. It's perfectly acceptable and represents great value for your euro.

ALPUENTE
Strictly speaking, Alpuente, 8km east of Titaguas along the CV-345, belongs to the Serranía and isn't a part of the Alto Turia. Whatever its geopolitical position, it's one of the prettiest villages in the hinterland and is well worth the short detour. The old part clings to the western slope of Monte Las

Lomas, a narrow spur jutting between the taller, near vertical cliffs that flank it on either side. Enter through the old city gateway, its thick walls angled to make unwelcome penetration all the more difficult. Stroll its few streets with their pleasant wooden and wrought-iron balconies, then make the less than five-minute climb to the **Mirador de Angel Comes**, a viewpoint squeezed between the much-restored remains of Alpuente's castle (now a delightfully appointed private home) and a crumbling tower looming from the rock above. Here, you can look down upon the 14th-century church of **La Virgen de la Gracia** that, with its cupola of mellow tiles and octagonal tower, are rare in these parts, then take a short, 10-minute walk along the path that threads around the spur.

The village has a small **ethnological museum**, housed in a restored medieval bakery, but you'll be lucky to find it open. Around 2.5km north-east is a 15th-century aqueduct with 13 pointed arches stretching across the valley.

ARAS DE ALPUENTE

At the southern end of the village, arches of roses trained across the narrow, dusty streets scent the air when they're in season, while at the heart of the main square, Plaza del Olmo, a giant elm tree provides welcome shade.

Aras has a small **Museo Municipal** containing locally found artefacts. Until the museum moves into new premises, which are currently under restoration and when it may observe more regular hours, you have to be fairly tenacious to visit at it. Go to Restaurante Los Tornajos (see later in this section) and ask for Pepe el Maestro who, if he's around, will be happy to open up for you.

To enjoy a magnificent panorama, take the CV-355 north-east towards Losilla for 5km, then double back up a dirt track for 1.75km to the Ermita de Santa Catalina (1178m). From this isolated 18th-century chapel, a patchwork of orchards, vineyards and cereal fields pervade the wide plain below. Before you descend, drink deep and fill your water bottles from the Ermita's cool spring.

Casa Rural de Aras (☎ *92 210 20 39, Calle Luis Amigo 46*) €18 per person Mon-

Fri, €27 Sat & Sun. Apartments within this gracious renovated town house all have rooms with bathroom, heating and access to self-catering facilities.

Restaurante Los Tornajos (☎ *96 210 20 88, Carretera de Valencia s/n)* Menú €9, mains around €7.50. It's not simply because this bustling bar and restaurant is the only eatery in the village that we recommend it. Portions are plentiful and the cooking both traditional and with aspirations. For traditional fare, have as a starter their *gazpacho de la casa*, a small frying pan of seasoned, shredded chicken and rabbit which has nothing in common with Andalucía's cold summer soup of the same name. For the latter, try the *trucha* (trout) from the trout farm in Tuéjar, which comes with cream and kiwi fruit on the side.

RINCÓN DE ADEMUZ
postcode 46140 • pop 3200
• elevation 825m

Here, in the 'corner of Ademuz', the regions of Valencia, Aragón and Castilla-La Mancha meet. As the locals graphically put it, you can sit in Valencia looking north with your left foot in Castilla and your right in Aragón. It's an odd little enclave, separated from Valencia proper by a narrow neck, barely 5km wide. The Rincón is linked umbilically and in spirit to the Comunidad Valenciana by the Río Turia and, politically, by nearly 800 hundred years of affiliation, ever since the Rincón was recovered from the Moors. That is, except for 20 brief months of amputation in the 19th century, after which it was regrafted onto Valencia as a result of popular pressure.

It's good walking territory. Villages are linked by a network of signposted trails that follow drover's roads and centuries-old paths which, until the internal combustion engine and the construction of concrete highways, were the only means of communication.

Ademuz, 35km northwest of Aras de Alpuente, is the main town – although it's scarcely a town – of this anomaly. Recaptured from the Moors in 1210, it was the first Valencian pueblo to be liberated and remains proud of this record. Unlike most other villages and hamlets of the Rincón, it has a modicum of accommodation and makes a good base for walking.

Villages are connected by ancient trails, nowadays signed with the familiar yellow-and-white Pequeño Recorrido (PR; short walk) symbol, as are a couple of ancient drovers routes. For guided walks (€4.20 per person, minimum of six people), horse riding (€9 per hour), bike hire (€9 per day) or a leisurely two-hour descent of the Río Turia by canoe, you can contact *Ademuz Aventura* (☎ 630 924149 or 96 330 56 81, e dprcop@ santandersupernet.com). Active at weekends and during July and August (we strongly recommend that you call in advance to reserve a spot), they occupy a pleasant, restored building at Calle Solano 6, just off Plaza del Ayuntamiento, the Town Hall square. Whether or not you walk, ride or paddle with them, you can stay in their attractive doubles with bathroom for €36.

Hostal Casa Domingo (☎ 978 78 20 30, fax 978 78 20 56, e casadomingo@ctv.es, Avenida Valencia 1) Singles/doubles with bathroom €18.20/31.20. Occupying the town's largest building except for the parish church, what appears to be just another concrete roadhouse is, in fact, rather cosy and rooms have TV and heating. You couldn't describe the vast *restaurant* dining room as intimate but it does serve up an ample *menú del día* (€9) that changes daily. Mains cost €9 to €11.50 and there's a generous range of meats – roast, grilled or stewed.

For late-night, weekend-only fun – these places are as dead as their own doornails on other nights, except in late July and August when they might getting going on any old night – try the golden quadrangle, each within 100m of the other and all on Avenida Valencia. The pubs *Scorpio* and *El Rincón* are good for starters before moving onto one or both of a pair of discos that eyeball each other: *Disco-Pub Stylo* and, across the road beneath Hostal Casa Domingo, *Disco Molino*.

You're unlikely to find a more dynamic community than that of **Puebla de San Miguel** anywhere in Spain. With less than 100 souls (expanding to over 700 in August when its emigre sons and daughters return to

their roots), its nucleus is *Bar San Miguel*, cheek by jowl with the 18th-century parish church. Here, you can eat, drink, buy local honey, sign up for one of the village's *refugios* (simple mountain refuges) and collect a guide – the mayor himself if you're lucky – to show you around the small **ethnographical museum** *(admission free)*.

The museum has a collection of artisans' tools and machinery. Beside it is a huge cylindrical grape-fermenting tank, used to store and pound grapes. The wine from these grapes used to be distilled into *aguardiente*, the local firewater, that would be dispatched to Valencia City and nearby Teruel in Aragón. Soon to be on display are the remnants of a dinosaur skeleton, found locally quite by chance and which is currently being analysed.

From the village, a way-marked trail leads to the summit of **Calderón de las Barracas** (also called Alto de las Barracas), at 1839m the highest point in the Comunidad.

Within the village's lands are five simple buildings that have been adapted as *refugios*, mostly used by walkers. Costing €6 per person, they can be reserved by calling the town hall (☎ 608 277428) or, like just about every other deal in town, by calling into Bar San Miguel.

Requena-Utiel

REQUENA
postcode 46340 • pop 19,100
• elevation 690m
Just off the A-3 motorway and 71km west of Valencia, Requena is a bustling commercial centre from whose heart rises a little, walled, medieval town, established by the Muslims in the 8th century. Requena's former wealth came from silk; at one time it had 800 active looms, making this tiny town Spain's fourth-biggest producer. Nowadays it's primarily wine country, producing robust reds and sparkling *cavas*.

Information
The tourist office (☎ 96 230 38 51) is near the entrance to the old town at Calle García

La Tomatina

Buñol? It'll make you see red!

If you happen to be in Valencia on the last or penultimate Wednesday in August (the date varies), you can participate in one of Spain's messiest and most bizarre festivals. Held in the town of Buñol (about 40km west of Valencia just off the N-111/A3 highway and on the Requena/Utiel local train line), La Tomatina is, believe it or not, a tomato-throwing festival.

Buñol is an otherwise drab industrial town. Its outskirts are overshadowed by a massive, smoke-belching cement factory, while the old town is dominated by a crumbling 12th-century stone castle.

The festival's origins, although relatively recent, are already the subject of myth. And while it mightn't last long, it attracts up to 30,000 visitors to a town that normally has just 9000 inhabitants.

Here's how it goes: just before noon on the day of the festival, truckloads of ripe, squishy tomatoes (125,000kg is one estimate) are delivered to (thrown at) the waiting crowd, and for the next hour or so everyone joins in a frenzied, cheerful and anarchic tomato war. The most enthusiastic participants chant *'tomate, tomate, queremos tomate!'* ('tomato, tomato, we want tomato!').

After being pounded with pulp, expect to be sluiced down with hoses by the local fire brigade. The mayhem takes place on the town's main square and Calle del Cid.

At 1pm an explosion signals the end and the drenched participants don their stash of fresh clothes. Most people come for the day, arriving on the morning train from Valencia and heading back in the afternoon.

If you prefer to remain dry, you can watch the spectacle on Canal 9, Valencia's local TV channel. They mount a camera behind a shop window and pay a willing youth to wipe off the dripping tomato juice from the lens with a squeegee mop.

Montés s/n. It opens 9am to 2pm, Tuesday to Friday, and 10am to 2pm plus 4pm to 7pm, Saturday and Sunday.

Things to See & Do

Enter the old quarter from its northern side, passing by the 10th-century Muslim **Torre del Homenaje**. Within the town walls are the Gothic **Iglesia de Santa María**, largest of the old town's three monumental churches, and which has a fine sculpted main portal. The **Iglesia de San Nicolás**, oldest of the trio, was originally built in the 13th century but was substantially altered in the 18th century. The west door of the third church, the **Iglesia de San Salvador**, rivals that of the Iglesia de Santa María in the richness of its stone carving. Seek out, too, sturdy manorial houses such as the **Casa del Arte Mayor de la Seda** (Silk Guild House), **Casa del Corregidor** (Mayor's House) and **Palacio del Cid**.

Also in the old town, Plaza de la Villa (also known as Plaza Albornoz) hides beneath it a network of interlinked **cuevas** (cellars), that were once used as storerooms (note the huge clay *tinajas*, storage jars twice as tall as a person, used for storing wine) and, during times of strife, as hideouts. Guided visits of the cellars (adult/child €1.80/1.20) descend from the entrance on the square at 11am, noon and 1pm, Monday to Friday and every half hour between 10.30am and 1.30pm, plus 4.30pm to 6.30pm on Saturday and Sunday.

The **Museo Municipal** *(adult/child €1.80/1.20; open 11am-2pm Tues-Sun)* is in the

Convento Carmelito near Plaza Consistorial in the new town.

Special Events

In February, inland a time of deepest winter, Requena holds its annual three-day Muestra del Embutido de Artesano, when such rich fare protects against the cold of the *meseta* (Spain's high inland plateau). It's a celebration of the sausage in all its manifestations, helped down with *copas* (glassfuls) of robust Utiel-Requena red wine.

In late August and early September, Requena's Fiesta de la Vendimia brings revellers from far and wide to participate in this hearty bacchanal, which celebrates the end of the grape harvest.

Places to Stay & Eat

Hotel Avenida (☎ 96 230 04 80, Calle de San Agustín 10), just off Avenida del Arrabal, has singles/doubles with bathroom and TV for €21.25/33.55.

If you can't visit the cuevas, eat at *Mesón La Villa (☎ 96 230 12 75, Plaza de Albornoz 13)* and ask your hosts to let you see theirs – briefly used by the local branch of the Inquisition to turn the screws on heretics.

Getting There & Away

Autolineas Alsina (☎ 96 349 72 30) runs over 12 buses daily (fewer at weekends) between Requena and Valencia (€3.65, one hour). Seven trains run daily to and from Valencia (€3.16, 1½ hours) and three run to Madrid.

FAUNA IBÉRICA

Around 10km east of Requena on the A-3, Fauna Ibérica *(☎ 96 213 80 76; adult/child €9/4; open 10am-8pm daily Apr-Oct, 10am-5pm daily Nov-Mar)* is a nature park where you can see Spanish wildlife, both rare and common, in a relatively natural setting. A walking trail 1600m-long passes by, among many other species, Iberian lynxes.

UTIEL

postcode 46300 • pop 11,800
• elevation 720m

Utiel, beside the Río Magro and 15km northwest of Requena along the A-3, is primarily

a wine-producing area – and wine is what merits you pulling off the motorway.

The **Museo del Vino** *(wine museum; ☎ 962 17 10 62, Calle Sevilla 12; admission free; open 10am-2pm Mon-Fri)* is within a one-time winery, the Bodega Redonda ('round bodega', which is exactly what it is), one block west of the train station. For a bottle or two of economical (costing €0.80 a litre on draught) everyday wine, fill up at the **Bodega Cooperativa Agricola de Utiel**, a huge complex 200m north of the station that has its retail outlet on Avenida Marín Lazaro. To come away with something altogether more subtle, cross the road to **Enoteca La Mesilla**, a specialist wine shop at No 11 that carries a great range of Utiel-Requena's finest wines.

Aficionados of ecclesiastical architecture might enjoy the massive, soberly decorated Isabeline Gothic church of **Nuestra Senõra de la Asunción**. The other monument of which Utielanos are proud of is the town's **bullring**, built in 1858 and rivalling Bocairent for the title of the Comunidad's oldest.

La Cueva (Calle Santísima Trinidad 21) Meals around €12. All tiles, brass lamps and copper pots, La Cueva is an agreeable place to dine.

El Carro (☎ 962 17 11 31, Calle Heroes del Tollo 25) Mains €12-15. Opposite the Guardia Civil barracks, El Carro offers fine cuisine and, naturally, equally fine local wines. For dessert, try some of their homemade ice creams such as, for the more adventurous, olive oil or rosemary flavour.

Seven trains (€3.16, 1½ hours) run daily to Valencia via Requena. Buses of Autolineas Alsina (☎ 96 349 72 30) stop on the west side of the Mercado Central (central market). Over 12 services (fewer at weekends; €4.10, 1¼ hours) connect Utiel and Valencia's main bus station, and also call by Requena.

AROUND UTIEL

Entre Viñas (☎ 962 13 90 71, fax 962 17 14 32, ℮ entrevinas@ainia.es) Singles/doubles with bathroom €40.25/54.10. Also known as Finca el Renegado, this huge former farmhouse, set amid vineyards and with a bodega right next door, has been tastefully restored

CENTRAL VALENCIA

and furnished. It also has a pair of apartments, each with two double bedrooms, living room and kitchen for €84.15 per night Monday to Friday, €102 on Saturday and Sunday. To get there, take the N111 westwards from Utiel then head south over the motorway and along the CV-452 for 4.5km.

For **Venta del Moro** continue along the CV-452 and turn right (west) at the junction with the CV-455. This small village is home to three open-air activity outfits that operate in the nearby Río Cabriel and local hills. Between March and November, *Avensport* (☎ 96 123 50 76, **W** www.avensport.com – *Spanish only)* offers a whole range of water sports – a 20km raft descent, canoeing, canyon clambering – plus walking and rock climbing. They also have a variety of simple, overnight accommodation options for between €6 and €18 per night if you're doing one of their activities.

Kalahari (☎ 96 377 44 44, **W** www .kalahariaventuras.com – *Spanish only, Calle Manzana 12)* offers much the same. You can reserve by phone or by calling in at their office, Calle Mar 47, Valencia City. *Ozono* (☎ 96 218 50 39, *Calle San Juan 14)*, the only one of the three with a permanent presence in the village, also offers horse riding and can arrange accommodation.

Hostal Ventamorino (☎ 96 218 51 77) has rooms with bathroom for €15 per person.

One bus a day connects Venta del Moro with Requena.

Xàtiva & Vall de Ayora

XÀTIVA (JÁTIVA)
postcode 46800 • pop 25,500
• elevation 120m

Xàtiva, easily accessible by train, makes a convenient day trip from Valencia. Snug at the base of the Serra Vernissa mountain range 60km south of Valencia City, it has a long history.

The nearby Cova Negra (Black Cave) revealed relics over 30,000 years old – and an intact Neanderthal skull. When the Iberians

held sway, the town was called Saiti and, together with Ilici (Elche) and Dianium (Denia), ranked as considerably more important in its distant day than Valencia City.

In the 11th century the Muslims built Europe's first paper manufacturing plant here, forming their product from a paste of straw and rice. After the Reconquista, Xàtiva became Valencia's second-largest city.

Xàtiva was the birthplace of the Borgia Popes Calixtus III and Alexander VI and also of the baroque painter, José de Ribera, known as El Espanoleto.

However, the town's glory days all but ended in 1707 when Felipe V's troops torched most of the town during the War of Succession.

Orientation
The east-west boulevard, which changes its name from Albareda (Alameda) Jaime I to Avenida de Selgas, is Xàtiva's main thoroughfare. Shaded by mature plane trees, it makes for a pleasant stroll. To its north are the train and bus stations. To its south lie the old quarter and all the main monuments. Higher and even farther south are the castle that dominates the town and Hostería Mont Sant, a luxury hotel that merits a visit, even for a brief drink in its gardens.

Information
The staff at Xàtiva's tourist office (☎ 96 227 33 46), Alameda Jaime I 50, are particularly friendly and well informed. It's open from 10am to 1.30pm and 4pm to 6pm, Monday to Friday, and 10am to 2pm, Saturday and Sunday, October to May. From June to September, it functions 10am to 2.30pm from Tuesday to Sunday.

The post office is on Alameda Jaime I.

Things to See & Do
What's interesting sits south and uphill from the Alameda. Ask at the tourist office for their multilingual pamphlet *Conjunt Històric Artístic*. Calle Angel, which becomes Calle Moncada, is flanked by noble mansions. Parallel Calle Corretgería has more modest but no less fascinating bourgeois residences.

CENTRAL VALENCIA

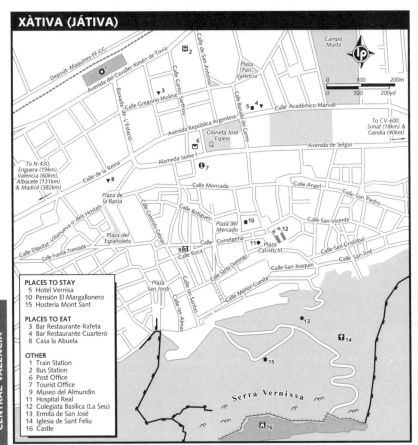

XÀTIVA (JÁTIVA)

PLACES TO STAY
5 Hotel Vernisa
10 Pensión El Margallonero
15 Hostería Mont Sant

PLACES TO EAT
3 Bar Restaurante Rafeta
4 Bar Restaurante Cuarteró
8 Casa la Abuela

OTHER
1 Train Station
2 Bus Station
6 Post Office
7 Tourist Office
9 Museo del Almudín
11 Hospital Real
12 Colegiata Basílica (La Seu)
13 Ermita de San José
14 Iglesia de Sant Feliu
16 Castle

In the past, Xàtiva proclaimed itself 'The City of 1000 Fountains' and the case remains a watery one. Copiously fed from the Bellús spring about 10km away, many houses had their own water supply way before the days of taps and faucets. The spring still supplies the town and feeds its splashing fountains.

The **Museo del Almudín** (☎ 96 227 65 97, Calle Corretgería 46; admission €2; open 9.30am-2.30pm Tues-Fri mid-June–mid-Sept, 10am-2pm & 4pm-6pm Tues-Fri mid-Sept–mid-June, 10am-2pm Sat & Sun year round), once Xàtiva's corn exchange, is a fine building in its own right. It houses

an impressive collection of archaeological relics and artworks from Roman and Islamic times, a couple of Riberas – and the famed portrait of Felipe V, hung permanently upside down in retribution for his pyrotechnic assault on the town.

The 16th-century **Colegiata Basílica** (Collegiate Church), also known as La Seu (the cathedral), merits a visit primarily for the rich treasures of its **museum** (☎ 96 227 38 36; admission free; open 10.30am-1.30pm Mon-Sat). In front of the main facade are a pair of bronze statues of Calixtus III and Alexander VI, the Borgia Popes born in Xàtiva.

On the opposite, west side of Plaza Calixto III is the **Hospital Real**, which is still used as a medical centre to this day. Its elaborate 15th-century facade, the only remaining element of the original building, contrasts favourably with the Colegiata Basílica's own uninspiring 20th-century eastern entry.

A visit to Xàtiva is incomplete without ascending to the **castle** (☎ *96 227 42 74; admission €1.90; open 10am-7pm Tues-Sun in summer, 10am-6pm Tues-Sun in winter)*, from where the views are inspiring. If you're without transport, you can avoid the steep uphill walk by taking a taxi from the rank by the train station, or the twice daily tourist train (see Getting Around, later). First occupied by the Iberians, the location has the remains of a palace, constructed by the Arabs atop this strategic site, and of a post-Reconquista Cistercian monastery. The ramparts, which snake the length of the hillside, remain largely intact. Access to the castle grounds is free.

On the way up, notice on your left the 18th-century **Ermita de San José**, closed to visitors and, to the right, the **Iglesia de Sant Feliu** *(admission free; open 10am-1pm & 4pm-7pm Tues-Sat May-Sept, 10am-1pm & 3pm-6pm Tues-Sat Oct-Apr, 10am-1pm Sun year round)*, built in 1269 and Xàtiva's oldest church.

Special Events

Xàtiva's biggest annual festival is the Feria de Agosto, which in 2000 celebrated its 750th anniversary. Originally permitted by royal decree of King Jaime I, it was until quite recently the Comunidad's largest livestock fair. Held along the Alameda Jaime between 14 and 20 August, it still has an animal element, plus a host of events from the seriously cultural to the popular and playful.

Places to Stay

Accommodation in town is fairly limited.
Pensión El Margallonero (☎ *96 227 66 77, Plaza del Mercado 42)* Simple rooms €12 per person. Three generations of the same family have run this pleasant pensión and restaurant.

Hotel Vernisa (☎ *96 227 10 11, fax 96 228 13 65,* e *hvernisa@servidex.com, Calle Aca-démico Marvall 1)* Singles/doubles/triples/ quads with bathroom €37/49/64/72. Rooms at the Vernisa, which is open year round, all have heating, air-con and TV.

Hostería Mont Sant (☎ *96 227 50 81, fax 96 228 19 05,* e *montsant@servidex .com)* Singles/doubles with bathroom from €78.15/90.15. Prices rise to €125 for a self-contained chalet. This charming alternative for those with decidedly fatter wallets has 15 beautifully appointed rooms with full facilities. On the road to the castle, it offers superb views over the town and valley, its restaurant is first class, and guests can enjoy the fine gardens and swimming pool.

Places to Eat

El Margallonero (Plaza del Mercado 42) Menú €8 Mon-Fri, €10 Sat. Open lunchtime only Mon-Sat. This pensión (see Places to Stay) runs a popular, bustling restaurant with a menú that's strong on traditional cooking.

Bar Restaurante Rafeta (☎ *96 228 33 13, Calle Gregorio Molina 11)* Meals around €10. Open lunchtime only Mon-Sat. Another simple, no-frills place, it's justifiably popular with workers at midday. For starters, try their *sopa de lentejas* which has lentils, meat and potatoes swimming in a tasty broth.

Bar Restaurante Cuarteró (☎ *96 227 55 82, Calle Académico Marvall 7)* Menú €12, meat mains €7.25-12, fish mains €9.50-14.50. Open Mon-Sat, closed mid-Aug–mid-Sept. Open all day, this place, also good for a snack, carries a good selection of wines.

Casa la Abuela (☎ *96 228 10 85, Calle de la Reina 17)* Menú €12, mains €9.50-13.25. Open daily, closed mid-July–mid-Aug. Casa la Abuela, Xàtiva's longest-established restaurant, is renowned for its a la carte regional cuisine. It's a must if the finances will stretch to it. It has a second, smaller entrance on Plaza de la Bassa.

For something equally special although without Casa La Abuela's long pedigree, head up the hill to *Hostería Mont Sant* (see Places to Stay, earlier).

Getting There & Away

Train and bus stations are both on Avenida del Cavaller Ximén de Tovia, although the

Arnadí

If it's an option on your dessert menu, go for the *arnadí*. If it doesn't, pick up a piece or two at a pastry shop in town. One variant has pumpkin as its base, the other sweet potato. Both kinds are laced with eggs, cinnamon, lemon, pine nuts, almonds and lots and lots of sugar. Traditionally an Easter-time sweetmeat and peculiar to Xàtiva, it's available around the calendar and is quite irresistible.

latter is usually deserted; the train is by far your best bet. Frequent local services connect Xàtiva with Valencia (€2.50, half-hourly) and most Valencia-Madrid trains stop here, too. You can also reach Alicante (€9-12, five daily) and Gandía (change in Silla; €2.50, frequent).

If you have wheels and are heading for Gandía and the Costa Blanca, the CV-600 via Simat de Validigna makes spectacular mountain driving or – with decidedly more input – cycling.

Getting Around

One of those rather naff trains on wheels (€2.60) does the run up to the castle. You might like to swallow your embarrassment and seriously consider it. It does a commentated run through the old part of town before heading uphill and saves you quite a lot of legwork. It chugs off from the tourist office at 12.30pm and 4.30pm, rain or shine, trippers or nay.

There's a large underground car park beneath Glorieta José Espejo, entered from Avenida República Argentina. Leave your vehicle there since it won't be welcome in the old quarter.

AROUND XÀTIVA
Enguera

Enguera, 19km from Xàtiva and 70km from Valencia, formerly made its money from the wool trade, as one or two ample 18th- and 19th-century bourgeois residences still attest. Nowadays, its wealth comes from fashioning wrought iron, working wood and

pressing virgin olive oil from the surrounding countryside.

Things to See & Do A short visit conveys well the sense of a typical medium-size Valencian community with its town hall, Unión Musical (headquarters of the town brass band) and Casa Fallera, social centre for Enguera's falleros and falleras. And, of course, there's the parish church, the stolid **Iglesia de San Miguel**, its ponderousness relieved to a degree by the more graceful bell tower. Typically, too, Enguera, like any self-respecting small town, has its **Casa de la Cultura**, a focus for cultural activities, and a tiny **museum** *(admission free; open 4pm-8pm Mon-Fri)*, a repository for local finds. In Plaza Manuel Tolsà, it occupies a wing of what was at one time a Carmelite convent.

Places to Stay & Eat Enguera has a few interesting possibilities.

Camping La Pinada (☎ 96 222 45 03, W www.paralelo40.org/pinada – Spanish only, Calle Paraje Piscina Municipal s/n) €2.40/7.20/2.40 per person/tent/car. Open year round. Admission to the adjacent Olympic-sized swimming pool is free if you're staying at this shady, recently established camp site. Not tasted Bulgarian cooking lately? In the bar is a chalkboard menu in Cyrillic script to cater for the sizeable Bulgarian community that lives hereabouts.

Casa el Borreguero (☎ 96 222 41 58, fax 96 222 56 53, Calle Santa Bárbara 21) €10.85 per person, €13.25 with bathroom. If you're planning to travel in the area, the furnished apartments of Casa el Borreguero, which has full cooking facilities, make a comfortable and economical base.

Cafe El Industrial (☎ 92 222 40 60, Plaza Valencia 2) It's worth seeking out this unexpected little gem dating back to the 1930s, which is tiled, pillared and has an elaborate stucco ceiling. It was originally a gentlemen's club for local captains of industry.

VALL DE AYORA

For centuries, this valley, which should more accurately be called Cantabán after the rivulet that meanders down it, was an important north-south communication route. In its time, it also marked the frontier between Christian and Muslim territory. Just about every village is dominated by a castle, nowadays much dilapidated, to which the locals would retreat when the going got rough. Long since at peace, the valley lives nowadays mainly from agriculture – in particular from its juicy peaches, prized throughout the region.

Ayora

Ayora, with over 5000 inhabitants, is the main settlement in the valley and is the town from which the valley gets its name. It may be relatively tiny but is Spain's principal honey-producing area. You'll find the sticky substance on sale everywhere.

Architecturally, the fine, freshly scrubbed Mannerist facade of the stolid parish church of **Nuestra Señora de la Asunción** is impressive. Inside, if you manage to find it open, are the Tablas de Yáñez de Almedina, an impressive 16th-century altarpiece, and Milagro del Ángel (Angel's Miracle) by Vicente López. For a good overview of town and valley, clamber up to the severely dilapidated castle. Take Calle San Nicolas and follow the signs through the Barrio de San Nicolas, where every house is whitewashed and doors and windows are outlined in blue, giving the district a Greek feel.

Restaurante El Rincón (☎ 962 19 17 05, Calle Parras 10) Mains €7.75-14.50. Down a street just off the Plaza Mayor, this is the place to sample the typical cuisine of the valley such as *gazpacho ayorino* (€7; a rich, rabbit and chicken stew served on a bed of crisp, unleavened bread). To stagger out truly filled and fulfilled on local produce, go for the *menú gastronómico* at €16.25.

On high days and holidays, folk flock from nearby villages to unwind in Ayora, which must have more bars and cafes than all the rest of the valley put together. Just see how they line the pedestrianised Calle Empedra, which takes off from the Plaza Mayor, and which itself is well endowed with pavement cafes.

Jarafuel

In addition to having the valley's only camp site, the other claim to fame of Jarafuel, 12km north of Ayora, is that it traditionally works *el almez*, a whippy, flexible wood that's bent into walking sticks and the traditional three-pronged wooden pitchfork. Bastones Martinez on Calle Juan XXIII 12 carries a huge selection.

Camping Las Jaras (☎ 961 89 90 84, Partida de las Rochas) €2.85/3/2.55 per person/tent/car. Open year round. On a hillside overlooking the village of Jarafuel, Las Jaras has a swimming pool and large bar/restaurant, and sites are shaded. Since space for casual campers is limited – most pitches are rented out by the year – it's prudent to book in advance.

Jalance

The N-330 highway bypasses the village of Jalance, 5.5km north of Jarafuel, but it would be a pity if you did the same. The village itself deserves a brief ramble before undertaking the easy 1km walk or drive up a signed dirt track to its ruined 11th-century castle. From here, there are splendid views of the pueblo, the broad Ayora valley – and the intrusive cooling towers of the Cofrentes nuclear power station, steam exuding from their flat tops like a pair of Tintin quiffs.

From the north end of the village, a narrow, sealed road leads off through an almond orchard and pine forest to the **Mirador Los Cañones de Júcar** (8.5km). This overlooks the sheer, rust-coloured cliffs that rear up from the Río Júcar, glinting far below.

A further 2km brings you to the **Cueva de Don Juan** (☎ 96 219 60 11 for information; open 10am-2pm Sat & Sun). At the head of a tight ravine that cuts into the Júcar valley, this 60,000-cu-metre cavern reaches into the hillside. The stalactites and stalagmites along this 500m guided walk may not be as spectacular as several elsewhere in Spain, but you'd be hard pressed to find a more lonely, less exploited spot.

Cofrentes

Cofrentes, 7km north of Jalance and at the

CENTRAL VALENCIA

confluence of the Ríos Júcar and Cabriel, has a small tourist office (☎ 961 894 316), Plaza de España 6, open 8am to 3pm, Monday to Friday. Outside these hours, the town hall at No 9 can help you. Looming over them and the rest of town is the much-modified **Arabian castle**, undergoing the latest of its many facelifts and transformations over the centuries. Most locals if they think of Cofrentes, recall the nuclear power plant whose gargantuan cooling towers were like a pair of giant egg cups sitting in your sight line from just about every possible angle.

***Balneario de Hervideros** (☎ 96 189 40 25, fax 96 189 40 05)* Singles/doubles from €38.60/64.30. Open Mar–Dec. If you feel the need to be rejuvenated, pass by this long-established health spa and rub shoulders with the clientele, whose average age must be well into the seventies, and walk away lighter of step. For a more long-lasting peeling back of the years, you can book yourself in for a huge array of water, mud and steam-based cures, therapies and massages (including the enigmatically named *clapping respiratorio*).

***Torreblanca** (☎ 961 89 40 69, Calle Santa Ana 3)* Singles/doubles €25.85/38.50. Open year round. Torreblanca offers a pleasant and more affordable alternative to the Balneario's fin de siecle charms. The rooms come with bathroom, TV and heating. Call Restaurante Torralba, on Calle Barrio Maestros s/n at the southern end of town, which belongs to the same family and acts as reception for the hotel.

Sierra de Mariola & Around

The Sierra de Mariola, popular with Valencianos in the know but relatively untrodden by the rest of the world, offers fine, easy to moderate walking, the opportunity for horse riding and some spectacular drives. The historic centres of its modest towns, which were among the first in the Comunidad to be industrialised, are all worth a brief stop. Typically, the small-scale sprawl of the *polígono industrial*, the area of light industry that keeps the place going, gives way to the nucleus of the old town, carrying on its business very much as though the Industrial Revolution was yet to happen.

Rolling gently and clad in forests of pine, holm oak and yew, the sierra is shared between the provinces of Valencia and Alicante. It's famous for its *neveras* (ice houses), broad, cylindrical structures where the winter snow on the mountains was compacted and stored, then, with the advent of spring, cut into blocks and transported to the coastal plains.

Among many signed trails are those leading to the summits of Montcabrer, the highest point in the sierra, Sant Jaume and El Portín.

Places to Stay

***Les Fonts de Mariola** (☎ 96 213 51 60, fax 96 235 00 31, e fontsmariola@infonegocio .com, Carretera Bocairent–Valencia km 9)* €2.70 each person/tent/car. Open year round. This, the Sierra de Mariola's only camp site, is beautifully situated at the heart of the wooded mountains, equidistant from both Alcoy and Bocairent. The GR7 long-distance trail passes right by and it makes a good base for some great medium-grade walking. It also has a few bungalows from €42.10, a pool and a small restaurant.

BOCAIRENT

postcode 46880 • pop 4700
• elevation 660m

Bocairent is one of the highest towns in the Comunidad. If you can, plan to visit at the weekend, when its small but impressive church museum and other attractions are open. The tourist office (☎ 96 290 50 62), at No 2 on the main Plaza del Ayuntamiento, is open 10am to 2pm and 5pm to 7.30pm, Tuesday to Sunday.

The town's chief drawcard is the **Covetes dels Moros**, just north-east of town on the far side of Río Clariano, which is here more stream than river. Although they are popularly known as the Caves of the Arabs, no-one really knows the origin or purpose of these 53 caves, cut into the soft limestone of

CENTRAL VALENCIA

The Original Freezer

Life has always been hard in the Sierra de Mariola. And until quite recently the existence of the *nevaters*, the snow gatherers, was tougher than most. When the heights turned white, they'd reach for a shovel and a couple of straw baskets and head for the snowline. The snow they collected would be heaped into a pile. Then the team would tread the mound to expel the air, make it more compact and compress it into ice.

The ice was transferred into a pit, or sometimes a cylindrical, above ground building like a gas holder. Here, the 'snow men' separated each layer with a coating of grass so that it could more easily be carved into manageable blocks, come summer. Once the pit was full – in the good years, that is, when enough snow fell – they covered this giant block of subterranean ice with a coating of wood-ash, then a final layer of fronds and branches as insulation.

When the Costa Blanca was sweltering in the summer heat, villagers would spend the hours of darkness hacking off slabs of ice, which they'd transport down to the plains by donkey or mule. This long-standing traffic ended abruptly with the invention of artificial refrigeration early in the 20th century.

You can still come across these deep, cylindrical pits – and, less frequently, their above-ground variant – throughout the Sierra de Mariola. Usually on harsher, north-facing slopes, typical ones are about 15m deep and 10m wide. Larger ones would have supporting beams of stone and roofs of wooden tiles. Smaller neveras would be topped by a domed, dry-stone roof.

the cliff wall. From town, it's a pleasant short walk along the riverbed and up to the caves, which are fun to explore if you're reasonably agile and don't mind crouching. They're open 11am to 2pm Tuesday to Sunday, and 5pm to 8pm Saturday and Sunday, and admission is free. Follow the signs, 'Ruta de les Covetes' from Plaza del Ayuntamiento.

The parish **church**, constructed on the site of an Arabian castle, is, unless you've a tolerance for rococo excess, decidedly over the top. What is altogether more restrained and worthwhile is the adjacent ecclesiastical **museum**, which has a chalice by Benvenuto Cellini and canvases by, among others, Juan de Juanes, Ribalta, Sorolla and Segrelles, a talented local painter whose distinctive hand you can see in many local churches and convents. Unfortunately for such a treasure, it's only open at 12.30pm on Sunday, after mass, although it's possible to visit at other times by ringing the tourist office in advance.

The **Plaza de Toros** *(admission free; open 1pm-2pm & 5pm-6pm Sat & Sun)*, hacked out of the rock in 1843, is the Comunidad's oldest bullring.

Now here's a novel theme for a sculpture. Such is the importance of Bocairent's main industry that there's even a **Monumento a la Manta**, literally, a Monument to the Blanket, wrought in iron, at the entrance to town beside the Puente San Blai!

ONTINYENT
postcode 46870 • pop 29,900
• elevation 385m

The spectacular drive between Bocairent and Ontinyent follows the narrow defile of the Río Clariano.

Ontinyent itself, compared to its more modest neighbours, is rather too big and too traffic-dominated for comfort. All the same, La Vila, the small old quarter, merits a stop and a stroll. Highlights are the impressive bulk of **Les Jutjats** (Los Juzgados), the former law courts, which were being fundamentally renovated at the time of writing, and the **bell tower** *(admission free)* of the Iglesia de la Asuncion de Santa Mari. Reaching for the sky and dominating the simple church beneath, it was begun in 1689 and took a full 20 years to complete. Amazingly, it's still there, having survived an earthquake in 1748 and a lightning strike a century later. It's open for visits on Sunday morning after mass.

The tourist office (☎ 96 291 60 90) is on Plaza Santo Domingo, a pleasant spot for a rest on a hot day beneath the shade of its plane trees. The office is open 10am to 2pm and 4pm to 7.30pm from Tuesday to Friday,

CENTRAL VALENCIA

10am to 2pm on Saturday and from 4pm to 7.30pm on Monday.

Ontinyent is on the train line between Valencia and Alcoy and is served by La Concepción buses running between Valencia and Villena.

IBI
postcode 03440 • pop 20,700
• elevation 816m
Until it could no longer compete with far-eastern imports in the early 1980s, Ibi accounted for 60% of the toys made in Spain and its products delighted children throughout Europe. The Paya factory, once the town's largest employer, has long since closed but its memory lives on in the **Museo del Juguete** *(☎ 96 555 02 26, Calle Aurora Pérez Callallero 4; admission €1.20; open 10am-1pm & 4pm-7pm Mon-Sat, 11am-2pm Sun)* and in the parallel and flourishing workshop that reproduces classic toys for a specialist collector's market. Both are just off the town's main Plaza de la Iglesia.

BANYERES DE MARIOLA
Banyeres de Mariola is another mountain town, all steep alleys and stairways. The town grew up from the base of its 13th-century castle, which at 830m, is the settlement's highest point. It was an important paper-producing town since the introduction of the industry by the Arabs in the 9th century, up until the middle of the 20th century. Down on the plain is Villa Rosario, once the home of a paper-mill owner, you can visit the **Museo del Papel (Museu Molí Paperes)**, which has a whole floor devoted to cigarette papers. Knock hard if it seems to be shut.

About 150m below Villa Rosario is the town's recently overhauled and well laid-out **Museo Arqueológico**, occupying the Torre de la Font Bona, a 17th-century tower.

ALBAIDA
Albaida, 'the white one' in Arabic, was so named by the Muslims because of the light-coloured rock on which it was constructed. Once famous for its wax production (in its time it rivalled mighty Barcelona in the quantity of candles that it turned out for both domestic and religious purposes), it's nowadays a textile town, producing bed linen and towels.

Looking down over the Plaza Mayor is the imposing, much-restored facade of the Palacio de los Marqueses de Albaida. Go through its deep archway to the **Iglesia Arciprestal**, Albaida's main church which has canvases by local artist José Segrelles. In the north-west corner of the square that bears his name is the **Museo José Segrelles** *(admission €3; open 10am-1pm & 4pm-6pm Tues-Fri, 10am-1pm Sat, 4pm-6pm Sun)*, a homage to this painter, born and brought up in Albaida, who was the decorator of many a local church and a student of Joaquin Sorolla.

The Palacio is home to Spain's only puppet museum, the **Museo de Títeres** *(open 4pm-8pm Tues-Sat, 11am-4pm Sun)*.

In front of the Palacio stand the church bells like giant inverted flower pots. Removed from the belfry, they're still tolled six times daily.

COCENTAINA
postcode 03820 • pop 10,600
• elevation 435m
For a bird's eye view, walk up the dusty signed path leading to a small, ruined tower that overlooks the small town of Cocentaina. Mature plane trees impart deep shade to the main square, **Pla de la Font**, where the town wash house is still fed from a spring just upstream. Small, pedestrianised **Plaza Cardenal Ferriz**, at its heart a brimming fountain, is bordered by Cocentaina's equally modest – in local terms – parish church and spruce houses in freshly painted pastel colours. The 16th-century **Palacio Condal** (Ducal Palace) with its tranquil Patio de Armas is currently being restored. The tourist office (☎ 96 559 01 59), within the Patio de Armas, opens 10am to 2pm, Monday to Saturday.

ALCOY (ALCOI)
postcode 03801 • pop 60,400
• elevation 565m
For 51½ weeks a year, there's not a lot to entice you to the rather lugubrious, mainly in-

dustrial town of Alcoy (Alcoi), 50km south of Xàtiva and the Comunidad's fifth largest town. But there's everything to draw you here for three days in April. Between the 22nd and the 24th, overlapping with St George's (Sant Jordi's) day, Alcoy celebrates its annual Moros y Cristianos festival around the clock (see the special section 'Fiestas' for details), which ranks as the Comunidad's most colourful event after Valencia City's Las Fallas.

Information

Alcoy has a recently established tourist office (☎ 96 553 71 55) at Calle San Lorenzo 2, just off the main Plaza de España. It opens 9.30am to 1.30pm and 5pm to 7pm Monday to Friday and 9.30am to 1.30pm on Saturday.

Things to See & Do

To get an idea of the splendour of the Moros y Cristianos costumes and a feel for the fiesta, call by the **Casal de Sant Jordi** (☎ *96 554 05 80, Calle San Miguel 62; admission €1; open 11am-1pm & 5.30pm-7.30pm Tues-Fri, 10.30am-1.30pm Sat & Sun).* Occupying an 18th-century noble mansion, it houses the festival's museum.

Decidedly less colourful but still worth a brief visit is Alcoy's **Museo Arqueológico Municipal** (☎ *96 553 71 44, Placeta del Carbó s/n; admission free; open 9am-2pm Mon-Fri year round & 10.30am-1.30pm Sat & Sun Oct-June).*

Alcoy boasts a pair of fine *modernista* buildings, the **Casa del Pavo** *(Calle Sant Nicolau)* dating from 1908, and a few doors away, the **Circulo Industria**, constructed four years earlier. For a piece of contemporary architectural splendour, look beneath the Plaza de España at the spacious, soaring **Lonja de Sant Jordi**, designed by the internationally renowned Valencian architect Santiago Calatrava (see the boxed text in the Arts section of the Facts about Valencia chapter).

Places to Stay

Hostal Savoy (☎ *96 554 72 72, Calle Casablanca 9)* Rooms €28.41. One block south of Plaza de España, Hostal Savoy is

markedly the cheaper of the only two accommodation options in town.

Hotel Reconquista (☎ *96 533 09 00, fax 96 533 09 55,* W *www.hotelodon.com)* Singles/doubles €50/72. Also in the heart of town, the Reconquista has a private garage (€7), an asset in a town where parking is at a premium.

Getting There & Away

There are four to five trains daily to Valencia (€6.25, 1¾ hours) via Xàtiva. From the nearby bus station, four to six services run to Valencia, at least 10 to Alicante and a couple a day to Gandía.

AROUND ALCOY

Hotel Els Frares (☎ *96 551 12 34, fax 96 551 12 00,* W *www.mountainwalks.com, Avenida Pais Valencià 20, Quatretondeta)* Singles/doubles €30/45-51. Closed 2 weeks in Jan & 1-21 July. This delightful British-run hotel and restaurant, the major building in a tiny hamlet, make a great base for a off-the-beaten-track holiday, whether hiking or just lazing. Els Frares also has the rare distinction in Spain of being a nonsmoking hotel. Reservations are essential for both hotel and restaurant. To get there, take the CV-70 south-eastwards from Alcoy for 12km and turn left (north-east) for Gorga and Quatretondeta.

Vall de Vinalopó & Around

VILLENA

postcode 03400 • pop 31,800

Villena, on the N-330 between Alicante and Albacete, is an upbeat place and the most attractive of the towns that dot the corridor of the Vall de Vinalopó.

Head for Plaza de Santiago at the heart of the old part of town. At No 5 is the tourist office (☎ 96 580 38 04). It opens from 8am to 3pm, Monday to Friday. Across the square at No 2 is the fine 16th-century **Palacio Municipal**. Penetrate to the two-storey central patio, with its Tuscan pillars and clean classical lines and enter the **Museo Arqueológico** (☎ *960 580 11 50 ext 69; admission free; open 10am-2pm & 5pm-8pm Mon-Fri, 11am-1pm Sat & Sun)*. The pride of its collection are 60 priceless gold artefacts weighing over 10kg and dating from around 1000 BC. The pieces were discovered quite by chance in an old riverbed, the Rambla de Pandero, which gives its name to the treasure.

On the west side of the square is the **Iglesia de Santiago** with its flamboyant, impressively restored interior. Unfortunately, although one of the Comunidad's finest Gothic-Renaissance buildings, it's only open during services although there are plans for the tourist office to provide access.

Perched high above town is the **Castillo de la Atalaya** *(admission free; guided tours 10.30am, 11.30am & 12.30pm Tues-Fri, 11am, noon & 1pm Sat & Sun)*. Constructed by the Arabs in the 12th century, this castle is splendidly lit up at night.

More recent and also worth a look is the recently restored **Teatro Chapí**, Villena's theatre. You'll be lucky to see inside its lavish interior, which can accommodate an audience of over 800, as it's usually closed to the public, but the exterior alone with its elegant facade and neo-Moorish side walls justify the short detour alone.

Villena celebrates its Moros y Cristianos fiesta (see the special section 'Fiestas' for more information) in spectacular style from 4 to 9 September.

Places to Stay & Eat

Hotel-Restaurante Salvadora (☎ *96 580 09 50, fax 96 581 34 66,* Ⓦ *www.hotelsalvadora .com – Spanish only, Avenida de la Constitución 102)* Singles/doubles €25.25/37.90. This is Villena's only hotel but it's a good one offering value for money. Pleasant rooms have full facilities including air-con and heating. The entrance, one block back from its restaurant, is at the junction of Calle Luis García and Calle Jacinto Benavente.

The **restaurant** and **bar** of the Salvadora is also about the best place in town to eat, especially if you want to taste some typical local food (mains cost €8 to €13). You can

sit at the counter and sample from their great selection of tapas or work your way through a *bocadillo* (under €3). It does a range of filling rice dishes at €6. To really sample the full range of their fare, go for the *menú degustación*, a set meal that changes monthly.

Restaurante Bar Wary Nessy (☎ *96 580 10 47,* Ⓦ *www.warynessy.com – Spanish only, Calle Isabel la Católica 13)* Open Tues-Sun. The quality of the food and originality of the menu more than matches this stylish place's attractive decor.

Bar-Restaurante La Teja Azul (☎ *96 534 82 34, Calle Sancho Medina 34)* Mains €11-13. Open Wed-Mon. Quite different in character to Wary Nessy but just as agreeable, this recently established place, all mellow brick and rough stone walls, goes for the rural and rustic look. Try their *arroz a banda* (€8) – rice is the house speciality – that's almost a meal in itself.

Entertainment

For a town of its size, Villena has an admirably high proportion of decent cafes, bars and pubs, among them these three to get you started: **Flannagan's** and **Sergeant Pepper's**, both on Calle Quevado, bring an Anglo-Irish flavour to the town. More typical is long-established, deep and cavernous **El Túnel** (☎ *96 580 70 94, Calle Maestro Chanza 6)*. It has regular photographic and painting exhibitions enlivening its walls and is open 3pm to 3am daily.

Getting There & Away

The Alsa company runs buses regularly to and from Alicante (€3.25). Ten trains link Villena with Madrid daily. Four trains also run to and from Valencia, and eight go to and from Alicante.

BIAR

Today, the small, light industrial towns and agricultural villages of the Vall de Vinalopó seem oblivious to their turbulent and precarious past. This region was once a wild frontier, an area of raid and counter-raid where castles were designed to defend and to deter.

One of Spain's oldest continuously occupied towns, Morella is crowned by its imposing ruined fortress.

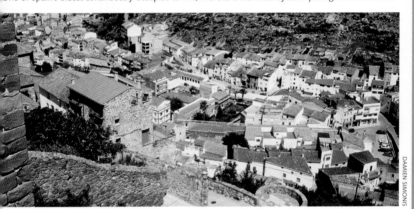

The rusty-roofed town of Vilafamés, viewed from its dramatically situated castle

Peñíscola clusters around the 13th-century citadel, which was Templar-built on Moorish foundations.

Guadalest's oldest area is reached via a tunnel.

Murals celebrate Requena's glorious harvests.

Xàtiva's 13th-century Iglesia de Sant Feliu

Thoroughly fortified – the medieval Castillo de Biar is surrounded by a double wall.

Biar, 8km from Villena along the CV-799, has the region's finest castle. The village straggles at its feet, clinging to the steep hillside. If Biar were nearer the coast, it would by now have been prettified and occupied by second-homers. As it is – and long may it stay – it remains a lively, working community, producing dolls, bedspreads, blankets and, especially, ceramics.

The tourist office (☎ 96 581 11 77) is on Avenida de Villena s/n, the ring road that encircles the old quarter. It opens 9am to 1pm and 3pm to 6pm daily.

Biar's parish **church** on Plaza de la Constitución has an impressive although much weathered 15th-century Plateresque facade. Just off the square is the **Museo Arqueológico** *(Calle Mayor s/n; admission free; open noon-2pm & 6pm-8pm Tues-Sat, noon-2pm Sun)*, Biar's diminutive museum of antiquities.

The 12th-century **castle** *(open 11am-1pm Tues-Fri, 10am-2pm & 4pm-6pm Sat, 10am-2pm Sun)* is just as well preserved and heavily restored as Villena's. Even if you arrive outside its limited mid-week visiting hours, you can still get a magnificent sweeping view of the wide Vall de Vinalopó from the base of its crenellated battlements.

Hotel Vila de Biar (☎ 96 581 13 04, fax 96 581 13 12, Calle San José 2) Singles/doubles/triples/quads €57.10/75.10/103/130.50 mid-Sept–June, €67.30/87.75/120/152.25 July–mid-Sept including breakfast. Behind the renovated facade of this one-time noble palace is a light, airy interior. Modern rooms have all facilities including air-con and heating.

ELDA
postcode 03600 • pop 51.500
Foot fetishists shouldn't miss the **Museo de Calzado** *(☎/fax 96 538 30 21, Avenida Chapí 32; adult/child €2.40/1.20; open 10am-1pm & 4pm-8pm Tues-Sat, 10am-1pm Sun)*. Elda vies with Elche for the title of shoe-making capital of Spain and its shoe museum is a true temple to leather. Above the mezzanine floor, with its row upon row of Heath Robinson drills, stamps and sewing machines, it's wall-to-wall footware: boots through the ages, shoes and slippers from around the world, fanciful designs that must have been absolute agony to wear and donated cast-offs from matadors, flamenco dancers, King Juan Carlos and Queen Sofía and other well shod greats.

NOVELDA
postcode 03660 • pop 23,800
If you're a fan of Art Nouveau and *modernismo,* make the 25km pilgrimage from Alicante to Novelda's wonderful **Casa-Museo Modernista** *(☎ 96 560 02 37, Calle Mayor 24; admission free; open 9.30am-2pm & 4.30pm-6pm Mon-Fri, 11am-2pm Sat)*. A bourgeois mansion completed in 1903, its stained glass, soft shapes in wood, period furniture and magnificent spiralling wrought-iron staircase take the breath away.

Peek, too, inside No 6 – these days the municipal library – and admire the exterior of the Cruz Roja (Spanish Red Cross) building at Plaza del Ayuntamiento.

You should also pay a brief pilgrimage to the **Santuario de Santa María Magdalena**, which shares a knoll with the Castillo de la Mola, 3km north-west of Novelda. The 12th-century castle, Arab in origin but much restored, has little to interest you apart from an odd – unique, even – tower in the form of an equilateral triangle. The sanctuary, by contrast, is a delight. Begun in 1918, it's like a doll's house equivalent of Gaudí's famous heavyweight Sagrada Familia in Barcelona. The mix of pebbles and boulders, which were lifted from the Río Vinalopó, marble and decorative brickwork, is embellished with tile work in abstract forms and vegetable motifs.

Central Valleys

VALL DE GALLINERA & VALL D'ALCALÁ
A few kilometres north of Alcoy, a judicious right (eastwards) turn at Muro d'Alcoy along the CV-700 sends you down a winding valley road past a series of pueblos, mostly of Muslim origin (look for village names beginning with 'Beni' – for example,

Benisivà, Benialí and Benissili – a sure-fire indicator). You are now in the heart of Valencia's cherry-growing country. The Vall de Gallinera is especially rich in the juicy red fruit, and the second half of March, when the trees are in blossom, is sensational. **Planes**, watched over by the ruins of an old castle, merits a short stop.

A tempting detour along the CV-712, about halfway between Muro d'Alcoy and Pego, leads down a second valley, the Vall d'Alcalá. The village of the same name is 12km down the road, and on the way you'll pass hill-top **Margarida**.

There's a modest *camping ground (☎ 96 551 43 33)*, with a cafe-restaurant, at Vall d'Alcalá. It's open from Easter to mid-October. *Casa Rural Almasera (☎ 96 551 42 32)*, in Margarida, offers singles/doubles for €24/36, including breakfast.

To gain access to the central valleys from the Costa Blanca, take the CV-700, signed Pego, where it leaves the N-332 to the north of Denia.

GUADALEST

The CV-755, which is an even more spectacular route, runs westwards from the coast between Calpe and Altea. Following a natural corridor connecting the coast with the interior, it makes for a very stimulating and scenic drive through wild countryside, even if you get no farther than the long-established settlement of Guadalest.

You'll be far from the first to discover the pueblo, which goes back to at least AD 715, when the Arabs were in residence. Guadalest remains about the only place in inland Valencia that tour buses have discovered in force. Coaches, heading up from Costa Blanca resorts, disgorge more than two million visitors annually, overwhelming the village's resident population of less than 200 souls. But get there early or after the last bus has pulled out and the place can be almost your own.

Crowds come in their hordes because the place *is* so pretty. Ignore the tawdry souvenir shops and tripper traps and look at the whole, reached by a natural tunnel and dominated by the Castillo de San José. And enjoy the experience of strolling through a traffic-free village.

There's a small tourist office (☎ 96 588 52 98) alongside the parking area on the road that bypasses the village.

Guadalest is ill served by public transport. One bus daily, Monday to Friday only,

Turrón, the Finger Lickin' Fudge

Call it fudge, call it nougat, neither translation quite captures Jijona's delightful almond-based confection. Records reveal that it's been made ever since the 15th century and a plausible case can be made for its introduction much earlier, when the Arabs held sway.

The village's factories work intensively from autumn into early winter to produce the slabs that Spaniards buy by the tonne to enhance their Christmas festivities.

The short production season begins in September, when harvested almonds are tipped by the truckload into the yards of Jijona's *turrón* producers. The almonds are crushed, then mixed in vats with liberal quantities of sugar, egg white and honey – traditionally only from bees that have feasted upon rosemary.

The best turrón is still blended by hand before being rolled and milled to achieve its firm texture, after which it's sliced into the standard shape that any sharp Spanish child can recognise from 50 metres. And – check the ingredients but we're sure we're right – genuine turrón contains not a trace of colouring or preservative.

Although bought in huge quantities around Christmas time, turrón is on sale throughout the year, just the same, just as delicious and at around half its peak price. For hiking, biking or just sloping around, there's no better source of instant energy.

leaves Benidorm, passing by the train station at 9am. For the return journey, it departs Guadalest at 12.30pm.

JIJONA (XIXONA)

If you love all things sweet, you really ought to pay a pilgrimage to Jijona, on the N-340 more or less midway between Alicante and Alcoy. This small town has two claims to fame. Nowadays, it's far and away Spain's principal producer of turrón, a kind of nougat with both soft and crunchy variants (see the boxed text). If you would like to replicate this most delicious of sweets at home, see the boxed text 'Turrón for Softies' in the Facts for the Visitor chapter. In the past, the place was also a stopover for porters bearing ice from the high hinterland to assuage the heat of a coastal summer. And so it lent its name to Jijona, a popular brand of ice cream that sells by the hectolitre throughout the land.

Costa Blanca

Alicante and the 'White Coast' are among Europe's most heavily visited regions. If you're after a secluded beach in midsummer, try elsewhere. But if you're looking for a lively social life, good beaches and a suntan...

However, the region isn't all concrete and package deals. Although the original fishing villages have long been engulfed by the sprawl of resorts, holiday villas and skyscrapers, many resort towns retain a small fishing fleet and the auctioning of the day's catch at *la lonja de pescado* (wholesale fish market) happens as though tourism has yet to arrive. A few kernels of the old towns have survived. The nuclei of old Xàbia and Calpe are particularly attractive and the historic part of Altea is a jewel by any criteria. All are better still out of high season.

During July and August your chances of finding accommodation anywhere are limited if you haven't reserved a spot. Out of season many places close, but those remaining open usually charge substantially less than in high summer and during national holidays.

Most buses linking Alicante and Valencia head straight down the motorway, some making a stop in Benidorm. A few, however, call by other intervening towns. Renfe trains connect Valencia with Gandía, while FGV narrow-gauge trains ply the scenic route between Denia and Alicante, stopping at all pueblos en route.

CULLERA
postcode 46400 • pop 21,000

Cullera, the first major resort south of Valencia is, strictly speaking, outside the Costa Blanca. All the same, for convenience and because it's very much of the same ilk as its sister resorts of Gandía and Denia, we've taken the minor geographical liberty of including it here.

Cullera is a very Spanish resort, where many people from Madrid and the north

keep second homes. The largest number of non-Spanish visitors come from France. Served by regular buses and trains, it makes for a convenient day's outing from Valencia.

Information
The main tourist office (☎ 96 172 09 74), in the town at Calle de Riu 38, opens 10am to 1.30pm and 5pm to 7pm, Monday to Friday. The office by the beach (☎/fax 96 173 15 86) on Plaza Constitución observes much the same hours and opens Tuesday to Saturday, as well as Sunday morning. There's another

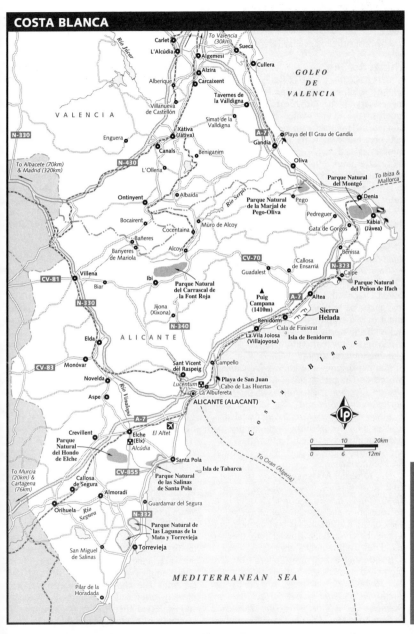

branch, open only in summer, near the lighthouse.

The post office is at Plaza San Isidro 1.

Things to See

Cullera has a fine sweep of sandy beach, extending southwards from the lighthouse to the estuary of the **Río Júcar**. Although so much of the river's waters have been siphoned off for upstream irrigation, it still puts on a brave show for its final couple of kilometres and is pleasant to stroll by. A more strenuous but scarcely demanding walk takes you up to Cullera's **castle** *(admission free; open 10am-1pm & 5pm-dusk daily)*. The small chapel just below it is the 19th-century **Santuario de la Virgen**. Both the chapel and castle offer splendid views.

Back at sea level, the **Museo del Arroz** *(☎ 96 173 26 43, Carretera Nazaret-Oliva; admission free; open 10am-1pm & 6.30pm-8.30pm Tues-Sun June-Sept, 10am-1pm Thur-Sun Oct-May)* occupies a deconsecrated chapel, the 13th-century Ermita de los Santos de la Piedra. The museum is all about rice, a crop that thrives in the paddy fields to the north and west of town, and it illustrates the cultivation process from planting to harvesting.

Another original museum is the **Cueva-Museo de Dragut** *(☎ 96 174 67 00, Plaza Doctor Fleming s/n; adult/child €3/1.80; open 9am-midnight daily June-Sept, 11am-2pm Sun & 4pm-7pm Sat & Sun Oct-May)*. It takes its name from the 16th-century pirate Dragut, who sacked the town in 1550, and illustrates piracy and plunder around the Mediterranean.

The **Torre del Marenyet** *(open 10.30am-1pm & 6.30pm-8.30pm Thur-Sun June-Sept, 10am-1pm Tues-Sat Oct-May)* is a defence point and watchtower on the south bank of the Río Jùcar. It is built at the point where the river once flowed into the sea and dates from Dragut's era.

Beside such exotic fare, Cullera's **Museo Municipal** and **Museo Fallero** *(both ☎ 96 173 26 43, Calle Cervantes s/n; admission free; open 10.30am-1pm & 6.30pm-8.30pm Tues-Sun June-Sept, 9am-1pm Tues-Sun & 6pm-8pm Mon-Fri Oct-May)* are rather overshadowed. The latter displays a selection of *ninots*, or effigies, from the town's annual Fallas celebrations.

Activities

The **Aquópolis** *(☎ 96 173 80 52; adult/child €11.75/8; open 11am-7pm mid-June–mid-Sept)* is a water park (a neat pun on the name of Athens' most famous temple) on the western side of town beside the Museo del Arroz. Its 'black hole' is not for the faint hearted.

Radical Surf School *(☎ 96 173 08 98)* and **Seasurf Patrol Escuela** *(☎ 96 172 50 93)*, both based on Playa Racó, offer windsurfing classes and board hire. **Club de Vela Garbí** *(☎ 696 04 67 62)* at Playa Cap Blanc gives both sailing and windsurfing classes. For diving, contact **Actividades Subaquáticas Delfín** *(☎ 96 172 16 34, Calle Guardia Civil 11)*.

Getting There & Away

Trains pass through Cullera, on the Valencia–Gandía line, every half hour. Nine Alsa buses run daily between Cullera and Valencia from the bus station on Avenida del Racó, set back from the beach area.

Getting Around

Rent A Car Cullera *(☎ 96 173 19 83)*, Calle Fray Pascual Jover 1, rents bicycles from €24/67.60/138 per day/three days/week and scooters from €15/27/42.

For a taxi, call ☎ 96 172 27 16.

SIMAT DE LA VALLDIGNA

If you've the least penchant for ecclesiastical architecture, consider making a detour westwards from the A-7 or N-332 to visit Simat, 20km equidistant from Cullera and Gandía. In this otherwise unexceptional village is the **Monasterio de Santa María de Valldigna** *(☎ 96 385 65 00; admission free; open 11am-1pm Wed-Fri, 10am-2pm Sat & Sun)*. Founded in 1298, this Cistercian monastery was the first to be established on Valencian soil in the wake of the Reconquista. The core of this large complex dates from the 14th and 15th centuries. The whole has been sensitively and recently restored after having been plundered and neglected after Spain's 1835 *desamortización* (confiscation of church lands).

GANDÍA

**postcode 46700 • pop 59,125
• elevation 22m**

Gandía, 65km south of Valencia, is a tale of two cities. The main town, once home to a branch of the Borja dynasty (more familiar to most people as the infamous Borgias), is a prosperous commercial centre.

Four kilometres away on the coast, Playa de Gandía has so far avoided the tawdriness of too many Costa Blanca resorts. Many consider its long, broad, sandy beach to be the best on the Costa Blanca. The beach is groomed daily by a fleet of tractors and backed by medium-rise hotels and apartments. Like Cullera, Gandía is a predominantly Spanish resort, especially popular with Madrileños and day visitors from Valencia. It enjoys a well deserved reputation for great summer nightlife. For the rest of the year – and unlike more international playgrounds such as Benidorm, Peñíscola or Torrevieja – the beach area is all but dead during the week, reviving itself on Friday and Saturday, when Valencia comes to town to party.

Information

Tourist Offices The main tourist office (☎ 96 287 77 88), Calle Marqués de Campo s/n, is opposite the train station. It opens 9.30am to 1.30pm and 4.30pm to 7.30pm (to 7pm in winter) Monday to Friday and 10am to 1.30pm on Saturday. The Playa de Gandía tourist office (☎ 96 284 24 07), Paseo Marítimo Neptuno s/n, is right beside the beach. It opens 10am to 2pm and 5pm to 8pm, Monday to Saturday, and 10am to 1.30pm Sunday between Easter and October. For the rest of the year, it opens only on Sunday morning.

Email & Internet Access Intern@aut@ (☎ 96 295 13 38), Calle Magistrado Catalá 5, some 200m south of the train/bus station, charges €2.40 per hour and also operates as a phone centre. It opens 9am to 10.30pm Monday to Saturday, and 11am to 1pm and 4pm to 10.30pm on Sunday.

Things to See

Gandía's one building of major historic interest is its magnificent **Palacio Ducal de los Borja** *(☎ 96 287 14 65, Calle Duc Alfons el Vell 1; adult/child €2.50/1.50; open 10am-1.30pm & 4.30pm-8pm Tues-Sat, 10am-1.30pm Sun).* A magnificent structure in itself, this home of Duque Francisco de Borja, dating from the 15th century with later accretions, is adorned with a collection of his personal belongings. One-hour guided tours in Spanish, with an accompanying leaflet in English, are available; they take place hourly (last tours begin at 12.30pm and 7pm).

Activities

There are two excellent Rutas Ecoturísticas (Ecotourism Routes). The 12km **Racó del Duc** walking and cycling trail follows an old train line through unspoiled countryside between the villages of Vilallonga (8km south of Gandía) and L'Orxa. **Entre Senill i Borrò** is a 13km walking trail through coastal marsh and dunes from Gandía to the coast. Both tourist offices have brochures in English describing the routes.

Gandía's small but active port is fun to browse around, especially at about 5pm when the fishing boats return.

Special Events

Gandía's Festival Internacional de Música offers concerts every Friday and Saturday evening during July and August. Embracing jazz, classical music and folk, events take place in the Casa de Cultura, Passeig de les Germanies, in Gandía. For more details, contact the tourist office.

Places to Stay

Camping Playa de Gandía has a couple of camping grounds, both quite a walk from the beach.

Camping L'Alquería (☎ 96 284 04 70, fax 96 284 10 63, ⓦ www.lalqueria.com, Carretera del Grau de Gandía s/n) €3.91/5.50/4.40 per person/tent/car. Open Apr-Oct. This large camp site, 1km inland beside the main road connecting Gandía and Playa de Gandía, has a pool as well as cabins and bungalows accommodating from two to seven people. For prices, consult its multilingual Web site.

COSTA BLANCA

Camping La Naranja (☎ *96 284 16 16, Camino Assagador de Morant s/n)* €3.60/5.40/3.60 per person/tent/car. Open mid-June–mid-Oct. About 800m from the sea, this shady site set amid orange groves, has a pool if you don't fancy the hike to the beach.

Hostels *Albergue Mar i Vent* (☎ *96 283 17 48, fax 96 283 11 21, Calle Doctor Fleming s/n)* Adult/child €7.20/4.80. Open Feb–mid-Dec. Some 5km south of Gandía beside Playa de Piles is the excellent beachfront youth hostel, Albergue Mar i Vent. The hostel rents bikes year round and offers windsurfing and canoeing instruction in summer. Take La Amistad bus (see Getting Around later) from opposite the train station.

Hotels *El Nido* (☎ *96 284 46 40, Calle de Alcoy 22)* Singles/doubles with bathroom €27/39, rooms €47-51.10 July & Aug. Open year round. Rooms are as cheerful as the owners at this highly recommended hostal, a block back from the beach. Its restaurant does a filling *menú* at €8.

Week-end (☎ *96 284 00 97, Calle Mare Nostrum 45)* Singles/doubles with bathroom €20/39, €26/51.50 June–mid-Sept. Open Mar-Nov. Calling itself both Week-end and Fin de Semana, the Spanish equivalent, this small, pleasant bar, a couple of blocks north of El Nido, has 11 comfortable rooms above it.

Hotel La Alberca (☎/fax *96 284 51 63, Calle Cullera 8)* Singles/doubles with bathroom €19.25/31.25, €21.25/45.70 high season. Rooms, all with heating and air-con, are comfortable and represent excellent value at this modern hotel, 300m from the beach.

Hotel La Safor (☎ *96 286 40 11, fax 96 286 41 79,* 🖂 *scampturia@tpi.infomail.es, Carretera de Valencia 40)* Singles/doubles/triples with bathroom & air-con €28/50/68, €37/60/75 high season. Up in town, Hotel La Safor is handy for bus and train stations. Prices include breakfast, and it has private parking (€8).

Hotel Cibeles Playa (☎ *96 284 80 83, fax 96 284 81 76,* 🖳 *www.hotelcibeles.com, Calle Clot de la Mota 9)* From €30 per

---

Fideuá

Locals claim that Gandía is where *fideuá*, a noodle-based variant of paella, was invented. The story goes something like this. A fisherman out trawling found himself clean out of rice and far from shore. Rather than go hungry, he threw into the pan a handful or two of noodles that he happened to have with him and simmered them with his usual ingredients.

If you only taste them once, Gandía, the town that has hosted the Concurso Internacional de Fideuá y Gastronomía every year since 1975, is the best place to try a plateful. The contest, held in June, is, alas, strictly for the pros but you'll find fideuá on offer in any self-respecting restaurant, whether in town or beside the beach.

---

person, from €61 Aug. Playa de Gandía's newest hotel, which opened in 2001, offers top-end comfort at top-end prices.

Places to Eat

The Paseo Marítimo Neptuno abounds in eateries and there are a few longer established places at the western end of the port and along Calle Verge.

Rosario (☎ *96 284 01 11, Calle Verge 14)* Open Wed-Mon (daily in summer). This bar, with its smallish restaurant to the rear, is run by a friendly young couple and is popular with locals in the know.

El Charro (☎ *96 284 63 64, Calle Verge 4)* Open Wed-Mon (daily in summer). Spilling onto the street and with an atmospheric interior, El Charro, is rather more than expensive than Rosario. It is another good place to sample freshly caught fish and also rich sausages and meat products from Salamanca, deep in Spain's interior.

If you fancy pushing your own boat out, Gandía boasts three magnificent, fish and seafood restaurants. Hugely popular, they primarily pull in the expense-account trade at lunchtime. Bring your credit card, or even two, as they don't come cheap.

As de Oros (☎ *96 284 02 39, Paseo Marítimo Neptuno 26)* Fish mains €7.80-16.85.

Open Tues–Sun lunch Feb-Dec, daily July-Sept. The majority of As de Oros' diners come from far and wide for its menú (€43.50). For a tasty and altogether more modestly priced alternative, try their *fideuá de mariscos* (seafood fideuá; minimum two people).

Kayuko (☎ 96 284 01 37, Calle Asturias 23) Menú €45. Open Tues–Sun lunchtime, daily July-Sept. In much the same mould, Kayuko also offers a rather less gut-busting *menú playa* (literally 'beach set menu') that costs €12.25.

Gamba (☎ 96 284 13 10, Carretera Nazaret-Oliva s/n) Open lunchtime only Tues-Sun. Run by three brothers and their wives ('we only open at lunchtime – otherwise it would be certain divorce,' explained the eldest), Gamba doesn't post a menu. It doesn't need to. Renowned internationally, it offers whatever is best and freshest that day. Prepare to pay around €45, including drinks.

Entertainment

There's great summer nightlife at Playa de Gandía. Places open daily between June and September and from Thursday to Saturday the rest of the year.

A dozen or so small bars, some no bigger than a shack, cluster around Plaza del Castell, barely 300m inland from the beach. Favourites include *Paco Paco Paco*, *Mama Ya Lo Sabe*, *Ke Caramba* and *La Década*. The really *in* place for a drink is *Por Quien Doblan las Campanas (For Whom the Bell Tolls; junction of Calle Catalunya & Calle La Rioja)* about 200m south.

After the bars close (around 3am), head for one of the discos that bang on till dawn: *Coco Loco (cnr of Paseo Marítimo & Calle de Galicia)* or *La Calle del Ritmo*, which is just south of the tennis club. Alternatively, follow your ears to *Bacarra (Calle Legazpi)*, two blocks from the beach.

Getting There & Away

Trains run between Gandía and Valencia City (€3.25, one hour) every half-hour (hourly at weekends). The stylish intercity bus station and train station are co-located.

Getting Around

La Marina Gandiense buses for Playa de Gandía (€0.90, every 20 minutes) stop outside the train station.

Autobuses La Amistad (☎ 96 287 44 10) run five buses daily, Monday to Saturday, between Gandía and Playa de Piles. Arrive on a Sunday and you'll have to hitch to the youth hostel in Playa de Piles.

El Port (☎ 666 826206), Calle les Barraques 11b, set back from the road, rents cycles and scooters. A dedicated cycle lane links the town and Playa de Gandía, running alongside Avenida Carretera del Grau. Another raised cycle path follows the Paseo Marítimo along the beach.

Call ☎ 96 284 30 00 for a taxi.

DENIA
postcode 03700 • pop 30,700

Denia is a popular, fairly pricey resort. The town itself is rather dull, apart from its small old quarter, but the beaches of Las Marinas to the north are good and sandy. Southwards, the fretted coastline of Las Rotas offers less-frequented rocky coves. Denia has a small fishing harbour and large marina. As the nearest mainland port to the Balearic Islands, it makes a good jumping-off point for Ibiza and Mallorca.

Known to the Romans as Dianium in honour of the goddess Diana, it was an important trading centre for goods imported from Italy and North Africa. Conquered by the Arabs around AD 713, Denia became an important *taifa* (independent emirate) in the 11th century as the Caliphate of Cordoba fragmented into smaller units. In the second half of the 19th century, it again enjoyed prosperity thanks to the raisin trade (see the boxed text 'Denia's Raisin d'Être').

Orientation

Avenida Marqués de Campo, running east-westwards from Glorieta del País Valencià, is Denia's unexceptional main street. On Saturday afternoons and all Sunday, it's closed to traffic. At its eastern end is the port, terminal for ferries to the Balearic Islands and, one block south, the tourist office and train station. Intercity buses put in at

Denia's Raisin d'Être

While the rest of the Comunidad Valenciana was producing sturdy wines and juicy table grapes, Denia and Xàbia let their own ample grape harvest simply shrivel. From the latter half of the 19th century and well into the 1930s, raisins were the mainstay of their economies.

The grapes, fresh from the vineyards, were briefly scalded in large cauldrons set over smouldering wood fires in order to kill off any yeasts and prevent fermentation. Then the harvest was spread onto cane racks, where over the days the sun's rays completed the desiccating process. The variety of grape was the *moscatel*, which is still used to ferment into a sweet dessert wine.

Raisins were the countryside's main product and the principal goods to be shipped through the ports of Denia and Xàbia. Cases were loaded aboard ships destined for Liverpool, London and Southampton, the UK taking almost half the annual production, while other cargo vessels headed for France, Germany, Baltic ports and even as far as Russia.

Plaza Archiduque Carlos, a 10-minute walk from the port.

Information

Tourist Offices The tourist office (☎ 96 642 23 67, 902 114162) is near the waterfront at Glorieta del Oculista Buigues 9. It opens 9.30am to 1.30pm and 4.30pm to 7.30pm daily (closed Sunday afternoon in winter). During the summer, there's an additional information kiosk open beside the port and another on Avenida Marqués de Campo.

Email & Internet Access CoCo (☎ 96 643 14 12), Calle Colón 39, opens 10am to 8pm, Monday to Friday, and 10am to 5pm, Saturday. It charges €3.60 per hour.

Things to See

Denia has three small museums that deserve a brief visit.

It's a fairly easy 15-minute walk from the port up to Denia's much-restored **castle** (☎ 96 642 06 56; adult/child €2.15/0.75; open at least 10am-1pm & 5pm-6pm). Between July and mid-September, you can save yourself this minimal effort by taking the wheeled train that sets off from the tourist office. On a knoll that offers fine views of town and coast, it houses Denia's **Museo Arqueológico** (admission included in castle ticket), which displays artefacts dating from Iberian times up until the 18th century.

The most interesting part of the **Museo Etnológico** (☎ 96 642 02 60, Calle Cavallers s/n; admission free; open 10.30am-1pm & 4pm-7pm Tues-Sat, 10.30am-1pm Sun) presents the raisin industry – their cultivation, processing and export. The rest has little of interest for the non-Spanish visitor.

The **Museo del Juguete** (☎ 96 642 02 60, Calle Calderón s/n; admission free; open 10am-1pm & 4pm-8pm daily) occupies Denia's former train station. Toy manufacturing was, until the second half of the 20th century, another important element of Denia's economy and this museum has a fascinating display of items made locally across the decades.

Pass by the shining new lonja around 5pm. Unlike other wholesale fish markets up and down the coast, which are strictly trade only, you can view the auctioning of the day's catch from the upstairs, exterior balcony. Sadly, electronic bidding at the push of a button has superseded the auctioneer's rat-a-tat delivery, but the sight of so much fish can still set the saliva glands working.

Activities

From the port, there are frequent brief sailings around the harbour and towards Cabo San Antonio.

Three signed **walking** trails, varying in length from 1.6km to 5.2km, lead from the entrance to the **Parque Natural del Montgó** (nature park), about 2.5km from the tourist office. Ask the office for its pamphlet *Rutas de Senderismo*. For the ascent of Montgó, a magnificent 753m-high slab of limestone, see Activities under Xàbia later in this chapter.

Fun & Quads (☎ *96 578 72 28, 639 542365,* W *www.funquads.com, Carretera Consolá del Mar 13a)* is for the seriously outdoor type, offering guided kayak trips and snorkelling, cycle tours and day walks. Rather belying their claim to be environmentally friendly, they also do tours with quads. They rent city and mountain bikes, too.

Denia, with its rocky coastline to the south extending to the protected marine reserve of Cabo San Antonio, is the Costa Blanca's most promising place for diving. Among its six schools are **Diving Center Costa Blanca** (☎/*fax 96 578 10 79, Edificio Mare Nostrum II, Carretera Las Rotas 38)* and **Dive Center Denia** (☎ *607 600900, Marina de Denia, Dique Sur 1)*, who operate from the pleasure-boat harbour.

If you're a windsurfer, **Las Molinas**, north of town, will blow your sail and mind. Slip your board in at Punto de los Molinos (6km north of town) or Les Deveses (12.5km north). For lessons and equipment hire, contact **Nova Denia** (☎ *619 533395, Las Marinas km 6)*.

For sailing courses or boat hire, **Ecomar** (☎ *96 642 27 83)* in the Marina will get you afloat.

Escuela de Equitación La Sella (☎ *96 576 14 55, Residencial La Sella, Pedreguer)*, a little out of town in the village of Pedreguer, offers accompanied horse riding and lessons.

Special Events

Many, even most, Valencian pueblos run bulls through the streets at fiesta time. But Denia and Xàbia share a unique variant. For a week during the first half of July and coinciding with the town's main fiesta, a special arena is set up near the old lonja and the young bloods of Denia try to entice or propel a bull into the sea. Check times at the tourist office.

Places to Stay

Camping About 10km north of town is the only one of Denia's five camp sites to offer a swimming pool, **Camping Los Llanos** (☎ *96 575 51 88, fax 96 575 54 25,* W *www .losllanos.net, Carretera Nacional 332 km 203)*. €3.60 each person/tent/car.

Los Pinos (☎ *96 578 26 98)* €3.60/3.60/ 3.60 per person/tent/car. South of town towards Las Rotas, Los Pinos is a shady and marginally cheaper alternative than Los Llanos.

Both are open year round.

Hotels *Hotel Costa Blanca* (☎ *96 578 03 36, fax 96 578 30 27,* e *marti.roig@ teleline.es, Calle Pintor Llorens 3)* Singles €24.50-30, doubles €42-81.50. A mere 50m from the train station and handy for the port, this hotel represents excellent value for money, except during July & August.

Hostal El Comerç (☎ *96 578 00 71, fax 96 578 23 00, Calle de la Via 43)* Singles/ doubles from €22.85/29.45, €31.85/49.30 July & Aug. Three blocks inland from Hotel Costa Blanca and with fewer frills, the rather sombre Hostal El Comerç could be your place if money matters.

Places to Eat

Avenida Marqués de Campo has a few worthwhile eateries while much of Explanada Cervantes and its continuation northwards is cheek-by-jowl restaurants.

Cafetería el Punt (*Avenida Marqués del Campo 31)* Menú €7.25. For modest, value-for-money food, you can rely on this unpretentious place, which is also good for tapas.

Gavila (☎ *96 578 10 66, Avenida Marqués de Campo 55)* Open Tues-Sun (lunchtime only Sun-Thur). Rather more stylish but still reasonably priced, Gavila is another popular choice on Denia's main thoroughfare.

Caña Azúcar (☎ *610 855853, Calle Fora Mur 3b)* Menú €8.50. Open Tues-Sun, last orders 9pm Mon-Fri. Tasty fare and imaginatively seasoned dishes are the name of the day at vegetarian Caña Azúcar, a handy stop-off on the way to or from the castle. The fruit juices (€2 to €2.50) are equally original, and they offer a huge variety of teas from around the world. Warmly recommended, even for the most committed carnivore.

Asador del Puerto (☎ *96 642 34 82, Plaza del Raset 10-11)* Meals €25-30. This is an excellent choice for either meat or fish dishes even if the service can incline towards the supercilious. Try their *cochinillo* (roast suckling pig), crispy on the outside and juicy within.

The terrace of **Restaurante Mena** (☎ 96 578 09 43) in Las Rotas has superb seascapes and views of the Cabo San Antonio. *Menús* range all the way from €21 to €36.

The **covered market**, at the northern end of Calle Carlos Senti, overflows into Calle Magellanes.

Entertainment
Denia's discos are mostly just north of town, set back from Las Marinas. Favourites include Maná-Maná and La Dolce Vita (at km 1) and Harley (km 4.5). On summer weekends, a free bus ferries ravers hourly between 1am and 6am from outside the tourist office to the northern pubs and discos.

Getting There & Away
Bus Buses for Valencia and Alicante call by Plaza Archiduque Carlos, where Alsa (☎ 96 643 50 45) has an office.

Boat From Denia's port, boats (adult/child €9.65/4.20 one way) run around Cabo San Antonio to Xàbia up to three times daily. On Tuesday and Friday, they make the longer run southwards to Calpe (adult/child €18/9 return), stopping in at Xàbia.

From the ferry terminal, Balearia Lines runs daily ferries to and from Palma de Mallorca, and both Ibiza City and San Antonio on the island of Ibiza.

Their superfast ferry, the Garcia Lorca (€55), can whiz you between Denia and Ibiza in just two hours and continues onto Palma de Mallorca (five hours). The normal ferry (€44) takes 4½ and nine hours respectively. Call ☎ 902 160180 for information and reservations.

Train From the station seven trains daily follow the scenic route southwards to Alicante (€6.6, 2¼ hours) via Calpe (€2.25) and Benidorm (€3.65).

Getting Around
Autobuses Denia (☎ 96 642 14 08) run buses hourly both northwards alongside Las Marinas and southwards to Las Rotas.

You can hire cycles from Motos Luis (☎ 96 578 18 66), Plaza Benidorm 5, and Fun & Quads (see Activities earlier for details).

You can ring for a taxi on ☎ 96 642 44 44 or ☎ 96 578 65 65.

XÀBIA (JÁVEA)
postcode 03730 • pop 23,350
Xàbia, the Comunidad Valenciana's most easterly town, stretches between a pair of promontories, Cabo de San Antonio and Cabo de San Martín. With as much as one-third of its resident population and over two-thirds of its annual visitors non-Spanish, Xàbia isn't the best place to meet the locals. This said, it's gentle, laid-back and well worth a visit early in the season, when the sun shines but the masses have yet to arrive.

In recent years, Xàbia, presaging what will probably occur elsewhere where development has outstripped resources, has experienced quite serious high-summer water shortages. These should be eased once the town's proposed desalination plant comes on stream, but if you've any civic sense, don't linger too long under the shower.

Orientation
Xàbia comes in three parts. The attractive old town is a couple of kilometres inland. El Puerto (the port) lies directly east of the old quarter while the beach zone of El Arenal, lined with pleasant bar-restaurants, is 2km to the south of the harbour.

Information
Tourist Offices Xàbia has three tourist offices. The main one (☎ 96 579 43 56, fax 96 579 63 17, e javea@costablanca.org) is in the old town's Plaza de la Iglesia. Another (☎ 96 579 07 36) is on Plaza Almirante Bastarreche beside the port, and there's a branch (☎ 96 646 06 05) serving El Arenal at Carretera Cabo de la Nao s/n.

For comprehensive information about the town, click on W www.xabia.org.

Email & Internet Access In El Arenal, Sarah Internet Cafe, Avenida de la Libertad 42, open 10am to 11pm, Monday to Friday and 2pm to 11pm Saturday, charges €4 per hour. On the fringe of the old quarter, Cafe Internet, Avenida Amanecer de España 19, observes office hours. It's open 10am to 6pm Monday to Friday and 10am to 2pm Saturday, and it charges a hefty €6 per hour.

Bookshops Bookworld (☎ 96 646 22 53), Avenida Amanecer de España 13, carries a good range of books in English and has a small German section as well.

Laundry Now, here's a rare find for Spain! In El Arenal at the southern end of Avenida del Pla, Lavandería Los Delfines is a laundrette where you can wash your own clothes (€4.80 wash only, €9.60 wash and dry). It is open 9am to 1pm and 4pm to 6pm Monday to Friday and 9am to 1pm on Saturday.

Things to See
Whether you want to walk, drive or dig into Xàbia's history, the town's tourist offices are particularly well endowed with literature in English.

To explore the old quarter's monumental buildings, pick up the English version of their excellent free booklet *Centro Histórico de Xàbia*. This details a couple of walks, one covering the medieval legacy and the other highlighting prominent 18th- to 20th-century buildings. Of particular interest are the fortified, mainly 16th-century **church of San Bartolomé** *(Plaza de la Iglesia; open 11am-1pm & 5pm-8pm Fri-Wed)* and the **Museo Arqueológico y Etnográfico** *(☎ 96 579 10 98; Calle Primicies s/n; admission free; open 10am-1pm & 6pm-8pm Tues-Fri & 10am-1pm Sat & Sun Mar-Oct, 10am-1pm only Tues-Sun Nov-Feb)*. The finest exhibit, albeit a reproduction of the original (which is displayed in the Museo Arqueológico Nacional in Madrid), is a magnificently wrought set of Iberian gold jewellery that was found by chance in 1904.

Activities
For walks around Xàbia, ask at the tourist office for their six *Ecotourist Route* pamphlets, each describing a signposted route in the vicinity. Varying in difficulty, and lasting

from one hour to half a day, they include a trail to Cabo San Antonio and – most challenging of the pack – the ascent of Montgó. For more detail and more ideas on walking, the map *Parque Natural de Montgò-Cap de Sant Antoni* (€7.50), published at a scale of 1:15,000 by the Institut Cartogràfic de Valencia, is a good buy.

In summer, there are free guided walks each week in Spanish and English to three of these six destinations. They're arranged by the tourist office, which also puts on a weekly guided tour in English of the old quarter.

In the port area, **Buceo Pelicar** *(☎ 96 646 21 83, Calle Sertorio 2 Local 9)*, offers diving courses. Another diving operator is **Buceo Cabo La Nao** *(☎/fax 96 579 46 53,* **W** *www.cabolanao.com – Spanish only, Comercial Jávea, Park 71)*, set back from Playa Arenal.

With a cabin just south of the port, **Centro de Actividades Náuticas Chambergas** *(☎ 96 394 22 44)* gives sailing classes, rents out sailing boats and canoes and organises guided canoe trips. Also in the port area, the **Club Náutico** *(☎/fax 96 579 10 25,* **W** *www.cnjavea.com – Spanish only)* provides sailing courses from May to mid-September.

For a brief and less-strenuous watery experience, hop aboard the pleasure boat that runs around Cabo San Antonio to and from Denia up to three times daily (adult/child €9.65/4.20).

A little inland, **Centro Hípico Jávea** *(☎ 96 597 40 21, Carretera Xàbia–Gata 80 km 4)*, offers horse-riding lessons and accompanied rides.

If you have wheels, the promontory of **Cabo de la Nao**, south of town, offers spectacular views while tiny **Granadella**, just to its south, has a small, relatively quiet beach.

Places to Stay
Camping *Camping El Naranjal (☎ 96 579 29 89, fax 96 646 02 56,* **e** *naranjal@ teleline.es, Camino dels Morers 15)* €3.50/3.75/3.45 per person/tent/car. Set back from El Arenal it's about 10 minutes' walk from the beach.

Camping Jávea (☎ 96 579 10 70, fax 96 646 05 07, **e** *camjavea@arrakis.es, Camino* *de la Fontana 2)* €3.60 each person/tent/car. Camping Jávea, a little more inland than El Naranjal, is handier for the port and old town.

Neither camp site is placed correctly on the otherwise accurate standard tourist office map of town.

Pensiones & Hotels *Pensión Carrió (☎ 96 579 12 19, Calle Virgen de los Ángeles 31)* Singles/doubles €18.05/30.05, €27.05/42.07 in high season. Open Mon-Sat Nov-Sept. On the fringe of the old quarter, this pensión, which has seven rooms, all with bathroom, heating and air-con, represents a real bargain.

The port area has some reasonably priced accommodation.

Pensión La Favorita (☎ 96 579 04 77, Calle Magellanes 4) Rooms €24 (€30 July & Aug), with bathroom from €27 (from €37 Jul & Aug). Open Feb-Nov. This popular, recommended place with simple rooms fills up quickly so it's prudent to book in advance once the tanning season arrives.

Hostal La Marina (☎ 96 579 31 39, Avenida de la Marina Española 8) Singles/doubles with bathroom €42/60. Open Feb-Nov. All rooms outside the summer season are €30, a bargain, at this English-owned hostel, right on the foreshore 200m south of the port.

Hotel Miramar (☎/fax 96 579 01 02, Plaza Almirante Bastarreche 12) Singles/doubles €26/46, €36/56 July-Sept. Hotel Miramar, right beside the port, offers cosy, well appointed rooms with bathroom and air-con. Those overlooking the harbour cost €9 more, but are especially attractive and worth the little extra.

Parador de Turismo de Jávea (☎ 96 579 02 00, fax 96 579 03 08, e javea@parador .es, Avenida del Mediterráneo 7) Singles/doubles €96.63/119.55. Although the exterior of Xàbia's modern parador is uninspiring, inside you'll find the comfort and service you'd expect from a member of this excellent state-owned chain.

Places to Eat

In the old town, there are two good options just off Plaza de la Iglesia.

Tasca Tonis (☎ 96 646 18 51, Carrer Major 2) This modest, economical place has a good selection of bar tapas and does decent rice dishes.

Tasca La Rebotica (☎ 96 579 28 55, Carrer de Sant Bertomeu 8) does a daily rice special and has a good selection of tapas, too. It's recently gone more upmarket but remains value for money.

The port area also offers a couple of tasty choice.

Kimera (☎ 96 579 66 63, Avenida Lipanto 14) Open Fri-Wed (daily in summer). This is a cheap, cheerful and friendly place to nibble on a tapa or two and down a *bocadillo* (French-bread sandwich) or *plato combinado* (combination plate).

Azorín (☎ 96 579 44 95, Calle Toni Llidó s/n) Meat mains €4-6.60, fish mains €3.60-8.50. Open Sun-Fri. Meals are very reasonably priced at this popular restaurant, set just behind the *paseo marítimo*.

The whole of the paseo marítimo at El Arenal is bordered by cafes, pizzerias and restaurants.

La Bohême (☎ 96 579 16 00) Meat mains €6-10.25, fish mains €9-17.50. At the northern, Parador end of the promenade, recommended La Bohême has a range of tapas the length of a tall blackboard and serves fine food.

Cristóbal Colón (☎ 96 647 09 58) Rice dishes €8-16, mains €6-14. Halfway along the promenade, this restaurant, which specialises in rice and fish, is hugely popular with both Spanish and foreigners. Like La Bohême, it has a large *terraza* (terrace) from where you can watch the world pass by. Both fill up quickly so stake your claim before the swarm of diners descends.

El Nilo (☎ 96 579 36 48, Avenida de la Libertad Bloque 2-2) Open Wed-Mon mid-Jan–Oct. For more exotic fare, head one block behind the shore to El Nilo, where Egyptian Sam keeps an excellent small restaurant serving *shawerma* (doner kebab; €4.25-5.50), falafel (€3), kofta and kebabs to eat in or take away at reasonable prices.

Xàbia's ***covered market***, selling foodstuffs, is on Plaza Celestino Pons, immediately north of Iglesia de San Bartolomé.

Entertainment

The terraza of the whimsically named *Montgo' di Bongo*, on the shore between port and playa heaves with night-time drinkers. Nearby, *La Siesta* also packs in the punters, while *Coco Loco* is a popular music bar at the southern end of Playa El Arenal.

Of the discos, *La Hacienda*, on the Cabo de San Antonio road to the north of town, pounds nightly during the summer months. Equally buzzing, and easier to get to and home from, is *Molí Blanc* on the southern fringe of the port area, which also comes alive at weekends throughout the year.

Getting There & Away

Up to six buses run daily to both Valencia (€7.10) and Alicante (€10.40). They stop in the south-eastern corner of Plaza del Convento in the old quarter.

Getting Around

Between July and September, Autocares Venturo buses (☎ 96 642 14 08) run every half hour from 8am to 10pm between pueblo, port and Playa El Arenal. For the rest of the year, the service is hourly until 7pm.

You can rent a cycle from Xàbia's Bike Centre (☎/fax 96 646 11 50), Avenida Lepanto 21. Two wheels will set you back €6/18/36 per day/three days/week.

To call a taxi, ring ☎ 96 646 04 04 or ☎ 96 579 32 24.

CALPE (CALP)

postcode 03710 • pop 20,650

The Gibraltaresque **Peñon de Ifach**, a giant molar protruding from the sea, dominates the seaside resort of Calpe. Like so many other places along the coast of the Comunidad, the small old town, all narrow streets and small plazas, contrasts with the high-rise apartment blocks and hotels of the modern development along the seafront. But the two are not divorced and the sea is but a spit away from Plaza del Mosquit at the heart of the old quarter.

Calpe, 105km from Valencia and 62km from Alicante, is very much a family resort. It's particularly popular with visitors and residents from Germany – among the town's annual celebrations, there's even a Hispano-German beer festival.

Orientation

Calpe is long and, for the most part, thin. Like Benidorm, it's oriented east-west and therefore enjoys particularly mild winters, even by the gentle standards of the Costa Blanca. Also like Benidorm, it's essentially two bays. In Calpe's case these are separated by the impressive mass of the Peñon de Ifach. The old town lies west of the Peñon. From it, the main street, Calle Gabriel Miró leads down to the beaches of Playa Cantal Roig and Playa Arenal-Bol. The fishing and leisure port lies just west of the Peñon. Most of the recent, and still continuing, development is east of the mountain, fronting Calpe's most attractive beach, Playa Fossa-Levante.

Information

Tourist Offices Calpe has three tourist offices, all open year round. The main one (☎ 96 583 85 32) is on Plaza del Mosquit in the old town. It opens 9am to 2pm and 4.30pm to 7.30pm Monday to Friday, and 9am to 2pm on Saturday. There's another beside the port (☎ 96 583 74 13). The third, (☎ 96 583 69 20), Avenida Ejércitos Españoles 44, is open 9am to 9pm daily in summer.

Email & Internet Access José and his colleagues behind the desk at DIP Digital Center, Calle Benidorm 15, speak excellent English. Internet access costs €2.40 per hour, with a minimum log-on charge of €0.60. The computers hum 10am to midnight, Monday to Saturday, and 4pm to midnight on Sunday.

Bookshops Gill, the English owner of Librería Europa (☎ 96 583 58 24), Calle Oscar Esplá 2, carries a good stock of titles in Spanish, French, German and English, including major Lonely Planet titles.

Things to See

Ask at the tourist office for their pamphlet *Routes Around Calpe*. Particularly interesting is route No 9, which guides you around the old town. Within the old quarter, west of Plaza de la Constitución, are three small museums that observe the same opening hours. Beside Plaza de la Villa are the remains of the town walls and the 15th-century Torreón de la Peça, a tower that's home to the **Museo del Coleccionismo** (*Plaza de la Villa s/n; admission free; open 10.30am-1.30pm & 5pm-9pm, Tues-Sun*), which houses a collection of cameras, photos and other interesting bric-a-brac.

Calpe's **Museo Arqueológico** (*Calle Francisco Zaragoza 2; admission free*) displays local finds, mainly from the Baños de la Reina (see later).

The **Museo Fester** (*Calle José Antonio 6; admission free*), in rude health despite its name, illustrates the town's two main festivals. There's a display of elaborate costumes worn in its Moros y Cristianos parades and some singularly tasteless ninots, the figurines that appear at Fallas time.

Beside the Paseo Marítimo (promenade) of Playa Arenal are a couple of reminders of Roman Calpe, both much battered by the sea. The so-called **Baños de la Reina** (Queen's Baths) were probably an ancient fish farm. Some 150m westwards, beyond the **Torre del Molí**, an ancient watchtower later recycled as a windmill, are the equally crumbling remains of some 5th-century Roman baths.

Activities

From the port, **boats** (*adult/child €9/7.25*) with an underwater-viewing chamber leave hourly for a cruise around the Peñon. On Tuesday and Friday, they cruise around the spectacular Cabo de la Nao to Denia (€18/9 return), stopping at Xàbia.

The 332m summit of the **Peñon de Ifach** makes for a magnificent, fairly strenuous walk. Allow two to 2½ hours to get there and back. Even if you don't fancy the ascent, take in the exhibition at its **Centro de Información** (*☎ 96 597 20 15; open 9am-3pm & 4pm-7.30pm in summer, 8am-3pm & 4pm-6pm in winter*). In July and August, numbers undertaking this popular walk are controlled. Pick up a ticket early in the day from the information centre. The Peñon is also a popular climbing venue with 21

designated routes. The centre has details on the routes and tourist offices carry a descriptive pamphlet, *Escaladas*.

España Bajo el Mar (*☎ 96 583 13 37*), at Puerto Blanco, west of the resort, offers diving courses.

Places to Stay

Camping **Camping Levante** (*☎/fax 96 583 22 72, e campinglevante@teleline.es, Avenida de la Marina s/n*) €4.25/3.60/4.35 per person/tent/car. Open June-Apr. Just a brief walk from Playa Levante, this is the best of Calpe's three camp sites.

Hotels There are a couple of good-value places to bed down in the heart of town.

Pensión Centrica (*☎/fax 96 583 55 28, Plaza Ifach 5*) Simple rooms €11 per person. Although it's under new management, rooms are as pleasant as ever at this welcoming, recommended place, just off Avenida Gabriel Miró.

Hostal Crespo (*☎ 96 583 39 31, Calle de la Pinta 1*) Doubles with bathroom €25-45 according to season. Open year round. A stone's throw from the beachfront, neat Hostal Crespo has eight rooms (four with sea views).

Pensión el Hidalgo (*☎ 96 583 93 17, Avenida Rosa de los Vientos 19, Edificio Santa Marta 1, 2nd floor*) Singles €15-21, doubles €24-30 Oct-May, €21-36 & €33-54 June-Sept. All rooms have a bathroom and prices include breakfast. Three blocks from Hotel Esmeralda and around a third of the price, Belgian-run Pensión el Hidalgo offers the best value accommodation on Playa Levante. Its entrance is just round the corner from Bar Calypso.

Hotel Esmeralda (*☎ 96 583 61 01, fax 96 583 60 04, w www.rocaesmeralda .com, Calle Ponent 1*) Singles €58-87, doubles €77.50-174 according to season. For top-end luxury, Hotel Esmeralda, a block back from Playa Levante, is hard to beat.

Places to Eat

There are plenty of restaurants and bars around Plaza de la Constitución and along the main Avenida Gabriel Miró.

Restaurante El Pati (☎ 96 583 17 84, Avenida Gabriel Miró 24) Menú €15. Although its prices have recently suffered a hike, Restaurante El Pati remains good, if no longer great value whether you go for a main course (€6-11) or chew on a pizza (€4.20-7.20).

La Cambra (☎ 96 583 06 05, Calle Delfín 2). Open Mon-Sat. A couple of blocks towards the waterfront and just off Avenida Gabriel Miró, La Cambra, all agreeably antique wood and tile, is, by common consent, one of Calpe's finest restaurants. Specialising in rice dishes, it also has a rich a la carte selection.

Restaurante Bodegón (☎ 96 583 01 64, Calle Delfín 6-8) Meat mains €6.50-15.65, fish mains €11-16. Just a bread roll's throw from La Cambra, the small bar of El Bodegón gives onto a cosy, intimate interior dining area.

Casa Rolando (☎ 96 583 10 52, Calle Doctor Fleming 3) Menú €12. Open Tues-Sun eve & Sun lunch. German-owned but with a Spanish chef, Casa Rolando, in addition to its fish specialities, offers wild game. Try, for example, its roast boar with red cabbage and – recall that German connection – potato (€11).

Los Zapatos (☎ 96 583 15 07, Calle Santa Mari7). Mains €13-17. Open Thur-Tues evenings year round, Sun lunchtime Dec-Oct. The a la carte menu is short and specialised at this highly recommended restaurant. To save yourself even such limited decision making, go for the *menú del día*, where both choice and servings are ample.

Club Náutico (☎ 96 583 93 56, Puerto Pesquero s/n) Menú €9.05. Open Tues-Sun. Among a cluster of good fish restaurants down by the port, that of Calpe's sailing club, open to everyone, offers great views of the port beyond the plate-glass windows, or from the terrace in summer. The range of tapas (around €5) is impressive. Alternatively, simply slip into the bar for a drink and the view.

Disha's (☎ 96 583 04 54, Calle la Niña 36) An Indian or Chinese restaurant has to be *really* special to get into a guidebook on Spain and Disha's, specialising in Punjabi cuisine, well deserves a mention. It also does takeaways.

Getting There & Around

The narrow-gauge railway between Denia and Alicante passes through Calpe. Northwards to Denia costs €2.25 (40 minutes, seven daily) while a ride via Benidorm (€1.40) to Alicante costs €6.35 (1 hour 40 minutes, seven daily).

Buses connect Calpe with both Valencia and Alicante. They pull in along Calle Capitán Pérez Jordá beside the Cruz Roja (Red Cross) station.

For a taxi, you can call ☎ 96 583 00 38 or ☎ 96 583 78 78.

ALTEA
postcode 03590 • pop 15,600

Altea, separated from Benidorm only by the thick wedge of the Sierra Helada, could well be a couple of moons away. Its beaches are mostly pebbles and rock – and that's what has saved it so far from the hordes, although the pile drivers are beginning to pound. Its beach and harbour are backed by a pleasant foreshore promenade and a strip of low-key development, although the traffic belching fumes along the main road through the modern town is a horror.

The whitewashed old town, perched on a hilltop overlooking the sea, is just about the prettiest pueblo in all the Comunidad Valenciana. Although scarcely tainted by mass tourism, despite its closeness to Benidorm just over the hill, Altea is threatened from another direction – over-gentrification from, in the main, its high proportion of non-Spanish residents. But it would be churlish to resent the often tasteful restoration and recuperation that has taken place and, for the moment at least, Altea remains well on the right side of twee.

Information

Altea's tourist office (☎ 96 584 41 14), on the beachfront at Calle San Pedro 9, opens 10am to 2pm and 5pm to 7.30pm weekdays and from 10am to 1pm on Saturday morning (Sunday morning as well from July to September).

Things to See & Do

The most enjoyable thing to do in Altea is simply to ramble from sea level up to Plaza de la Iglesia, the focus of the old town, then let your feet direct you a different way down.

Altea has an impressive new **arts centre**, just north-west of the old quarter. A splendid piece of contemporary architecture in its own right, it maintains a varied and active programme of events, mainly music, with some theatre and dance. For what's on, ring ☎ 902 332211 or call the tourist office.

Places to Stay

Hostal Fornet (☎ *96 584 30 05, Calle Beniardá 1)* Singles/doubles €12.85/20.60, €20.45/30.05 July & Aug, with bathroom €18.05/31.75, €30.05/45.10 July & Aug. Up in the old town, Hostal Fornet is a homely place offering simple, comfortable rooms.

At shore level, there are a couple of decent options as well.

Hotel San Miguel (☎ *96 584 04 00, Calle San Pedro 7)* Singles/doubles with bathroom €30/36, €36/41 July-Sept. Open Feb-Dec. With a restaurant beneath, Hotel San Miguel looks directly onto the beach.

Hotel Altaya (☎ *96 584 08 00, fax 96 584 06 59, Calle San Pedro 28)* Doubles from €45.10, from €60.40 July & Aug. Opened in 2000, Hotel Altaya, a very smart option indeed, also overlooks the seashore.

Places to Eat

Off Plaza de la Iglesia and especially down Calle Mayor, there's a profusion of cute little restaurants, many open evenings only except in high summer.

El Canonge (☎ *95 584 43 05, Calle Mayor 1)* Mains €7-15. Open Thur-Tues (daily in summer). Just off the plaza, this is a cosy, intimate place to dine. The food matches the attractiveness of the locale.

Oustau de Altea (☎ *96 584 20 78, Calle Mayor 5)* Mains €10-13.75. Open Apr-Jan. At this prize-winning restaurant, all dishes have cinema references. It sounds gimmicky but the food can stand proud on its own merits. Toy with a Sofia Loren salad or bite on an Al Pacino steak.

Sant Pere 24 (☎ *96 584 49 72, Calle San Pedro 24)* Meat mains €6-14.50, fish mains around €15. Down at sea level, Sant Pere 24, highly regarded both locally and from afar, specialises in rice and seafood. That odd name? It's simply the address of the place in Valenciano.

Entertainment

Bar La Plaza in the old town's Plaza de la Iglesia has live jazz on Friday evenings and also plays great music any time of day or night.

BENIDORM

postcode 03500 • pop 54,300

Benidorm sprawls along the coast, 40km north of Alicante and 147km south of Valencia. It's easy to be snobbish about a place that, with over five million visitors annually, long ago sold her birthright to cheap package tourism. However, while quite a few of the horror tales are true and although you have to poke around among the tawdriness, the place can still throw up a gem or two.

Here's a short salvo of statistics to give you an idea of the sheer enormity of what's reputed to be Europe's largest holiday resort. The town's 130 hotels and hostales enjoy a year-round occupation rate in excess of 90%. In addition, some 70 companies rent out a total of 5200 apartments. For do-it-yourselfers, there are nine camp sites in the environs of Benidorm with over 18,000 pitches between them. And to feed the masses, the town has over 600 restaurants and cafes, and this doesn't take into account the small bars that pop up on just about every street.

The 5km of white sandy beaches *are* backed by some hideous concrete high-rises and its streets *are* thronged with pink trippers. But Benidorm, although violated most summer nights by louts from northern Europe, still manages to retain a certain dignity. The foreshore is magnificent as the twin sweeps of Playa del Levante and the longer Playa del Poniente beach meet beneath Plaza del Castillo, where the land juts into the bay like a ship's prow. Behind as a backdrop to the beach looms the peak of

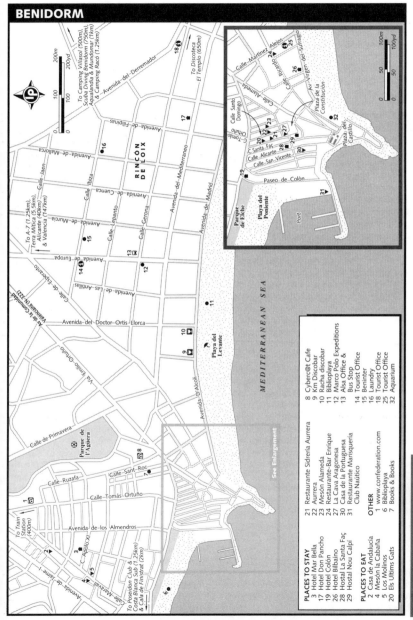

BENIDORM

PLACES TO STAY
3 Hotel Mar Bella
17 Hotel Don Pancho
19 Hotel Colón
26 Hotel Bilbaíno
28 Hostal La Santa Faç
29 Hostal Nou Calpi

PLACES TO EAT
2 Casa de Andalucía
4 Mesón la Cabaña
5 Los Molinos
20 Els Ultims Gats

21 Restaurante Sidrería Aurrera
22 Aurrera
23 Mesón Alameda
24 Restaurante-Bar Enrique
27 La Cava Aragonesa
30 Casa de la Portuguesa
31 Restaurante Marisquería
   Club Náutico

OTHER
1 www.confederation.com
6 Biblioplaya
7 Books & Books

8 Cyberc@r Cafe
9 Km Discobar
10 Racha discobar
11 Biblioplaya
12 Marco Polo Expeditions
13 Alsa Office &
   Bus Stop
14 Tourist Office
15 Beninter
16 Laundry
18 Tourist Office
25 Tourist Office
32 Aquarium

Puig Campana (1410m), like Mussolini's craggy Roman-nosed profile.

In winter, Benidorm is predominantly a haven for elderly northern European tourists. But during summer it's a destination for all ages – and becomes one of Spain's premier nightlife hot spots with a disco scene to rival that of Ibiza.

Orientation

Benidorm cuts neatly into two halves. Rincón de Loix and the Playa del Levante area east of Avenida de Europa is very much the preserve of package tourists from northern Europe. Here you'll find most of the major hotels and, on the downside, the majority of the tacky chip-butty British bars and nightspots. The narrower strip of development behind Playa del Poniente is more favoured by Spanish visitors.

The narrow streets of the original town of Benidorm form the thin end of the wedge (in physical terms only; it's actually the most interesting part of town). Behind the old quarter and west of Parque de l'Aguera is also a very Spanish area. Intercity buses stop on Avenida de Europa while the train station, a longer walk from the action, is at the town's northern limit.

Information

Tourist Offices The main tourist office (☎ 96 585 32 24) is on the fringe of what's left of the old town at Avenida Martínez Alejos 6. It opens 9am to 9pm Monday to Friday, July to September, and 9.30am to 1.30pm, plus 4.30pm to 7.30pm Monday to Friday, October to June. Saturday hours are 10am to 1.30pm and 4.30pm to 7.30pm year round. There are two smaller branches – in Rincón de Loix at the eastern end of Calle Derremador and on Avenida de Europa.

There are post offices at Plaza Doctor Fleming 1, Avenida de Europa 8 and Avenida del Mediterraneo 62.

Money Benidorm bristles with banks and exchange offices who are eager for your currency. Some of the latter are less than up-front (see the boxed text 'Small Change' for more information).

Small Change

Be wise to a frequent exchange-office scam. 'Bank rate X euros. No commission' state the seductive noticeboards. Look closely and you may see in much smaller letters, if it features at all, 'service charge Y'. So, for example, one office of red-nosed robbers quoted us an attractive rate, which at the time was €1.61 to the pound sterling. After they'd deducted service charges for less than two minutes of surly attention, we would have come away with a rate of €1.33, representing a cut of some 17% from the quoted amount. But we didn't. Instead we walked away, oblivious to the curses resounding in our wake. Do the same if an exchange office tries it on.

Email & Internet Access You can surf the Net at Cyberc@t Cafe (☎ 96 680 32 63), Calle Ruzafa 2, an underground cavern of a place that's open 10am to 2am daily. Rates are €3 per hour and there's a minimum fee of €0.60.

An easy walk away is www.confederacion.com (yes, that's the name, blazing out in blue neon) at Calle Tomás Ortuño 28. This places charges €2.40 per hour and is open 8am to 11pm daily.

Internet Resources For useful general information about the town you can pay a visit to the Web sites W www.benidorm.org or W www.planetbenidorm.com.

Bookshops If you've run out of reading material, Books & Books (☎ 63 012 07 76), Calle Sant Roc 17, in the old town, has both new and second-hand titles in English.

Laundry There's a self-service laundry at Calle Ibiza 14. It's open 9am to 8pm Monday to Friday and 9am to 2pm on Saturday, and charges €7.25 to wash and dry a load of up to 6kg.

Terra Mítica

Here on the outskirts of Benidorm is the theme park Terra Mítica, or Mythical Land

(☎ 902 020220, Ⓦ www.terramiticapark .com; adult/child €28.85/21.05 Mar-Oct, €21.50/15.70 Nov-Feb; open 10am-midnight mid-June–mid-Sept, 10am-dusk mid-Sept–mid-June), Costa Blanca's heavily promoted answer to Disneyland and to Port Aventura in Catalunya. A fun day out, especially if you're on holiday with children, it's Mediterranean in theme with areas devoted to ancient Egypt, Greece, Rome, Iberia and the Mediterranean islands. Buses run regularly from downtown Benidorm. A taxi costs around €8. (Note that in recent years Terra Mítica has closed between October and mid-February; at the time of writing the future off-season pattern was not clear.)

Aqualandia

You can happily slither and slide your way throughout a whole day at Europe's largest water park *(☎ 96 586 01 00, Ⓦ www.aqua landia.net; adult/child €14.30/8.30; open May–mid-Oct)*.

Mundomar

Right beside Aqualandia is Mundomar *(☎ 96 586 91 01, Ⓦ www.mundomar.es; adult/child €12/7; open 10am-dusk year round)* with its parrots, dolphins, sea lions and even bats.

For €21/11.50 you can buy a combined ticket, which needn't be used on the same day, giving admission to both Mundomar and Aqualandia.

Aquarium

Benidorm's privately run aquarium *(☎ 96 680 12 52, Calle Don Cosme Bayona – ex-Calle Horno – 5; adult/child €3.60/1.80; open 11am-1pm & 4pm-8pm daily)* is just below the church in the old quarter.

Boat Trips

Excursiones Marítimo Benidorm (☎ 96 585 00 52) do trips to the Isla de Benidorm, a wedge-shaped island, for €9/7.20 per adult/child. Boats leave every 45 minutes between 10am and 6pm. From Monday to Saturday they also do a cruise (€13.25/9.65) towards Calpe, departing at 11am and returning at around 3.30pm. Every Tuesday, a boat (€12/8.50) leaves at 10am, returning at

about 2.30pm, allowing plenty of time for shopping at the weekly market of Altea, the next pueblo up the coast from Benidorm.

If you're in a group, it could be worthwhile hiring a boat from **Charter Naútica Benidorm** *(☎ 96 585 06 33, 608 076124)*. A craft accommodating up to 12 passengers costs €72 for one hour and €114 for two.

Both companies have their offices at the port.

Diving

From April to October, **Scuba Diving Benidorm** *(☎ 96 680 97 12, Ⓔ diving@dragonet .es, Avenida Otto de Habsburgo 10)*, near Benidorm Palace nightclub, does diving courses for all levels. Based behind the Playa del Poniente, **Poseidon Club** *(☎ 96 585 32 27, Ⓔ poseidon@xpress.es, Calle Santander 9)* organises dives and runs courses from March to January. **Costa Blanca Sub** *(☎ 96 680 17 84)*, just up the street at No 20, functions from March to mid-January. All three can offer diving courses in English.

Waterskiing

Offshore from Playa del Levante, a cable contraption will drag you around a trapezoid circuit. Between May and October, Carlos *(☎ 96 680 04 18)*, who has an office at the port, can set up boat-hauled water skiing plus parachute skiing and banana-raft riding.

Mountain Biking

Marco Polo Expeditions *(☎ 96 586 33 99, Avenida de Europa 5)* rents mountain bikes and also arranges guided rides, ranging from their gentle Family Tour to a more demanding 35km off-road bash.

Walking

Should Benidorm's frenetic pace get you down, pick up a free copy of *Routes Across Sierra Helada* from the tourist office. Then pull on your walking shoes and take one of the walks into the hills to the north of town to enjoy the superb seascapes and views of the bay.

On the south side of Benidorm a freshly signed footpath leads from Cala de Finistrat, ending beside the tourist office in La Vila Joiosa (Villajoyosa), from where you can take a train or bus back to Benidorm. Allow about 2½ hours for the walk.

Marco Polo Expeditions (see Mountain Biking earlier) also arranges day walks.

Biblioplaya

At an altogether more relaxed pace, Biblioplaya – a library on the beach – is an excellent local initiative. Right on the beach and in the shade, you can catch up on the news absolutely free. The two centres – one on the Playa del Levante (open April to September), the other on the Playa del Poniente (open April to November) – carry major European newspapers. The UK selection, confined to the tabloids and Rupert Murdoch's *The Times*, isn't as enjoyable as it could be.

Places to Stay

Camping Of the two Category 1 camp sites around Benidorm, *Camping Villasol* (☎ 96 585 04 22, fax 96 680 64 20, W www .camping-villasol.com, Avenida Bernat de Sarrià s/n), which costs €4.17/4.35/8.53 to €5.64/6.10/15.26 per person/tent/car according to season, is nearer to town.

Largest of the Category 2 sites – and therefore offering the best chance of an available pitch in high summer – is *Camping Racó* (☎ 96 586 85 52, fax 96 586 85 44, e campingraco@inicia.es) costing €4.25/ 4.50/4.80 per person/tent/car.

Both of these sites are open year round.

Hotels Since almost everyone's on a package deal, Benidorm's accommodation can be expensive for the independent traveller. Our recommendations are all in or near the old town. Another option, if you're keen to save money and aren't too concerned about indulging in Benidorm's nightlife, is to stay in nearby La Vila Joiosa and travel to Benidorm by bus or train.

For discounted hotel and apartment rates (sometimes quite substantially so) contact Beninter (☎ 96 585 70 60, fax 96 586 79 68), Calle Ibiza s/n. You can also reserve online at W www.beninter.com.

If you're planning to be in town for a number of nights, pick up the long list of apartment operators from one of the tourist offices and ring around. Most normally require a minimum stay of one week but many are more flexible during times other than high summer.

Hotel Nou Calpí (☎/fax 96 681 29 96, e hotelnoucalpi@hotmail.com, Plaza Constitución 5) Singles/doubles with bathroom €21-30, €24-42.10 July-Oct. This pleasant, friendly, recently refurbished place is in the heart of the old town.

Hostal La Santa Faç (☎ 96 585 40 63, fax 96 681 22 48, e hotelsantafaz@ctv.es, Calle Santa Faç 18) Singles/doubles/triples €48/67/99. Recently renovated, this place has rooms with all facilities, including aircon. It's open from April to October only.

Hotel Mar Bella (☎ 96 585 49 58, fax 96 681 13 45, Calle Apolo XI 34) Singles/ doubles €18/26 per person (up to €93 per double July & Aug). Here, a little away from the main hotel zones, well appointed rooms have heating, air-con and bathroom.

Hotel Don Pancho (☎ 96 585 29 50, fax 96 586 77 79, W www.don-pancho .com, Avenida del Mediterraneo 39) Singles €69.75-104, doubles €93.75-136.45 including breakfast according to season. If you want to mix it with the package groups, one of the better options is the vast, 252-room, four-star Don Pancho.

Major hotels can be reasonable value out of season. *Hotel Colón* (☎/fax 96 585 04 12, Paseo de Colón 3) offers winter singles/ doubles with balcony and sea views for €27/39, rising to €39/60 in August.

Hotel Bilbaíno (☎/fax 96 585 08 04, e bilbaino@arrakis.es, Avenida Virgen del Sufragio 1) Singles/doubles €30/48.10, €45/83 May-Sept. Originally constructed in 1926 and subsequently remodelled, Hotel Bilbaíno was Benidorm's very first hotel. Overlooking the action end of Playa del Levante, its winter rates are especially attractive.

Places to Eat

Restaurants offering really good local cuisine are as rare as space in summer to spread your beach towel. On the other hand, there's many a place where you can eat economically and reasonably well. In the very Spanish wedge formed by Avenida de Jaime 1 and the Parque de Elche, there are a multitude of modest eateries serving decent, if unexceptional fare.

Los Molinos (☎ 96 585 19 49, Calle Maravall 18) Menú €6, bocadillos €2-2.50. You can eat inside or on the street corner terraza at this no-frills ('economical snacks, home cooking' proclaims the huge signboard in Spanish), good value-for-money place.

Just across the road, *Mesón la Cabaña (Calle Maravall 18)* does a marginally – and surely by no means fortuitously? – cheaper menú at around €5.80. They'll also serve you six sizzling, freshly grilled sardines for €1.80. Their €9 *menú especial*, with a choice, *inter alia*, of grilled shrimps or boiled scampi for starters, followed by steak, sole or sea bass and including bread, dessert and wine represents exceptional value. Outside are enticing photos of each dish with its price so you can just point.

Farther up the same street, *Casa de Andalucía (Calle Maravall 33)* does the same sardine offer, is equally good value and, as the home of Benidorm's Andalucian cultural centre, brings a slice of the south to town. Dry sherry (ask for a *fino*) is the most popular drink.

For a more upmarket concentration of local and Spanish regional restaurants and tapas bars – Basque in plenty, Galician and Cantabrian – take your pick from those lining Calle Santo Domingo at the Plaza de la Constitución end. Drift into *La Cava Aragonesa (☎ 96 680 12 06)*, which has a magnificent selection of tapas and juicy canapes and serves good wine by the glass. Scarcely less tempting is *Aurrera (☎ 96 680 92 97)*, occupying both sides of the extremity of the short passageway between square and street. Both are mostly standing room only. If you're after a sit-down meal, drop below ground to the related *Restaurante Sidrería Aurrera* where mains cost €9 to €15. Beneath La Cava Arag-onesa at semibasement level and specialising in Basque cuisine, it's also ideal for studying the legs of passers-by. Cider, cloudy

and fermented in the bottle, is the preferred tipple. Just along the street at No 12, *Els Ultims Gats*, which is open evenings only and is steeped in atmosphere, is a favourite with Catalan visitors and board-game aficionados.

A few paces away on a parallel street, you can guarantee that the produce is fresh and the ingredients are of a high quality at *Mesón Alameda (☎ 96 680 0176, Calle Martínez Oriola s/n)*.

Casa de la Portuguesa (☎ 96 585 89 58, Calle San Vicente 39) Open daily. Dishes €8-11.50. Casa de la Portuguesa, with its tables spilling into the street in the summer months, is a favourite with Benidorm's movers and shakers. Despite this, prices remain very reasonable (fish dishes cost around €11, meat dishes €8.50 to €11.50 and excellent rice platters €8 to €10).

Restaurante-Bar Enrique (☎ 96 586 09 35, Calle Ricardo 3) Open daily June-Oct, closed Tues Nov-May. For fish and seafood, visit this long-established restaurant, which does a great value menú at €8.50 and where generous fish mains cost €9 to €14.

More upmarket, *Restaurante Marisquería Club Naútico (☎ 96 585 54 25, Paseo Colón s/n)* Meals €21-30. Recently inaugurated as part of the port renovations, this restaurant is designed with flair and overlooks the small harbour. It's another place to scoff the riches of the sea, whether you're sampling tapas at the bar or enjoying a full meal inside or on the large terraza (where you can also simply sip a drink and enjoy the view).

Benidorm may be in Spain – although in some areas you have to look carefully – but one of life's gastronomic delights is a full, bloating English breakfast with all the sauces and trimmings as you nod in the sun on the terraza of one of the many British bars around Rincón de Loix and the old town. Tad and Lesley from Castleford, Linda and Darren from Skegness, Fred and Freda from Blackpool proffer their siren signs, playing on tribal loyalties.

Entertainment

You don't need any help from us to stumble across, into and out of Benidorm's hundreds of bars, cafes and pubs. Between June and

September, big beats throb nightly from a cluster of discos on the northern fringe of town. Head inland up Avenida de Europa to the intersection with Avenida de la Comunidad Valenciana (the N-332).

Biggest of all is *Ku*, shaped like a stranded flying saucer. Too spaced out? Cross the road to its rival, *Km*. Beside Km is *Racha* (check out [W] www.gruporacha.com for what's upcoming), opposite its near namesake *Pacha*. *Penelope* ([W] www.penelopedisco.com), part of a Spanish chain, is another major player. If, as dawn rises, you crave yet more, drop into the Morning Dance Club at *Scream* (also confusingly called *Manssion*). No, we're not recommending a sedate promenade cafe where oldies foxtrot to wheezing trios; this place actually cranks up at 6am.

Most places close outside summer and Easter week although Km plays to a year-round weekend beat. Down in town, Km and Racha, too, operate year-round discobars. Both are small beer compared to their N-332 sweatshops but are well worth dropping into. In Rincón de Loix, *El Templo* (☎ 96 585 04 00), at Hotel Palm Beach, charges a €6 admission. It's open nightly in July and August and at weekends during the rest of the year.

In the old town, you'll find several gay and lesbian places, ranging from the discreet and intimate to more in-your-face, along the three parallel streets of Calles Santa Faç, San Vicente and Alicante.

Getting There & Away
Bus Alsa (☎ 96 680 39 55) buses run north and south along the Costa Blanca to and from Valencia (€9.50, seven daily) and Alicante (€3, every half hour). They also run hourly to and from La Vila Joiosa (€0.75). Their office (set back in La Nuria shopping mall) and bus stop are at Avenida de Europa 8.

Train Benidorm lies on the narrow-gauge railway line linking Alicante and Denia. Fares include La Vila Joiosa (€0.70), Alicante (€2.82) and Denia (€3.50).

Getting Around
Bus Nos 1 and 7 run between the train station, the town centre and Rincón de Loix,

which is also served by Nos 2 and 8. From the centre, Nos 3 and 5 run along Playa del Poniente.

Call ☎ 96 586 26 26 or ☎ 96 586 18 18 for a taxi. Approximate prices are €9.75 to Altea, €10.85 to La Vila Joiosa and €50 to Alicante airport.

You can hire mountain and town bikes from Marco Polo Expeditions (see Mountain Biking earlier in this section).

LA VILA JOIOSA (VILLAJOYOSA)
postcode 03570 • pop 23,700
La Vila Joiosa ('Happy Town') is, in fact, a fairly staid place for most of the year. Known to the locals simply as La Vila, it perks up in summertime, dons its glad rags and has a Moros y Cristianos fiesta that can rival anywhere bar Alcoy. It's a much more tranquil resort than Benidorm or Alicante, those rowdy neighbours up and down the coast. Popular in particular with Madrileños, many of whom own apartments here, and yet to be overrun by package tourism, it remains a very Spanish resort with a small but active fishing port. If money's a consideration, it also works out cheaper than Benidorm, which is only a short bus or train ride away.

Happy Town is also Chocolate Town, headquarters to Valor, the Spanish equivalent of Cadbury or Hershey. The cocoa connection is a longstanding one, going back to the 18th century when La Vila Joiosa imported cocoa beans by the tonne from Ecuador and Venezuela to then distribute throughout Spain and Western Europe.

Information
Tourist Offices The tourist office (☎ 96 685 13 71), overlooked by the remains of the city walls, is at Avenida del Pais Valenciá 10. It opens 10am to 2pm and 5pm to 8pm from Monday to Friday and 10am to 1pm on Saturday (also 5pm to 8pm Saturday and 10am to 1pm on Sunday from mid-June to the end of September).

Email & Internet Access You can log on at Milenium, beside Hogar del Pescador (see Places to Eat later in this section) on Avenida del País Valencià.

Things to See & Do

The small old quarter tumbles down to the foreshore. Of particular interest are the houses, painted in a variety of pastel shades, that overlook the riverbed of the Río Amadorio on its western side. Improbable tradition has it that each was uniquely decorated so that returning sailors of La Vila Joiosa could recognise their home from far out at sea. Here, too, is the **Iglesia de Nuestra Señora de la Asunción**, a fortified church that more than once served as a refuge for the townspeople when Turks and Barbary pirates came raiding.

Valor, Spain's largest cocoa company, maintains La Vila Joiosa's **Museo del Chocolate** (*☎ 96 589 09 50, Avenida Pianista Gonzalo Soriano 13; admission free; tours on the half hour 9.30am-12.30pm & 3.30pm-5.30pm Mon-Fri)*. The museum tells you all you want to know and more about the manufacturing and marketing of chocolate.

The **Museo Arqueológico y Etnográfico** (*☎ 96 589 01 50, Calle Baranquet 16; open 9.30am-12.30pm & 5pm-8.30pm Mon-Fri)* is rather a grand name for this museum housing La Vila's collection of local finds, co-located with the town library.

Good for the body and soul is highly recommended **Terra Ferma** (*☎/fax 965 89 03 92, W www.terraferma.net, Calle Lepanto 13)*, a small, environmentally committed walking and climbing outfit. They can arrange anything from a one-day break in the hills to a week of trekking in the Sierra Aitana. Prices are very reasonable and staff speak excellent English.

Special Events

La Vila Joiosa's Moros y Cristianos celebrations, occupying a whole week at the end of July, are held in honour of Santa Marta, the town's patron saint. Uniquely for mainland Spain, they re-enact the sea raid and disembarking of marauding Turks (the boats that bear the invaders once served as lifeboats on transatlantic liners).

Places to Stay

Camping *Camping Playa de Torres (☎ 96 681 00 31, fax 96 681 01 73, e capto@ctv.es,*

Partida Torres Norte 11) From €3.15 each person/tent/car. Open year round. Playa de Torres is an attractive, well maintained camp site beside a relatively secluded beach a little north of town.

Hostales & Hotels *Hostal Rosa (☎ 96 685 09 19, Calle Quintana 46)* €15 per person Oct-June, €18 July-Sept. Rooms are simple, clean and good value at Hostal Rosa, one block south of the main drag.

Hostal el Mercat (☎ 96 589 59 33, Calle Jaime Soler Urrios 2) Singles/doubles/triples €18/33/42, €30/48/60 mid-July–mid-Sept. Open Jan-Nov. Rooms with all facilities are excellent value at this spruce hostal, opened in 2000, which overlooks the covered market.

Hotel el Montiboli (☎ 96 589 02 50, fax 96 589 38 57, e montiboli@alc.servigroup.es) Singles/doubles from €73.30/161.65. Perched on a knoll overlooking the sea 3km south of town, El Montiboli is one of Spain's loveliest and most tasteful hotels.

Places to Eat & Drink

Hogar del Pescador (☎ 96 589 00 21, Avenida del País Valencià 33) Menú €11.45, fish mains €7.25-12. Open Tues-Sun. This ranks among the best places in town for fish, seafood and rice dishes. For a special treat, tuck in your bib and settle down to its special *menú degustación* of delights from the sea at €33.

Bar l'Hort (☎ 96 685 35 99, Avenida del Puerto s/n) You won't come across many locals in Bar l'Hort but what you will find is delicious Filipino cooking served up by Venus, wife of the British owner. Let her tempt you with her Thai chicken or chicken ginger (€6.75).

Entertainment

If you fancy frittering away some of your hard-earned holiday money, visit La Vila Joiosa's *Casino (Carretera La Vila Joiosa-Benidorm km 3.5)*, north of town and the only gambling joint on the Costa Blanca. It brings in various top-line Spanish artists for its dinner-and-show spectacle; readers report that, while the show sparkles, the food is decidedly dull.

Bullfighting posters plaster the walls and memorabilia of the bullring fill every available space at **Rincon de Pepe** *(Plaza Castelar)*, where the wine, straight from the barrel, is as rough and ready as the clientele.

Getting There & Around

La Vila is on the Denia-Alicante train line (for the centre of town, get off at the Creueta–Vila Joiosa station). Buses run at least hourly (€0.65, 40 minutes) to and from Benidorm, and over 15 times daily to and from Alicante.

To call a taxi, ring ☎ 96 589 45 45.

ALICANTE (ALACANT)
postcode 03002 • pop 277,000

Alicante is the Comunidad Valenciana's second-largest town. Dynamic and brimming with fresh projects, it has transformed itself in less than a decade from a rather seedy port to an attractive town that improves with every visit. And unlike its coastal neighbours, it's a real town living for much more than tourism alone. Fit in a minimum of one night to experience its frenetic – and very Spanish – nightlife.

Orientation

Palm trees shade pedestrian Explanada de España, rich in cafes and running parallel to the harbour. Around Catedral de San Nicolás are the narrow streets of El Barrio (the old quarter), which has most of the cheaper accommodation options and the best nightlife. El Barrio is bordered by the Rambla de Méndez Núñez, the principal north–south artery where you'll find the regional tourist office. To the west of this boulevard are the main post office, bus and train stations.

Information

Tourist Offices There are no fewer than five tourist offices around town. The main, regional one (☎ 965 20 00 00, fax 96 520 02 43), Rambla de Méndez Núñez 23, opens 10am to 7pm (to 8pm June to September) Monday to Friday, plus 10am to 2pm and 3pm to 7pm or 8pm on Saturday. The principal municipal ones (offering a better, larger-scale town map) are at the bus station and town hall.

Post Alicante's main post office is at the intersection of Calle Alemania and Calle Arzobispo Loaces.

Email & Internet Access Yazzgo Internet, Explanada de España 3, opens 8.30am to 10pm daily and charges €3 per hour. If you prefer to log on late – and save a copper or two – go for UP Internet, Calle Ángel Lozano 10, open 10am to 2am Monday to Thursday, to 4am Friday and Saturday and to midnight Sunday. With 37 machines, it charges €2.70 per hour (€1.50 after midnight).

Laundry For €6, 5 à Sec will wash and dry a machine load. It's at Calle Calderón de la Barca.

Dangers & Annoyances

Be especially wary of pickpockets and bag snatchers around the bus station and along the Paseo Explanada de España.

Things to See & Do

The 16th-century **Castillo de Santa Bárbara** *(☎ 96 516 21 28; admission free; open 10am-8pm Apr-Sept, 9am-7pm Oct-Mar daily)* overlooks the city. Inside is the **Collección Capa** *(admission free; open 10am-2pm & 5pm-8pm Tues-Sat Apr-Sept, 10am-2pm & 4pm-7pm Tues-Sat Oct-Mar, 10am-3pm Sun year round)*, which is a permanent display of contemporary Spanish sculpture. A lift (€2.40 return), reached by a footbridge opposite Playa del Postiguet, ascends deep within the mountain. Alternatively, you can walk up the snaking minor road that takes off a little north of the Estación de la Marina.

Alicante's latest treasure is its avant-garde and completely revamped **Museo Arqueológico Provincial** *(MARQ; ☎ 96 514 90 00, Plaza Doctor Gómez Ulla s/n; admission €6; open 10am-2pm & 4pm-8pm Tues-Sat & 10am-2pm Sun)*, housed in the former Hospital de San Juan de Díos, which merits a visit in its own right. It has a strong collection of ceramics, particularly Islamic, across the ages and Iberian art and artefacts. On the outskirts of town (yet easily walkable), it's served by bus Nos 2, 6, 9, 20 and 23; there's a taxi rank right outside. A combined ticket for the museum and the Roman site of Lucentum costs €9 (see Around Alicante later in this chapter).

The **Museo de la Asegurada** *(☎ 96 514 09 59; admission free; open 10am-2pm & 5pm-9pm Tues-Sat Apr-Sept, 10am-2pm & 4pm-8pm Tues-Sat Oct-Mar, 10.30am-3.30pm Sun year round)* occupies Alicante's oldest building on Plaza Santa María. It has an excellent collection of modern art, including a handful of works by Dalí, Miró, Picasso, Chillida and Sempere.

On the same plaza, the 14th-century **Iglesia de Santa María** *(open 10.30am-1pm & 6pm-7.30pm)* has a flamboyant, 18th-century facade and ornate, gilded altarpiece, both strongly contrasting with the nave's Gothic simplicity of line.

The **Museo de Bellas Artes Gravina** *(MUBAG; ☎ 96 514 67 80, Calle Gravina 13; admission free; open 10am-2pm & 4pm-8pm Mon-Sat, 10am-2pm Sun)*, Alicante's museum of fine arts, occupies the Palacio de Gravina, a fine 18th-century mansion.

Also worth a visit is Alicante's **covered market** (see Places to Eat later), bustling, colourful and a cornucopia of the best and freshest food. A pleasing construction dating from 1921, it was strongly influenced by the *modernismo* trend of the day. Emphatically of the 21st century is the new development of shops, bars and restaurants beyond Hotel Melia along the port's eastern flank and, opposite on the western mole, **Panoramis**, a vast shopping and leisure complex.

Kontiki (☎ 96 521 63 96) runs a boat (€12), departing at 11.15am, to the popular **Isla de Tabarca** (see Around Santa Pola later in this chapter), an island 11 nautical miles south.

The commercial port and the more evident pleasure boat harbour take up most of central Alicante's foreshore. Immediately north is the sandy beach of **Playa del Postiguet**. Larger and less crowded beaches are at **Playa de San Juan**, easily reached by bus No 21 or 22. Between the two is the headland of Cabo de Las Huertas whose secluded, rocky coves – Cala Judios, Cala Cantalares and Cala Palmera – are a popular nudist area.

Special Events

Alicante's major festival is the Fiesta de Sant Joan, spread either side of 24 June, when Alicante stages its own version of Las Fallas (see the special section 'Fiestas' for details), with fireworks and satirical effigies going up in smoke all over town.

Places to Stay – Budget

Camping *Camping el Molino (☎/fax 96 565 24 80, Avenida de Elda 35)* €3.50/3.65/3.50 per person/tent/car. At Playa de San Juan, Camping el Molino, the nearest camp site to Alicante, is 700m from the beach.

Camping Costa Blanca (☎/fax 96 563 06 70, W www.campingcostablanca.com, Calle Convento s/n) 2 people tent & car €18. About 10km north of Alicante on Campello's outskirts, Camping Costa Blanca has a good pool and cafe. The *trenet* (little train; see Getting There & Away later in this section) passes right by.

Camping Bon Sol (☎ 96 594 13 83, fax 96 566 39 41, Camino Real de Villajoyosa 35) €3.45/5.10/3.45 per person/tent/car. This friendly camp site, altogether smaller than the other two, is only 200m from sandy Playa de Muchavista, a seamless extension to Playa de San Juan. Take the trenet to the La Sofra stop.

All camp sites are open year round.

Hostels *Albergue Juvenil La Florida (☎ 96 511 30 44, fax 96 528 27 54, e laflorida_ivaj @gva.es, Avenida Orihuela 59)* €4.80/6.60 under/over-25s. This large 188-bed, Hostelling International-affiliated place, normally a student residence, functions as a youth hostel from July to September. It's comfortable; 168 of those beds are in single rooms, there's a cafeteria and even air-con. About 2km west of the centre on a busy main road, it's accessible by bus No 3.

Hostales & Pensiones There are a few cheap hostales in El Barrio.

Hostal Les Monges Palace (☎ 96 521 50 46, fax 96 514 71 89, Calle San Agustín 4) Singles/doubles with shower €22/33, with bathroom €30/49. Just behind the town hall, this place represents outstanding value for money (the 'Palace' part was appended when

ALICANTE (ALACANT)

PLACES TO STAY
2   Hostal La Lonja
14 Pensión La Milagrosa
16 Hostal Les Monges
    Palace
32 Eurhotel Hesperia
35 Hostal Portugal
51 Hotel Mediterranea Plaza
54 Hotel Tryp Ciudad
    de Alicante
58 Hotel Melia Alicante

PLACES TO EAT
4   La Rotonda
6   Rincón de Antonio
11 Restaurante Marrakech
13 Restaurante Mixto
    Vegetariano
15 Restaurante El Canario
26 Restaurante Nou Manolin
30 Piripi
36 Tienda Open 25
47 El Buen Comer

48 Boutique del Mar
52 Restaurante Casa Ibarra

BARS & CLUBS
3   Cafe Or i Ferro
5   El Caribe
17 La Llum
19 Desdén Café Bar
20 Celestial Copas
22 La Naya
23 Cherokee
24 Havana
27 Boys Bar & Horus
31 La Cúpola Azul
39 Santa Fe
40 Fitty
41 Eclipse; Xanadu; El Sarao
42 Santiago de Cuba
44 Z
45 Cafe-Pub Piscis
59 Compañía Haddock;
    Pub Moncloa
60 Tropiscafo; Coyote Ugly

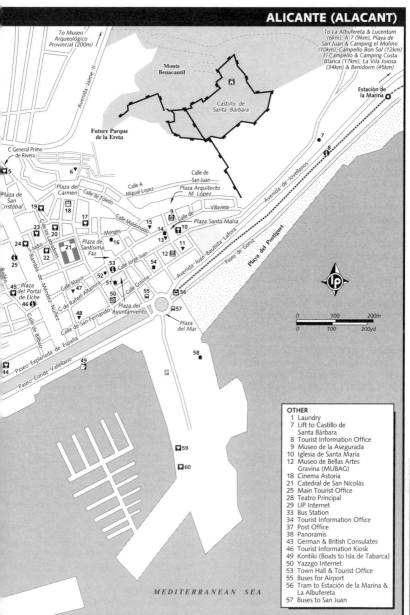

ALICANTE (ALACANT)

To Museo
Arqueológico
Provincial (200m)

To La Albufereta & Lucentum
(6km), A-7 (9km), Playa de
San Juan & Camping el Molino
(10km), Campello Bon Sol (12km)
El Campello & Camping Costa
Blanca (17km), La Vila Joiosa
(34km) & Benidorm (45km)

Monte
Benacantil

Estación de
la Marina

Castillo de
Santa Bárbara

Avenida de Jovellanos

Future Parque
de la Ereta

C General Primo
de Rivera

Calle de
San Juan

Plaza Arquitecto
M López

Villavieja

Plaza del
Carmen

Calle A
Miguel López

Calle de Toledo

Plaza de
San
Cristóbal

Plaza
Santa María

Calle Maldonado

Monges

Plaza de
Santisima
Faz

Plaza del
Ayuntamiento

Plaza del
Portal
de Elche

Calle Mayor

Calle Jorge Juan

Calle Gravina

C de Rafael Altamira

Calle de San Fernando

Rambla de Méndez Núñez

Calle de Bilbao

Paseo Explanada de España

Paseo Conde Vallellano

Avenida Juan Bautista Lafora

Paseo de Gomiz

Playa del Postiguet

Plaza
del Mar

Plaza de
los Luceros

MEDITERRANEAN SEA

Monges

0   100   200m
0   100   200yd

OTHER
1 Laundry
7 Lift to Castillo de
  Santa Bárbara
8 Tourist Information Office
9 Museo de la Asegurada
10 Iglesia de Santa María
12 Museo de Bellas Artes
   Gravina (MUBAG)
18 Cinema Astoria
21 Catedral de San Nicolás
25 Main Tourist Office
28 Teatro Principal
29 UP Internet
33 Bus Station
34 Tourist Information Office
37 Post Office
38 Panoramis
43 German & British Consulates
46 Tourist Information Kiosk
49 Kontiki (Boats to Isla de Tabarca)
50 Yazzgo Internet
53 Town Hall & Tourist Office
55 Buses for Airport
56 Tram to Estación de la Marina &
   La Albufereta
57 Buses to San Juan

COSTA BLANCA

they upgraded!). To really pamper yourself, ask for a room equiped with sauna and Jacuzzi (singles/doubles for €49/78). All rooms are individually and tastefully decorated and have heating, satellite TV and aircon (€4.20 supplement for the cheaper rooms). There's also a private garage (€6). Look out for the small Dalí original at reception.

Pensión La Milagrosa (☎ 96 521 69 18, *Calle de Villavieja 8)* €12-18 per person according to season and facilities. With less character but still quite acceptable, 40-room La Milagrosa has a small guest kitchen and roof terrace. Ask for a room overlooking Plaza de Santa María.

Hostal Portugal (☎ 96 592 92 44, *Calle de Portugal 26)* Singles/doubles €16.25/25.25. Bang opposite the bus station, this slightly old-fashioned place has clean, spacious rooms.

Places to Stay – Mid-Range & Top End

Hostal La Lonja (☎ 96 520 34 33, fax 96 520 35 27, e *hlonja@offcampus.net, Calle Capitán Segarra 10)* Rooms €46.40. The spruce Hostal La Lonja, just behind the covered market, offers reasonable value.

Hotel Tryp Ciudad de Alicante (☎ 96 521 07 00, fax 96 521 09 76, e *tryp.alicante@ solmelia.es, Calle Gravina 9)* Singles/doubles €63.10/68. Only the name has changed at this modern, stylish three-star hotel, a member of the Melia chain. Weekend rates at €48.10/57.75, including buffet breakfast, are a particularly good deal.

Eurhotel Hesperia (☎ 96 513 04 40, fax 96 592 83 23, e *hotel@hesperia-eurhotel .com, Calle Pintor Lorenzo Casan-ova 33)* Singles/doubles €81.50/93.15, private garage €7.50. Handy for the bus station, this is another good mid-range possibility.

Hotel Mediterranea Plaza (☎ 96 521 01 88, fax 96 520 67 50, Plaza del Ayuntamiento 6)* Singles/doubles €69.50/86, €111.35/125 Aug–mid-Sept. Service is excellent at this recently inaugurated hotel, which couldn't be more central. It has a gym and sauna – although a sauna in summer in Alicante would probably figure low on your wish list.

Hotel Melia Alicante (☎ 96 520 50 00, fax 96 520 47 56, Playa del Postiguet s/n)* Singles/doubles €116.50/141.25. Rooms from €86.60 including breakfast at weekends. In one direction, this huge four-star hotel overlooks the beach, in the other the spanking new portside development of bars and restaurants.

Places to Eat

La Rotonda, a simple bar opposite the covered market's flower stalls, does very reasonable tapas and bocadillos. Its terraza is a good spot to sit and view market life.

Restaurante El Canario (*Calle de Maldonado 25)* is a no-frills local eatery with a hearty menú (that's still composed on a typewriter. Remember them?) for under €6.

Restaurante Mixto Vegetariano (☎ 96 520 08 42, Plaza de Santa María 2)* Menú €7.50. Just around the corner from El Canario, this is another equally simple, low-ceilinged place with a vegetarian and – paradoxically – meat menú. If you prefer, you can combine dishes from both or go a la carte. Sit out on their small terraza and let the view of the church of Santa María's elaborate facade add piquancy to your meal.

Restaurante Casa Ibarra (*Calle de Rafael Altamira 19)* Menú €8. This is one of several budget places around Plaza del Ayuntamiento. It also has plenty of tapas ('squids to the Roman' is the engaging translation of one seafood dish) as well as fish and grilled-meat options.

El Buen Comer (☎ 96 521 31 03, Calle Mayor 8)* Meals around €20. El Buen Comer has a fancy, upstairs, a-la-carte restaurant. Downstairs and on the street terraza, there's a good selection of more modest dishes. Try their *lubina a la sal* (sea bass baked inside a crust of salt; €11.15).

For great atmosphere head up to the ***Rincón de Antonio*** (*Calle de Rafael)* in the Barrio de Santa Cruz. Here on the steep, stepped lane above Plaza del Carmen is local life – Alicantinos enjoying themselves on the street.

For Moroccan food, ***Restaurante Marrakech*** (☎ 96 521 37 63, Calle de Gravina 15)* is a good, if a tad expensive, bet. Hearty *tajines* (a North African stew) will set you back around €8.

Boutique del Mar *(☎ 96 520 60 09, Calle San Fernando 16)* Meals around €20. Open Tues-Sun. Stylish yet reasonably priced, this place serves up among the best in local fish and seafood dishes. It offers a plentiful range of rice dishes such as *arroz negro, arroz a banda* or *arroz marinera* (€6.75-7.75) and seafood choices (€3-7.50). The midday menú costs €11, while the much more elaborate *menú especial* is €21.

Restaurante Nou Manolín *(☎ 96 520 03 68, Calle Villegas 3)* Meat mains €12-16, fish mains €15-21. This restaurant, specialising in Mediterranean cuisine, is another favourite among discerning – and well heeled – Alicantinos.

Self-Catering Browse around the huge, two-storey *covered market (Avenida de Alfonso X El Sabio)*. After hours, ***Tienda Open 25*** *(☎ 96 513 41 53, Calle del Pintor Lorenzo Casanova 1)* is a 24-hour store.

Entertainment

Bars & Discos The old quarter around Catedral de San Nicolás is wall-to-wall bars. Most stay open until 2am early in the week and until 4am or 5am at weekends.

Havana *(☎ 96 521 69 26, Rambla Méndez Nuñez 26)* Open 8am-1am Sun-Thur, 8am-5am Fri-Sat. Havana is atypical in its opening hours; a lively bar by day, it becomes ever more animated as the night wears on and the dancing begins.

El Caribe *(Calle General Primo de Rivera 14)* Open 8.30pm-3am Tues-Thur, 10.30pm-4.30am Fri-Sat. Strictly Latino, El Caribe offers free classes in salsa and merengue.

On Calle de los Labradores is ***La Naya***, a cocktail bar adorned with paintings by local artists. The heavenly (and weird) ***Celestial Copas***, on Calle de San Pascual, has a kitsch collection of religious art/junk and great music. Farther up on Calle de Santo Tomás, look out for ***Cherokee*** at No 8 and the nearby ***Desdén Café Bar***. On the corner of Calle de Montengon and Calle del Padre Maltés, tiny ***La Llum*** is a sweatbox dance-bar that heaves late into the night.

The area farther west between Rambla de Méndez Núñez and Avenida del Doctor Gadea is a more concentrated and equally hectic option.

People and pounding music spill out of ***Santiago de Cuba*** onto its open-air terrace on Explanada de España. There's more action a block back along Calle de San Fernando. ***Santa Fe***, on the corner of Avenida del Doctor Gadea, is a sophisticated place to kick off the evening. A few steps east, any pretensions are left behind in a blur of mixed drinks and dancing. ***Fitty*** at No 57 is happening, and if for any reason it's not, dive into one of its neighbours ***Eclipse***, ***Xanadu*** or ***El Sarao***.

Just off Plaza Gabriel Miró, recently opened ***Z*** has quickly built up a faithful following. A slick disco with a dress code and €6 cover charge, it's open nightly until dawn, Tuesday to Sunday.

El Barrio bars no longer have the night to themselves. Down by the harbour, Paseo del Puerto, tranquil by day, is a doubledecker line of bars, cafes and discos with their own nocturnal following, mainly the late, late night owls. Those with stamina play the Barrio from midnight to around 4am, then slip into the stream of fun-seekers flowing towards the port, where the action continues until well after dawn.

In the port area, if you don't recognise ***Compañía Haddock*** by the noise, you will from the image of Tintin's pipe-smoking companion. Directly above – and risking bringing the roof down on a good night – is ***Pub Moncloa***. A couple of doors along, ***Tropiscafo*** beams out good recorded jazz, while beside it ***Coyote Ugly*** sometimes has live music.

Finally, if you're still on your feet and, in the unlikely event that the port begins to pall, you can take the night ferryboat over to the Panoramis complex, where the opportunities for nocturnal action are almost as rich.

During summer the disco scene at Playa de San Juan gets thumping. In fact, there are dozens of discos all along the coast from Alicante to Denia, served by the *Trensnochador*, a Ferrocarriles de la Generalitat

COSTA BLANCA

Valenciana (FGV) night train that ferries partygoers to and fro hourly between 11pm and 7am, July to September. *Búhobus* (the 'Night Owls Bus') is a similar service running between Alicante and San Juan.

Gay & Lesbian Venues Alicante has an active queer scene. In El Barrio, there are several fairly strong dives, not for the faint-hearted. *Cafe Or i Ferro* (*☎ 96 521 54 16, Calle Belando 12*) by contrast is a pleasant, welcoming place with a young clientele. It opens around 4pm and continues until late. *La Cúpola Azul* (*Avenida Óscar Esplá 2*) functions as a discopub while *Venial Club* (*☎ 96 611 75 51, Avenida Condes de Soto Ameno 16*) is on the outskirts of town in the San Blas suburb.

Back in El Barrio, there's something for everyone at Calle César Elguezábal 11. *Boys Bar*, a late-night venue, speaks for itself, while next door *Horus* is strictly for the girls. *Cafe-Pub Piscis* (*Calle Bailén 4*) is another lesbian hangout.

Theatre & Cinema The small *Cinema Astoria* (*☎ 96 521 56 66, Plaza del Carmen*) sometimes screens undubbed films. Alicante's main venue for the performing arts is the *Teatro Principal* (*☎ 96 520 23 80, Calle del Teatro 16*).

Getting There & Away

Air Most visitors arrive to Alicante by air. In 2000, of the record 6,038,000 passengers who passed through Alicante's El Altet airport, over three quarters came from abroad. Gateway to the Costa Blanca, the airport (information ☎ 96 691 91 00) is served by charters from all over Europe. It also hosts a number of scheduled flights to and from destinations within Spain – including Palma de Mallorca, Ibiza City, Barcelona and Madrid – and the rest of Europe. For more details, see the Getting There & Away chapter.

For the latest bargain flights to European destinations, pick up a copy of the *Costa Blanca News* or *Weekly Post* and check the advertisements. Two of the major cut-price operators, both of whom have offices at Alicante airport, are Servitour (*☎ 96 568 26 42,* **W** www.servitour.es), who sell tickets for Go, as well as charters, and V. Travel 2000 (*☎ 96 691 94 60*). Both will accept reservations by phone if you use a credit card.

There's a small tourist office in the airport arrivals area.

Bus There are up to 12 motorway buses daily to Valencia, as well as other much slower buses that pass through all the Costa Blanca coastal towns, such as Benidorm and Calpe.

Bussing It from Alicante

Destinations served from Alicante bus station (☎ 96 513 07 00) on Calle Portugal include:

Destination	fare (€)	duration (hours)	daily frequency	bus company
Alcoy	6	1½	4	Travicoi
Benidorm	3	50 mins	every 30 mins	Alsa/Enatcar
Bilbao	29.25	12	2	Bilman Bus
Denia	6.40	2½	8	Alsa/Enatcar
Elda	2.25	40 mins	15+	Alsa/Enatcar
Madrid	21	5	7	Alsa/Enatcar
Seville	39	11½	2	Alsa/Enatcar
Valencia	12.35	2¼ to 2½	up to 12	Alsa/Enatcar
Villena	3.25	1¼	10+	Alsa/Enatcar
Xàbia	5.60	2	7	Alsa/Enatcar

The fertile plain of *la huerta* produces prodigious amounts of fruit, vegetables, olives and almonds.

A 332m-high rocky molar looms over Calpe.

Hilltop Altea's tile-topped church

Elche's basilica: site of a yearly medieval drama

INGRID RODDIS

Benidorm's sprawl, fronted by its broad, sweeping foreshore, retains some dignity in the dusk.

MICHAEL TAYLOR

Until you're blue in the face?

Watching the night whizz by in Barrio de Santa Cruz, Alicante

MARK DAFFEY

La Vila Joiosa: geometric sun-bathed calm, a stone's throw from bouncy Benidorm

The left-luggage office (☎ 96 513 07 00) opens 8am to 8.30pm Monday to Saturday and 10am to 1pm and 3.45pm to 7pm on Sunday. A medium-size backpack or suitcase costs €2.50.

Train Alicante has two train stations. From the main Renfe Estación de Madrid (☎ 90 224 02 02), Avenida Salamanca 1, sleek Altaria trains run to Madrid (€33.70, 3½ to 3¾ hours, seven daily). Other destinations include Valencia (€8.60 to €18.65, 1½ to two hours, up to eight daily) via Villena and Xàtiva; Barcelona (€32.45 to €36, 3½ to 4½ hours, six daily); and Murcia (€3.50, 1½ hours, up to 20 daily) via Orihuela. The high-speed *Euromed* train to Valencia and Barcelona leaves up to six times daily. The left-luggage office (☎ 96 592 38 50) opens 6am to midnight and charges €3 per item per day.

Estación de la Marina, the FGV station (☎ 96 526 27 31), is at the far north-eastern end of Playa del Postiguet. A narrow-gauge service, commonly called the trenet, follows a coastal route, at times scenically stunning, northwards as far as Denia (€6.35) via Playa de San Juan (€0.70), Benidorm (€2.85) and Calpe (€4.35). Trains run as far as Altea hourly until 8pm and every two hours continue to Denia (last train 7pm). For details of summer night trains, see Entertainment, earlier. The station is an easy walk from Plaza del Mar or, if you're encumbered with luggage, train passengers can make the short tram journey (see Getting Around) for free.

Boat There is a regular ferry connection (☎ 96 514 15 09) to Oran in Algeria, but until things calm down there you'd be mad to get aboard.

Getting Around
El Altet airport is 12km south-west of the centre. SuBús/Alcoyana (☎ 96 526 84 00) runs buses every 40 minutes between Plaza del Mar (the stop in front of the pharmacy) and the airport, passing by the west side of the bus station.

Reliable local car-hire companies operating from the airport include Javea Cars

(☎ 96 579 3312, fax 96 579 60 52, ₩ www .javeacars.com), Solmar (☎ 96 646 10 00, fax 96 646 01 09, ₩ www.solmar.es) and Victoria Cars (☎ 96 579 27 61, fax 96 583 20 00, ₩ www.victoriacars.com). All are normally substantially cheaper than the multinationals.

A tram service runs from Plaza del Mar to La Albufereta, passing by Estación de la Marina (free for trenet passengers).

For a taxi, you can call ☎ 96 591 05 91 or ☎ 96 510 16 11.

AROUND ALICANTE
Lucentum
The Roman town of Lucentum, forerunner of Alicante, was constructed on the Tossal de Manises, an area of higher ground previously inhabited by the Iberians. It's a mere hillock 38m above sea level but, for purposes of defence and as a lookout point, every single metre above sea level counted. The site *(☎ 96 514 90 00; admission €4.80; open 9am-noon & 7pm-10pm Mon-Sat June-Sept, 10am-2pm & 4pm-6pm Mon-Sat Oct-May, 9am-noon Sun year round)* is nowadays dominated by the high-rise apartment blocks of La Albufereta. To get there, take the trenet to Lucentum station or bus No 9, 21 or 22.

ELCHE (ELX)
postcode 03200 • pop 196,800
• elevation 86m
Just 23km south-west of Alicante, Elche (Elx) is the Valencia Comunidad's third-largest city. It's renowned for the Misteri d'Elx, its annual mystery play (see the boxed text later in this chapter for more details) and for its palm groves, originally planted by the Muslims, which are the most extensive in Europe. The Arabian irrigation systems converted the region into a rich agricultural district that still produces citrus fruit, figs, almonds, dates and cotton to this day. Elche is also a university town with a strong industrial sector – notably its shoe factories, most of which are still fairly small scale and artisan.

Although its suburbs sprawl grimly, the central area with its large municipal park and extensive palm groves is refreshingly green.

Misteri d'Elx

The Misteri d'Elx, a two-act lyric drama dating from the Middle Ages, is performed annually in Elche's Basílica de Santa María.

One distant day a casket was found washed up on Elche's Mediterranean shore. Inside were a statue of the Virgin and the *Consueta*, the music and libretto of a mystery play describing Our Lady's death, assumption into heaven and coronation. Thus far is legend, but what experts agree upon is that the Misteri story, declared a Unesco World Oral Heritage event, goes back in more or less its present form to at least the latter part of the 15th century.

The story tells how the Virgin, realising that death is near, asks God to allow her to see the apostles one last time. They arrive one by one from distant lands and, in their company, she dies at peace. Once received into paradise, she is crowned Queen of Heaven and Earth to swelling music, the ringing of bells, cheers all round and – hey, we're in the Comunidad Valenciana – spectacular fireworks later that same evening.

The mystery's two acts, *La Vespra* (the eve of her death) and *La Festa* (the celebration of her assumption and coronation) are performed in Valenciano by the people of Elche themselves on 14 and 15 August, respectively. Public *ensayos* (dress rehearsals) take place on the three previous days – and, in fact, are a better bet since the three-hour performance combines both Vespra and Festa. Best of all is the 13 August Ensayo, following which Elche celebrates its Nit de l'Albá, a night of spectacular fireworks, its high point on the stroke of midnight when, with the town lights doused, a spectacular *palmera* (a simulated palm tree in flame) briefly fills the sky above the Basilica. Full performances of the Misteri are also given in even years at the end of October and on 1 November to mark All Saints Day.

If your visit doesn't coincide with the real thing, you can see a multimedia presentation – complete with a virtual apostle – in the **Museu Municipal de la Festa** (☎ 96 545 34 64, *Carrer Major de la Vila 27; admission free; open 10am-1pm & 4.30pm-8.30pm (5pm-9pm in summer) Tues-Sat, 10am-1pm Sun)*. The museum, which displays a wealth of paraphernalia relevant to the mystery, runs its 35-minute spectacular (admission €3) with optional English commentary at 10.30am, 11.30am, 12.15pm, 5pm, 6pm and 7pm (and 8pm in summer).

Orientation

The city is neatly split north-south by the Río Vinalopó. The older quarter, where you'll find most of the parks and monuments, lies on its eastern side.

Train and bus stations are beside each other on Avenida de la Libertad (also called Avenida del Ferrocarril), north of the centre. From either station: exit, turn left along Avenida de la Libertad then go left again down Paseo de la Estación. Flanking the attractive, landscaped Parque Municipal, it will bring you in less than 10 minutes to the tourist office and town centre.

Information

The tourist office (☎ 96 545 27 47) is on the south-eastern corner of the Parque Municipal.

It opens 10am to 7pm Monday to Friday and 10am to 2pm at weekends.

The main post office is at the southern end of Avenida del País Valenciá, just north of the Santa Teresa bridge.

Entre Acto Cybercafe (☎ 96 545 07 02), Calle Santa Barbara 15, opens 3pm to 11pm Monday to Thursday (to 2am Friday and Saturday) and charges €3 per hour with a minimum fee of €1.25.

Things to See

Palm groves dominate the city and its environs. Within them are over 200,000 trees, just about one for every inhabitant of Elche, and the whole has been designated a Unesco World Heritage Site. Some trees are pretty dishevelled and much in need of a haircut but

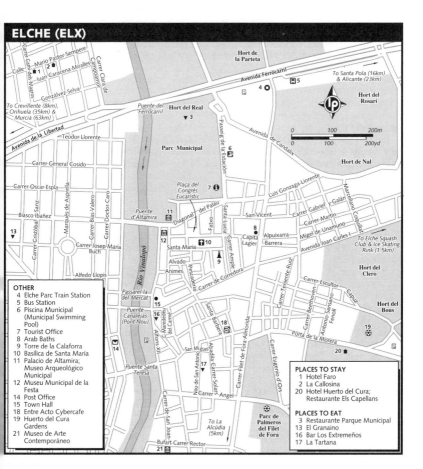

ELCHE (ELX)

OTHER
4 Elche Parc Train Station
5 Bus Station
6 Piscina Municipal
(Municipal Swimming
Pool)
7 Tourist Office
8 Arab Baths
9 Torre de la Calaforra
10 Basílica de Santa María
11 Palacio de Altamira;
Museo Arqueológico
Municipal
12 Museu Municipal de la
Festa
14 Post Office
15 Town Hall
18 Ente Acto Cybercafe
19 Huerto del Cura
Gardens
21 Museo de Arte
Contemporáneo

PLACES TO STAY
1 Hotel Faro
2 La Callosina
20 Hotel Huerto del Cura;
Restaurante Els Capellans

PLACES TO EAT
3 Restaurante Parque Municipal
13 El Granaino
16 Bar Los Extremeños
17 La Tartana

both the **Parque Municipal** and newly spruced-up **Parque de Palmeras del Filet de Fora** are pleasant to stroll through. Many have pointed tips like giant toothpicks wrapped tight in fibre mats or black plastic. This is to deny the top fronds light and keep them white and etiolated for future decoration. You can bet fairly safely that, wherever you are in Spain, just about any palm leaf taken to church on Palm Sunday or woven into intricate dollies will have been grown in Elche.

Opposite the hotel of the same name (see Places to Stay), the **Huerto del Cura** (☎ 96 545 19 36; admission €2.50; open 9am-8.30pm daily in summer, 9am-6pm daily in winter) is a lovely private garden and an oasis of calm with its tended lawns, colourful flowerbeds and freakish eight-pronged palm tree.

The narrow streets of the old and fairly compact Vila Murada (Walled City) are also well worth a wander. Little of the original walls remain, although the **Torre de la Calaforra**, originally constructed in the 12th century, stands solid as a reminder of Elche's Arab heritage. Just north of it, the vast 18th-century baroque **Basílica de Santa María** (open 7am-1.30pm & 5.30pm-9pm) is the

COSTA BLANCA

venue for performances of the Misteri d'Elx (see the boxed text earlier). One block eastwards are the renovated 12th-century **Baños Àrabes** *(Arab Baths;* ☎ *96 545 28 87, Plaza de Santa Lucia; admission free; open 10am-1.30pm & 4.30pm-8pm Tues-Sat, 10.30am-1.30pm Sun)*, which have an impressive audiovisual presentation. Ask them to roll the optional English soundtrack.

The east wing of the 15th-century **Palacio de Altamira** is home to Elche's **Museo Arqueológico Municipal** *(☎ 96 545 36 03, Plaça del Palau; admission €0.60; open 10am-1.30pm & 5pm-9pm Tues-Sat in summer, 10am-1.30pm & 4.30pm-8pm Tues-Sat in winter, 10.30am-1.30pm Sun year round)*. Although small, it's worth popping in to see the sculptures dating from the Iberian period.

The **Town Hall** has a pair of 15th-century portals and, up in the Torre de la Vela at its north-east corner, a pair of engaging little 17th-century figures, Calendura and Calendureta, who pop out to strike the hour.

Equally modest and farther south is the town's **Museo de Arte Contemporáneo** *(☎ 96 545 49 82, Plaça del Raval s/n; admission free; open 9.30am-1.30pm & 5pm-8pm Tues-Sat, 10.30am-1.30pm Sun)*.

Activities
If the summer heat begins to sap your energy, dunk yourself in the **Piscina Municipal** *(Municipal Swimming Pool; Paseig de la Estación)*, a little north of the tourist office. Alternatively you could perform a few pirouettes around the **ice-skating rink** *(☎ 96 545 34 46, Calle Mallorca 37)* within Elche Squash Club. Or, to become briefly airborne, drift over the palm groves in a **hot-air balloon**. Call ☎ 96 663 74 01 for details and current prices.

Organised Tours
From mid-July until the end of August, guided tours of the historic quarter leave from the tourist office at 11.30am and 5.30pm. Conducted in Spanish with highlights explained in English, they last about two hours and cost a bargain €3 plus admission fees (see Things to See earlier for more details), where required.

Special Events
Elche's second-most expansive spectacle after the Misteri (see the boxed text earlier) is its Palm Sunday procession, which also dates from the Middle Ages.

Places to Stay
Budget choices in Elche are very limited.

Hotel Faro *(☎/fax 96 546 62 63, Camí dels Magros 24)* Simple singles/doubles with ceiling fan €10.85/21.60, €12/24 July-Sept. This little gem is friendly, spotlessly clean and unrivalled in its category.

La Callosina *(☎ 96 546 00 76, Calle Mario Pastor Sempere 15)* Simple singles/doubles €13.25/25.20, doubles with bathroom €28.20. If Hotel Faro's full, this place, just around the corner, makes a comfortable and economical alternative.

Do yourself a favour – save up, come on a weekend and book into Elche's longest-standing luxury lodgings.

Hotel Huerto del Cura *(☎ 96 661 00 11, Calle de la Porta de la Morera 14)* Singles/doubles €93.15/100 Mon-Thur, doubles €66.10 Fri-Sun. Set in lush gardens and shaded by huge palms, this magnificent spot, an Elche institution, has tennis courts, a gym, sauna, solarium, a wonderful kidney-shaped pool and spa, and bungalow-style rooms – you're right in the city centre but it feels like a tropical island. During the week it's popular with businesspeople and priced accordingly, but at weekends it's a real bargain. Complete the cosseting by dining in *Els Capellans*, the hotel restaurant, which concentrates on local cuisine.

Places to Eat
Carrer Mare de Déu del Carmé *(Calle Nuestra Señora del Carmen)* has a cluster of good, cheap-and-cheerful places, including *Bar Los Extremeños* at No 14, which serves great tapas. On summer evenings almost the whole length of this short street is set with tables.

Restaurante Parque Municipal *(☎ 96 545 34 15, Parque Municipal s/n)* Mains €9-11.50. Although this vast emporium to eating can accommodate almost 2000 diners, its cuisine is far from institutional. In fact, whether you choose the terrace or cavernous, air-con interior, it's one of the best places in town for sampling local cuisine at other than fancy prices. Try their good daily menú at €9.85, go for one of their splendid rice dishes such as *arroz con costra* or splash out a little more for their local specialities menú at €15.65. The restaurant also has the distinction of being open for business from 9am to 11pm continuously every single day of the year.

El Granaino (☎ 96 666 40 80, Calle Josep María Buch 40) Mains around €12. Open Mon-Sat. Many discriminating diners drop by just to pick and choose from the rich variety of tapas at the bar of this long established restaurant. Penetrate deeper and you can choose from its equally broad range of local and Andalucian dishes.

La Tartana (☎ 96 542 57 87, Calle Nou de San Antonio 17) Mains €9-12. Open Tues-Sat & Sun lunch. La Tartana occupies attractive old premises in the historic quarter. Although it hasn't been established as long as El Granaino, it too offers regional cuisine at slightly more modest prices.

For that special occasion, get your glad rags on and head for *Els Capellans*, restaurant of the Hotel Huerto del Cura (see Places to Stay earlier).

To relax tired feet, treat yourself to a drink sitting out on one of the pleasant *terrazas* on the north side of Plaça del Congrès Eucarístic.

Local specialities to look out for include *arroz con costra*, a rice dish similar to paella that's topped by an egg crust; *cocido con pelotas*, a stew in which meatballs float; and, for dessert, *tortá d'Elx*, a rich confection with almonds and syrup. If you've a sweet tooth, be sure to pick up a packet of Elche dates or some sweetmeats based upon dates before you leave town.

Getting There & Away

Bus AM Mollá operates buses every half-hour to and from Alicante (€1.40) and Santa Pola (€0.90) on weekdays (fewer at weekends). Alsa runs four buses daily to Valencia (€8.60) via Elda and Villena and seven to and from Murcia (€3.10).

Train The town, sitting on the Alicante–Murcia train line, has a couple of stations, Elche Carrús and Elche Parc. Around 20 trains stop daily at each, heading north-east to Alicante (€1.60), where there are reasonable connections for Madrid, Valencia and Barcelona, and south-west to Murcia (€2.20) via Orihuela.

AROUND ELCHE
Alcúdia

The well signed Alcúdia archaeological site, huge and most of it yet to be excavated, is set back from the CV-855, 3.5km south of the tourist office. It was here that the Dama de Elche, a masterpiece of Iberian art, was unearthed in 1897. The original now graces the Museo Arqueológico Nacional in Madrid, but in the site's south-eastern corner a replica protrudes from the dusty earth. It's framed by slabs of stone, exactly as she was rediscovered, leading experts to believe that she had been deliberately hidden away.

At the heart of the site is the **Museo Arqueológico** (☎ 96 661 15 06, *Partida Atzavares Baix 138; adult/child €2.40/1.80; open 10am-2pm & 4pm-8pm Tues-Sat Apr-Sept, 10am-5pm Tues-Sat Oct-Mar, 10am-2pm Sun year round*). The museum displays the rich findings from a settlement that was occupied continuously from Neolithic to late-Visigoth times. On a lectern in each gallery you'll find an excellent summary in English of its contents and historical background.

ORIHUELA
postcode 03360 • pop 53,500

On the banks of the Río Segura and about 50km south-west of Alicante, Orihuela sits at the base of a barren mountain of rock. Although the district capital of the Vega Baja region, it has something of a down-at-heel air these days. But it wasn't always this way. In the 200 years after its designation as a bishopric in 1564, it enjoyed wealth and prestige as a fresh construction boom brought new splendours to stand beside the town's existing Gothic treasures. If you're at all interested in ecclesiastical architecture, it's worth setting aside a good half day to explore the town's heritage.

Orientation

From the combined bus and train stations, a walk of less than 10 minutes along Avenida de Teodomiro, then Calle Calderón de la Barca, brings you to the Río Segura and the old quarter spreading back from the river's north bank.

The main route to and from the A-7 heads northwards along Ronda de Santo Domingo, which becomes via Avenida Doctor García Rogel, passing beside Convento de Santo Domingo.

Information

Tourist Offices The tourist office (☎ 96 530 27 47), at Calle Francisco Die 25, occupies the ground floor of the neobaroque Palacio de Rubalcava. It opens 10am to 2pm and 5pm to 8pm Tuesday to Saturday, and 10am to 2pm on Sunday and Monday.

Post & Communications Orihuela's post office is on Plaza Nueva.

Things to See & Do

Admission to the historic buildings of the old quarter is free except where indicated. At places where a fee is charged, students are exempt. Afternoon opening and closing times are shunted back by one hour between October and May.

The town's most impressive complex is the 16th-century **Convento de Santo Domingo** *(Calle Adolfo Clavarana s/n; open 9.30am-1.30pm & 5pm-8pm Tues-Sat, 10am-2pm Sun)*. Set apart from Orihuela's other historic buildings, it functioned as a university from when it was recognised by papal bull in 1569 until the suppression of religious orders early in the 19th century. Nowadays, almost 200 years later, it again enjoys an educational role, housing both a secondary school and a branch of Alicante University's department of tourism. The entrance in the south-west corner gives onto the early-17th-century *claustro del convento* (convent cloister). Beyond it is the baroque *claustro de*

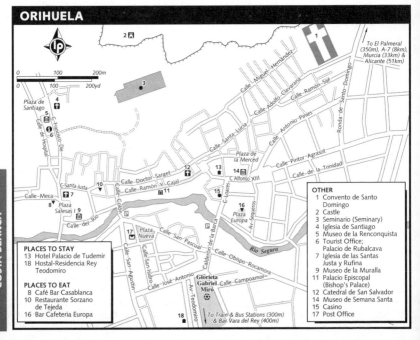

ORIHUELA

0   100   200m
0   100   200yd

Plaza de Santiago

To El Palmeral (350m), A-7 (8km), Murcia (33km) & Alicante (51km)

Plaza de la Merced

Plaza Europa

Plaza Nueva

Río Segura

Glorieta Gabriel Miró

To Train & Bus Stations (300m) & Bar Vara del Rey (400m)

PLACES TO STAY
13 Hotel Palacio de Tudemir
18 Hostal-Residencia Rey Teodomiro

PLACES TO EAT
8 Café Bar Casablanca
10 Restaurante Sorzano de Tejeda
16 Bar Cafetería Europa

OTHER
1 Convento de Santo Domingo
2 Castle
3 Seminario (Seminary)
4 Iglesia de Santiago
5 Museo de la Renconquista
6 Tourist Office; Palacio de Rubalcava
7 Iglesia de las Santas Justa y Rufina
9 Museo de la Muralla
11 Palacio Episcopal (Bishop's Palace)
12 Catedral de San Salvador
14 Museo de Semana Santa
15 Casino
17 Post Office

COSTA BLANCA

la universidad (university cloister) with its heraldic logos and slender Corinthian pillars, constructed a century later. Between the two is the original refectory, its walls very Valencian with their ornately decorated 18th-century tiles portraying idyllic pastoral scenes. The church, and especially the icing-sugar stucco on the interior of the dome, will be over the top for many visitors' tastes. More sober is the apparently disproportionate altarpiece by Juan de Juanes, moved from a side chapel to take the place of the larger original, which was destroyed during the Civil War.

The 14th-century Catalan-Gothic **Catedral de San Salvador** *(Calle Doctor Sarget; open 10am-1.30pm & 5pm-7.30pm Mon-Fri, 10am-1.30pm Sat)* is, as so often in Spain, built on the site of a mosque. In dimensions more like that of a parish church – which it originally was until Orihuela's elevation to bishopric – than a mighty cathedral, it has, among its other charms, three splendid portals. At the rear and giving onto a charming little cloister is its **Museo Diocesano** *(admission €0.60; opening hours as per Catedral de San Salvador)*, whose religious art collection includes Velázquez's *Tentación de Santo Tomé* (Temptation of St Thomas). A block away along pedestrianised Calle Ramón y Cajal, pause to look at the sober baroque facade of the **Palacio Episcopal** (Bishop's Palace).

The **Iglesia de las Santas Justa y Rufina** *(Plaza Salesas 1; admission €0.60; open 10am-1.30pm & 5pm-7.30pm Mon-Fri, 10am-1.30pm Sat)* is named in honour of the town's two patron saints. Grafted onto its Gothic core, which includes a fine tower graced with gargoyles, are elements – such as the Renaissance facade – which were added later.

The 14th-century **Iglesia de Santiago** *(Plaza de Santiago 2; admission €0.60; open 10am-1.30pm & 5pm-7.30pm Mon-Fri plus Sat morning)* is also primarily Catalan-Gothic with later accretions.

Signs indicating the new **Museo de la Muralla** *(☎ 96 674 31 54, Calle del Río s/n; open 10am-2pm & 5pm-8pm Tues-Sat, 10am-2pm Sun)* were, at the time of writing,

inadequate. Look out for the entrance just inside the main door to the Universidad Miguel Hernandez, Orihuela branch. A 20-minute guided tour in Spanish (an English leaflet is promised) leads you through the vast underground remains of the city walls, Arab baths and domestic buildings.

The **Museo de Semana Santa** *(Plaza de la Merced 1; admission €0.60; open 10am-1pm & 5pm-7pm Mon-Fri, 10am-1pm Sat)* displays the costumes, paraphernalia and giant thrones (such as 'El Lavatorio', which is not what you might think) used during the town's spectacular Holy Week processions.

Spare 10 minutes for the tiny **Museo de la Renconquista** *(Calle Francisco Die, admission €0.30; open 11am-1pm & 5pm-7pm Mon-Fri)*, which exhibits costumes and mementos from Orihuela's Moros y Cristianos fiestas across the years. Take a peek, too, into the town's **Casino** *(Calle Cardenal Loaces 1)*. Constructed in 1887, it is, like its equivalent in Torrevieja, essentially a gentlemen's club without a one-armed bandit in sight. The doorman will be happy to let you in for a brief look around its rich decor – as long as you aren't wearing shorts (we did say it's a *gentlemen's* club!).

Crowning the mountain that dominates Orihuela are the ruins of a **castle**, originally constructed by the Muslims. Your reward for the stiff climb up is great views of town and plain. If you find this daunting, the panorama is almost as impressive from the terrace beside the **Seminario**, an altogether easier ascent.

For a walk that's strictly level, go past the Convento Santo Domingo and along Avenida Doctor García Rogel to reach **El Palmeral**, 625 hectares of palm grove and Spain's largest after Elche.

Special Events

Orihuela's Easter Week processions rival in fervour and splendour those of Andalucía to the south. The Fiesta de la Reconquista is a week-long jollification, held around 17 July, the date of the town's repossession from the Arabs, where competing bands of Moors and Christians take to the streets and fight mock battles. For four days around 15 August, Orihuela holds its annual Feria del Ganado, a big livestock fair.

Places to Stay

Hostal-Residencia Rey Teodomiro (☎/fax 96 674 33 48, Avenida Teodomiro 10) Singles/doubles with bathroom €22.60/39.40. This spruce option in the more modern part of town is handy for both bus and train stations. Rooms have TV, air-con and heating.

Hotel Palacio de Tudemir (☎ 96 673 80 10, fax 96 673 80 70, e palacio.tudemir@ shserotel.com, Calle Alfonso XIII 1) Singles/doubles €84.15/102.25. This recently opened four-star hotel occupies a tastefully renovated 18th-century palace. Its weekend offer at €66.10 (which also applied to the whole of July and August in its first year of operation and may continue) is particularly good value for money.

Places to Eat

Bar Cafeteria Europa (☎ 96 674 26 78, Plaza Europa s/n) Meals around €9. Here, you get hearty, slap-it-down fare at popular prices.

Café Bar Casablanca (☎ 96 530 10 29, Calle Meca 1) Tapas from €1.50. This unpretentious place has a wide selection of tapas. It may look closed, but go down Calle Meca and in through the door flanked by a pair of, in summer, most welcome air-con units.

Bar Vara del Rey (☎ 96 674 56 58, Avenida Teodomiro 56) Tapas from €1.65. Open Tues-Sun. Handy for bus and train stations, this place serves tapas throughout the day and also does a bargain midday menú at €6.

Restaurante Sorzano de Tejeda (☎ 96 674 51 03, Calle Doctor Sarget 4) Mains €10.85-16.25. Open Mon-Sat. Famous for its rice dishes, this restaurant, which also occupies a former palace, offers elegant dining. The daily menú costs €15.65 (€9.65 at the bar).

For something special, go for the *restaurant* of Hotel Palacio de Tudemir (see Places to Stay). Mains cost between €11 and €19 and they do an inventive menú of regional specialities (€25.40) that changes weekly.

Getting There & Away

Bus and train stations are combined at the Intermodal, an airy new structure at the southern end of town.

Alsa serves Alicante and Murcia (both destinations eight times daily), Agostense goes to Guardamar (€3, 1¼ hours, up to six daily) while Costa Azul has nine buses daily to and from Torrevieja, and eight to and from Murcia.

Orihuela is on the Alicante–Murcia train line. For details, see Getting There & Away under Elche, earlier.

Getting Around

If you're driving, avoid claustrophobia in Orihuela's narrow streets by leaving your vehicle in the large Entrepuentes car park beside the river. For a taxi, call ☎ 96 674 02 02.

SANTA POLA

postcode 03130 • pop 17,750

Despite the increasing impact of tourism, Santa Pola, 18km south of Alicante, remains an important fishing port. From its harbour, base of the local fishing fleet and haven to hundreds of pleasure vessels, boats leave for the popular **Isla de Tabarca** (see Around Santa Pola later in this section), just 3.5 nautical miles offshore.

Santa Pola's other traditional industry has been for centuries the conversion of seawater into that most basic of commodities, salt. At its rear is the **Parque Natural de las Salinas**, a set of lagoons and salt pans that are today a protected nature park.

Although most of Santa Pola's beaches are backed by jungles of concrete, they're more than worthwhile if you keep your gaze fixed firmly on the briny. Spread yourself on sandy **Gran Playa**, **Playa Lissa**, west of the harbour, or **Playa de Levante** to its east.

Information

The helpful tourist office (☎ 96 669 22 76) is at the entrance to town, beside El Palmeral park and just off the large roundabout at the heart of Plaza de la Diputación. It's

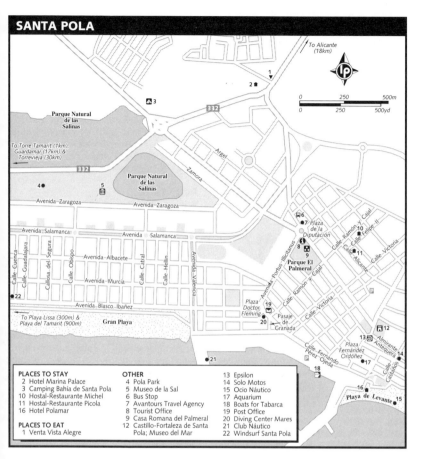

SANTA POLA

To Alicante (18km)

Parque Natural de las Salinas

To Torre Tamarit (1km), Guardamar (17km) & Torrevieja (30km)

Parque Natural de las Salinas

Avenida Zaragoza
Avenida Zaragoza

Avenida Salamanca
Avenida Salamanca

Calle Cuenca
Calle Guadalajara
Calleosa del Segura
Calle Obispo

Avenida Albacete

Calle Catral
Calle Hellín

Avenida Murcia

Avenida Valencia

Avenida Blasco Ibáñez

To Playa Lissa (300m) & Playa del Tamarit (900m)

Gran Playa

Plaza de la Diputación

Calle Ramón y Cajal
Calle Felipe II

Calle Victoria

Calle Alicante

Parque El Palmeral

Avenida Portus Illicitanus
Avenida Ramón y Cajal

Plaza Doctor Fleming

Pasaje de Granada

Calle Victoria

Plaza Doctor Fernández Ordóñez

Calle Fernando Pérez Ojeda

Calle Almirante Antequera

Calle Castillo

Boats for Tabarca

Playa de Levante

PLACES TO STAY
2 Hotel Marina Palace
3 Camping Bahía de Santa Pola
10 Hostal-Restaurante Michel
11 Hostal-Restaurante Picola
16 Hotel Polamar

PLACES TO EAT
1 Venta Vista Alegre

OTHER
4 Pola Park
5 Museo de la Sal
6 Bus Stop
7 Avantours Travel Agency
8 Tourist Office
9 Casa Romana del Palmeral
12 Castillo-Fortaleza de Santa
 Pola; Museo del Mar

13 Epsilon
14 Solo Motos
15 Ocio Náutico
17 Aquarium
18 Boats for Tabarca
19 Post Office
20 Diving Center Mares
21 Club Náutico
22 Windsurf Santa Pola

open 10am to 2pm and 5.30pm to 8.30pm Monday to Saturday from 22 June to 20 September (afternoon hours 4pm to 7pm, rest of the year).

The post office is located on Plaza Doctor Fleming.

For surfing of the electronic kind, visit Epsilon at Calle Almirante Antequera 8.

Things to See
The well preserved 16th-century **Castillo-Fortaleza de Santa Pola**, these days besieged by 20th-century high-rise architecture, is on Plaza del Castillo. Around the

fortress's stark courtyard are a small chapel, bar and the **Museo del Mar** (*☎ 96 669 15 32, adult/child €1.50/0.60; open 11am-1pm & 2pm-7pm Tues-Sat Sept-June, 11am-1pm & 6pm-9.30pm Tues-Sat July & Aug, 11am-1.30pm Sun year round*). The sea is the leitmotif of this small, recently revamped museum, which also illustrates the history of Santa Pola through dioramas and pictures.

The equally compact **Museo de la Sal** (*☎ 96 669 35 46, off Avenida Zaragoza; admission free; open 9am-2.30pm daily*) occupies a converted salt mill at the edge of

**In the pink at Santa Pola's
salty nature park**

the Parque Natural de las Salinas and tells the story of salt production. If the season is right, you can look through their telescope and see the flamingos strut and trawl for the tiny invertebrates that constitute their diet. If you're coming by car, either take the signed turn-off on the N-332 (northbound only) or park on Avenida Zaragoza and walk across the flats.

Just west of the museum and also on drained land is **Pola Park** (☎ 96 541 70 60), an amusement park, open 7pm to 2am in July and August, and weekends only during the rest of the year.

In the nine tanks of Santa Pola's **Aquarium** (☎ 96 541 69 16, Plaza Fernández Ordóñez s/n; adult/child €2.40/1.20; open 11am-1pm & 6pm-10pm daily mid-June–mid-Sept, 10am-1pm & 5pm-7pm daily mid-Sept–mid-June) swim, crawl and creep examples of off-shore marine species.

There are few extant remains of Portus Illicitanus, the Port of Illice (today's Elche) and the Roman precursor of Santa Pola. The most significant are those of the **Casa**

Romana del Palmeral in the Parque El Palmeral, just behind (south of) the tourist office. Once a resplendent villa, within its low walls are some fine polychrome abstract mosaics, clumsily restored with thick wedges of mortar.

If you're around as the sun goes down and have wheels, take the brief trip out of town to Torre Tamarit, once a watchtower and now a crumbling hunk of masonry. From here, the sunset over the salt pans, especially in winter, can be so spectacular that it's been known to draw spontaneous applause.

Activities
Windsurfing and Canoeing From mid-June to mid-September, both **Ocio Náutico**, on Playa de Levante, and **Windsurf Santa Pola**, on Gran Playa (☎ for both 68 959 60 67, W www.ociomas.com) hire windsurf boards (€21 per hour) and also offer classes (15 hours from €110). Canoe rental costs €5 for a single and €9 for a double.

Diving Opposite the post office, **Diving Center Mares** (☎ 96 669 29 86, Pasaje de Granada 5, W www.natural.es/scubaelx) offers, among several learning patterns, a 10-hour open water PADI course (€290) between June and September. Dives, available year round, cost €14.50 (€31.25 with full equipment hire).

Sailing The **Club Náutico** (☎ 96 541 24 03) on the west side of the marina, runs a sailing school. Courses of 20 hours for both beginners and more advanced sailors cost between €150 and €180. If you fancy something more physically taxing, it also offers lessons in rowing (five hours from €30).

Special Events
On 16 July, Santa Pola pays homage with processions and fireworks to the Virgen del Carmen, patron of fisherfolk. Throughout the first week of September, the Virgen de Loreto, patron of the town, is celebrated with a bang since her festival coincides with the town's Moros y Cristianos celebrations. It's a time for yet more processions, even more splendid fireworks and a spectacular

re-enactment of the landing of the Muslim invaders, who every year come off worse.

Places to Stay

Camping *Camping Bahía de Santa Pola (☎ 96 541 10 12, fax 96 541 67 90)* €3.55 each person/tent/car. Open year round. This camp site, on the outskirts of town just off the N-332, provides free showers and has a bar-restaurant, pool and shop.

Hotels *Hostal-Restaurante Michel (☎ 96 541 18 42, fax 96 541 19 42, Calle Felipe II 11)* Singles/doubles with bathroom & air-con €27/33 including breakfast, rooms €39.25 in summer. The rooms here are pleasant and the downstairs restaurant, recently refurbished, does a good menú at €8.75.

Hostal-Restaurante Picola (☎ 96 541 18 68, fax 96 541 10 44, Calle Alicante 64) Singles/doubles with bathroom & ceiling fan €27/33, €30/36 in summer. Just around the corner from Hostal-Restaurante Michel, this is an equally attractive budget option.

Hotel Polamar (☎ 96 541 32 00, fax 96 541 31 83, e info@polamar.com) Singles/doubles/triples/quads with breakfast €39.10/63.15/92/108.25, €54.10/81.20/110.60/126.25 July & Aug. Ask for a room with sea views at this pleasant three-star hotel, right on the beachfront.

Hotel Marina Palace (☎ 96 541 13 12, fax 96 541 16 02, w www.hotelmarinapalace.com, Carretera Alicante-Cartagena km 17) Singles €45.90-61.40, doubles €83.35-102.75 according to season. This top-end hotel offers a gym, pool, tennis court and all the usual comforts.

Places to Eat

Venta Vista Alegre (☎ 96 541 10 02, Carretera Alicante-Cartagena km 89) Mains €6.50-11. Pretty it ain't, with its kitsch flamingo-coloured curtains and pastel walls, but you'll eat heartily at this noisy, bustling roadside hostelry. Try the fish mixed grill (€10.85).

Getting There & Away

Buses stop 30m north-west of Plaza de la Diputación. Buy tickets in advance from Avantours travel agency in the square. Buses of Autocares Baile (☎ 96 592 53 65) serve Alicante hourly (every half hour in July and August). Costa Azul (☎ 96 592 46 60) runs northwards to Alicante and southwards to Torrevieja via Guardamar eight times daily. Enatcar has eight buses daily to and from Madrid (€22).

For details on boats to and from Isla de Tabarca, see Around Santa Pola.

Getting Around

Solo Motos (paradoxically meaning Only Motorbikes; ☎ 96 541 42 81), Calle Castaños 17, rents bicycles at €12/32.50/63 per day/three days/week and 50cc scooters for €30 per day.

For a taxi, call ☎ 96 541 35 36.

AROUND SANTA POLA
Isla de Tabarca

A mere 7km from Santa Pola and 17km south of Alicante, Tabarca, 1800m long and 400m across at its widest point, is the only permanently inhabited island in the Comunidad Valenciana.

Tabarca's history is rather more interesting than its present. In the 1760s, the entire population of Tabarka, an island off the coast of present-day Tunisia belonging to Genoa, was captured and imprisoned by the Arabs. Carlos III, king of Spain, negotiated the people of Tabarkas release and granted them this small island off the Alicantino coast. So it was that a colony of Genoese fisherfolk and their families, some 600 souls in all, established themselves on what was originally called Nueva Tabarca (New Tabarca), a name which stuck and quickly supplanted the original name of San Pablo.

Nowadays, day visitors by the thousand invading from coastal resorts, seriously outnumber the handful of permanent inhabitants, among whom you'll still find a few who bear Italian family names.

You go to Tabarca as much to enjoy the short sea journey and the surrounding waters as for the island's limited pleasures. On approaching it, the glass-bottomed boat lingers above huge beds of shaggy seaweed abounding in fish. If this isn't enough for

COSTA BLANCA

you, you can take the plunge in a yellow submarine that nudges out from Tabarca's harbour for short trips (€6). Or else just pack your snorkel and mask and explore the permitted offshore areas of the first of Spain's marine reserves, declared in 1986.

It can make a good day out: the journey, a little swimming and snorkelling, a laze by the water (head towards the lighthouse to seek out your own personal rock and escape the crowded beach) and lunching on something fishy in one of the several restaurants between port and pueblo.

The village itself, mainly squat two-storey structures, many neglected and unoccupied, is quickly explored. Its soft sandstone church has been hideously plastered over in unfaced concrete. And, quite inexcusably, scrap iron and sundry junk litters too much of the rest of the island.

At the end of the day, Tabarca's greatest pleasure, granted only to the very few, is having the island almost to yourself once the hordes have retreated.

Hotel Casa del Gobernador (☎ *96 596 08 86, fax 96 596 12 72,* W *www.casadel gobernador.com, Calle Arzola 2)* Singles/ doubles with bathroom & air-con €42/55, €52/64.75 June-Sept. The old Governor's Residence – a grand term for such a Spartan building – has been restored and converted into a pleasant, welcoming hotel.

Hostal Masín (☎ *96 596 05 09, Carrer d'en Mig 22)* Doubles with breakfast & air-con €58.50, €67.75 June-Sept. This significantly overpriced Hostal is the only other accommodation option on the island. Consider it only if the last ferry's steamed out and the Casa del Gobernador is full.

Boats (adult/child return €9.65/6.60) pull out from Santa Pola more or less every half hour on a voyage lasting 20 to 30 minutes. Tabarca is also accessible from Alicante and Torrevieja (for details, see the relevant Getting There & Away sections).

GUARDAMAR DEL SEGURA

Guardamar, 37km south of Alicante, sits at the mouth of the Río Segura. Its recent history is one of misfortune. Originally perched on a hillock, the town was all but flattened by an earthquake in 1829. Then, once the population had decamped to the plain between hill and shore, their houses were all but buried on more than one occasion by the unpredictable, shifting sand dunes blown grain by grain towards them by stiff offshore winds.

The town itself is a rather scruffy, soulless sort of place. What brings holidaymakers here in increasing numbers is the 14km of relatively underdeveloped beach that stretches north and south. They also come for the splendour of those very dunes – now tamed by magnificent pine groves and sturdy agave cactus that the villagers planted so that their roots would spread and help to pin down the wayward monster blown in from the sea.

Guardamar's tourist office (☎ 96 572 72 92) is at Plaza de la Constitución 7, just off the main Calle Mayor. In summer, it opens 10am to 2pm and 6pm to 9pm Monday to Saturday and 10am to 1.30pm on Sunday, observing shorter hours during the rest of the year.

After the 1829 earthquake, the **castle** on the hillock was shattered almost to its foundations. All the same, it's worth the brief ascent to the much restored ramparts and solitary cannon at their southern end for an overview of the town, dunes and coastline.

The vast dunes hug the town on the seaward side. Park is a misnomer for these wild, relatively unstructured areas. Penetrate the Parque Reina Sofía in the heart of the small town and, especially, the Parque Alfonso XIII, which stretches northwards. Crisscrossed by tracks and lanes and shaded by pines, this area is great for jogging, walking or biking.

Right beside those dunes – appropriately enough – is Drometour (☎ 629 68 39 36), an outfit that offers half-hour camel rides (€5/3.75 per adult/child). You'll find it beside the new marina at the mouth of Río Segura. Alternatively, follow signs from the roundabout at the northern entry to town.

The seasons in Guardamar are punctuated by its fiestas: the Holy Week processions; the Hogueras, celebrating with fire the simultaneous feast of San Juan (St John) and the summer solstice; and, most exuberant of all, the town's spectacular, even by exacting local standards, Moros y Cristianos, an explosive week of gunpowder and lavish processions in the second half of July.

Camping Marjal (☎ 96 672 70 70, Carretera Alicante-Cartagena km 76) 2 people, tent & car €18/21/27 low/medium/high season. Camping Marjal doesn't come cheap but this much garlanded camp site is well worth your euros if you want a degree of comfort above the average tent village. It's open year round.

·TORREVIEJA
postcode 03180 • pop 50,200
Torrevieja, 47km south of Alicante, is a heavily developed resort which attracts a high proportion of northern European visitors. It still manages to retain just a twinkle or two of its former charm – such as the elegant casino just west of the tourist office

– and has good beaches, a pleasant harbourside promenade, some reasonable restaurants and a decent nightlife.

Unlike most Spanish towns, even the oldest, early-19th-century part follows a strict grid pattern. This is because Torrevieja, like so many former mining villages in Britain, was once a company town. When in 1802 the Salinas (salt lagoons) company moved in, it set the pattern for Torrevieja. And salt, while it can no longer rival tourism as a revenue earner, still remains important; over half a million tonnes are exported annually.

Orientation
Torrevieja, bounded by the Circunvalación ring road, runs parallel to the coast from the northern suburbs of La Mata to Rocío del Mar in the south. West of the ring road stretch the extensive salt lakes of the Parque Natural de las Lagunas de la Mata y Torrevieja.

From the south, enter by the old N-332, which runs to the heart of town. From the

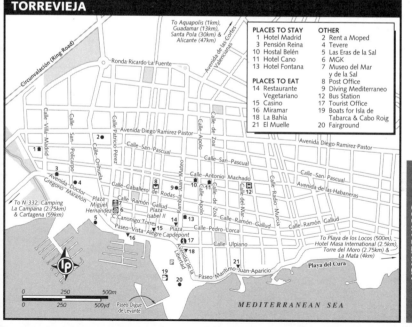

TORREVIEJA

PLACES TO STAY	OTHER
1 Hotel Madrid	2 Rent a Moped
3 Pensión Reina	4 Tevere
10 Hostal Belén	5 Las Eras de la Sal
11 Hotel Cano	6 MGK
13 Hotel Fontana	7 Museo del Mar y de la Sal
PLACES TO EAT	8 Post Office
14 Restaurante Vegetariano	9 Diving Mediterraneo
15 Casino	12 Bus Station
16 Miramar	17 Tourist Office
18 La Bahía	19 Boats for Isla de Tabarca & Cabo Roig
21 El Muelle	20 Fairground

MEDITERRANEAN SEA

COSTA BLANCA

north, peel off the ring road at the exit after La Mata to take Avenida de las Cortes Valencianas, passing by one of the Comunidad's ugliest monuments – a tall phallic monster, candy-striped with the red and yellow of the Valencian flag.

From the bus station walk westwards along Calle Antonio Machado then cut down any of the intersecting streets to reach the port and tourist office.

Best of the beaches are **Playa de la Mata**, longest and particularly popular with Scandinavian visitors, **Playa de los Locos**, literally, 'Beach of the Crazies', and **Playa del Cura**, the equally enigmatically named 'Beach of the Vicar'.

Information
Tourist Offices The tourist office (☎ 96 570 34 33) is on the waterfront at Plaza Capdepont. It opens 9am to 1.30pm and 4.30pm to 7pm weekdays & 10am to noon Saturday, October to mid-June. Between mid-June and September it opens continuously 9am to 8pm, Monday to Saturday.

Ask for a copy of *Hello Torrevieja*, a bilingual, bimonthly publication listing what's on around town. Free from the tourist office and major hotels, it will set you back €2.50 at a newsagencies. Another free-listings publication in English is the *Torrevieja Monthly*, which appears – you guessed it – every month.

Post The post office is on Calle Caballero de Rodas.

Email & Internet Access MGK, Plaza Miguel Hernandez 2, open 10am to 2pm and 6pm to 9pm, Monday to Saturday, charges a bargain €1.80 per hour, with a minimum fee of €1.

Things to See
The **Museo del Mar y de la Sal** *(Museum of the Sea and Salt; ☎/fax 96 670 68 38, Calle Patricio Pérez 10; admission free; open 10am-1.30pm & 5pm-9pm Tues-Sat, 10am-1.30pm Sun)* is a hotchpotch of ships in glass cases, naval bric-a-brac, some interesting photos and – this a local speciality

– models of Torrevieja's Casino, a windjammer, the parish church, even a crane, all made from encrusted salt. As for the salt in the museum's title, you'll learn much more by visiting the Museo de la Sal in Santa Pola (see Santa Pola earlier for details). Also, by briefly visiting **Las Eras de la Sal** *(admission free; open 11am-2pm & 7.30pm-11pm daily)*, the reconstructed Torrevieja warehouse and wharf where, from 1777 to 1958, salt from the pans was loaded aboard sailing ships bound for Cuba and other transatlantic destinations.

For a drink in exquisite surroundings or merely a snoop around, you shouldn't leave Torrevieja without visiting its recently renovated **Casino**. Constructed in 1896, it's a gloriously over-the-top, fin de siecle creation, rich in Art Nouveau and a model for similarly inspired excess in nearby Orihuela and Murcia. Don't miss the gorgeous pastiche of its Arabian room.

Activities
Diving Mediterraneo *(☎ 96 570 43 09, e torreviejasub@terra.es, Rambla Juan Mateo 37)*, a diving school with an international flavour, hires equipment, organises

JANE SMITH

Habaneras

The Habaneras song crossed the Atlantic on the ships that ran the line, only to return to the Mediterranean, borne by the trade winds and winds of trade.

Torrevieja is the town of the Habanera, a genre of 2:4 time song, performed individually or chorally. But why, you may ask, should this Valencian resort town be the Spanish capital of a musical form named after the Cuban capital, La Habana (Havana)?

The Habanera's journey was a long, bidirectional one. Emigrants from Spain to the New World and Cuba (the latter, predominantly from the Canary Islands, that volcanic string off the coast of Africa) took with them the popular music of their homeland, in particular the *contradanza*. Cuba's rich, distinctive folk music owes its origins to the melodies sung by these early settlers, often blended with African rhythms and forms, brought across the ocean by slaves destined for the Caribbean.

In the mid-19th century, Torrevieja had the largest sailing fleet on Spain's Mediterranean coast. Trade was good and lucrative and Cuba was the most popular destination. Tiles and salt by the tonne were shipped out, while vessels returned laden with sugar and exotic woods. The journey was long and often tedious and sailors would sing and strum on the guitar melodies they'd picked up in ports.

Habaneras are songs of the sea but also of the hearth. Back home, the melodies passed to sailors' wives, who sang them as lullabies and cradle songs. The words tell of longing, absence and separation, of girls, friends, wives and homeland left behind, and of unrequited love.

Torrevieja, as it established its own traditions and identity, took the Habanera and made it its own. The original melodies were arranged and adapted for choral singing and in 1955 the first Habanera choral festival and competition was held. Nowadays, choirs from four continents attend the weeklong festival, held in late July or August and televised throughout the Spanish-speaking world. It takes place in the small theatre at Eras de la Sal – right beside the jetty where the ships that first bore the Habanera would moor.

dives and also does courses in English. **Tevere** (☎ *96 571 65 55, Calle San Policarpo 8)* offers similar services although for the moment cannot offer instruction in English. Based a little out of town but operating from Torrevieja is **Scubatribe** (☎ *96 671 99 36, 62 960 81 02,* **e** *scubatribe@ ctv.es,* **w** *www.scubatribe.freeservers.com)* who have English-native-speaker instructors available.

For more frivolous water fun, visit **Aquapolis** (☎ *96 571 58 90; adult/child €12/8; open 11am-7pm daily June-Sept).* A free bus service to this water park operates from the bus station.

Between June and September **Marítimas Torrevieja** (☎ *96 670 21 22)* sail to the Isla de Tabarca (see Around Santa Pola earlier in this chapter) twice daily. The return fare costs €15.65/11.50 per adult/child. They also do a daily run (adult/child €9.65/6 return), leaving at 11.30am, to Cabo Roig, a promontory south of town that makes a pleasant picnic spot. Alternatively, take their half-hour evening cruise along the coast (€5/3 adult/child).

Once the beach work for the day is over, catch the evening breeze with a stroll along the **Paseo Dique de Levante**, a recently inaugurated 1.5km walkway and jetty that cradles the harbour in its scrawny arm.

A more challenging walk takes you northwards beyond Playa de los Locos and beside a more rugged, less-developed stretch of coastline as far as Torre del Moro, the tower after which Torrevieja (Old Tower) is named. It's rather an insignificant affair but the view from its base is worthwhile.

Less energetically, fritter away a few euros at Torrevieja's **fairground**, which warms up as the day cools and evening approaches.

Special Events

Like many maritime communities, Torrevieja honours the Virgen del Carmen, patron of fisherfolk and sailors, on her special day, 16

July, with festivities on land and sea. For a week in late July or August, the Certamen Internacional de Habaneras y Polifonía draws local and international choirs (see the boxed text 'Habaneras'). The first half of December is devoted to events in honour of La Purísima Concepción, the Most Pure of Conceptions (OK, so it loses something in translation!), one of the many names of the Virgin Mary, patron of the town. The big day, with processions and general festivities, is 8 December.

Places to Stay

Camping *Camping La Campana (☎ 96 571 21 52, Carretera Torrevieja-Cartagena km 4.5)* €8.50 per site & €3 per person. Open Apr-Sept. This, Torrevieja's nearest camping ground, is 4.5km south of town on the N-332.

Hotels *Pensión Reina (☎ 96 670 19 04, Avenida Doctor Gregorio Marañón 22)* Singles/doubles/triples with minuscule bathroom €16.75/24/35, €15/28.75/38 July & Aug. Rooms are rather shabby at this friendly enough place, as cheap as you'll find anywhere in Torrevieja.

Hostal Belén (☎ 96 570 56 85, Calle Apolo 45) Singles/doubles €14.75/24.60 in low season, €18/30 in high season. Spruce and central, this place represents excellent value. It has private off-road parking (€6 per night) and rooms have bathroom, TV, air-con and heating.

Hotel Cano (☎ 96 670 09 58, Calle de Zoa 53) Singles/doubles with bathroom €27/36, €33/48 July–mid-Sept. One block east of Hostal Belén, the Cano has comfortable, modern rooms with TV and air-con.

There are some more upmarket hotels on offer as well.

Hotel Madrid (☎ 96 571 00 38, fax 96 670 12 12, e hmadrid@eresmas.com, Calle Villa Madrid 15) Singles/doubles €45/60, €54/78.25 July & Aug, including breakfast. This place has comfortable rooms with all facilities.

Hotel Masa International (☎ 96 692 15 37, fax 96 692 21 72, e hotel-masa@arrakis .es, Avenida Alfredo Nobel) Singles €38.60-64.50, doubles €58-83.75 according to season. This clifftop hotel, first of the expanding Masa chain to be established, is remote from all downtown frenzy. It has its own pool, sauna and off-road parking.

Hotel Fontana (☎ 96 670 11 25, fax 96 571 44 50, e fontana@visual.es, Rambla Juan Mateo 19) Singles €46.75/64.50, doubles €67.75/103 according to season. Complete with pool, pub and restaurant, the Fontana is a tour-group favourite.

Places to Eat

Plenty of restaurants clustered around the waterfront offer cheap meals and international menus. For something more local, head for the south side of the old market and the small Plaza Isabel II, known informally to locals as 'La Calle de La Hambre' (Hunger Alley). Here, you can enjoy great grilled fresh fish, sitting out on one of the restaurant terraces.

Restaurante Vegetariano (☎ 96 670 66 83, Calle Pedro Lorca 13) Sandwiches €3-4.25, salads €3.60-7.25, mains €5.50-7.50. Open Tues-Sun. You don't patronise this little vegetarian haven, run by a Spanish-Australian couple (the didgeridoo above the bar's a good clue), because it's the only meat-free joint in town. You go because the food's great by any canon of taste and the folk are friendliness itself. You'll need to reserve in advance at weekends.

El Muelle (☎ 96 670 41 72, Paseo Marítimo Juan Aparicio, junction with Calle del Mar) Pizzas €7.20-10.20, mains €9-13.20. Open daily, year round, this highly regarded place is right on the prom with the Mediterranean before you.

La Bahía (☎ 96 571 39 94, Avenida de la Libertad 3) Mains €9.75-13.85. Open Tues-Sun. Finish off with one of their scrummy desserts (€2.40-3.90), confected on the spot, at this stylish, split-level place.

Miramar (☎ 96 571 34 15, Paseo Vista Alegre s/n) Mains €10-15. Open daily Dec-Oct, Wed-Mon Dec-June. Try one of their inventive rice and seafood dishes such as *arroz con rodaballo y bonito* (rice with turbot and tunny fish; €11.25).

Torrevieja also abounds in cafes serving coffee that ranges from bilge-water to a very tasty sip indeed.

Getting There & Away

The bus station (☎ 96 571 01 46) is on Calle Antonio Machado. There are up to six buses daily to Madrid (€23.25) via Albacete (€10.75) and Villena (€5).

Autocares Costa Azul runs eight buses daily to both Cartagena (€3.10, 45 minutes) and Alicante (€2.75, 50 minutes).

Getting Around

Line A runs between Torrevieja and La Mata every 30 minutes (every 15 minutes in July and August).

We advise you to dump your car in the huge open-air car park beside the fairground. Torrevieja is no place for newcomers to drive around and maintain their equanimity.

For a taxi, you can call ☎ 96 571 22 77 or ☎ 96 571 10 26.

Rent a Moped (☎ 67 037 61 36), at Calle San Pascual 74, hires out cycles for €9/18/36 per day/three days/week and require a €30 refundable deposit. They also rent 50cc scooters for €12/36/72 and larger models for €18/54/108.

Language

The following guide provides a list of useful words and phrases in the two official languages of Valencia: Castilian Spanish and Valenciano. For cultural information on the languages of the region, see the Language section in the Facts about Valencia chapter. For a more detailed guide to Castilian Spanish, get a copy of Lonely Planet's *Spanish phrasebook*.

Castilian Spanish

Spanish nouns and adjectives are marked for gender. Where two optional endings (for example, *diabetico/a*) are given in the following words and phrases, the first is for a male speaker, the second for a female speaker.

Pronunciation

Vowels Unlike English, each of the vowels has a uniform pronunciation that doesn't vary. For example, the letter 'a' has one pronunciation rather than the numerous ones we find in English, such as in 'cake', 'care', 'cat', 'cart' and 'call'. Many words have a written accent. This acute accent (as in *días*) indicates a stressed syllable; it does not change the sound of the vowel. Vowels are pronounced clearly even if they are in unstressed positions or at the end of a word.

a   somewhere between the 'a' in 'cat' and the 'a' in 'cart'
e   as in 'met'
i   somewhere between the 'i' in 'marine' and the 'i' in 'flip'
o   similar to the 'o' in 'hot'
u   as in 'put'

Consonants Some consonants have the same pronunciation as their English counterparts. The pronunciation of others varies according to which vowel follows. The Spanish alphabet also contains the letter ñ, which is not found in the English alphabet. Until recently, the clusters **ch** and **ll** were also officially separate consonants, and you're likely to encounter many situations – for example, in lists and dictionaries – in which they are still treated that way.

b   soft, as the 'v' in 'van'; also (less commonly) as in 'book' when word-initial or when preceded by a nasal such as 'm' or 'n'
c   as the 'th' in 'thin'
ch as in 'choose'
d   sometimes not pronounced at all
g   as in 'go' when initial or before 'a', 'o' or 'u'; elsewhere much softer. Before 'e' or 'i' it's a harsh, breathy sound, a bit like 'ch' in Scottish *loch.*
h   always silent
j   a harsh, guttural sound similar to the 'ch' in Scottish *loch*
ll similar to the 'y' in 'yellow'
ñ   a nasal sound like the 'ni' in 'onion' or the 'ny' in 'canyon'
q   always followed by a silent 'u' and either 'e' (as in *que*) and 'i' (as in *aquí*); the combined sound of 'qu' is like the 'k' in 'kick'
r   a rolled 'r' sound; longer and stronger when initial or doubled
s   often not pronounced, especially at the end of a word; thus *pescados* (fish) is pronounced 'peh-cow' in Andalucía
v   same as 'b'
x   as the 'x' in 'taxi' when between two vowels; as the 's' in 'say' before a consonant
z   as the 'th' in 'thin'

Greetings & Civilities

Hello.	*¡Hola!*
Goodbye.	*¡Adiós!*
Yes.	*Sí.*
No.	*No.*
Please.	*Por favor.*
Thank you.	*Gracias.*
You're welcome.	*De nada.*
Excuse me.	*Perdón/Perdone.*
Sorry/Excuse me.	*Lo siento/Discúlpeme.*

Useful Phrases

Do you speak English?	*¿Habla inglés?*
Does anyone here speak English?	*¿Hay alguien que hable inglés?*
I (don't) understand.	*(No) Entiendo.*
Just a minute.	*Un momento.*
Could you write it down, please?	*¿Puede escribirlo, por favor?*
How much is it?	*¿Cuánto cuesta/vale?*

Getting Around

What time does the ... leave/arrive?	*¿A qué hora sale/ llega el ...?*
boat	*barco*
bus (city)	*autobús/bus*
bus (intercity)	*autocar*
train	*tren*
metro/ underground	*metro*

next	*próximo*
first	*primer*
last	*último*
1st class	*primera clase*
2nd class	*segunda clase*

I'd like a ... ticket.	*Quisiera un billete ...*
one-way	*sencillo*
return	*de ida y vuelta*

Where is the bus stop?	*¿Dónde está la parada de autobús?*
I want to go to ...	*Quiero ir a ...*
Can you show me (on the map)?	*¿Me puede indicar (en el mapa)?*
Go straight ahead.	*Siga/Vaya todo recto/ derecho.*
Turn left.	*Gire a la izquierda.*
Turn right.	*Gire a la derecha.*
near	*cerca*
far	*lejos*

Around Town

I'm looking for ...	*Estoy buscando ...*
a bank	*un banco*
the city centre	*el centro de la ciudad*
the embassy	*la embajada*
my hotel	*mi hotel*
the market	*el mercado*

Signs – Castilian Spanish

Entrada	**Entrance**
Salida	**Exit**
Abierto	**Open**
Cerrado	**Closed**
Información	**Information**
Prohibido	**Prohibited**
Habitaciones Libres	**Rooms Available**
Ocupado/Completo	**No Vacancies**
Comisaría	**Police Station**
Servicios/Aseos	**Toilets**
Hombres	**Men**
Mujeres	**Women**

the police	*la policía*
the post office	*correos*
toilets	*los aseos/servicios*
a telephone	*un teléfono*
the tourist office	*la oficina de turismo*

the beach	*la playa*
the bridge	*el puente*
the castle	*el castillo*
the cathedral	*la catedral*
the church	*la iglesia*
the hospital	*el hospital*
the lake	*el lago*
the main square	*la plaza mayor*
the old city	*la ciudad antigua*
the palace	*el palacio*
the ruins	*las ruinas*
the sea	*el mar*
the square	*la plaza*
the tower	*el torre*

Accommodation

Where is a cheap hotel?	*¿Dónde hay un hotel barato?*
What's the address?	*¿Cuál es la dirección?*
Could you write it down, please?	*¿Puede escribirla, por favor?*
Do you have any rooms available?	*¿Tiene habitaciones libres?*

I'd like ...	*Quisiera ...*
a bed	*una cama*
a single room	*una habitación individual*
a double room	*una habitación doble*

a room with	*una habitación*
a bathroom	*con baño*
to share a dorm	*compartir un dormitorio*

How much is it ...?	*¿Cuánto cuesta ...?*
per night	*por noche*
per person	*por persona*

| Can I see it? | *¿Puedo verla?* |
| Where is the bathroom? | *¿Dónde está el baño?* |

Food

breakfast	*desayuno*
lunch	*almuerzo/comida*
dinner	*cena*

I'd like the set lunch.	*Quisiera el menú del día.*
Is service included?	*¿El servicio está incluido?*
I'm a vegetarian.	*Soy vegetariano/ vegetariana.*

Time & Dates

What time is it?	*¿Qué hora es?*
today	*hoy*
tomorrow	*mañana*
yesterday	*ayer*
in the morning	*de la mañana*
in the afternoon	*de la tarde*
in the evening	*de la noche*

Monday	*lunes*
Tuesday	*martes*
Wednesday	*miércoles*
Thursday	*jueves*
Friday	*viernes*
Saturday	*sábado*
Sunday	*domingo*

January	*enero*
February	*febrero*
March	*marzo*
April	*abril*
May	*mayo*
June	*junio*
July	*julio*
August	*agosto*
September	*setiembre/septiembre*

Emergencies – Castilian Spanish

Help!	*¡Socorro!/¡Auxilio!*
Call a doctor!	*¡Llame a un doctor!*
Call the police!	*¡Llame a la policía!*
Where are the toilets?	*¿Dónde están los servicios?*
Go away!	*¡Váyase!*
I'm lost.	*Estoy perdido/a.*

October	*octubre*
November	*noviembre*
December	*diciembre*

Health

I'm ...	*Soy...*
diabetic	*diabético/a*
epileptic	*epiléptico/a*
asthmatic	*asmático/a*

I'm allergic to ...	*Soy alérgico/a a ...*
antibiotics	*los antibióticos*
nuts	*las nueces*
penicillin	*la penicilina*

antiseptic	*antiséptico*
aspirin	*aspirina*
condoms	*preservativos/ condones*
contraceptive	*anticonceptivo*
diarrhoea	*diarrea*
medicine	*medicamento*
nausea	*náusea*
sunblock cream	*crema protectora contra el sol*
tampons	*tampones*

Numbers

0	*cero*
1	*uno, una*
2	*dos*
3	*tres*
4	*cuatro*
5	*cinco*
6	*seis*
7	*siete*
8	*ocho*
9	*nueve*
10	*diez*
11	*once*
12	*doce*

13	*trece*
14	*catorce*
15	*quince*
16	*dieciséis*
17	*diecisiete*
18	*dieciocho*
19	*diecinueve*
20	*veinte*
21	*veintiuno*
22	*veintidós*
23	*veintitrés*
30	*treinta*
31	*treinta y uno*
40	*cuarenta*
50	*cincuenta*
60	*sesenta*
70	*setenta*
80	*ochenta*
90	*noventa*
100	*cien/ciento*
1000	*mil*

one million   *un millón*

Valenciano

Pronunciation
The sounds of Valenciano are not hard for an English-speaker to pronounce. You should, however, note that vowels will vary according to whether they occur in stressed or unstressed syllables.

Vowels
a	when stressed, as the 'a' in 'father'; when unstressed, as in 'about'
e	when stressed, as in 'pet'; when unstressed, as the 'e' in 'open'
i	as the 'i' in 'machine'
o	when stressed, as in 'pot'; when unstressed, as the 'oo' in 'zoo'
u	as the 'u' in 'humid'

Consonants
c	hard before 'a', 'o', and 'u'; soft before 'e' and 'i'
ç	like 'ss'
d	pronounced 't' at the end of a word
g	hard before 'a', 'o' and 'u'; as the 's' in 'measure' before 'e' and 'i'
h	silent
j	hard before 'a', 'o', and 'u'; as the 's' in 'pleasure' before 'e' and 'i'
r	approximately as in English; also pronounced at the end of a word
rr	rolled at the beginning of a word, or 'rr' in the middle of a word
s	as in 'so' at the beginning of a word; as 'z' in the middle of a word
x	as the 'ch' in 'church'; sometimes as 'sh'

Other letters are pronounced as per their English counterparts. There are a few odd combinations:

l.l	repeat the 'l'
tx	like 'ch'
qu	like 'k'

Greetings & Civilities
Hello!	*Hola!*
Goodbye.	*Adéu!*
Yes.	*Sí.*
No.	*No.*
Please.	*Per favor/Si us plau.*
Thank you (very much).	*(Moltes) gràcies.*
You're welcome.	*De res.*
Excuse me.	*Perdoni/Perdone.*
May I?/Do you mind?	*Puc?/Em permet?/ Amb Permís?*
Sorry. (forgive me)	*Ho sent/Perdoni/ Perdone.*
What's your name?	*Com et dius?* (inf) *Com es diu?* (pol)
My name's ...	*Em dic ...*
Where are you from?	*D'on eres?*

Language Difficulties
Do you speak English?	*Parla anglès?*
Could you speak in Castilian, please?	*Pot parlar castellà per favor?*
I (don't) understand.	*(No) ho entenc.*
Could you repeat that?	*Pot repetir-ho?*
Could you please write that down?	*Pot escriure-ho, sisplau?*
How do you say ... Valenciano?	*Com es diu ... en Valencìa?*

LANGUAGE

Getting Around

What time does the ... leave?	*A quina hora ix ...?*
boat	*el barco/el vaixell*
bus	*autobús*
flight	*el vol*
train	*el tren*

I'd like a ... ticket.	*Voldria un bitllet ...*
one-way	*d'anada*
return	*d'anar i tornar*

Where is (the) ...?	*On és ...?*
bus station	*l'estació d'autobusos*
city centre	*el centre de la ciutat*
train station	*l'estació de tren*
tourist office	*l'oficina de turisme*
metro/ underground	*la parada de metro*

How do I get to ...?	*Com puc arribar a ...?*
I want to go to ...	*Vull anar a ...*
Please tell me when we get to ...?	*Pot avisar-me quan arribem a ...?*

baggage claim	*recollida d'equipatges*
departures	*eixides*
exchange	*canvi*
platform	*andana*

Around Town

I'm looking for ...	*Estic buscant ...*
a bank	*un banc*
the city centre	*el centre de la ciutat*
the police	*la policia*
the post office	*correus*
a toilet	*els serveis/services*
a restaurant	*un restaurant*
the telephone centre	*la central telefònica*
the tourist office	*l'oficina de turisme*

the beach	*la platja*
the bridge	*el pont*
the castle	*el castell*
the cathedral	*la catedral*
the church	*l'església*
the hospital	*el hospital*
the lake	*el llac/l'estany*
the old city	*el barri antic*

Signs – Valenciano

Entrada	**Entrance**
Eixada	**Exit**
Obert	**Open**
Tancat	**Closed**
Informació	**Information**
Comissaria	**Police Station**
Serveis/Services	**Toilets**

the palace	*el palau*
the ruins	*les ruïnes*
the sea	*la mar*
the square	*la plaça*
the tower	*la torre*

What time does it open/close?	*A quina hora obrin/tanquen?*

I want to change ...	*Voldria canviar ...*
some money	*diners*
travellers cheques	*xecs de viatge*

Accommodation

Is there a campsite/ hotel near here?	*Hi ha algun càmping/ hotel a prop d'açí?*
Do you have any rooms available?	*Hi han habitacions lliures?*

I'd like ...	*Voldria ...*
a single room	*una habitació individual*
a double room	*una habitació doble*
to share a dorm	*compartir un dormitori*

I want a room with a ...	*Vull una habitació amb ...*
bathroom	*cambra de bany*
double bed	*llit de matrimoni*
shower	*dutxa*

How much is it per night/person?	*Quant val per nit/persona?*
Does it include breakfast?	*Inclou el desdejuni?*
Are there any cheaper rooms?	*Hi ha habitacions més barates?*
I'm going to stay	*Em quedaré*

for (one week).	*(una setmana).*
I'm leaving now.	*Me'n vaigara.*

Food

breakfast	*desdejuni*
lunch	*dinar*
dinner	*sopar*
Can I see the menu, please?	*Puc veure el menú, per favor?*
I'd like the set lunch, please.	*Voldria el menú del dia, sisplau.*
The bill, please.	*El compte, sisplau.*
dessert	*postres*
a drink	*una beguda*
Bon appétit/Cheers!	*Salut/Bon profit!*

Drinks

tiger nut drink	*orxata*
fruit juice	*suc*
mineral water (plain, no gas)	*aigua mineral (sense gas)*
tap water	*aigua de l'aixeta*
soft drinks	*refrescos*
coffee ...	*cafè ...*
with liquer	*carajillo*
with a little milk	*tallat*
with milk	*amb llet*
black coffee	*cafè sol*
long black	*doble*
iced coffee	*cafè gelat*
decaffeinated coffee	*cafè descafeinat*
tea	*te*
a beer	*una cervesa*
a champagne	*un cava*
a rum	*un rom*
a whisky	*un whisky*
muscatel	*moscatell*
a glass of ... wine	*un got de vi ...*
red	*negre*
rosé	*rosat*
sparkling	*d'agulla*
white	*blanc*

Shopping

Where can I buy ...?	*On puc comprar ...?*
Where is the	*On és ... més proper/*
nearest ...?	*propera?*
bakery	*el forn*
bookshop	*la llibreria*
camera shop	*la botiga de fotos*
department store	*el gran magatzem*
greengrocer	*la botiga de verdures (or fruiteria)*
launderette	*la llavanderia*
market	*el mercat*
newsagency	*el quiosc*
pharmacy	*la farmàcia*
supermarket	*el supermercat*
travel agency	*la agència de viatges*
condoms	*gometes higiénics*
deodorant	*desodorant*
razor blades	*fulles d'afaitar*
sanitary napkins	*compreses*
shampoo	*xampú*
shaving cream	*crema d'afaitar*
soap	*sabó*
sunblock cream	*crema solar*
tampons	*tampons*
tissues	*mocadors de paper*
toilet paper	*paper higiènic*
toothbrush	*raspall de dents*
toothpaste	*pasta de dents*
magazines	*revistes*
newspapers	*diaris*
postcards	*postals*
envelope	*sobre*
map	*mapa*
pen (ballpoint)	*bolígraf*
stamp	*segell*

Time, Dates & Numbers

What time is it?	*Quina hora és?*
It's one o'clock.	*És la una.*
It's two o'clock.	*Són les dues.*
It's quarter past six.	*Són les sis i quart.*
It's half past eight.	*Són les vuit i mitja.*
today	*avui*
tomorrow	*demà*
yesterday	*ahir*
in the morning	*al/del matí*
in the afternoon	*a la/de la vespreda*
in the evening	*a/de la nit*
Monday	*dilluns*

LANGUAGE

Tuesday	*dimarts*	5	*cinc*
Wednesday	*dimecres*	6	*sis*
Thursday	*dijous*	7	*sét*
Friday	*divendres*	8	*vuit*
Saturday	*dissabte*	9	*nou*
Sunday	*diumenge*	10	*deu*
		11	*onze*
January	*gener*	12	*dotze*
February	*febrer*	13	*tretze*
March	*març*	14	*catorze*
April	*abril*	15	*quinze*
May	*maig*	16	*setze*
June	*juny*	17	*désset*
July	*juliol*	18	*divuit*
August	*agost*	19	*dinou*
September	*setembre*	20	*vint*
October	*octubre*	30	*trenta*
November	*novembre*	40	*quaranta*
December	*desembre*	50	*cinquanta*
		60	*seixanta*
0	*zero*	70	*setanta*
1	*un, una*	80	*vuitanta*
2	*dos, dues*	90	*noranta*
3	*tres*	100	*cent*
4	*quatre*	1000	*mil*

Glossary

abierto – open
agua de Valencia – Buck's Fizz; cava, fresh orange juice and a dash of vodka
albergue juvenil – youth hostel; not to be confused with *hostal*
all-i-pebre – hunks of eel in a peppery sauce
alpargatas (espardenyes in Valenciano) – traditional Valencian jute sandals
apartado de correos – post office box
artesonado – coffered ceiling, usually *mudéjar* (see below)
ascensor – lift (elevator)
aseos – toilets
autonomía – autonomous community or region: Spain's 50 *provincias* are grouped into 17 of these, one of which is the Comunidad Valenciana
autopista – tolled dual-lane highway
autovía – toll-free dual-lane highway
ayuntamiento – city or town council or hall
azahar – orange blossom

bacalao – codfish; a type of Spanish techno music, often spelt *bakalao*
barranco – dry river bed
barrio – district, quarter of town or city
biblioteca – library
bici – bicycle
bici de montaña/todo terreno (BTT) – mountain bike
bocadillo – French-bread sandwich
bodega – literally, a cellar (especially a wine cellar); also means a winery, or a traditional wine bar likely to serve wine from the barrel
bollo – bread roll
boquerones – fresh anchovies
buceo – scuba diving
butaca – airline-type seat
buzón – letter box

cabo – cape (headland or promontory)
cajero automático – cash machine, automated teller machine (ATM)
calle – street

cama – bed
cambio – in general, change; also currency exchange
capilla – chapel
capilla mayor – chapel containing the high altar of a church
carta – menu
casa rural – a village or country house or farmstead with rooms to let
casco – literally 'helmet'; often used to refer to the old part of a city as *casco antiguo/histórico/viejo*
castellano – Castilian; a term often used in preference to *español* to describe the national language
castillo – castle
catedral – cathedral
cava – Spanish equivalent of champagne
cena – dinner
centro commercial – shopping centre/ mall
cercanías – local trains serving Valencia, Alicante and nearby towns
cerrado – closed
certificado – registered mail
cervecería – beer bar
chorizo – red sausage
comida – food; lunch
Comunidad Valenciana – the official name of the Valencia region, often used to distinguish it from Valencia City or Valencia province
ciudad – city
claustro – cloister
comedor – dining room
completo – full (eg, of hotel, camp site)
comisaría – National Police station
consigna – left-luggage office or lockers
copa – a drink (literally, a glass); *ir de copas* means to go out for a few drinks
coro – choir (part of a church, usually in the middle)
correos – post office
cortes – parliament, national/regional assembly
costa – coast
cristiano – Christian

cuenta – bill (check)
cueva – cave

desayuno – breakfast
diapositiva – slide film
ducha – shower

entrada – entrance
ermita – chapel
estación de autobuses/ferrocarril – bus/train station
estación marítima – ferry terminal
estanco – tobacconist's shop
este – east

farmacia – chemist's shop (pharmacy)
faro – lighthouse
ferrocarril – railway
fideuá – a paella made with noodles instead of rice
fiesta – festival, public holiday or party
fin de semana – weekend
feria – (trade) fair

GR – Sendero de Gran Recorrido; long-distance trail
gremio – guild or trade association
Guardia Civil – police

hostal – commercial establishment providing accommodation in the one- to three-star category; not to be confused with *albergue juvenil*
hostal-residencia – *hostal* without a restaurant
huerta – market garden, orchard

iglesia – church
IVA – *impuesto sobre el valor añadido* or value-added tax (VAT)

kiosko – kiosk; newspaper stand

lago – lake
largo recorrido – long-distance
lavabo – wash basin
lavandería – laundry
llegada – arrival
librería – bookshop
lista de correos – poste restante
litera – couchette or sleeping carriage

lonja – wholesale market or exchange

madrileño – someone from Madrid
madrugada – the 'early hours', from around 3am to dawn – time for *la marcha* (see below)!
marcha – the action, 'the scene'; also *la movida*
mariscos – shellfish, seafood
marisquería – seafood eatery
menú del día – fixed-price multi-course meal available at lunchtime, sometimes in the evening too; often shortened to *menú*
mercado – market
merienda – afternoon snack
meseta – the high tableland of central Spain
mirador – lookout point
modernista – modernist
montaña – mountain
moro – 'Moor' or Muslim (usually in a medieval context); common and slightly pejorative term for North Africans
movida – see *marcha*
mudéjar – a Muslim living under Christian rule in medieval Spain; also refers to their decorative style of architecture
municipio – town council or hall
muralla – city wall
museo – museum

nevera – ice house
norte – north

oeste – west
oficina de turismo – tourist office; sometimes called an *oficina de información turística*

palacio – palace
parador – one of a chain of state-run, high-class hotels, often set in magnificent castles or mansions
parque – park
paseo – promenade; boulevard
paseo marítimo – seaside promenade
pensión – guesthouse; modest private hotel
pescado – fish
piscina – swimming pool
plato combinado – literally 'combined

plate'; a largish serving of meat/seafood/omelette with trimmings

playa – beach

plaza – public square

plaza mayor – main square

plaza de toros – bullring

PR – Sendero de Pequeño Recorrido; short-to medium-length signed trail

pueblo – village

puente – bridge; also means the extra day or two off that many people take when a holiday falls close to a weekend

puerta – gate or door

puerto – port; mountain pass

provincia – province; Spain is divided into 50 of them

ración – meal-sized serving of *tapas*

rastro – flea market

real – royal

Reconquista – the Christian reconquest of the Iberian Peninsula from the Muslims (8th to 15th centuries)

refugio – shelter or refuge, especially a mountain refuge

Renfe – Red Nacional de los Ferrocarriles Españoles, the national rail network

retablo – altarpiece

río – river (*riu* in Valenciano)

romaría – festive pilgrimage or procession

salida – exit or departure

salinas – salt pans

santuario – shrine or sanctuary

secano – an area of unirrigated land

Semana Santa – Holy Week, the week leading up to Easter Sunday

señorial – noble

servicios – toilets

sierra – mountain range

siglo de oro – golden age

s/n – *sin número* (no number), sometimes used on street addresses

sur – south

taifa – small Muslim kingdom in medieval Spain

tapas – bar snacks traditionally served on a saucer or lid *(tapa)*

taquilla – ticket window

tarjeta de crédito – credit card

tarjeta telefónica – phonecard

temporada alta/media/baja – high/mid/low season

terraza – terrace; often means a cafe or bar's outdoor tables

tienda – shop; tent

torre – tower

tostada – slice of toast with jam or similar

turrón – a kind of nougat

urbanización – suburban housing development

valle – valley (*vall* in Valenciano)

vía pecuaria – drovers' road

zumo de naranja – fresh orange juice

Food Glossary

Spain has such huge variety in food and food terminology from region to region that you could travel the country for years and still find unfamiliar items on every menu you encountered. Still, you should be able to decipher a good half of most worthwhile menus with the help of the lists in this glossary.

Ways of Cooking & Preparing Food

a la brasa – chargrilled
a la parrilla – grilled
a la plancha – grilled on a hotplate
a la vasca – with parsley, garlic and peas; a Basque green sauce
adobo – a marinade of vinegar, salt, lemon and spices, usually for fish before frying
ahumado – smoked
albóndiga – meatball or fishball
aliño – anything in a vinegar and oil dressing
allioli (or **alioli**) – garlic mayonnaise
asado – roasted
caldereta – stew
caldo – broth, stock, consomme
casero – home-made
cazuela – casserole
cocido – cooked; also hotpot/stew
croqueta – croquette
crudo – raw
escabeche – a marinade of oil, vinegar and water for pickling perishables, usually fish or seafood
estofado – stew
fideuá – a *paella* made with noodles instead of rice
frito – fried
gratinado – au gratin
guiso – stew
horneado – baked
horno – oven
olla – pot
paella – rice, seafood and meat dish
pavía – battered fish or seafood
pil pil – garlic sauce usually spiked with chilli

potaje – stew
rebozado – battered and fried
relleno – stuffed
salado – salted, salty
seco – dry, dried
tierno – tender
zarzuela – fish stew

Basics

aceite (de oliva) – (olive) oil
ajo – garlic
arroz – rice
azúcar – sugar
bollo – bread roll
confitura – jam
espagueti – spaghetti
fideo – vermicelli noodles
harina – flour
macarrones – macaroni
mayonesa – mayonnaise
mermelada – jam
miel – honey
pan – bread
panecillo – bread roll
pimienta – pepper
sal – salt
salsa – sauce
soja – soya
tostada – toasted roll
trigo – wheat
vinagre – vinegar

Soups & Snacks

bocadillo – bread roll with filling
ensalada – salad
entremeses – hors d'oeuvres; starters
gazpacho – cold, blended soup of tomatoes, peppers, cucumber, onions, garlic, lemon and breadcrumbs
media-ración – half serve of *tapas*; see *ración*
meriendas – afternoon snacks
montadito – small bread roll with filling, or a small sandwich, or an open sandwich (often toasted)
pincho – a *tapa*-sized portion of food; also a *pinchito* (see Carne & Aves)

pitufo – small filled baguette or roll
ración – meal-sized serving of *tapas*
sopa de ajo – garlic soup
tabla – selection of cold meats and cheeses; literally a board
tapa – snack on a saucer or lid *(tapa)*

Frutas (Fruit)
aceituna – olive
aguacate – avocado
cereza – cherry
chirimoya – custard apple, a tropical fruit
frambuesa – raspberry
fresa – strawberry
granada – pomegranate
higo – fig
lima – lime
limón – lemon
mandarina – tangerine
manzana – apple
manzanilla – a type of olive (also means camomile and a type of sherry)
melocotón – peach
melón – melon
naranja – orange
pasa – raisin
piña – pineapple
plátano – banana
sandía – watermelon
uva – grape

Vegetales/Verduras/Hortalizas (Vegetables)
alcachofa – artichoke
apio – celery
berenjena – aubergine, eggplant
calabacín – zucchini, courgette
calabaza – pumpkin
cebolla – onion
champiñon – mushroom
col – cabbage
coliflor – cauliflower
espárragos – asparagus
espinacas – spinach
guindilla – chilli pepper
guisante – pea
hongo – wild mushroom
judías blancas – butter beans
judías verdes – green beans
lechuga – lettuce
maíz – sweet corn

patata – potato
patatas a lo pobre – literally 'poor man's potatoes' (potato dish with peppers and garlic)
patatas bravas – spicy fried potatoes with mayonnaise
patatas fritas – chips, French fries
pimiento – pepper, capsicum
pipirrana – salad of diced tomatoes and red peppers
puerro – leek
seta – wild mushroom
tomate – tomato
verdura – green vegetable
zanahoria – carrot

Legumbres (Pulses) & Nueces (Nuts)
almendra – almond
alubia – dried bean
anacardo – cashew nut
cacahuete – peanut
faba – type of dried bean
garbanzo – chickpea
haba – broad bean
lentejas – lentils
nuez – nut; also walnut
piñón – pine nut
pipa – sunflower seed

Pescados (Fish)
anchoa – tinned anchovy
atún – tuna
bacalao – cod
boquerones – anchovies marinated in vinegar or fried
caballa – mackerel
cazón – dogfish
chanquetes – whitebait (baby fish – illegal but not uncommon)
dorada – sea bass
lenguado – sole
merluza – hake
mero – halibut, grouper, sea bass
mojama – cured tuna
pescadilla – whiting
pescado frito – small fried fish
pez espada – swordfish
platija – flounder
rape – monkfish
salmón – salmon

salmonete – red mullet
sardina – sardine
trucha – trout

Mariscos (Seafood)
almejas – clams
bogavante – lobster
calamares – squid
cangrejo – crab
cangrejo de río – crayfish
chipirón – small squid
cigala – crayfish
frito variado – a mixture of deep-fried seafood
fritura – same as *frito variado*
gamba – prawn
langosta – spiny lobster
langostino – large prawn
mejillones – mussels
ostra – oyster
peregrina – scallop
pulpo – octopus
puntillita/o – small squid, fried whole
sepia – cuttlefish
vieira – scallop

Carne (Meat) & Aves (Poultry)
beicon – bacon (usually thinly sliced and pre-packaged; see *tocino*)
bistek – thin beef steak
butifarra – thick sausage (to be cooked)
cabra – goat
cabrito – kid, baby goat
callos – tripe
carne de caza – game meat, such as venison or wild boar
caza – hunt, game
cerdo – pig, pork
chivo – kid, baby goat
chorizo – red sausage
chuleta – chop, cutlet
churrasco – slabs of grilled meat or ribs in a tangy sauce
codorniz – quail
conejo – rabbit
cordero – lamb
embutidos – the many varieties of sausage
faisán – pheasant
filete – fillet

hamburguesa – hamburger
hígado – liver
jabalí – wild boar
jamón (serrano) – ham (mountain-cured)
lengua – tongue
lomo – loin (of pork unless specified otherwise), usually the cheapest meat dish on the menu
longaniza – dark pork sausage
morcilla – blood sausage – ie, black pudding
pajarito – small bird
paloma – pigeon
pato – duck
pavo – turkey
pechuga – breast, of poultry
perdiz – partridge
picadillo – minced meat
pierna – leg
pinchito – small kebab
pollo – chicken
rabo (de toro) – (ox) tail
riñón – kidney
salchicha – fresh pork sausage
salchichón – cured sausage
sesos – brains
solomillo – sirloin (usually of pork)
ternera – beef, veal
tocino – bacon (usually thick; see *beicon*)
vaca, carne de – beef
venado – venison

Productos Lácteos (Dairy Products) & Huevos (Eggs)
leche – milk
mantequilla – butter
nata – cream
queso – cheese
revuelto de ... – eggs scrambled with ...
tortilla – omelette
tortilla española – potato omelette
yogur – yoghurt

Postres (Desserts) & Dulces (Sweet Things)
bizcocho – sponge cake
churro – long, deep-fried doughnut
galleta – biscuit, cookie
helado – ice cream
natillas – custards

pastel – pastry, cake
tarta – cake
torta – round flat bun, cake
turrón – almond nougat
yema – candied egg yolk

Other
caracol – snail
empanada – pie
hierba buena/menta – mint
migas – fried breadcrumb dish

ON THE ROAD

Travel Guides explore cities, regions and countries, and supply information on transport, restaurants and accommodation, covering all budgets. They come with reliable, easy-to-use maps, practical advice, cultural and historical facts and a rundown on attractions both on and off the beaten track. There are over 200 titles in this classic series, covering nearly every country in the world.

 Lonely Planet Upgrades extend the shelf life of existing travel guides by detailing any changes that may affect travel in a region since a book has been published. Upgrades can be downloaded for free from **www.lonelyplanet.com/upgrades**

For travellers with more time than money, **Shoestring** guides offer dependable, first-hand information with hundreds of detailed maps, plus insider tips for stretching money as far as possible. Covering entire continents in most cases, the six-volume shoestring guides are known around the world as 'backpackers bibles'.

For the discerning short-term visitor, **Condensed** guides highlight the best a destination has to offer in a full-colour, pocket-sized format designed for quick access. They include everything from top sights and walking tours to opinionated reviews of where to eat, stay, shop and have fun.

CitySync lets travellers use their Palm™ or Visor™ hand-held computers to guide them through a city with handy tips on transport, history, cultural life, major sights, and shopping and entertainment options. It can also quickly search and sort hundreds of reviews of hotels, restaurants and attractions, and pinpoint their location on scrollable street maps. CitySync can be downloaded from **www.citysync.com**

MAPS & ATLASES

Lonely Planet's **City Maps** feature downtown and metropolitan maps, as well as transit routes and walking tours. The maps come complete with an index of streets, a listing of sights and a plastic coat for extra durability.

Road Atlases are an essential navigation tool for serious travellers. Cross-referenced with the guidebooks, they also feature distance and climate charts and a complete site index.

LONELY PLANET

ESSENTIALS

Read This First books help new travellers to hit the road with confidence. These invaluable predeparture guides give step-by-step advice on preparing for a trip, budgeting, arranging a visa, planning an itinerary and staying safe while still getting off the beaten track.

Healthy Travel pocket guides offer a regional rundown on disease hot spots and practical advice on predeparture health measures, staying well on the road and what to do in emergencies. The guides come with a user-friendly design and helpful diagrams and tables.

Lonely Planet's **Phrasebooks** cover the essential words and phrases travellers need when they're strangers in a strange land. They come in a pocket-sized format with colour tabs for quick reference, extensive vocabulary lists, easy-to-follow pronunciation keys and two-way dictionaries.

Miffed by blurry photos of the Taj Mahal? Tired of the classic 'top of the head cut off' shot? **Travel Photography: A Guide to Taking Better Pictures** will help you turn ordinary holiday snaps into striking images and give you the know-how to capture every scene, from frenetic festivals to peaceful beach sunrises.

Lonely Planet's **Travel Journal** is a lightweight but sturdy travel diary for jotting down all those on-the-road observations and significant travel moments. It comes with a handy time-zone wheel, a world map and useful travel information.

Lonely Planet's eKno is an all-in-one communication service developed especially for travellers. It offers low-cost international calls and free email and voicemail so that you can keep in touch while on the road. Check it out on **www.ekno.lonelyplanet.com**

FOOD GUIDES

For people who live to eat, drink and travel, **World Food** guides explore the culinary culture of each country. Entertaining and adventurous, each guide is packed with detail on staples and specialities, regional cuisine and local markets, as well as sumptuous recipes, comprehensive culinary dictionaries and lavish photos good enough to eat.

LONELY PLANET

OUTDOOR GUIDES

For those who believe the best way to see the world is on foot, Lonely Planet's **Walking Guides** detail everything from family strolls to difficult treks, with 'when to go and how to do it' advice supplemented by reliable maps and essential travel information.

Cycling Guides map a destination's best bike tours, long and short, in day-by-day detail. They contain all the information a cyclist needs, including advice on bike maintenance, places to eat and stay, innovative maps with detailed cues to the rides, and elevation charts.

The **Watching Wildlife** series is perfect for travellers who want authoritative information but don't want to tote a heavy field guide. Packed with advice on where, when and how to view a region's wildlife, each title features photos of over 300 species and contains engaging comments on the local flora and fauna.

With underwater colour photos throughout, **Pisces Books** explore the world's best diving and snorkelling areas. Each book contains listings of diving services and dive resorts, detailed information on depth, visibility and difficulty of dives, and a roundup of the marine life you're likely to see through your mask.

LONELY PLANET

OFF THE ROAD

Journeys, the travel literature series written by renowned travel authors, capture the spirit of a place or illuminate a culture with a journalist's attention to detail and a novelist's flair for words. These are tales to soak up while you're actually on the road or dip into as an at-home armchair indulgence.

The range of lavishly illustrated **Pictorial** books is just the ticket for both travellers and dreamers. Off-beat tales and vivid photographs bring the adventure of travel to your doorstep long before the journey begins and long after it is over.

Lonely Planet **Videos** encourage the same independent, tough-minded approach as the guidebooks. Currently airing throughout the world, this award-winning series features innovative footage and an original soundtrack.

Yes, we know, work is tough, so do a little bit of deskside dreaming with the spiral-bound Lonely Planet **Diary** or a Lonely Planet **Wall Calendar**, filled with great photos from around the world.

TRAVELLERS NETWORK

Lonely Planet Online. Lonely Planet's award-winning Web site has insider information on hundreds of destinations, from Amsterdam to Zimbabwe, complete with interactive maps and relevant links. The site also offers the latest travel news, recent reports from travellers on the road, guidebook upgrades, a travel links site, an online book-buying option and a lively travellers bulletin board. It can be viewed at **www.lonelyplanet.com** or AOL keyword: lp.

Comet, our free monthly email newsletter, is loaded with travel news, advice, dispatches from authors, raging debates, travel competitions and letters from readers. To subscribe, click on the newsletters link on the front page of our Web site or go to: **www.lonelyplanet.com/comet/**.

Planet Talk is a free quarterly print newsletter, full of travel advice, tips from fellow travellers, author articles, news about forthcoming Lonely Planet events and a complete list of Lonely Planet books and other products. It provides an antidote to the being-at-home blues and helps you dream about and plan your next trip. To join our mailing list contact any Lonely Planet office or email us at: talk2us@lonelyplanet.com.au.

Lonely Planet Guides by Region

L onely Planet is known worldwide for publishing practical, reliable and no-nonsense travel information in our guides and on our Web site. The Lonely Planet list covers just about every accessible part of the world. Currently there are 16 series: Travel guides, Shoestring guides, Condensed guides, Phrasebooks, Read This First, Healthy Travel, Walking guides, Cycling guides, Watching Wildlife guides, Pisces Diving & Snorkeling guides, City Maps, Road Atlases, Out to Eat, World Food, Journeys travel literature and Pictorials.

AFRICA Africa on a shoestring • Botswana • Cairo • Cairo City Map • Cape Town • Cape Town City Map • East Africa • Egypt • Egyptian Arabic phrasebook • Ethiopia, Eritrea & Djibouti • Ethiopian Amharic phrasebook • The Gambia & Senegal • Healthy Travel Africa • Kenya • Malawi • Morocco • Moroccan Arabic phrasebook • Mozambique • Namibia • Read This First: Africa • South Africa, Lesotho & Swaziland • Southern Africa • Southern Africa Road Atlas • Swahili phrasebook • Tanzania, Zanzibar & Pemba • Trekking in East Africa • Tunisia • Watching Wildlife East Africa • Watching Wildlife Southern Africa • West Africa • World Food Morocco • Zambia • Zimbabwe, Botswana & Namibia
Travel Literature: Mali Blues: Traveling to an African Beat • The Rainbird: A Central African Journey • Songs to an African Sunset: A Zimbabwean Story

AUSTRALIA & THE PACIFIC Aboriginal Australia & the Torres Strait Islands •Auckland • Australia • Australian phrasebook • Australia Road Atlas • Cycling Australia • Cycling New Zealand • Fiji • Fijian phrasebook • Healthy Travel Australia, NZ & the Pacific • Islands of Australia's Great Barrier Reef • Melbourne • Melbourne City Map • Micronesia • New Caledonia • New South Wales • New Zealand • Northern Territory • Outback Australia • Out to Eat – Melbourne • Out to Eat – Sydney • Papua New Guinea • Pidgin phrasebook • Queensland • Rarotonga & the Cook Islands • Samoa • Solomon Islands • South Australia • South Pacific • South Pacific phrasebook • Sydney • Sydney City Map • Sydney Condensed • Tahiti & French Polynesia • Tasmania • Tonga • Tramping in New Zealand • Vanuatu • Victoria • Walking in Australia • Watching Wildlife Australia • Western Australia
Travel Literature: Islands in the Clouds: Travels in the Highlands of New Guinea • Kiwi Tracks: A New Zealand Journey • Sean & David's Long Drive

CENTRAL AMERICA & THE CARIBBEAN Bahamas, Turks & Caicos • Baja California • Belize, Guatemala & Yucatán • Bermuda • Central America on a shoestring • Costa Rica • Costa Rica Spanish phrasebook • Cuba • Cycling Cuba • Dominican Republic & Haiti • Eastern Caribbean • Guatemala • Havana • Healthy Travel Central & South America • Jamaica • Mexico • Mexico City • Panama • Puerto Rico • Read This First: Central & South America • Virgin Islands • World Food Caribbean • World Food Mexico • Yucatán
Travel Literature: Green Dreams: Travels in Central America

EUROPE Amsterdam • Amsterdam City Map • Amsterdam Condensed • Andalucía • Athens • Austria • Baltic States phrasebook • Barcelona • Barcelona City Map • Belgium & Luxembourg • Berlin • Berlin City Map • Britain • British phrasebook • Brussels, Bruges & Antwerp • Brussels City Map • Budapest • Budapest City Map • Canary Islands • Catalunya & the Costa Brava • Central Europe • Central Europe phrasebook • Copenhagen • Corfu & the Ionians • Corsica • Crete • Crete Condensed • Croatia • Cycling Britain • Cycling France • Cyprus • Czech & Slovak Republics • Czech phrasebook • Denmark • Dublin • Dublin City Map • Dublin Condensed • Eastern Europe • Eastern Europe phrasebook • Edinburgh • Edinburgh City Map • England • Estonia, Latvia & Lithuania • Europe on a shoestring • Europe phrasebook • Finland • Florence • Florence City Map • France • Frankfurt City Map • Frankfurt Condensed • French phrasebook • Georgia, Armenia & Azerbaijan • Germany • German phrasebook • Greece • Greek Islands • Greek phrasebook • Hungary • Iceland, Greenland & the Faroe Islands • Ireland • Italian phrasebook • Italy • Kraków • Lisbon • The Loire • London • London City Map • London Condensed • Madrid • Madrid City Map • Malta • Mediterranean Europe • Milan, Turin & Genoa • Moscow • Munich • Netherlands • Normandy • Norway • Out to Eat – London • Out to Eat – Paris • Paris • Paris City Map • Paris Condensed • Poland • Polish phrasebook • Portugal • Portuguese phrasebook • Prague • Prague City Map • Provence & the Côte d'Azur • Read This First: Europe • Rhodes & the Dodecanese • Romania & Moldova • Rome • Rome City Map • Rome Condensed • Russia, Ukraine & Belarus • Russian phrasebook • Scandinavian & Baltic Europe • Scandinavian phrasebook • Scotland • Sicily • Slovenia • South-West France • Spain • Spanish phrasebook • Stockholm • St Petersburg • St Petersburg City Map • Sweden • Switzerland • Tuscany • Ukrainian phrasebook • Venice • Vienna • Wales • Walking in Britain • Walking in France • Walking in Ireland • Walking in Italy • Walking in Scotland • Walking in Spain • Walking in Switzerland • Western Europe • World Food France • World Food Greece • World Food Ireland • World Food Italy • World Food Spain **Travel Literature:** After Yugoslavia • Love and War in the Apennines • The Olive Grove: Travels in Greece • On the Shores of the Mediterranean • Round Ireland in Low Gear • A Small Place in Italy

Lonely Planet Mail Order

Lonely Planet products are distributed worldwide.They are also available by mail order from Lonely Planet, so if you have difficulty finding a title please write to us. North and South American residents should write to 150 Linden St, Oakland, CA 94607, USA; European and African residents should write to 10a Spring Place, London NW5 3BH, UK; and residents of other countries to Locked Bag 1, Footscray, Victoria 3011, Australia.

INDIAN SUBCONTINENT & THE INDIAN OCEAN Bangladesh • Bengali phrasebook • Bhutan • Delhi • Goa • Healthy Travel Asia & India • Hindi & Urdu phrasebook • India • India & Bangladesh City Map • Indian Himalaya • Karakoram Highway • Kathmandu City Map • Kerala • Madagascar • Maldives • Mauritius, Réunion & Seychelles • Mumbai (Bombay) • Nepal • Nepali phrasebook • North India • Pakistan • Rajasthan • Read This First: Asia & India • South India • Sri Lanka • Sri Lanka phrasebook • Tibet • Tibetan phrasebook • Trekking in the Indian Himalaya • Trekking in the Karakoram & Hindukush • Trekking in the Nepal Himalaya • World Food India **Travel Literature:** The Age of Kali: Indian Travels and Encounters • Hello Goodnight: A Life of Goa • In Rajasthan • Maverick in Madagascar • A Season in Heaven: True Tales from the Road to Kathmandu • Shopping for Buddhas • A Short Walk in the Hindu Kush • Slowly Down the Ganges

MIDDLE EAST & CENTRAL ASIA Bahrain, Kuwait & Qatar • Central Asia • Central Asia phrasebook • Dubai • Farsi (Persian) phrasebook • Hebrew phrasebook • Iran • Israel & the Palestinian Territories • Istanbul • Istanbul City Map • Istanbul to Cairo • Istanbul to Kathmandu • Jerusalem • Jerusalem City Map • Jordan • Lebanon • Middle East • Oman & the United Arab Emirates • Syria • Turkey • Turkish phrasebook • World Food Turkey • Yemen **Travel Literature:** Black on Black: Iran Revisited • Breaking Ranks: Turbulent Travels in the Promised Land • The Gates of Damascus • Kingdom of the Film Stars: Journey into Jordan

NORTH AMERICA Alaska • Boston • Boston City Map • Boston Condensed • British Columbia • California & Nevada • California Condensed • Canada • Chicago • Chicago City Map • Chicago Condensed • Florida • Georgia & the Carolinas • Great Lakes • Hawaii • Hiking in Alaska • Hiking in the USA • Honolulu & Oahu City Map • Las Vegas • Los Angeles • Los Angeles City Map • Louisiana & the Deep South • Miami • Miami City Map • Montreal • New England • New Orleans • New Orleans City Map • New York City • New York City City Map • New York City Condensed • New York, New Jersey & Pennsylvania • Oahu • Out to Eat – San Francisco • Pacific Northwest • Rocky Mountains • San Diego & Tijuana • San Francisco • San Francisco City Map • Seattle • Seattle City Map • Southwest • Texas • Toronto • USA • USA phrasebook • Vancouver • Vancouver City Map • Virginia & the Capital Region • Washington, DC • Washington, DC City Map • World Food New Orleans **Travel Literature**: Caught Inside: A Surfer's Year on the California Coast • Drive Thru America

NORTH-EAST ASIA Beijing • Beijing City Map • Cantonese phrasebook • China • Hiking in Japan • Hong Kong & Macau • Hong Kong City Map • Hong Kong Condensed • Japan • Japanese phrasebook • Korea • Korean phrasebook • Kyoto • Mandarin phrasebook • Mongolia • Mongolian phrasebook • Seoul • Shanghai • South-West China • Taiwan • Tokyo • Tokyo Condensed • World Food Hong Kong • World Food Japan **Travel Literature:** In Xanadu: A Quest • Lost Japan

SOUTH AMERICA Argentina, Uruguay & Paraguay • Bolivia • Brazil • Brazilian phrasebook • Buenos Aires • Buenos Aires City Map • Chile & Easter Island • Colombia • Ecuador & the Galapagos Islands • Healthy Travel Central & South America • Latin American Spanish phrasebook • Peru • Quechua phrasebook • Read This First: Central & South America • Rio de Janeiro • Rio de Janeiro City Map • Santiago de Chile • South America on a shoestring • Trekking in the Patagonian Andes • Venezuela **Travel Literature**: Full Circle: A South American Journey

SOUTH-EAST ASIA Bali & Lombok • Bangkok • Bangkok City Map • Burmese phrasebook • Cambodia • Cycling Vietnam, Laos & Cambodia • East Timor phrasebook • Hanoi • Healthy Travel Asia & India • Hill Tribes phrasebook • Ho Chi Minh City (Saigon) • Indonesia • Indonesian phrasebook • Indonesia's Eastern Islands • Java • Lao phrasebook • Laos • Malay phrasebook • Malaysia, Singapore & Brunei • Myanmar (Burma) • Philippines • Pilipino (Tagalog) phrasebook • Read This First: Asia & India • Singapore • Singapore City Map • South-East Asia on a shoestring • South-East Asia phrasebook • Thailand • Thailand's Islands & Beaches • Thailand, Vietnam, Laos & Cambodia Road Atlas • Thai phrasebook • Vietnam • Vietnamese phrasebook • World Food Indonesia • World Food Thailand • World Food Vietnam

ALSO AVAILABLE: Antarctica • The Arctic • The Blue Man: Tales of Travel, Love and Coffee • Brief Encounters: Stories of Love, Sex & Travel • Buddhist Stupas in Asia: The Shape of Perfection • Chasing Rickshaws • The Last Grain Race • Lonely Planet ... On the Edge: Adventurous Escapades from Around the World • Lonely Planet Unpacked • Lonely Planet Unpacked Again • Not the Only Planet: Science Fiction Travel Stories • Ports of Call: A Journey by Sea • Sacred India • Travel Photography: A Guide to Taking Better Pictures • Travel with Children • Time & Tide: The Islands of Tuvalu

LONELY PLANET

You already know that Lonely Planet produces more than this one guidebook, but you might not be aware of the other products we have on this region. Here is a selection of titles that you may want to check out as well:

Andalucía
ISBN 1 86450 191 X
US$17.99 • UK£10.99

Barcelona
ISBN 1 86450 143 X
US$14.99 • UK£8.99

Madrid
ISBN 1 86450 123 5
US$14.99 • UK£8.99

Canary Islands
ISBN 1 86450 310 6
US$15.99 • UK£9.99

Spain
ISBN 1 86450 192 8
US$24.99 • UK£14.99

Catalunya & the Costa Brava
ISBN 1 86450 315 7
US$17.95 • UK£11.99

Walking in Spain
ISBN 0 86442 543 0
US$17.95 • UK£11.99

World Food Spain
ISBN 1 86450 025 5
US$12.95 • UK£7.99

Spanish phrasebook
ISBN 0 86442 475 2
US$5.95 • UK£3.99

Europe on a shoestring
ISBN 1 86450 150 2
US$24.99 • UK£14.99

Western Europe
ISBN 1 86450 163 4
US$27.99 • UK£15.99

Mediterranean Europe
ISBN 1 86450 154 5
US$27.99 • UK£15.99

Available wherever books are sold

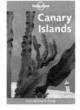
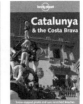

Index

Text

Bold indicates maps.

Bold indicates maps.